New Voices in American Poetry —1979

Compiled by the editors of Vantage Press

VANTAGE PRESS
New York / Washington / Atlanta
Los Angeles / Chicago

Contents

New Voices in American Poetry — 1979

APOLOGIES TO MR. PAGLIACCI

Once the lights are up,
The curtains pulled, or parted,
People like a good show—
Now, let's be gay and lighthearted!

* * *

COURAGE—RARE!

The lunch is in the sack.
The appointment is approved,
And, The Day is at hand.

Now, let's pray
For courage rare,
To meet again
That strange and
Ever-frightening friend:
"The Audience."

The New Group—
New friends out there,
New joys and ideas to share,
New fun, and dreams to plan.

Once at the podium,
I grip the roster strong,
I turn my eyes upward in prayer.
Why were there no tried and true
And trusted friends to link
To carry this new idea,
This new career—
To win the Press,
And save the Day!

1

PEGGY SUE ACORD

LIFE CYCLE

A tiny plant one day began to grow
Beneath a shaded tree.
And as it pushed its way toward life I wondered:
Just who would see
This tiny plant so beautiful
That bloomed in this debris.
The stones closed in the thin, frail stem,
And leaves long dead and sod
All but covered the lonely plant
That grew before its God.
Many a careless wanderer trampled through the wood,
And passed close by the shy young plant
But never chanced to see the tiny bloom,
The lovely bloom —
Except, the woods —and me.
The little plant —it lived.
It grew. It flowered. And it died.
It gave back to its maker earth, its life. And
No one cried —except, perhaps, the winds —they mourned,
When to the woods they came. They blew about the leaves.
The little plant was gone.
Perhaps the clouds far in the sky
Came rumbling close and missed the tiny, timid plant
And took repose near a mountain height;
And told the eagles it was gone, this bloom from off the earth
That we could not aware its void —for we knew not its worth.
And —all God's creatures stood —as one.
Wept soft as falling rain. Because —
They searched the earth for one —and —that one, of them,
Was gone.

UNIVERSE

It began with One
and gradually fragmented
so that nothing could be recognized —
or even strongly remembered.
We encountered one another in wholesomeness,
that which was pure and true.
Our fires joined and the
calmed waters' mist rode the wind
which blew sweet breaths of refreshment.
The Earth was firm and warm
And I was never more happy.
Then irksome and chilly winds interrupted
the blissful State of Affair.
Marked changes surfaced
upon the state of wholesomeness
—and Oneness.
Clouds ran—stripping naked,
darkly dancing over trees and mountains.
And scalded waters failed to quench
The now uncontrollable fires that erupted
out of the bowels of the Earth.
And in this state it was difficult to recall
that it all began with One
and gradually fragmented
so that nothing could be recognized—
or even strongly remembered by anyone —
except those who endeavor
to return the State of Affair
to One.

MY LORD AND I

"In my Father's house are many mansions:
　　I go to prepare a place for you."

In God's celestial city
　　A home's reserved for me,
Where, by His grace so boundless,
　　His blessed face I'll see.

I'll hear His voice so tender,
　　The voice that calmed the sea:
He talked with Paul and Peter,
　　He'll even talk with me.

I'll walk with Him in glory
　　Across the crystal sea:
Enjoy the royal splendor
　　Throughout eternity.

MISSING YOU

"For now we see through a glass darkly:
　　but then, face to face:
　　　　Now I know in part,
　　　　　　But then, shall I know
　　　　　　　　Even as also I am known"
　　　　　　　　　　(1 Cor. 13:12).

I miss you in the morning
　　When the rose is bathed with dew,
And when the twilight deepens
　　I miss my walk with you.

The Sun has lost his splendor
　　And the Moon—her glory, too.
The Robin tells the Sparrow
　　How much I'm missing you.
The starlit sky at midnight
　　The roar of the pounding sea
Winds sweeping o'er the desert
　　Bring back sweet memories.

At last! the day-star shineth
　　Night fades from the Eastern sky
Some day!—there'll be no parting
　　Where roses never die.

THE SONG OF AGES

A storm of time, a vision of many lands,
a screaming of life,
a sigh of all the seas,
in the ocean of time;
the hope of just one minute, one second,
one minimal part of time,
waiting for the secret of life
because all of us we have deeply
in our hearts,
that roaring, that weeping,
that sighing, that waiting,
that asking;
our confused race through the forest of fire,
forest of life,
where each tree is smoke, fog,
ghost and coal,
always asking, searching
for the secret of life.

OVER THE WIND OF TIME

Over the wind of time,
when stars lie in a death of eternal days and nights,
when the robe of sand doesn't cover
any more the abyss of space and time,
when the light forever meets the darkness forever.
Far away over the wind of time
my soul is going and calling my mind.
Looking for the reason of being,
total and partial minimal object,
crossing the body of matter
and searching for the eternal rhythm of life.
My feelings tremble, impulsed by the secret of ages,
knowing that life begins and ends forever
and reflecting their image over the specter of infinity.
The writing follows the internal energy and
continues the cadence of many unknown feelings
and beings.
The nature becomes evolved in its own echo,
everlasting essence.
Laws make the man, the Nature, the total of creation,
and over the wind of time they ride beyond the Infinity.
Where the Being was, is, and will be.
Amen.

THE WHEEL OF TIME

The thrilling of time strikes my veins,
Looking for the meaning of the second gone
and returned in the next wave of the sea of life.
We caress the image of love,
made passion, fire, dust, ashes,
looking for the meaning of hours
and through the mirror of time
we see the future becomes past
and the past becomes future.
And we weep, knelt in the path of silence,
embracing the sun of forever light
lost in the shadow of our souls.
We come, darling, from the mystery,
and to the mystery we go,
and the only force we have
to break the face of the wind of time
is our love
united to the song of creation,
beyond the dawn of man.
We destroy the barriers of dimensions,
when we kiss each other,
in the present of centuries
before the dawn of man . . .
Together we are tied to the wheel of time . . .

DREAM . . .

The specter of ages chants the everlasting song,
love your fate, son of man,
no other truth has given to you that Life.
You suffer with the thorns and claws,
of dimensional flesh,
but that anguish,
that impels the hand in the first and last
grabbing of space and time,
before and after the beating of heart,
expresses the force beyond Infinity,
the re-encounter of Life with Life,
separated only by the temporary sequence
of one human life . . .
The Infinity looks for the Infinity,
the Rhythm for the Rhythm,
as the Secret searches the Truth,
and the Sun searches its light . . .
In the beginning was the Presence
and at the end will be the Presence . . .
resting forever beyond the silence of time . . .
and smiling at the Secret of Life.

SCOTT R. ALLEN

MY FATHER'S LIFE

The tears shed by my father will increase;
Today there are none, but a sorrow surrounding his eyes
Is the warning to be careful in the time that lies ahead.
Each morning it seems that once again I have done
Little or nothing for anyone. I include myself in this,
But mostly my father looks on through weathered eyes.
He does not see where it leads; why did I not follow
In his footsteps? Surely the path was clear . . .
Sunday mornings he steps up into the pulpit
And delivers the word as it has been revealed; secretly
It is clear that what he wants is to step off into
The purple windows, dropping the limitations of fifty years
Behind in order to enter the stained-glass world of God,
Who is no doubt in wait behind the morning star.

* * *

VIEW FROM THE STEEPLE

You can see her now only at a distance,
Shrouded and torn by haze.
She is for you an open silk-screen;
It will brighten under new light.
Oh, young and tender fern!
"I see for you there is another . . ."
It falls dimly, echoes
Cool and hauntingly lovely . . .
It is water from a new spring
On your tongue,
Soon learning to run
Into an old and supple dam.

10

I NEVER DREAMED

I never dreamed you'd mean so much to me,
That everyday seemed so much easier, simply knowing you were
    near.
Lonely nights so often I wish you to be
Warming a part of me, a part I hold so dear.

I never dreamed I'd want to be part of someone,
As much as I want to be a part of you;
Wanting to share the good and bad, the lost and won,
Of every day and night spent without you.

I never dreamed I could speak to someone with my eyes
And the gentle touch of my frightened hand,
Or to have answers to questions that don't quite rise
Out of my mind of a mysterious land.

I never dreamed it could be so easy to love someone;
But you made it so easy —in everything —
Not only to love you, but for me to express more than once
The feelings that have so much difficulty seeing reality.

I never dreamed that you'd become my life
To a point that so often I don't understand.
Or that once too often I'd like to be your wife,
Which is something I'd say to you in hesitance.

I never dreamed the love I feel for you could be so real;
But even more so, the love you return to me —for you.
Your real existence could in time become very unreal,
But no one can ever take away what I feel so deeply for you.

INVISIBLE LOVE

You can't see love, some people say,
But I saw love just yesterday,
in the sun above and the flowers below
and love so bright in the rivers that flow.

A child shows love in so many ways:
on warm nights and cold, cold days
he snuggles up and sits real near,
and shows love in his eyes so dear.

Take time to look and you too will see
love in a honeycomb built by bees.
Love is a cloud so high above,
and falling rain speaks of love.

A big broad smile can show us love,
and a bright colored leaf from a branch above.
So many beautiful things I see
can only be God's love to me.

Starting today, look around
and you too will see love abound.
Receive love, but don't forget to give
and you will see love as long as you live.

MERRY-GO-ROUND
Thought Exercise In (No In) Contra-Finite Perspective

All seriousness aside; let's be frivolous.
Finicky finite knowledge, forced to circle, can say but this:
Our hip to earth and self is vain need to know earth and self.
Big savvy must be roll-over slave to bright eye and fun skin?
"See it sharp, know it sure," goes the returning suasion;
"Intellect, aptly schooled in proven reality, is good life."
Prim sirs: straight-projection ruins any slick and curling pat.
When we were groping clods we knew (eyeball, skin and ear,
Nose and tongue) earth was concretely still and square; now
We're technological circuit-makers, turning abstract; but no
Time yet to doubt earth is round and rolling for us. Were we
Handless and awareless non-persons would earth swing free?
Are we concept-bound to concept round to stay bound; concepts
Being void? Earth's an idea of changing mold in forging hands
As all objects are? Could gravity center be a nest of fingers
On a futile palm and science: let's pretend a solar system?
Does the logic by which we perceive, equally also deny?
How say it to see it; square and round? Two simple shapes;
Home to eye, fine to feel; too bad both seem too odd in the
Dimension of dimensionless space.
Behold sure real as zero; call it earth, square or round, then
Try to make sense, wandering lost in a thriving chaos of
Rising prices. Senses involve senses; not objects:
You need to love you; five reasons close to. Proofs in
Purpose pertain to no exterior; they do roundly assert and
Reassert self, like repeated blasts on a New Year's horn,
Or grasping drags on a cigarette—idly taking in that dreamy
(Not flavor but) taste—so round, so fully packed; a neat and
Dexterous fit; so reassuring at the eerie tips of finitude.
We never see a bug; we see the self as a bug: nixed in endless
Space; subtle hand is a trick, so twisting, on pliant man?

Something as something projected, extends in conflict;
Hand-styled something as mind-image nil, projects in harmony.
Project, we must project, force of mind; despite a seizing,

Holding, staying urge that juts from every bone. Signs bulge
Indicating hand-mind split aspects in something-nothing
Are mythic values of five hand-serving senses.
For example: our one access to material identity is the
Unidentified awareness image; not a so-seemly physical sense.
To realize such must be the busy mental case; we need only
Ponder this in full: at the present-instant mention,
(If you'll excuse the crude and prying question); were you
Coincidentally aware of the paper object these words
Are printed on? I'll presume your final position would be
Negative and go on to draw the following conclusion:
Sight does not cause awareness; awareness causes sight.
"So what? A tree is a tree. We co-exist, the tree and I."
Would reachless tree direly need to move us to a sight
Of its own bigness, greenness, stately worth, etc., or is
Crying want ours alone to move our seeing, knowing selves
To see the tree; however, we may attribute and so, briefly
See it? Among minds and things, what is, is what attributes.
Intensely prehensile man equates real nil as
Real something in the flash-mood of a most relative being;
Senses not sensing hint,
There's nothing to sense but self?
Awareness might be the greatest energy on earth;
That's if we cannot bear to offend sacred hands
And accept mere attention as indeed
Earth itself.

LOVE THE CHILDREN

In the stillness of my quaint
    cubicle abode,
While pondering quietly my
    singular state,
From out of some vast
    inexplicable somewhere
A thought did intrude
    upon my place.

And so, without edit or
    proper rehearse
But with love, of necessity,
    I share with you in verse
That persistent thought that
    overtook me so complete;
So stilled my night that I
    could not sleep:

Take the children to your heart,
    it was,
As you would Me.
For isn't it true
That, but for a few short
    hours of time, there go you?
Take the children to your heart;
    let them be.

GINGER'S GARDEN

Autumn's a
departing time,
as with the leaves.
There she stands,
raking through her memories.

Winter is
a dying time,
cold and bleak.
She is left
to sleep this deathless sleep.

Spring comes in,
new life unfolds
around old reasons.
She has spent
hard cycles with her seasons.

Summer is
a living time,
time to pardon.
Now she'll turn
and leave the winter garden.

WHY I LOVE AMERICA

I love America because of its purity and vitality.

I love America because it has room for the rich and help for the poor, but most of all it helps all endure!

I love America for one reason in all; I love America because it is a classic and home of the brave, the proud, and the tall.

So if you still ask or wonder why I love America, I will repeat 'til I die:

America has room for not only I; America has room for the sick, the poor, the weak, and the forelorn;

The sad and the helpless, and the aliens of far and near; The old and the young, and the babies newborn.

Now, what more can you ask and what am I after?

I ask only that America stay with her heritage forever and hereafter.

* * *

SECRETS

As my face grows cold
The wind creeps upon my cheeks,
And it whispers the secret of
Tomorrow's dreams . . .

DIG THESE FOUR-LETTER WORDS, MAN

One never can tell what JOYS can come from four-letter words.
How much they tell, how much they hold!
Just four letters—some spell out very bold
The meaning of so many things—just as TRUE and CLEAR,
Giving one a chance to prove what's GOOD and DEAR.
      There's LIFE—that's heavensent,
      Dynamic vibrating, with rhythm bent.
How about the SUN'S GLOW,
And the RAIN that makes the streams flow?
And a SEED—just put it in th SOIL
And out of these four-letter words a TREE will grow.
There's LOVE—how much those four letters hold!
How DEAR they make one feel and give
      HOPE to the SOUL.
Those four-letter words can make the sun shine,
And to just be a-LIVE is sublime.
      MAMA and PAPA and HOME—
      What four-letter words could better be
      To fill a LIFE with WORK and LOVE and to
          help one LIVE satisfactorily
A FOND LOVE for LIFE gives that WARM GLOW
That's willing to HELP another to know
These four-letter words could fill a LIFE TIME.
In a MIND filled with words like these
There's no place for words of vulgarity.
      WORK is the four-letter word that keeps one
          in the perfect role
      Of developing in himself both MIND and SOUL,
      WORK develops that muscle and brain,
So that satisfaction is the wonderful GAIN.
Speak good English and good English will speak
      for you.

REVEALING

How wonderful to read so much in a flower
Or in the life of the Coral Sea
Or anywhere in the briny deep
Or anywhere on earth the miracle of birth
Showing Nature does not sleep.
    It's so wonderful to perceive
    The rhythm of life.
    Resting in an egg or a seed.
The miracle, a babe of whatever kind
Coming to this earth.
Or to see a bird on the wing
Or just resting in a tree —
All are fulfilling the cycle for eternity.
    None of these preach,
    They don't have to converse;
    They just live and breathe and reflect
    The allness of God throughout the universe.

SHATTERED DREAMS

My shattered dreams —
like a broken pane of glass —
lie at my feet
in many sharp fragments.

There is no way I can avoid walking over them
in my journey through life.

Each time I pass over my shattered dreams,
the pain of being cut again
makes me fearful.

Like broken glass cutting into flesh,
the sharp edges of my shattered dreams
cut into me, exposing my emotional weak spots,
and cause me to bleed numerous regrets.

The wounds caused by my shattered dreams
will one day heal,
but forever they will leave on me a scar.

Everyone has their shattered dreams;
there is no bandage to shield you from the pain,
only the promise that time will heal.

THE 4 D's

disappointed in my parents 'cause they treat me like a child,
they nag me till I could go wild.
can't blame it all on them, though,
disappointed in myself also.
after four years of college, thought I knew me;
only thing I can do well is go crazy.

disgusted with my present work,
might as well have majored in being a jerk.
can't take any more of this shit,
and that ain't the half of it;
hate this job, this I know,
the harder I try to get out, the deeper in I go.

discouraged from going to all those interviews,
they just give me the blues;
no matter if they are friendly through and through
everyone sings the same song:
sorry, we can't use you.

disillusioned from all the above,
hate my job, confused about myself, nobody to love.
it's like beating my head against a wall,
disappointed, disgusted, discouraged, disillusioned—
that about says it all.

CINDY ATTISANO

DREAM CHILD

The past is gone to stay,
the future's only one step away,
I live every tomorrow and yesterday,
but I can't live today.

They call me dream child;
my only reality is in my mind,
always one step ahead,
or one step behind.

Never cared much for today,
maybe 'cause today is so hard to face.
I'll take my dreams,
let the rest of the world have poverty, war, the arms race.

This thing called time is only what was or what will be,
the here and now have no meaning for me;
that's 'cause I've found no happiness in today,
but eternal joy and hope
in tomorrow and yesterday.

In my dreams there is no true hate, strife, or sorrow;
seemed good till I discovered,
there is also no true love or kindness,
just empty hopes of endless tomorrows.

This is the way I've chosen it to be;
each of us must find our own reality,
my dreams make me free and wild,
a dream child.

THE GRAND ILLUSION

Wishing for something that never could be,
hoping that he would want me,
living from day to day and waiting for his letters to come,
waiting, hoping . . . for nothing and no one.

Waiting for him became a madness,
the only thing that came was emptiness and sadness;
so wrapped up in self-deception I couldn't tell
I was trapped in my own self-made hell.

I wanted him so bad and so strong
but a person can only wait for so long.
I had to draw the line somewhere,
because waiting and hoping became too much to bear.

That empty mailbox staring back at me
finally brought me down to reality.
I had only seen what I wanted to see,
you and me just weren't meant to be.

Waiting for something that never came
I might still be waiting, and who is to blame?
all this sorrow and confusion
was caused by me and my grand illusion.

I FLY ALONE

I fly alone
In this Space of existence—
God's Heaven high above me,
Man's Earth, far below;
With my head, a-guiding;
On my two wings, a-gliding—
I fly alone
In this Space of existence.

I fly alone
To My Place of existence,
From the heredity of my birth,
To the goal of My Becoming:
Despite advices
Of all who love me,
And devices
Of those who're far more learned,
I fly alone
To My Place of existence.

I fly alone
In this Life of existence,
My thoughts, words, and deeds
Are mine alone to own;
Through the storms of conscience
And promptings of the soul,
For this Life that I own,
I fly alone.

AUTUMN CONTRASTS

Silver velvet is receding
As gold is moving in its place;
The yellows are looking mellow;
Purples and reds are losing face.

All glowed last eve in their sun baths
Until Sol let the curtain fall.
When he upped the curtain this morn,
They were shimmering in the mall.

* * *

AUTUMN GLORY

Robed in intricate colors,
Bathed in dew-pearls in the night,
Kissed by soft morning sunbeams
Autumn glory comes to light.

* * *

AFTER THE RAIN

Pearly eardrops bedeck it
After early morning rain;
Then six sprays of bright scarlet
Sing Lady Pine their refrain.

* * *

NATURE'S GIFTS

It makes a halo of diamonds,
It puts pearls in my hair;
It makes rose petals on my cheeks
And sweetens the morning air.

DECLARATION OF PEACE ON EARTH DAY

As I held my tiny newborn babe
So closely in my arms
In greatest fascination
I beheld his infant charms;
I knew instantly a mother's pride and joy.
The moment I held my little baby boy
I thought not of future tragedy
As happy congratulations were offered me.
Time passed by from year to year
Now so suddenly I shed
Sorrow's most bitter tear
For amidst war's battlefield
Far upon a distant shore
My son lies dead,
To smile and laugh or cry no more
As I ask why, oh why?
Was he in vain to die?
That we may dwell in PEACE
They say
I wonder when war will cease.
Now this I pray:
Let one and all in every nation
Speak out for PEACE in hopeful jubilation

Look towards the bright tomorrow
For the PEACE yet to be gained by such tragic sorrow
Though it is not within my power
To declare
PEACE and freedom everywhere
On this day, in this hour,
In memory of the brave for the life they gave
I boldly dare
To declare
June 5th to forever be
Set aside
In Loving Memory
Of all
Who have answered the call
In the quest of PEACE have died.

THE PERFECT ROSE

Spring touches the rosebush, its life to renew,
    And a beautiful rosebud is born,
Caressed by the sunshine and kissed by the dew
    Unfolding to greet the morn.

And soon it unfurls to a rose full-blown
    All fragrance and heart of gold;
Resplendent and regal, a queen on a throne,
    Perfection! A joy to behold.

Ere long its petals fall one by one
    And the beautiful rose is no more.
Springsong is over, the story is done
    And never a hand can restore.

Yet a thousand times it blossoms again;
    It blooms and it buds and it blooms
In the aura of memory, in sun and in rain,
    Its image, so comely, resumes.

In the blush of the morning when zephyrs caress
    And sweet summer wafts her perfumes,
Comes a vision, the soul to delight and to bless,
    For it blooms, it buds and it blooms—

The perfect bud on the verdant bush
    Or a full-blown rose so pink and lush
As pure and sublime as the song of a thrush—
    Ah yes, it buds and it blooms.

MAREATTA CHIVVIS BAKER

THE WANDERER

How you doin', "Old Man" cat?
You've been gone these past five days!
Your ears are frayed, your fur's a mat!
Why can't you mend your evil ways?

All the neighbor folk complain;
You are known for miles around—
How you fight and show disdain
And rend the night with fearful sound.

But here you are a-lookin' up
With piteous cry so full of want;
And here I come to fill your cup,
To stoop and stroke your frame so gaunt.

Dear Father, when I'm weak, and worn
It comforts me to feel and know
E'en though I stand all tattered, torn,
That you my cup will overflow.

TO WAIT FOR ME

My love, I see you standing by the gate
In patience waiting though the hour is late;
So gracious and so kind—how can it be
That you can love a tardy one like me?

When I am old, when chill the night and damp,
Your memory sweet will warm me—and my lamp
Rekindled by the tender thought of you
Will leap again to steady ruddy glow.

The sun will paint the sky, come break of day,
Bright flowers will spring up along my way
And I will ask again: how can it be
You cared enough to wait so late for me?

THE PURPLE HEART

I named a dance the Purple Heart
And composed it for my father.
He died before the dance complete.

Although he but heard
He named the music:
"Dance, baby, to Carl Nielson."
Carl lived in Denmark
And knew the First World War.

In my dance, I think Paschandelle:
The sour grounds of Belgium's battle.
I am my father; I dance in a hurry
For my father is dead. . . .

I am he and for him I dance
You see my dance in purple
It is a heart, named for you
For love, love of you, and all
        You had for this country.

What is my dance but this poem?
Oh, war no more!
I dance this grief of pain
This heart that is my wound,
        Your grave:
        My life between the dance is still.

I THANK THEE

I thank Thee for Your blessings, Lord,
    And for Your goodness, too,
Your needed inspiration
    In the tasks I plan and do.

I thank Thee, too, for breath of life,
    For friends that I admire,
For family and loved ones
    And the goals that I desire.

I thank Thee for Your wisdom
    Your true guidance and Your light,
Your very strong protection
    Every day and through the night,

But most of all I thank Thee, Lord,
    For Your deep love for me,
And for Your ever presence
    May it thus forever be.

MY GOAL

I'd like to think when I am gone
    That I had filled a worldy need,
To have given more than gained
    In every thought and word and deed.

That I had learned Christ's teachings well
    And practiced them in every way,
Lived not for just myself alone
    But for another's need each day.

And in my search for life's true goal
    Discovered well the meaning of
True living with a peace of mind
    Found only in the joys of love.

For all of this I'd hope and pray
    And only one thing more I'd ask:
That I had earned my daily bread
    With every good and worthwhile task.

THE CHAMPION

He was a champion through and through
    And lived it every day,
He was forever thankful, too,
    For gifts that came his way.

He was a winner in his heat
    More humble with each loss
A doer from the very start
    True bearer of his cross.

He'd known the joys of victory
    Had worn the winning crown,
And dreamed that he would one day be
    A leader of renown.

Eventually he reached his star,
    Yet he remained most true
To his ideals and he went far
    In gaining heaven, too.

THOUGHTS ON A TRAIN RIDE

TO MY KATIE

Blue eyes—I call you "Blue Eyes,"
And when your true eyes look into mine,
Daydreams begin to hold me—
Gay dreams of love enfold me.
Blue eyes, I never knew eyes
Could show the blue skies the way to shine.
All on a day my heart's flown away,
Because your blue eyes looked into mine.
Your Tom

* * *

TO MY TOM

I have a friend—his name is Tom,
I met him on a train one Monday morn.
His hair is light—his eyes are blue;
His smile is great and his manners, too.
We laughed and laughed and hardly knew
The time had passed until the whistle blew.
He entered my life when I needed a friend,
And brought peace and gladness that will ne'er end.
Because he cares and oft' tells me so,
My heart is light and my life aglow.
Each day we live where'er we be,
I belong to him and he belongs to me.
Our love for each other will always remain—
A love that was born while riding a train.
Your Katie

POSTSCRIPT TO THOUGHTS ON A TRAIN RIDE

My friend has gone and left me—
I feel I am all alone,
Since God saw fit to call him to
    His heavenly home.
My life is sad and lonely—
My days without a smile,
But I shall see my friend again in
    God's after-a-while.
        Your Katie

* * *

DA-BU

She wakes me in the morning as soon as it is light;
Watches o'er me during the day and guards the house at night.
She warns of all visitors before they ring the bell,
And dances when she sees me as if her love to tell.
She is beautiful to see and a pleasure to know—
She is my German shepherd —a friend where'er I go.

TO MY FRIENDS AT CHRISTMAS

At Christmas time, as I remember friends
along life's way
Who have helped and inspired me to do
my best each day,
I think of you especially and all
your friendship means,
And wish for you God's blessing in
fulfilling all your dreams.

* * *

WHERE IS JUSTICE?

Where is justice—the promise of "liberty and justice for all"?
Is it in the Traffic Court where the evidence seems slanted
     against one client and in favor of another?
Or is it found in the placing of an epileptic child in a State
     Hospital for the mentally ill because of the ignorance and
     fear of his family members?
Or in the refusal of credit or of employment to one strictly on
     account of his or her age?
Should justice not be found in our honest treatment of each other
     day by day,
As we pass on the street or meet in the home or office?
If justice is not found there, then justice is dead and the Great
     American Dream has become a nightmare.

OUR STRAWBERRY QUEEN

Our strawberry patch that spring was so good,
It made an abundant supply of one of our favorite foods.
Since we could use those berries in so many ways,
I took care of them about every other day.
The only bad thing, I was about the only one to pick,
Everytime I would pick them, it would make my poor legs sick!
I'd stoop, squat, moan and groan about how this "low-stooping"
    job,
Affected me, but then everytime I'd start to sob,
"I'm not doing that another time," I would vow,
I couldn't do this to my child, Bernie, as he loved them so!
After picking one day, I moped in, just able to drag,
My husband had written on a tall brown paper bag.
In big bold letters he had printed some words,
He and Bernie were smiling about to converge,
They made a big to-do over crowning me "Our Strawberry
    Queen"!
And seemed proudest of me that I'd ever seen!
With that crown standing high on my head, I felt just like crying.
Why, you big dunce, I told me, why don't you stop some of that
    sighing?
After that I decided if I had to complain, it would help
All of us, who would be better off, if I told it just to myself!

* * *

SLEEPY HEAD

Each morning I have two very big jobs,
Of waking up two sleepyheads, but see—
Instead of it being my young son who's bad,
My worst problem is waking up me!

38

MAN

I love the way your mind travels with your soul
through the streams of my eternal heart.

I have finally left the moment when I could move
from childhood and enter the boundaries of
womanhood for you.

I am now woman while you still remain man, the
center of my internal and external universe.

I am free to be my true self for the man who
once held me in his arms.

I have the freedom to love that same man and my
universal philosophy of the world in my own bright
light for my purpose of living and being.

We are both free to be friends and lovers—even
enemies—if that is what we choose to fit the
route of our lives' course.

We are free to grow, to think our own thoughts, to
have our own feelings, and to do our own explorations
and discoveries in either our experiences of togetherness
or in our separate experiences.

Please, man, always remember that I am for you and
with you in everything that you will ever do.

My wish is for you to someday gently touch me softly,
yet swiftly, in the understanding of our "love" and
our separate capacities of living.

FORESIGHT

The things most shared by all mankind,
Made wordless by feeling, that inchoate thing,
Seeing fall of a leaf that names the season,
The harvest time that with rhyme and reason,
Fills the mind with a sure token—
Presaging the garnering, the gathering,
With no word spoken, all think in unison
Of the change in the year's rhythm
From summer to fall, with winter coming.
Yet, after the first sorrow as the green dies,
Memory leans forward to the day when all will know
On a sudden, stepping into a cold dawn,
An unexplained whisper in the soft wind sings
Of the death of winter, though snow is all around.

Or, as when, from a fireside, where thought is known
Even before speech, suddenly by a glance, a slower step,
Deep breath from each, that earth has lost all weight.
How known by leaf, by air, by slowed step?
We cannot say: we will not say we know,
But, knowing, have no need to say—
So, whether by morn, or noon or end of day,
The changes fall, we know, not by ear or sense—
That falling leaf, and balm of spring, and passing breath,
Change will come, be welcome recompense.

FREEDOM

I live all alone in my own little house,
I have a good cat, so we never have a mouse!
(I mean to say, if one comes, HE has a mouse!)
If I don't eat at proper times, there's no one to see,
If I'm hungry, I eat an apple and drink a cup of tea
(I mean I have it ANY time, not at five o'clock tea).
If I have a book that leads me on and on,
I read all night and into early dawn
(I mean to say I FINISH it in day that follows dawn).
I like a guest or two who will enliven my day,
I like to entertain them in my most lavish way
(I mean, I like the ones who say they like my way)!

* * *

TIME FLIES

The years fly over us like great birds of passage,
Speeding Time rushes us forward, trains us to grasp its tools.
Gifts are handed all who reach and firmly grasp
The new and strange, the strange and new.

Symbols pack the mind, the mind, confused and repetitious,
Sorts all, striving to understand,
It patiently weighs their meaning: trivia beside momentous
      happening.
It holds the accumulated thought of long virtuous generations
Sowing their ethics to the latest generation.

LEAF WIND

There is a wind always, much or little,
Then, there is leaf-wind: it matters where you are—
If wind is high, the low earth will never feel it!
When is a high wind high? That is a misnomer:
The low wind, sweeping the earth, develops gales,
Besides floating breezes, where trees are
Leaf-wind is spraying sound in ever-breaking billows,
Striking the land with whispered cadence,
Or roaring through treetops with the swish of whips.

Who that hears leaf-wind can forget it?
If he live in deserts, or on the gale-borne sea,
Listening to wind-sound shuddering over ocean,
He hears leaf-rustling, dreams bring
The soft communion of leaf with leaf,
With wind bearing them, up and over and down.
The cherished pictures of forests made of earth's masterpieces
Holding grave symphonies with the wind-conductor,
Who has forgotten, who can forget.

* * *

EARTH-BEAT

Repeat, repeat, repeat, repeat,
Progression of seasons year-long,
Life-long, age-old, world-old, planet-wise.
Spring grows, glows, extends, covers earth
Halfway 'round, sphere-shaped planet
Spinning, spinning.

Leaf-long summer burns chlorophyll,
Lighting world-space with green glow.
Sun-fire, earth soil, water airborne
Multiply grass blades, leaves flow, high, low,
Collect, accumulate more, more —
No one numbers, none counts ever.

Autumn-long in sun desertion,
Green seas recede, retire, cease tire,
Glow burns low, lower,
Ashes of green, gray-brown leaves fall,
Prodigal summer is spent, fall dies
Into winter, long rest prevails.
Again sun-joy reverberates, Nature's
Gongs clang—wind's bells, water music
Pipe processions marching once more,
Out of earthly air and rain here,
Here the planet rhythms repeat,
Repeat, repeat, repeat, repeat.

* * *

LIGHT

Vast candles of the sun and moon that light our lives,
Day in and out, with transient moon,
Life's own gift, light —
Scheherazade tale never told,
Are loved more at each hour's passing —
Our grateful sighs in-breathing —
Between the white light and the gold.

HOME CHOICE

There are those who deem a city,
Towered and filled with avenues for crowds,
The achieved monument to gracious life,
Acme of the civilized, the goal of all.
But can those crowded ways
Hold joys of little towns?
Here treelined streets,
Bordered by grass and flowered gardens,
Tended by loving hands,
Living here and now,
Have homes amid their gardens,
With birds upon their boughs.

* * *

ROAMER

Home is where the heart is, and the heart has wings,
What four walls can hold the joyous soul that sings
Songs of multitudinous things—
What the earth has, he reaches for; whatever life brings,
A wasteland, a badland, those that seem like heaven,
The wanderer must have them all, his soul has its own leaven.
When comes again the singing in the blood
Visions in the mind of vaster space drown humdrum with a
    flood,
Desire for the desert over-masters thought of daily food,
Remembering happy living, though the life was rude.

TRUE FIRE

How much of water that flings over the cataract
Covers my flaring flame?
How much of a cloud that leans over the whirring earth
Can extinguish my light, and be wholly to blame?
What puts out my burning?
Shall leap ocean eternally turning, wave over wave?
Herein I feel vibrant and brave,
My hot breathe is only the least of my living,
My true fire is breathless, God-given, mind-giving.

* * *

LEARNED DIPLOMACY

I ride on this whirlwind and that,
No matter what storm shall arise,
I shall ride it out if I am wise . . .
Like a witch without a cat,
Broomstick, or acquaintance with a bat.

When need shall arise,
Those things known without help of eyes,
Come to my rescue, saying only,
"This, too, shall pass."
Instinctively I feel this truth:
So I learn to accept a condition
Not made by me, or if,
In my ignorance,
I find myself entrapped—
I learn to be a diplomat!

SONG FOR SORROW

Day is cold, love's old, and the night is void,
Life's rocks are jagged, tomorrow barren, shrill,
Oh, riddle me nothing that lies over the hill.

My love is faithless, and my heart stands still,
Yet here is ribbon for my smooth, shining hair;
Tomorrow may bring what tomorrow will.

These fair flowers have heartened my will,
I lift my head, and my nostrils fill,
Yet riddle me nothing that lies over the hill.

Heart whispers, "Cling to no man and smile still."
The pale, gold sky is sweet, though chill,
Tomorrow brings what tomorrow will.

* * *

NEIGHBORS

Birds telling tales to the world,
Or murmuring secrets to each other,
Twitter and carol in my trees.
There they are at home, as I upon the ground.
I listen to their twittering,
Rejoicing in their joy.
My trees are home to birds
Because they never leave.

Long ago I lived in northern climes,
Now I have my home
In a sunny, southern land,
Where birds live all year
I have a strong belief
That they know me much better
Than I know them—
Since I have never harmed them,
They hop close to me when
I throw them crumbs or grain.

* * *

EARTHBORN

From these dark roots have sprung,
Green and yet greener stalks each spring,
Dying with the year, and though
Next year still young, a better, stronger growth
Flowered from the hidden source.
What did the plant learn, there in the dark?
To clutch the earth, and by it rise.

* * *

BUTTERFLY SYMPHONY

A butterfly moves to melody
Of her own making.
Her singing wings fall upon air,
In a delicate timing,
The delighted eye is led to rhythm,
Beholding the motion—
Song made alive in silence.

47

SUMMER NIGHT

If you believe summer nights
were made for love you will believe
anything. So deep in my mind I seem
to find a possessive demon with no
self-control and contagious enrage
against bottled tears that will sell for
only pity.

So deep in my mind I can't seem
to find a label to describe what I feel.
Nothing to peel off and hang on my wall.
And no wind can blow it out to sea to
sink like pirates' treasure.

I know that you are causing this
and imaginary dreams that are too real to
hide in my eyes. So simple to hit and stab
with anger. A painful scene with no in-between.

So deep in my mind I seem to find
a knot that gets tighter in struggle to unwind.
So utterly simple to say I love you. "I love you."

So deep in my mind I can't seem to find
the key that unlocks sunshine inside. Teardrops
numbing my smile to ice. How often I've seen
myself hugging you tight and kissing your mouth
on a warm summer night.

NONE IS FORSAKEN

I build a kingdom of jagged rocks
that are smooth as marble, worn smoother
through the decades. Of molded mud that is
golden dust, frequently touched by a monarch
angel of great design. Pronounced beauty so
detailed a dream descended beneath waves that
brushed the sky in shimmering brilliance.
Walk the shore, oh lonely lass,
reflect the heart chaining the feet that
calculate every step. So unforeseen years ago
the patterned life you were to have led.
Nooks and crannies held livid times that were
put to past with no memory hold.
With placid walls I built monstrous
caves to store my secrets, and caressing hands
that drew such smiles on daisy chains. Dared
flickering ashes to burn such dreams as
barefoot nymphs alight in trees.
Sit by the water, oh lonely lass,
release tight grasp on muddled thoughts.
None is forsaken. Put the seashell close and
listen to the minstrel abducting you to starry
nights. Loosen up, lonely lass, for none is
forsaken, all is begun.

COME, WALK WITH ME

Come, walk with me in sunshine
    For the days are bright and warm.
I must sow good deeds today
    Throughout this world of scorn.

Guide me, oh, so gently,
    Please guide the steps I take.
Guide me over the hurdles
    For you know it's getting late.

Walk with me through sorrow
    For I bear a heavy load;
Many a burden I seem to have
    Upon this rocky road.

Come, walk with me in shadows,
    The days are getting dim.
Soon it will be time to go
    For we belong to Him.

Oh, Master, walk with me
    As along the path I trod,
Soon I'll enter through the gate
    To be at home with God.

THANK GOD

Thank God for two eyes
    That show me the way;
I can see God's country
    And the children at play.

Many thanks for two ears
    And the voices I hear,
Of laughter and singing
    Of loved ones down here.

Two hands He gave me
    I do all that I can;
I go to help neighbors
    And work in His land.

Thank God for two feet
    Tho' they've grown old,
Soon they will walk
    On the streets of pure gold.

Thank God for a mouth;
    I can whistle and sing;
I can give praises to God
    For those wonderful things.

Thank God for these blessings
    May I use them wisely each day,
And may I always remember
    To give thanks as I pray.

MAN'S PHYSICAL WORTH

Man's physical body was once worth
Less than a dollar bill;
But since prices have gone up
And keep on spiraling still,
His physical body should be worth
At least five times that much;
But with all due consideration,
It is not a bargain as such.

His eyeglasses cost him plenty,
He goes blind when he gets the bill.
And at the family drugstore,
He goes bankrupt buying a pill.
Expensive are his false teeth
When his own begin to rot.
There's so many replacements to buy,
Necessities that must be bought.

A look at the doctor frightens him
When he thinks of a hospital ward,
With some kind of an operation,
That in no way can he afford!
Still it seems kind of silly
When sinus keeps his nose runny,
To put so much expense
On a body not worth the money.

It certainly is no wonder at all
That people up and die
To escape the miseries of old age—
It is not hard to see why.
The body is steadily growing weaker
With more and more expense.
Why hold to a body worth no more
Than five dollars, twenty-five cents?

DEMOCRACY'S ROOTS

For the independence we now enjoy
Someone else had to pay;
The signers of the Declaration
Became martyrs in their day.
Vandals looted the valuable properties
Of Ellery, Clymer, Wallon and Hall.
Bennett, Heyward, Rutledge and Middleton —
All lost possessions beyond recall.

Thomas Nelson, Jr.'s home was destroyed
(He advised General Washington to fire).
Nelson died bankrupt and in need
When independence was his only desire.
Frances Lewis had his home destroyed,
Enemies jailed his wife and caused her death.
John Hart's children fled for their lives;
He escaped as his wife drew her last breath.

Norris and Livingston suffered similar fates,
Such were the sacrifices that were made
By the fifty-six signers of the Declaration.
No higher price could have been paid.
Carter Braxton, planter and trader
Saw his ships swept from the sea;
Sold his home and all his possessions,
Paid his debts, and died in poverty.

Nine men died from wounds and hardships,
Two lost sons in the Revolutionary war,
Two had sons captured and tortured
For the cause they were fighting for.
Democracy's roots have been fed by blood
And watered by human tears.
Sacrifices that only a grave could hold
Nurtured democracy through the years.

THE SINKING OF THE USS *ARIZONA*

The USS *Arizona* on a calm Sunday Morning
Was taking in the warmth of the sun;
Safely resting at Pearl Harbor
While her inspection was being done.

Unaware there could be any danger lurking
Close enough it could be a threat,
The crew was efficient, strong and willing,
Mastered every test they had met.

Then thundering explosion jolted the *Arizona*
As five torpedoes ripped her port side,
Piercing shells penetrated her upper deck
In nine minutes she sank and the crew died.

Agony twisted the faces of men in the water
Oil smeared some men more dead than alive,
As the Japanese cowardly bombed Pearl Harbor
And few were destined to survive.

The *Arizona* crew stayed with their ship
And are still considered on active duty,
In the deep blue waters of Pearl Harbor
Amid all the tropical island beauty.

Each morning the American flag is raised
On memorial built where the ship went down.
And if you listen closely on a clear night
You hear a ship's warning sound.

Trust each nation as far as it is safe to
Back it up with a strong defense;
Never forget Pearl Harbor and the *Arizona*
And protect your country with common sense.

LET IT DRY

An injustice is like mud on clothes:
When wet it will smear and spread.
If you give it time to dry
Then it will brush off instead.

When you're injured and offended,
It is better to let the mud dry.
Wait until you're cooled off a bit
Let a little time pass you by.

When you've been hurt and slighted,
Have an anger you cannot deny,
The mud will brush off much easier
If you give it time to dry.

* * *

THERE'S A REASON

There's got to be a reason
For everything we do.
There's got to be a reason
For the sorrows we pass through.

There's got to be an answer
To the questions that are raised.
If we could only find them
We all would be amazed!

Take the potter's clay and mold it,
Temper it with fire and heat
To have a useful vessel
For the service it must meet.

Earth's kiln is where we're tempered,
Fires of life but mold the soul—
Perfection is the object
Of our destiny . . . and its goal.

THE GIFT

Someone sent me a present:
it was boxed in autumn chill
wrapped in a white snowy day
tied with dark bare branches
and a bow of fallen leaves . . .

I turned it over:
it made no sound but numbed my fingers
and sent frozen flakes swirling around me
like strange flecks inside a paperweight . . .
I untied the bow
the leaves rattled with November
I pulled the ribbons off snapping brittle bark
I opened the box scattering snowdrifts . . .

And there came out a sigh like that heard
in the tops of conifers on a winter night
and a gust of wind
blowing over frozen snow, making tiny scraping sounds
as it sent fragments of ice end over end
sequining in the moonlight
And the soft flutter of wings
so faint I wasn't sure I heard them
And a clicking sound like snow falling from branches . . .
I searched the box
it was very still as the snow blew around me
I stood wondering, then I knew
the gift I received
was a box of silence. . . .

TICKING

Walking in salt spray
on a stretch of beach
a glint of light
pierced the side of my eye.
I turned and saw nothing but pebbles,
stones, water sanded
from the sea's tumbler
worn smooth.
As I walked it flashed again
bobbing like code.
I followed and there
on this plain of silence
half hidden in other circles
was a gold watch ticking.

I walked again
on an endless stretch
crossing galaxies,
scatterings of sand stars,
past planets stone cold
worn by time,
when a glint of light
struck the side of my eye.

Traveling to its origin
I found a timepiece:
the marbled earth
swirling among
dark stones
ticking.

WINTER VASE

My frozen jar
made of porcelain stars
spinning with snow scatterings
molded to earth's wheel;

Holding a bouquet of fence posts,
corn stalks, broken dry weeds,
and bare branches.

Gray days make dark water:
it runs under your silent surface
and all things sleep below . . .

PEREGRINE

Lord, please grant me wings
that I may soar up to the sky,
and leave behind this human land
so filled with inhumanity.
Thus, from the highest tree,
I may survey the course that
I should take . . .
Should it be east? Or west?
Perhaps the north . . . or south?
I'll let my whim dictate.
And then I'll fly away,
gliding with the wind
t'wards new horizons every day,
in search of fields of green,
where often rainbows shed
their lovely hues.
There, in the sun, I'll laugh
and play with others of my kind
until the day is gone.
Then, like the sun, I'll hide away
in newfound shelters every night,
to rest and dream of new adventures
that await me with each dawn.

THE CAT IN THE CONFEDERATE COAT

It was nearly a year ago
That there lived a cat whose greatness showed.
A Persian cat; a Persian king;
A southern warrior brave and true.
With silver paws
(With children) withdrawn claws
And a coat of velvet gray-blue.

O Cat! O King!
O Magnificent thing!
A general to the end!

With a coat like lavender
And eyes like copper
He was a king,
And rightly so,
With courage to the end,
And all that heaven could send;
A tattered Confederate coat.

He was a lion on the battlefield,
But really just a kitten at heart.
But I ignored him, while he implored me,
In fact, I hated him from the start!
Then one day he looked at me
With that famous Persian stare.
My heart melted, and oh glory!
He hooked me then and there.

He was a general, a kitten, a lion
But always a king,
And rightly so.
He always had courage to the end
And what God did send:
A gentle, loving soul.

He had copper eyes
That asked "Why?
"Why do you ignore me so?"
He couldn't understand;
It wasn't him;
I was mourning for someone I used to know.
He begged with me, he pleaded with me;
He loved me more than I will ever know.
Yet I just walked away
And left, sitting there,
The cat with a heart of gold.

Every part of him seemed to cry, "Why?
"Why must I suffer so?"
But he knew, ah, he knew that
Like General Lee he was fighting a lost battle
For a love he would never know.

My love finally came
But alas, too late!
The old general breathed no more.
He was killed by a reckless driver
On one frosty cold morn.
And I was left with one final thought:
"Prince, please forgive me!" I cried,
"I should have learned to love you sooner,
Oh, how could I have been so blind?"

Everyone speaks of the passing of things
On the time that gently floats,
But the South rings
And the woods still sing
Of the cat in the Confederate coat.

SHARING THOUGHTS

You may ask, what is poetry?
It is the imagination of the soul.
Thoughts that are in the heart and mind
That inspire us to put our thoughts in words
So that others may know the heart and soul
Of the poet. Imagination lives
Everywhere in our hearts and mind,
That is why poets write poetry,
So that others can read a few kind
And beautiful thoughts put in writing.

* * *

THE GIFT OF LIFE

What is life? Life is something given to us.
Without our knowing, we are to receive it—
How we take care of the gift of life is up to us.
Others may tell us how to use it
But only we ourselves can really take care of it.

Our gift may be short, or it may be many years long.
When the day comes to give back the gift to God
Who gave it to us for awhile, be it short or long,
If only it could be as clean and pure
As the day it was given to us to use.

But that very seldom happens to us.
All we can do is take care of our gift
Of life in the very best way we can,
By speaking no evil of anyone
Or hurting any living creature.

To keep love and kindness in our hearts,
To do to others as we would have others do unto us,
Maybe that is all God will ask of us.

OUR TIME

Life is made up of time.
As time goes on its way
How little we think of the hours
As our time on this earth slips away.

We think of time never ending.
Which is very true, my friend,
But time has a way of running out,
One day our time will end.

The hours of our life are made up of time—
Make use of each precious day,
Time is our life, so treasure it
Before time slips away.

* * *

ONLY MEMORIES

My days were filled with sunshine,
My skies were bright and blue.
Then dark clouds came our way,
And today, I don't have you.

The world is green and beautiful,
The morning is a melody.
Each day is a new beginning
But I can't forget yesterday.

What is left for me to dream
Now that you have gone?
Yesterday brought me sadness
Today the sun shines, but brings no gladness.

For all the things that made us happy—
The sky, the sun, the flower,
And all the lazy days of summer,
But without you, I have only memories.

* * *

A WINTER'S SKY

Looking up I saw a dark cloud above me.
Heavy, hanging low, were pillows of gray.
Nearer and nearer, and yet so far.
I could almost feel winter's embrace.

Bleak clouds of cold and charcoal gray,
Scattering and moving in for winter's stay,
Winds whipping leaves along the ground,
Making a soft and rustling sound,
I knew winter was on its way.

Then as I watched I saw,
A few snowflakes falling.
Drifting down so soft and slow,
I knew by morning winter would have arrived,
And the leaves of yesterday
Would be covered with snow.

WINTER WINDS

As the blustery winds of winter howl,
Blow cold, blow strong this winter eve,
I watch the willows bend like reeds.
As strange fantastic shadows weave,

Now taking on a cold gray light.
Slowly, slowly taking on the dark of night,
Blow cold, blow strong, oh winter winds.
I throw upon the winds a dream,
The endings of my favorite theme

What are we but a ray divine,
Longing, hoping for a warmer clime.
Blow cold, blow strong, oh winter wind,
My soul in thought goes out to find

To hear a pure eternal prayer
Which nature sends from every shrine
To the great soul that's everywhere.
It sends a prayer so divine
To me on winter winds.

LOVE'S CONFESSIONS

My Dear,
The touch of your hand resting on mine
    Keeps my heart beating in time,
And softly; you speak my name.
Then, Dear,
The look of your eyes gazing in mine
    Keeps my head floating so high,
And softly; you speak my name
And Luv,
The warmth of your body pressed close to mine
    Keeps my being weak with desire
And softly; I speak your name . . .

* * *

LOVE'S FAREWELL

Tell my heart this is not so:
Your long farewell—
The short hello—
What did pass was too quick to go
So tell my heart this is not so . . .

THE RIGHT TO LIFE

Would a farmer plant seeds, then dig them up;
Or break the jug before he fills the cup,
Or gardeners crush a bud before it blooms,
Or reaches vases to grace dining rooms?
Should someone climb a tree to rob a nest,
Deprive us of a song bird at its best,
Pouring forth songs of joy on morning air,
Sweet melodies in the evening to share?

When is a life a life, and who should take
It from its bed and kill it for whose sake?
Love that is given free can come to shame,
And who is who, and who shall give the name.
As man: God has commanded not to kill,
Nor wantonly away new life to spill,
Deprive an innocent the light of day;
Medical science, and law have their way.

The babe that never reached its mother's breast,
There lulled by her sweet lullaby to rest,
Or in its crib learn how to stand, and climb,
Then learn to walk just one step at a time.
Missing with mother those trips to the store,
Or to bask in the sun outside the door,
As all the beauties of the world unfold,
With nature's many wonders to behold.

Never from work to greet father's return;
Moments of play for which all children yearn,
Nor days in school or games with others played,
Or homes of friends at which it could have stayed.
They missed graduation from grade and high,
And college, where they might have reached the sky.
Who can say what zenith they would attain
Or recognition in a world of fame.

Little souls out in the limbo floating,
Forgotten, and passed off without noting,
Like chaff of the fields, then blown away,
Nothing to nothing, never here to stay.
Without a future, and without a past;
From out the right to life they then are cast,
Not given the thought of what they might have been.
At Judgment Day, who shall atone this sin?

Something not wanted should not be begun,
All that begins has a place in the sun.
Needless, senseless, devoid of all reason,
For a brief thrill; the feelings then pleasing.
All things that mate bring new life still,
This is the way of life, it is God's will.
The love of man and wife, this is the thrill;
When once conceived, no one a babe should kill.

WESLEY D. BERRIER

WHAT HAVE I TO OFFER?

What have I to offer, love,
As could the kings of old?
To seek to win your favors, love,
By giving things of gold?
In flaunting you for all to see
And heralding your charms,
In hope that one might chance to be
The one who shared your arms?

Would you choose among the lot
For treasure such as this,
Or seek a love for feelings sought
More worthy of your kiss?
If so, my humble gift, my queen,
Would surely measure much.
A heart of riches felt —not seen—
And the key lies in your touch.

For I am not of noble birth
Nor heir to titled lands,
I only pray my effort worth
The softness of your hands.
In your eyes I've found my worldly reign,
Your laughter is my crown.
In wealth I could not hope to gain
The happiness I've known.
For time has seen its share of kings
And watched their kingdoms fall,
But for love of you and all it brings
I need not be king at all.

IF YOU WILL GIVE YOUR HEART TO ME

I promise you a heart that's true
A smile, a shoulder when you're blue.
A helping hand, when things go wrong
A kiss to last you all night long.
A place that's warm—a love so deep.
Two arms to hold you when you sleep.
A dream for all eternity
If you will give your heart to me.

* * *

MAKING LOVE

Making love is like a song
The lyrics often few,
But the music has a different tone
Each time we start anew.
And through the years it's turned to gold
Its ring through seasons grew
And when I'm old I'll still be glad
To sing the same old song with you.

THE HIGH-SCALIN' MAN

I knew him first at Hoover Dam,
A high-scalin' brute of a man.
With his safety belt and a long, long line
Across the rocks he ran.
He would hold his line with just one hand
And leap from crag to crag.
At night he would sit at the local bar
And drink and curse and brag.

The tales they told of this fearless one
Grew long as the years went by,
But one I know to be the truth,
Of it I cannot lie.
I was one of the engineers
That worked high up on the rocks.
We painted lines and marked the points
For locating the powder shocks.
We worked on lines held at the top
And tried not to think of the cliffs below.
We were callous to danger and the threat of death
And fear we just didn't know.

One day while reaching out with paint brush in hand,
As I stretched to make a broad cross,
A loud clatter from above, "Headache!" yelled the men,
And warning cries from the boss.
Small rocks hurtled past like slugs from a gun.
I clung to the cliff with fear in my heart,
Like a lizard crouched in the sun.

I looked to my line so high overhead
And gave it a gentle pull.
My heart stood still and sick I was,
It was loose in my grasp and
Came slithering down in long loops and full.
My fingers clung to the jutting rocks,
The weight would surely tear me away.
A tug at my belt and I began to slide
And all I could do was pray.

Faster I fell, as time stood still,
And I knew that this was the end,
When out of the sky it seemed to me
Flew an angel with help to lend.
Just as I reached the fatal edge
There came a lusty whoop
And two strong legs clamped around my waist,
And I was caught in a mighty swoop.
For "Fearless Fred" had seen my plight
And without an instant's pause,
He started a run from the end of his line
And snatched me from death's jaws.

They hauled me up for the Doc to see
And check me for broken bones.
Unhurt I was but my spirit gone
To work on the rocks and stones.
No more could I climb the canyon walls,
But was sent to the safer flat.
I never saw him again, who saved my life,
And remorseful I was for that.

Later I went to Grand Coulee Dam
And the Hungry Horse watershed.
And wherever I worked I would always hear
The tales of "Fearless Fred."
Especially the one where he saved a man
By grabbing him out of the air,
And I told no one I was the man
For I was sure no one would care.

For the glory belonged to the high-scalin' man
That so carelessly seemed to fly,
And to his breed where dams are built
Where they work until they die.
For by such are made the works of man
Of blood and sweat and tears.
So here's to these hard-boiled climbing men:
Our honor. Our praise. Our cheers.

TO A FRIEND

Stilled are the eager helpful hands,
The smile erased.
The quickly moving step no longer comes.
The facile, seeking mind no longer seeks,
For it has found and on that other shore for which we long
He dwells with Him,
And once again takes up with greater zeal
A new and nobler task for which he trained on earth.

* * *

ESCHATOLOGY

The City sleeps.
The flashing Eye of the Needle* keeps
Watch over the slumbering host.
The radiant eastern sky etches the ragged peaks;
To the west the jagged coast.
With the burgeoning day, the tiny morsels of humanity stir,
And wind, fog, rain or freeway frantic sounds will not deter
Them from their vocational rounds.
But o'er it all or in or around there dwells some Super
Cosmos that gently stirs the throng with selective finger
And decides that this day there are those who will
No longer linger, but fly this plastic scene, mourned
For a fleeting second and then no one longer weeps.
The City sleeps.

*Seattle's Space Needle

75

THE HELPING HAND

As I walked the beach in the early morn and watched the rising
    mist,
The solar disc burst into gold as the mountain crags it kissed.
The young day quickly came to life with a promise of something
    new
And I felt my soul would surely burst with the good deeds I must
    do.

I met a man with a catch of fish that was more than he could lug
But to help would leave a fishy smell so I passed by with a
    shrug.
A car was mired in the sand and help was sore in need,
But I thought of my aching vertebrae and skipped another deed.

I left the beach and returned to town and wandered up the street;
Anxiety marked the faces of all I chanced to meet.
I heard that a fishing boat was down and all were feared lost.
I thought of the loneliness of the sea as the victims were
    water-tossed.

Again I felt that helpful urge and hurried to offer aid.
They looked at me and said, "Too old," and, "Probably
    afraid."
Then I realized to be of help one must do the little deeds.
One must recognize the common folks and face up to their needs.

You can't just pick your mighty works, but always be prepared
To step right in and be of help, indulge in problems shared.
There is no halfway point to care for those in need—
You must jump right in and help their happiness to speed.

PURPLE COW

Now Donald had a purple cow,
With character obtuse,
A silly, bovine animal,
This lovely creature, puce.

Her face was sad and lonely,
Her eyes were limpid blue.
Her sides were slick as slick could be.
Her voice a husky "Moo!"

Hip bones high and rugged
With skin draped gently o'er;
One horn curved north, the other south,
Her teeth, they numbered four.

A peaceful gal? without a doubt,
With attitude deliberate,
Until poor Donald came along
Her creamy flood to liberate.

But here the tranquil mood is gone,
The placid picture changes,
For this mild-mannered looking babe
Came from the mountain ranges.

She eyed the gleaming pail askance,
She frowned upon the stool.
The look she gave our Donald lad
Was unladylike and cool.

Our hero slapped her on the flank
And gruffly said, "Move over."
The purple one just sneered at him
And rudely chawed her clover.

Don sat himself with graceful poise
And gently took a hold.
The lady curled her upper lip,
Her eyes, she wildly rolled.

The milker took a firmer grip
And tugged experimentally.
The cow inhaled a lusty breath
And bawled unsentimentally.

She flipped her tail and took the boy
Across his noble brow.
He murmured softly to himself,
"Dat-rat this gol-durn cow!"

He grabbed the waving member
And to it tied a brick
She calmly wound up once or twice
And tossed it in the creek.

But patience has its just reward
The milk began to flow.
The foamy flood rose to the brim
And Donald rose to go.

But fickle fortune sometimes smiles
Then turns it to a sneer.
The purple one chewed thoughtfully
And twitched a mulelike ear.

She slowly rolled her gentle orbs.
She shyly switched her tail.
Then carelessly she raised her foot
And placed it in the pail.

Now Donald *had* a purple cow,
The reason for this fable.
But if you stop at Donald's house
There's beefsteak on the table.

I'LL MEET YOU AT . . .

Why is it when I wait for people they're always late?
And if they are to meet me I'm always early and that makes me
    surly
because they're late and made me wait.

Or else the place I pick to meet has a name like something
down the street and we wait at different ends of the block,
and each will swear he's where he should be and exactly where
he would be just like he said.

And if you're waiting for your wife and her coat is red,
there's suddenly a convention of red-coated women and you're
    dead.

And then there's the wait in ladies' unmentionables.
They pursue the bra with spirit unquenchable.
The contents call for material stretchable.
Not too loose and not too tight.
They're after a fit that's right, just right.
They try on this and try on that,
They're either too lean or much too fat.
And when they come out and you say, "What a fit!"
They look at you and start to hit you because they're
still wearing the same old baggy bit.
You might as well quit.
So this is it!

THE LONG NIGHT

The night is long.
I lie and think how wrong I've been.
Why doesn't God punish me for the things I've done?
I cannot sleep for fear of things to come,
Of punishment that will be mine,
I know not when.
I moan and toss in tensioned agony.
Why won't sleep come?
Then clear the answer comes.
For God, turned into man so long ago
Redeemed me, long before I came along,
Upon a cross-shaped tree
He hung that I might be free.
His blood with water mingled from His side
And fell to the ground for me.
Peaceful rest is mine.
I drift off to sleep untroubled
Content to lie in His loving arms.
The night, no longer long and terror-filled
Becomes a friend and folds me close
In restful slumber.

RELUCTANT LEAF

I saw a leaf upon a tree.
Obstinately he clung, as if he were loathe
To join his brothers on the ground.

It was as if he knew that when he fell
He would join the limbo of forgotten foliage
And mingle with the mold of years

So we like that leaf upon the tree
Are loathe to fall, lest we
Are lost to memory beneath the sod.
But we, unlike the leaf, possess a soul
That does not fall
But rises up and joins God.

* * *

HIZ MIZ

The gal I like is glamorous Liz
She types a letter like a whiz
But she makes me mind my own darn biz
For when I tried to steal a kiz
The look she gave me friz my phiz
She's got a husband and the trouble is
She's hiz.

JUST FOR TODAY FOR TODAY

Just for today I will try to live as if this were my last
    and tackle all my problems at once.
I cannot do something for twelve hours that would appall me
    if I felt that I had to keep up the dreary routine for a
    lifetime.

Just for today I will be snappy. This assumes to be true what
    Edward Francis Albee said: "Never give a sucker an even
    break."

Just for today I will try to adjust everything to my own desires
    instead of the usual phony trip of pretending
        everything is all right the way it is.
I will make luck if I can and rig the dice if I cannot.

Just for today I will try to avoid learning something useless.
Who needs skills and talents that I will never use again?
If there is a way I can keep my mind blank when I'm angry, I
    will.

Just for today I will exercise my ethics in three ways:
    I will do somebody I hate a good turn
        and make it obvious that I have better manners than he
    does—
            if anyone figures out the game, it won't count;
    I will rudely fart off at least two things I don't want to do
        and stick someone else with the errands—just for
    exercise;
    I will not show anyone that my feelings are hurt;
        they may be hurt, but today I will not show it—
            I'll just insult them back twice as hard.

Just for today I will be disagreeable. I will look as cold as I can,
    dress inconspicuously, raise my voice, be discourteous,
        criticize constantly.
I will find fault with anything, but not try to improve
    or regulate
    any idiot
Because I need all my time to myself.

Just for today I will ignore a program.
I will break all possible routines.
I will save myself from two pests: boredom and senility.

Just for today I will have a quiet half-hour all by myself for
    tension.
    During this half hour, sometime,
I will try to come up with a new scheme, or plot for my life.

Just for today I will be afraid.
    Especially I will be afraid to enjoy what is beautiful
        and to believe that as I give to the world,
            so the world will give to me,
Because if I do,
I won't be able to get down to the groveling and hypocrisy
    expected of me.

* * *

THE NINTH REALITY

A man of knowledge is a warrior, said the old Indian.
And Carlos Castaneda wrote it all down for us.
There is objective reality and seven subjective states, said the
    Indian.
That makes eight, Castaneda tells us.
There is a ninth reality.

83

Apollo lifts us to new heights of achievement,
Dionysius drags us to the garden of earthy pleasures,
Who was the liar who said these are opposites?
Wherefore desire and achievement cut and dryad?
There is a ninth reality.

Ye who pray to an inhuman image of a humorless Christ
Or ye who believe in the sanctity of the laboratory!
Thine is the false dichotomy which sought after Phaedrus—
A dichotomy itself weaker than Poincare and Pirsig.
Arete is the ninth reality.

Mark Twain told us the Germans have an awful language.
Kipling said they were lesser breeds without the law.
Their school aborts, digitalizes, polysyllablizes, cartographs life.
A growing cancer makes ugly, long words besmirching the
        sublime.
For to poison arête.

To dessicate, control, describe, encapsule arête, O!
One must needs play the rôle of objective technocrat
If planners could but rely on an idea factory;
But the ugly words are too bald a grab for power.
This is war.

One must needs play the rôle of objective technocrat
Lest one live a peon to buy chemicals for one of seven other
        stupors, heh.
Which choice made Jack London? George Gershwin?
Would He who made the tyger love sociologists?
Excellence is Kinde.

Sadness is not an interface of dysfunctional rôles.
Sadness is not a quantifiable maladjustment.
Sadness is a proper desire for new thought.
Sadness is a correct rejection of all extant choices.
This is a sad century.

Frank Lloyd Wright did not build beyond freedom and dignity.
A warrior may bring fire to his fellow man
And be ordered to blow out the candle ere adolescence.
Though a reluctance to choose of the known is hated,
Arête endures.

So take up the right man's burden!
Support the excellent, suspect the smug,
Do not render unto Caesar the things that are God's,
Stand up snottily to Yosemite Sam like Bugs Bunny.
Later peace, later.

Christ will come accompanied by Leroy Anderson's "Sleigh
    Ride."
After Zeus falls, he will again befriend Prometheus.
The patient Yaqui taught Castañeda narratives over anthropology.
Then, brotherhood: Only a warrior may master any of the nine.
The nine, the nine, the nine.

ST. PAUL

when I am wearied by belly-worshippers,
by the modern prophets who reject
the old wooden campaign pulpit of hope
for the newer, colder, hollow concrete platform,
and by the one-eyed oracle in the living room
preaching its "price is righteousness" gospel;

when I am weighing paganries against hypocrisies
and find both pressing against my ears,
when secular sermons chase my sacred symphonies
in a winded whirl around my inner life,
making me profane my temples with crimson anger
and ready to scream like a heathen at the heathens

he hears the thought of the cry,
and between the eyes and the hurricane
he reaches down with strong, sinuous words
and lifts my tired mind from the wreckage
of latter-day pseudo-sainted prosperity
to rock it to sleep in a simple, unfashionable manger.

DAMN THEM ALL

Damn the meek and miserable world, damn them all, let me be
    heard!
Destroy my pride and damn my name, credit me only with sin
    and shame,
For I care not for this god-forsaken place.
Rip my dreams from my pitiful heart and leave but a trace to
    torment me on and on.
You bring me nothing to which I can conceal, among the .
    paradise we all know is not
real.
Damn the mountains, damn the streams, damn them all, I say!
We shall all seek a glorified means to be heard, seen, and finally
    vanish from
the face of reality.
Hear my spoken word and let ye witnesseth the horrible sight,
For a man holds no means of escape without one final fight.
Take ye notice of a broken man; damn me now and watch me
    grow.
Wish me lame and wish me blind and wish me a horrible fate of
    death
But pool your madness, hate, and fears;
Concentrate your thoughts and let them not reach my listening
    ears.
The day has come, my unfortunate friend, for a man reborn to
    take revenge.
I care not for your feeble cries for help so distant,
I deal not in mere violence, but a revenge far more intriguing and
    persistent.
You know not the pain which I plan,
A revenge so long coming for someone who has witnessed the
    torments of hell.
You have taken away the last of my dreams and left me hanging
    by a thread.
I shall not take rest knowing my assailant still gloats of his
    victory surpassed,

I have a destiny planned for your tomorrow, which will soon
    become a dreaded past.
What it is you know not.
But it is certain I am the man to whom they look for his
    command.
Now you watch your back with care;
Your fear flows with much regret of past humiliation inflicted
    upon me.
You crawl on your knees, begging my mercy, disregarding pride
    and courage.
I have found my revenge, breaking your spirit.
You know not the pleasure I squeeze from your pitiful cries.
No, I care not how or why you perform your torture.
Now I, your sole god, laugh at you, enjoying my revenge.
I may sleep soundly now, carrying with me
A misguided soul, now too broken to see.

(James J. Black)

* * *

CAN WE BE FRIENDS?

Can we be friends?
Can we be more?
Can I give you the love
You've been searching for?
If I ask for your love
Will you tell me no?
If I ask for your hand
Will you tell me to go?
If I say that I love you
Will it be in vain?
If I tell you I need you
Will you think I'm insane?
When you hear these words
Will you shy away?
Or will you love me enough
That you'll want to stay?

(Pat Lynch)

EACH IN SEPARATE WAYS

The time is now, we must go on
But each in separate ways.
You know that we don't get along,
Our love has gone astray.
Each time we're near I always feel
That you love someone new,
And way down deep inside my heart
I know I don't love you.
Your eyes don't look the way they did
When you were loving me,
For they look upon another's heart
And he is all you see.
But mine have also turned away
To look upon another.
Maybe this time will be better;
We truly love each other.   (Pat Lynch)

TRIBUTE TO A PHILOSOPHER

He wasn't famous nor was he rich
But I remember each word of that philosophy of his;
His years gave him wisdom and experience to share,
In the hours of my need, his words still fill the air.

He didn't hail from Harvard,
But wisest just the same
Of all the teachers in the school
And the college I acclaim.

Maybe I'm the only person
Who saw him as he was,
For he was a very perceptive man
He's now watching from above.

I'm sure he'd send a message down
If he could just get through;
I know what he'd say about my life today:
"Girl, I'm very proud of you."

His passing was unnecessary
And until the day I die,
I'll loathe the day he was put to rest
In the quiet countryside.

No, he was not rich and famous
His funeral was quiet and sad,
And I'll never forget that wonderful man—
For that great man was my dad.

MORNING SUICIDE

Death—   Grief covered me as it should,
            My daughter gone, who was so dear!
            Pain crowded in so hard and near,
            But I think no one really understood.

Funeral—   Friends came as I knew they would,
            Some close and held dear—
            They came so very near,
            But I think they never really understood.

Time—   My sister and my son did what they could,
            They were both so faithful and dear,
            Both came so very near,
            But I think they never really understood.

Years—   My husband's love helped as it should,
            We shared many memories dear.
            He came so very near,
            But I think he never really understood.

Age—   Deep sleep is coming, as smooth as polished wood,
            And life seems not to be so dear,
            As death slowly claims me near,
            I think I never really understood.

THE YOUNGS PRAIRIE COMMUNITY

Please come with me; come, lightly trip along
and trek into these yesterdays among
the hills and valleys of a rural land.
So long ago it seems; the rushing sand
of time has dropped its multitude of grains
since I came to Riviera's seacoast plains.
Land of my birth—to Elgin, Texas town,
I must return and southward wander down
along nostalgia's lonely lane that led
straight back to our so long ago homestead.
I have a picture in my heart of all
the way it used to be—the house, the hall,
the porch, the cistern, and hard-packed yard ground
worn bare where running children raced around.
There in the house I see the old wood stove
with big flat top and cabinet above,
the long shed room with beds, the corner shelves,
and tall wardrobe. I see again ourselves
at night around the fireplace room, and hear
again the laughter of that distant year.

And this comes back; the chains are jangling now
and Papa has unhitched the middle-buster plow
and leaves it at the turning row to stand
all night in quiet surveillance of the land.
The mules come briskly in, they know that feed
and rest and everything they want or need
awaits them at the barn. With corn and hay
put out and milking done we make our way
back to the house with supper in the air.
I see again the coal oil lamp's weak flare
and all of us around the dining room
where chatter chased the last vestige of gloom.

Three miles or so we walked to school each day,
down turning rows and through the woods the way
we always went. With books and dinner sack
we gathered schoolmates at each crossing track.
Beside a sandy road our schoolhouse stood,
a two-room school for our small neighborhood.
Boys in knee pants and lovely lassies there
went winding through the lanes to old Youngs Prairie.
Wolf over the river, fox in the middle, too,
we played until the school bell sent us through
the doors. We said a prayer then, God's Prayer,
the children's voices loud and strong I hear,
and see again Miz Janey and Miz Baker
head bowed, appealing humbly to their Maker.

Great wonders were at school in our bookcase
of Siegfried's fight and Atalanta's race;
but when we came to tales of ancient Troy
I found a harvest of unending joy.
At home we made our spears and swords and shields
and lived again Homeric battlefields;
such dreams forever boy—a host, someday,
of warriors would I lead into the fray.
(But dreams change course—years later latched below
with stinking sweating men, a troopship slow,
the black and steamy South Pacific night
and Private Hector not so full of fight.)

Springtime was lovely in this rolling land
where roadside flowers made a border band
of beauty for the cotton, corn, or maize.
The dusty cotton choppers spent their days
in endless whacks along the rows and then
the cultivators turned from end to end
the fertile soil. Serenely one saw life
roll infinitely beyond the petty strife
of daily things. But time was drawing near
when these unpressured thoughts would disappear,
for looming ominously and soon
great changes were to bring a rural gloom.

A tale keeps going round, and in our home
or school we hear of people who have gone
and moved into the black gulf coastal lands.
No gullywashers there, no blowing sands,
they say, but deep and fertile gumbo soil
where farming can be done with little toil.
Soon Papa gets the fever, and then all
of us begin to feel migration's call.

Our last day came, a still and sunny day,
our things were in the freight car on its way.
That eve we sat on boxes, floors, or kegs,
and ate onions, hoecakes, and scrambled eggs;
we made our pallets round the fireplace floor
and slept that night where we would sleep no more.
Soon morning came in slender slips of gray,
and all was bustle to get under way.
Then down the lane we slowly moved at last
and took these memories of a precious past;
but I looked back before we made the bend
and my old home this message seemed to send:

"Farewell, my people of these former years;
love stills my heart, my eyes are filled with tears.
No more my racing kids in overalls
and bent-bill caps will answer supper calls.
No ante-over, no blind man's bluff, no hide-and-seek,
or jacks; no longer now my windows keep
the norther's blast away. No back-log fire
will crackle round my hearth and no grandsire
will light his pipe with coals; exploring boys
will travel not my ceiling beams. These joys
and sorrows of the past have fled and soon
a midnight fire will send me to my doom."

We turned the bend—I cried a little bit,
but this today is what I think of it;
nothing is perfect, our yesterdays were not,
but they are there—beautiful memories of what
we were, and they are there for us to borrow
until we reach a time with no tomorrow.

RANJAN BORRA

A FANTASY OF LOVE

When you open your eyes, my love,
      Let your lips be moistened by that morning kiss
          we used to share,
And you stretch your hands to feel
      My face leaning over you in eagerness
          to smell your hair!
Let's rise from bed, my darling,
      Hand in hand, arm in arm in togetherness
          and let's laze and dream,
Let's walk again, sweetheart,
      To that shining camelot where our love
          once reigned supreme!
On this special day of ours
      May we spend time together and recapture
          the hours of ecstasy,
Stolen kisses, sweet embraces,
      Whispering into each other's ears in our
          world of fantasy!
Let languid hours loll by,
      And to the strains of an afternoon serenade
          let's talk of love,
And as darkness ends the day,
      With the touching of our lips at midnight
          let's soar above!

A RETURN TO THE SEA

I return to the sea
  that always brought you back to me.
When our souls were segregated
  on the shores of two continents,
The rolling waves reverberated
  with sighs of our separation;
The wind-chased dark clouds
  breaking in curls over the expanse
Mirrored your sensuous locks
  clustering around the countenance;
The racing moon reflected
  your face in shadow and substance,
While the ocean, your promised love,
  remained unchanged and forever.

I return to the sea
  but things are not as they used to be.
In the sound of surf-breakers
  the serenade has fallen asleep;
The wings of soaring sea gulls
  no longer search for togetherness;
The celestials, bereft of beauty,
  are flotsam in the firmament,
Unchanged only are the ocean
  and my lonesome heart forever.

HAIKU

Do not believe them,
Brown Garden, when snows whisper:
"Spring will not return."

Blazing streak of light—
Little time to word the wish
Before the star fades.

The ribbons of dawn
Uncurl to release earth from
Packaging of night.

Burdened by leaf mould,
Sweet trailing arbutus blooms
Where knees touch the earth.

Silky catkins on
Gray pussy willow boughs need
Only a meow . . .

A field of lilies
Stretches miles to the mountains:
I want only one.

A strand of cobweb
Easily accommodates
Perfect rainbows . . .

The eagle flies high
But his gray lonely shadow
Never leaves the ground.

R. N. BOW

THE DOVE OF EASTER

There is a secret place of love,
A place of quiet and rest,
With the light shining from above,
When we give to God our best;

There is a place of rest and love,
By simply trusting in Him,
The spirit of a heavenly dove,
Always abiding within;

Oh, spirit of the heavenly dove!
Forever abide with me;
Peaceful rest and wonderful love;
We worship and adore thee;

There is a secret to success,
'Tis not by might or by power;
He, the dove of righteousness,
A pillar and a mighty tower.

There is a flight of golden stairs,
Over the side of the mountain,
We with Jesus are His heirs,
Through the crystal fountain;

Oh, spirit of the heavenly dove,
Measureless, so rich and pure;
There is a place in His great love,
Forever it shall endure.

REALIZATION

Let the night DAY, when my love has come;
Let the reeds play, when my love has come;
Let my heart see, when my love has come,
that my love has not come . . . to me.

* * *

MORNING

Each morning I can hardly wait
for its beginning light
to search out all the miracles
that happened overnight.

An opening bud, a baby leaf,
are treasures I hold dear,
but dearest is the thought:
God's hand was touching here.

* * *

DRAT!

Each year I do the same old thing—
shed my woolies at hint of spring;
Lie in bed with a pink begonia;
Lie in bed with a near-pneumonia.

* * *

PARADOX

Gratitude is two-faced;
It boomerangs on you;
Any obligation
builds resentment, in review.

FANTASY

My heart runs ahead to meet you,
like a clover-drunk colt, running free—
reckless, through fields of impatience—
unbridled, untamed, exultant!

The pulse of my heart is bacchantic
as I twirl and leap through space,
dancing to some unseen orchestra
whose music excites wild abandon . . .

A million voices sing your name;
A million mirrors reflect your beloved face;
While my heart runs ahead to our meeting,
and I, shall be coming . . . soon!

* * *

EARTHBOUND

Some far star beckons me
and holds me, in hypnosis,
while all my eager senses span the height.
The carefree clouds about ignore my subjugation
but sympathetic rains
weep along with me.

Meanwhile, I plod my usual course,
silencing my spirit,
buried beneath the business of essentials.
I would jettison this inequity—if I could—
but here am I, poised, predestined, passionate,
and . . . staved to Earth.

VIKING LIMERICK

There is a fine craft named Viking
And it did things so much to our liking
That we named it One—
Though it weighed + a ton—
As it flew faster to Mars than lightning.

There on the charts for her planning
Were numerous figures left standing
But when her time came,
Her numbers played "GAME"
And all teams cheered the Mars landing.

The first thing we saw close on Mars—
An incredible picture (framed 'bars')—
Was her land, deflatted—
Yet quite plainly nonmatted—
Rolling sands 'n rock (much like ours).

We all grew excited again
When we saw snow-capped mountains, but then
Dr. Klein said, "It's sun
Shining on some
Of those far-off Mars mounds, men!"

There is this fine craft, the Lander,
Of which we have never known grander,
A Viking for ventures,
Another for clinchers—
Can't walk like a goose, but it'll gander.

THE CLINGING JEWELS

The party—and I have no jewels to wear!
My wrists—they are so bare.
But, no, little hands are clinging there.
Around my neck there are no lustrous pearls
But, wait, soft loving arms are clinging there.
On my fingers there are no diamond rings
But the sparkle in my children's happy eyes
Is as bright as in any diamond lies.

I will take my children for my jewels
I will wear them proudly as my crown.
My jewels will grow and multiply
As the years go rolling by.
Others may wear their cold, hard jewels;
I will take mine, the clinging kind.

* * *

GRANDMOM TO GRANDDAUGHTER

In my heart there is so much love
    The earth cannot contain it nor the planets above.
As the years pass look back, look back for me—
    I'll be there if only in memory.
All the mists and miasmas over land and sea
    Can't prevent my love from following thee.
It will be there as a whisper in your mind,
    A feeling in your heart,
A conviction in your soul:
    My love you will know.

PAULINE J. BOYD

THE WEAVER OF WORDS

The rain drops, drops, drops
Like words in my mind
That have no meaning of any kind.
The drops unite into steady streams
That trickle down my window screens,
Sinking into the ground below.
Finally, the meaning becomes clear
When bright flowering blossoms reappear.

Thus would I like my words to unite
To become swift flowing sentences as I write
Weaving life's tapestries with words so beautiful and right,
Full of meaning, singing, a poet's delight.
I take my pad—the dawn begins—
Still nothing flows from my rhyming pens.
The words remain words in the morning light.
Someday, maybe, but not tonight.

* * *

THE GLOWING CANDLE

Let's climb another mountain
Let's reach for another star,
They are just over the horizon—
Not so very far.

If the mountain proves too high
And the star too far
And reality lost in a misty dream,
At least we will have had our effort and our gleam.

PAULINE J. BOYD

THE SOLACE OF NIGHT

Under the canopy of stars he lies
Restless, searching, he can only sigh:
"Must I struggle and strive until the end,
Will I hear no melody in the wind,
Will I find no mystery in a rose,
Will I find life to be a fraud, a pose?

"Will there be heights no one can climb,
Will there be depths we all must know,
Unfair deeds that no one can mend?
On the fields of night I lie, let peace descend.
Wrapped in the silence of the stars,
Welcomed by the lonely hills, I sleep."

* * *

THE WORLD AS IT IS TODAY

The deeds are done.
How wide the ripples run!
Far, far out they go
Far beyond the sight of eye,
Far beyond the living lives,
Far beyond the centuries.
East, west, north, south, ocean, air.
The ripples continue, are always there,
Diversifying, multiplying, adding,
So what could it mean
But that we have made the world as it seems.
Some is good,
Some is not.
Only God can sort it out.

MY GIFT

I held my beautiful, smiling baby, eight months old,
Gently, protective and, oh, so lovingly in my arms.
Then I looked again, she wasn't there at all—
But a beautiful woman, stately and tall
Was holding me protectively.
I looked over and my smiling beautiful baby was still on the
    wall!

But I hadn't lost her, not at all.
In a few minutes, it seems,
        Life changes,
And this beautiful woman is my baby on the wall, all
        grown up.
Life with its complexities, life with its changes
        Can never change this:
    This beautiful woman with love and wisdom,
        And the loving baby on the wall,
            Are one and the same—
                My daughter!

* * *

GHOSTS OF THE PAST

Precious moments in our lives
We often do not recognize,
Until time has swept them all away
Past recalling in any way
        Except in memory!
They are so painfully sweet and beyond recall
You almost wish memory would fail
And avert the lonesomeness of it all.

THE LAMP

I look out from my lonely room.
Wild and black are the winds.
White and cold is the moon,
But no colder than my heart
Full of lost hope and the shadows of fear.

I doubt if he will come at all.
I look up at the stars —
And yet—and yet—the stars do fall.
A knock at the door.
I do not hope.

I open the door wide
And he steps inside.
The darkness falls away —
Love, our lamp, to light the way!

* * *

LOVE RETURNS

Songs of the night sing me to sleep
Where dreams and fantasies awake in the deep.
What will they mean when the early light beams?
Disillusion and despair is usually the theme.

But shining reality will rise with this sun
Keeping me happy till day is done:
When I look into the shadows you will be there,
And gone forever my hopeless despair.

LOOKING BACK

Oh, these archives are so dusty
    They're so impersonal and so cold!
But the information hidden here—
    Is like tiny bits of gold.

So I'll keep on looking backward
    Searching for footprints of the past.
Finding names and dates and places—
    For these all interest me at last.

I'll wander through the many cemeteries
    Where bones lie quietly in repose.
I'll study the weatherbeaten headstones—
    More vital information to disclose.

I'm finding it to be so true
    That I'm made of many strains.
My ancestors were such hardy souls—
    And they suffered many pains.

They handed down to me so much
    Treasures gained by those so brave.
Freedom and liberties won by blood, or life—
    Which they so proudly gave.

I hope some day to meet all my kin
    Who wait at Heaven's door.
Their names and deeds I'll learn them then—
    I won't be searching any more.

GRASS

The sea has its crested waves of recognizable form,
The river its eddy and swirl and many voices.

But the grass! . . . The wind bloweth where it lists
And the grass bows.
"Thou canst not tell whither it goeth."
It takes no pattern.
It obeys no recognized law.
It is like a beautiful creature of a thousand wayward moods.
Its voice is like nothing else in the world.
It bids you rest and bury your head
In the green coolness.
Breathe of its breath and of the breath of the good earth
From which man was taken and to which man
Will return.
If you lend an ear and are still
You will hear wondrous things of the earth.
Of life in mineral and stone —
Of life in pulsing sap—
Of a green world that the stars saw
Before man trod it under foot.
The green emerald which will have its place
With the rset of the wonders of God.

THE TWO CYPRESSES

Standing on a mountain, side by side
Were two cypresses.
Strong—majestic—of almost equal height
They stood alone.
We said . . . on one occasion . . .
Do you remember? . . .
That those two trees were we two.
Just as their roots twined and intertwined
Beneath the earth
And their branches twined and intertwined
Above the earth
So we two would be united
In life and in immortality.
Their fate would be our fate.
If one of them were cut down
So one of us
Would come to an end.

The two cypresses are still standing.
No storm has torn them apart.
No axe has been put to their roots.
The birds still sit in the branches
At twilight
Twittering their love.

And we two???
We two are still alive —
Near each other—
But mad conceits no longer
Buzz in our brains.
You have gone your way—
I have gone mine.
I know very little of you . . .
You know nothing of me.

And yet!!!
Whenever I pass those two black brothers
I lower my head.
I realize—though you've forgotten —
What a beautiful thing
Our love was.
I don't know whether I still live
In your memory
But oh, my love . . .
How you do linger in mine!!

DAWN

The air is sharp-set.
A delicate rime frosts roof and roads.
The sea lies hazy and still
Like a great pearl.
Suddenly . . . the sky stirs,
Flush upon flush of warm rosy light appears.
The sky's face passes
From misty pearl
To heart of flame opal,
From opal to gleaming sapphire.
The gray dawn wakes and steals
With trailing robes
Across the earth's floor.
At her footstep the birds awake
And cry their greeting.
The sky, flushed and pale, is conscious
Of coming splendor.
Dew hangs heavy
On leaf and blade.
Down from the sea . . .
A cool, fresh wind is blowing.
The fields ripple
Like a silvery lake in the breeze.
It is beautiful—inexpressibly beautiful—
The unused day.
It is untouched—unsoiled—
Day . . . just begun.

THE FEEL OF FREEDOM

The feel of freedom, to be yourself,
The feel of freedom, to speak your thought,
The feel of freedom, to do as you please.

The feel of freedom, to be yourself,
To enjoy that glorious sky above.
Be glad you have your wits and health,
To soak up the elements of God's love.

The feel of freedom, to speak your thoughts,
To come and go, or just to watch others go to and fro.
To accomplish the things you want in life,
To love, help, and enjoy peace, not strife.

The feel of freedom, to go through life as you please,
And know God cares and knows your needs.
Not hurting anyone with the freedom that's yours,
To ignore the rights of others is not
Freedom anymore.

The feel of freedom is not to infringe,
But that life, through love, peace and
        Helping all mankind brings freedom
To all men.

DEFIANCE

trust is suffering, what I did before I thought;
trust is suffering, no matter what I believe;
giving is receiving, creed of the monist school;
sacrifice is suffering, when done too much daily.
cultist . . .
I'll have no guilt for striking you
I see no pleasure or joy in your spiritual way;
there's no middle way reason in your eyes,
no gentleness would do anything.
how your vengeance copies the oppressor!
aren't you happy, mind-messiah, at your bodies,
unhappy whores, and vegetables that kill:
there's many no-names your spaceships can't convince.

* * *

BYRON AFTER SHELLEY

a poor world, losing Socrates to Christ and India
whose irrational hordes beat heads
the syncretic churches offer a trade-off . . .
beat your torso and study their law books
the business teams preach murder instinct
governments have likes and dislikes;
this scene seems as eternal as dual myth.
there's no finish to hatred, unless
each moves on to find a companion
each works with sympathies in likable labors
each feels limits backed by custom and law;
for lack of all of these
I complain like Byron after meeting Shelley
a fierce, individual bleeding.

CITY HUSTLER

Those who rule by fear, say:
Clean your rump, and show courtesy,
Tomorrow you'll be eaten by holy society;
Keep your feelings in the closet,
Your perceptions mean nothing, or too much,
Your sensual touch is out of order;
In the time that all learn what is good
The status seekers and police types lose their marks.
God forbid! if the workaholics settle in one place
Most people would die of reflection.
Fear, taboo, merit, defend against
What anarchy, feeling, commune, go together;
Tolerate only the ones most clean and quiet
The religious heroes in marble and dead trees.
Do not follow alternates to cold, straight polity.
Industry must destroy so that we fear God.

* * *

LIBERTARIAN

Continued readiness, so much like paranoia,
Continued prudence, so much like delusion:
Mind dwells on parts, forces the issues into trade!
Gentleness leaves open doors where new habits gather.
Relaxed muscles—so unlike fascists' ideal
Unchanging spiritual rocks invulnerable
Super-objectives of those who traded away play as fantasy.
Struggle as foremost is a pathology trip—
May rules be subject to change,
May no violence bind.

FRENCH TENDERLOIN

I am a dualist son:
keep the monist god and monist money
I fear one order parallels the other
the city is electric cord on a faceless wall
a philosophy of mass moving murder;
stay safe only on the edge
crave a series of new social communities
squeamish conscience-objector
dying with the peasants whom the church does shield.

* * *

IN THE FOREST

all is one, a basic fact;
everyone learns from their own feelings
as their mind envelopes this jungle world.
I want the peace of the garden,
the statue that doesn't really belong
in seasonal flowering plants;
whiteness warm in the sun
but christ and the devil drag me into charity or greed:
such mythic fights double the fatigue of responding.

* * *

PLANNINGS

you must act good to get lucky;
you must act bad to cover all areas;
is that why ruins excite me?
sun fills the spaces
but does not build or rearrange.
you must ask to please
but imagination holds so many undiscussed schemes.

CORINE BRASHER

THOUGHTS AND DEEDS

It's not what we have or what we need,
But what we do to show a good deed.
This is what makes a friend all aglee
And gives them a reason to want to be.
Of my thoughts each day, I have to choose
Which of my talents God wants me to use
To bring some joy for a friend's happiness,
May the Lord guide me to always bless.
May I be the person that God wants me to be
And not to hurt others who have hurt me.
Of all the deeds that we have done so far,
Are we proud of ourselves for what we are?
Have we brought joy or have we caused a heartbreak?
A true friend brings happiness and never an ache.
Some deeds don't seem to always turn out for good
Though through our dreams, we thought they would.
If our dreams are no more than intentions only
We will probably fail a friend who is very lonely.
The Lord tells us that we can't love by spoken words alone,
But in deed and truth our love is shown.
May I be that special kind of friend to everyone
That my thoughts are put into active deeds well done.
Happiness is not what we take, but what we give
And life is not just as we pray, but how we live.
I hope that I can be the same kind of friend,
Just as Jesus is my friend and I can trust in Him.

THE PEDDLER

Get out of here, Satan,
And leave me alone.
I don't want you here,
This is my home.
Don't try to tempt me
To go down the wrong path.
You will only make God
Show His wrath.

I have a little temple
Where God does live.
My little temple of faith
Wants nothing that you give.
For when Jesus knocked
I let Him come in.
He holds the key to my temple of faith
And He does not welcome sin.

I could put a padlock
On each and every door
But you would only try to intrude
Just as you have many times before.
You might as well quit knocking
I will not let you in.
Satan, you are just a nuisance
For trying to peddle sin.

ABOVE ALL THINGS

Each time that I get on my knees and pray
Do I always ask God to show me the way?
I ask Him for forgiveness of each sin,
Though sometimes I hardly know where to begin.

He is a rewarder of those who diligently ask,
But our sins cannot hide behind a mask.
He knows my every thought and everything I do,
But He tells us, "Repent and I will forgive you."

I sought the Lord and He heard me.
He is the only one who could set me free.
He delivered me from all my fears
And He has heard my pleas for all these years.

I'm nothing without God, I readily confess.
He is the only one that can bring true happiness.
For when I have faltered, He takes me under His wings
And whispers, "I still love you, above all things."

* * *

CHAIN OF LOVE

Friendship is built on faith and trust
That is bonded together like the links of a chain.
Although our souls be rent in twain,
May God grant that chain will never rust
Until old friends meet again.

That chain of love has many a link
One for each memory that friends always share.
And are locked together with friendship prayer.
Each link is like a bond of strength
Whence comes from God, who will always care.

QUENCHED, AT LAST

"I thirst!" He cried—that man upon the cross
Of Calvary, the One they there impaled
Because His doctrine had reduced to dross
Their earthy, earthbound schemes of selfish rule.
Oh, how they hated Him who used to say
That one to save his soul must sometimes die.
"Well, now," they said, "let Him for His soul pay
The price He fixed: at cost of His own life."
"I thirst!" He cried. In vinegar they soaked
A sponge in hopes that this would seal His lips,
This stale and putrid sop at Him they poked.
It was too late to stifle His last cry.
"It's·finished!" . . . over now, God's thirst for men,
From all eternity unslaked till then.

* * *

THE SADNESS OF BEAUTY

Things beautiful a sometime sadness brings,
A melancholy with a sense of pain,
Esthetic sadness rooted in desire
Of something, someone not to have again.
I hold her aging photograph: her eyes
Still bright as if she gazed on Beauty's face;
Her countenance revealing all her love
For children who were often commonplace.
Now half a century and more is gone.
These paper eyes don't move; these paper lips
Now speak no ever-gentle, soft-voiced words . . .
Her photo my gnarled hand more tightly grips.
Her phantom crowds the window of my soul.
We'll see each other still, though ages roll.

120

ONE WHO CAME BACK

Some are convinced that of the many who
    Before us passed Death's narrow portal through,
None have returned, their kinsmen to acquaint
    The way they passed, to furnish them a clue.

There many are who toward the end of life
    Concern themselves about all who have left
The joys and sorrows of this mortal scene,
    Their only brethren quitting quite bereft.

Through Death's dim, cloistered passage they emerged;
    Yet who of them against the bars have surged
To break the news of that strange "otherworld,"
    To tell us where the destined roads converged?

Came one with deathless urge who crossed the breach,
    Our spirits with her messages up buoyed,
The blessed Virgin Mary heaven-sent,
    Who frequently has bridged the cosmic void.

Oh, blest Maria, thou, who through the years
    Returning here to earth hast calmed our fears,
Trace yet again for us the distant path,
    Long ere the tryst with our Creator nears!

We come in water, and we leave in ash,
    Poor, fitful creatures! Still, the way we know,
Not from the Dead; from Thee, from Death assumed.
    Maria, come; and say: "My child, let's go!"

AN OLDER LOVE

(For older youngsters and
   junior Senior Citizens)

I wish I knew you when
We were younger and stronger;
I wish I knew you then
And our love would be for longer.

But it's not the last inning—
Let it be the beginning
Of a beautiful love.

I wish I knew you when
Things went wrong
You would have been
My life's song.

Even now, you are making me
Younger and stronger;
I wish I knew you longer.

I wish I knew you when
Things went amiss;
I would still have your kiss
The best kind of bliss.

But what's wrong with starting now
To take our vow?
We can be together every day
And travel together the rest of the way.

MARLENA BRISKIN

SEPTEMBER

I haven't seen you since September
When all the leaves were red and gold.
I haven't seen you since September
When to me your love you told.

You went away when love was blooming
You went away but I'm assuming
That you'll be back before September.
You'll be back when you remember
And all the leaves are red and gold
And stay with me 'til we grow old.

WOMEN INDISPENSABLE

"Woman, oh woman, whatever she be,
Whatever she is, she's necessary."
This familiar phrase, often quoted in jest,
Really honors a woman and praises her best.
Ever since her creation (Biblically) from the rib of man,
She has affected life's course with her feminine plans.
In tribute to the Black woman this fits her to a "t,"
Her inherent power and talents run the gamut from "a to z."
A variety of definitions describe her nomenclature,
She's the alpha of the human race, analogous to "Mother Nature,"
Her roots are in the valley of the Nile and Euphrates where Black
        people reigned
And initiated a culture from which the world learned and gained;
Down through the pages of time she's embarked
And on each page made a definite, momentous mark.
She's helped shape the destiny of the entire world,
And within its history she's conspicuously furled.
Long before there was a "Mayflower" or even America was found
The beautiful Black woman was a creature of renown;
She's a human dynamo, though delicate and sweet,
And embodies attributes that make living complete;
She's the daughter of "Mother Nature" and old "Father Time,"
Whose African heritage reflects charm and greatness sublime.
In Biblical history she was a versatile star,
And all through her existence has a distinguished repertoire.
During the era of slavery her courage was well-known,
She bore the brunt of the burden to maintain her home,
She gave her all to protect her people from serfdom's disaster,
Even succumbed to the sadistic wiles of her slave master.
She was inspirational, courageous and a formidable protector,
Through her many hardships she was never a family defector.
Whatever her complexion, hair style or fashion taste,
The Black woman has remained the queen of her race
This lovely lady has been exploited without reason,
Because of her blackness she's experienced all kind of treason,
But despite this she fights for liberty and justice for all,
She has endless endurance and on her faith she stands tall.
She's the image of Venus, "goddess of beauty and love,"

She can be cataclysmic or as gentle as a dove;
She's a human commodity so essential to life.
She's ambiguous, equivocal and of no one certain type.
She's considered the weaker sex but has strength to impart,
The problems of the world lay heavily on her heart.
She can cope with all of this and still replenish the earth,
It's difficult to evaluate this woman and her worth.
'Tis said that behind a happy and successful man a woman is there,
Be she mother, wife, grandmother, daughter, sister or just a friend
      who cares.
A woman can exert her infiuence for either good or bad,
She can be delightfully happy or dangerously sad,
She's a variety of moods from termagant to tender
And can enhance or destroy the dignity of her gender.
The role of the Black woman is quite sui generis,
And one that she handles with excellent finesse.
Today's woman's duties are ambiguously defined,
Complex and compound are the ways they're designed;
There are many innovations in this computerized age
Of independent automation and calculators that gauge
Previously, "women's suffrage" and now women's liberation
Makes her perspective seem a formidable sensation.
On her bid for her rights she's considered audacious,
But, as a matter of fact, she's quite perspicacious;
She's a martyr who takes very seriously her task
Of securing for her counterparts the rights for which they ask,
Non discrimination, equal opportunity and socio economic benefits,
For this cause she vigorously and vehemently emits.
There are women who feel they are not emancipated
And that, as a woman, they are much underrated,
But a woman is vitally essential to life's plan,
'Tis said she was created to fulfill the life of man,
To be his earthly glory and make his world complete,
The essence of his entity, a veritable helpmeet.
Regardless of the whys and wherefores of this woman and her place,
She can compete with and challenge any background, creed or race.
There is certainly no one like her, with her blessed femininity,
With one hand she rocks the cradle while the other guides our destiny.
We can draw our own conclusions of the Black woman and her role,
"Yes, woman, oh woman, whatever she be,
Whatever she is, she's necessary."

PROFESSIONS

The oldest profession of course we all know
    but a newer one is horning in.
And though we doctors try our best to show
    compassion and skill—but let us begin.

Never in the history of this strange world
    has one profession been so greedy
They have cheated and gouged and false charges hurled
    and converted doctors to the ranks of the needy.

Of whom am I speaking such vileness and guile?
    why, lawyers, of course, and their filthy ways.
Attorneys and judges still crooks all the while
    as they twist the truth to anything that pays.

This country was great with the divinest of starts,
    with laws to protect the richest or poor.
A constitution was made by men with real hearts
    and courts and elections to protect freedom's door.

With gentle subversion and careful erosion
    lawyers changed all that and proceeded corrupt.
They invade all segments of life with corrosion
    to divide and change, confuse and disrupt.

And wealth and power were logical results
    of actions protected by self-made laws.
Law schools were jammed with more of the cults
    who wanted more riches from loopholes and flaws.

They bled the poor and probated the old,
    they cheated the rich and stole from the dead.
If a law didn't fit they changed it for gold
    and elected each other to be corporate heads.

All this time, another profession
    proceeded in blind faith diseases to cure.
.Unaware of the danger and now in confusion
    must admit naivete in their trust—for sure.

In making their very livelihood vulnerable
    to attack by this beast of violent prey
They left the soft under belly exposed and gullible
    to the barbs and hooks and shades of gray.

And before awareness, a new term was born
    then another and more to attract us.
Informed consent, *res ipsa loquitur* was torn
    from pages which eventually read "malpractice."

Now without hope for justice or relief,
    their faith nearly gone, the doctors are pleading
For help from the courts of the land in belief
    that some miracle will save them from gouging and
    bleeding.

Where will it all end—this fraternicide
    of the medical profession by the legal?
In violence, retribution, a sickness and suicide?
    in strikes and pestilence and vengeful upheaval?

Or will the lawyers come to their senses
    and turn off the greed and give us some hope,
And apply the ethics of the healing profession
    to the ills of our country at the end of its rope?

SEASOUND

Gently I am moved
by the sound of the sea
as I sit so alone
    in misery,
with my burdens getting harder to bear
I reach out to you
to find you're not there . . .
had that last wave
swept you from under my love—
    yes,
forever from my reach.

* * *

DISTANCE

Please let me inside . . .
I'm so cold,
so far
    from home.

* * *

SILENT LOVE

Thunderous roar
upon surf-tormented shore . . .
    blackened skies
seen through her eyes . . .
    silent rain
of a love in vain.

WANDERER

I possess not the sea
nor the river's chill;
I walk the shore alone
until my lake be still . . .

To wander with the being
of former soul unknown,
to follow present footsteps
again in search I roam.

* * *

QUIETUDE

Tonight there are no words:
silence surrounds thee
dreams engulf thee
the sea is in slumber . . .

* * *

OUTREACH

I reach out to you,
my silent one,
afraid and so alone
to grasp the emptiness of space . . .
was it in a dream
that I saw you last?
yes, you were walking
and I was unable to follow . . .

DEEP

O, heavy is my depression
as of winter awaiting spring
everlasting state of being
        to I, once a king . . .

Weeping upon emptiness
darkened corners alone,
dreaming of an island
where I've made my home.

Yet it lies deep inside
buried with the years,
while often at dusk I search
a quiet rage of tears . . .

Passing through this garden
a mist of morning dew,
careful not to awaken
this thought of loving you . . .

DEMONS

There lurks a demon
Deep in dark recess
Of a convoluted crevice
In my brain.

A mixed connection
Made by a frightened infant
Controls my destiny
And distorts the data
Programmed into that wondrous computer in my head.

How many such demons lurk in your brain?

Do infantile fears and childish ignorance
Of lifetimes ago
Rule the adult of today?

Help us!

Doctor, help us!

God, help us!

Mother, help me!

Mama!

'TIS SO
(About my experienced truth in verse)

A drunken car driver caused this adverse personal episode
By depriving me of my desired mortal body abode,
And consequently left me as a patient in three hospitals
With three death certificates as completed with usual details.

In three seconds after mortal death number one, I arrived at our
    moon's edge,
The inside of which showed no water, animal, or plant life nor
    hedge,
But only three relatively large observable volcano crater holes
And other geological structures simulating development in
    planned molds.

Deprived of mortal sensations before my transcient skips,
I comfortably completed all three interplanetary tirps
To another solar planet which was occupied by post mortals on
    high,
Separated by sex, and all were mature and happily learning to
    progress thereby.

Deceased mortals, as my father's and mother's spirits were there;
They recognized me and called me by my mortal name to avoid
    scare.
Father was more handsome and Mother more beautiful than
    mortality entails.
They asked me eight questions concerning me and my mortal
    details.

My second mortal death took me to spirits of my wife's mortal
    parents.
A third interplanetary escapade also occurred by deceased
    necessity.
All observed spirits (near 500,000) wore garments but had no
    bald heads, nor obesity;
Thereafter I personally received consent and permission to again
    enter mortality.

I LIBERATED MY SPIRIT

In a real episode in my life, almost totally sublime, I as man
in an unavoidable car wreck in seconds of time became a spirit
eternal, and did unavoidably definitely recline; as a spirit, I
entered their world in ten seconds in interplanetary rhyme.

Spirits spoke another language but also mine and their own as
well. I asked several questions from their authoritative personnel
and was granted permission to look into and beyond their veil;
also into acquaintances and secrets in unavoidable complete
        detail.

I saw the spirits of my mortal parents who had died eternal life
to gain. They recognized me and called me by my name, Royal,
and bid me to refrain from talking about returning to earth but
to happily there remain, but I had too much on earth that needed
care there to refrain.

So I went back from the spirits' planet to earth and mortal body
in one second. In this trek I died three times by M.D.s' accurate
recorded record. I'm still living in earnest acclaim and certain
knowledge beckoned, that there's life eternal over there and
spirits galore also genetically related.

Life yet has unsolved secrets and unanswered truths which may
be galore; yet they may be unanswered today or tomorrow as
        eternity
trespasses some more. But the enclosed secrets are solved, so
abide by them in sincere store, or you may flunk the test related
to sincere, eternal progress forevermore.

TOMORROW IS VERY CERTAIN

Tomorrow is a definite certainty;
My experience dictates this to me.
In it no facts were hidden certainly;
I recall its definiteness with glee.

Shortly after a fatal car accident,
My spirit definitely left my mortal body
And went to that planet where the spirits went
And communicated freely with many almighty.

I returned with permission to care for my wife
Who was ill and relied on help from me.
I again became mortal for another life
But she demised and left me to lonesome be.

My preference for locale is with her,
Where man dwells as spirit formerly.
If sealed he and his wife remain together
As happy spirits for life and for eternity.

SYMPHONY OF NIGHT

Hark! The symphony of night
    Halts the firefly in his flight;
The softness of the waning moon
    Greets the newborn day too soon.

Lovers bide their time and then
    Turn to each other's arms again;
Shades of light of the new day
    Smooth each bothersome care away.

Billowy clouds mount in the sky
    Driven by something greater than I;
Weary workers find surcease
    Of daily chores. Night brings them peace.

The sun sinks at close of day
    Into the waters across the bay,
The swallow falters in his flight
    Again we hear the songs of night.

* * *

THOUGHTS WHILE DRESSING FOR A DATE

When the Sun sinks low in the West
    And slowly slips from view
The whispering leaves grow calm,
    The clouds are a brighter hue.

The first bright star appears,
    And the shimmer of its light
Seems to try to tell me
    That the Moon will be up tonight.

1941

No mother's hand will fix the pillow
    To go beneath his head
His pillow will be a knapsack:
    This soldier boy is dead.

His hand is on his rifle
    His blouse is gory red
He was shot going over:
    This soldier boy is dead.

He left a sweetheart on the step
    "I'll be back," he said.
His plane fell in the ocean:
    This soldier boy is dead.

Why can't we see as we look back
    At Flanders with poppies red
For a score of years we've shed our tears:
    Those soldiers too are dead.

To what avail with shells like hail
    The doughboy's blood was shed?
Because some loathe democracy
    Our soldier boys are dead . . .

* * *

A SUMMER DAY

The solemnness of a hillside glen
    The murmur of a stream
The warmness of a summer day
    Let me sit and dream . . .

COME AUTUMN

I see late summer shadows, the sun within my reach,
Open skies wiped clean by the wind's hint of autumn.
I feel crisp fres nights and days easy like a breeze,
The leaving of summer; the beginning of a dream.
The boughs seem less burdened and the barns are all bulging,
The water still beckons; the sea is still calling.
And still the roses keep on blooming; but the butterfly regrets
That time is ever moving; come autumn we'll forget.

* * *

WITH THIS RING

We are in love, or so we say,
Yet you're not here, you're far away.
You still need time to make your plans,
But when you're not here I clasp another's hand.
He offers more, he shows more affection,
So I must choose between this and your seeming rejection.
I still need you, and so I break his heart
By telling him that we must part.
Back to you I go, with his wish for well
But what will happen, you never can tell.
He says I lost a good thing
But you won me back with this ring.
This ring means so much and even more,
I thought it meant I wouldn't be alone any more.

LOVE

Love is the theme in everyone's dream, constantly filling the soul
with bliss. Thus, desire we all require of our loved ones
        unappealed
till trials and troubles creep in, causing sins we fail to amend too
late for our Saviour to adhere. Thus wasting our blessings down
        here
through each struggle and strife, we build a better life by
        witnessing
each day for Christ.

Love is a transparent oil used on the hub of this fast-spinning
        world.
Without it everything squeaks and decays, regardless of the way it
might turn, causing the hopes and dreams of men to burn.

Love is nature's drug; a God-given brand will support a man and
        help
him to aspire to excelling plans beyond the imagination of many
        of
his pals, who took an overdose by chasing all the gals.

Love is the theme of a man's life, but a stale brand will make
        him
"hug" another man's wife, thus not only wrecking his life, but
causing destruction of the respect, admiration and loyalty of all
those knowing him.

It must be used according to the original prescription and without
deception to evade can cause effects on his soul, by absorbing his
strength of withstanding the jolts of this world, or soon into space
he is furled and forgotten, even before his bones are rotten.

Though we are cast in consternation by close observation of plans
placed in our hands, there is nothing to fear if God is near.

OUR RECORD IS RECORDED

When we report to God's court, we must not find our records
bare. We are told we must share His love to other souls,
and our hopes and faith display as we travel life's way.
In the Bible we are told faith without work is dead.
Therefore, we must work for life's bread. It is also
taught our report is automatically recorded and we are
systematically rewarded, judged also as to what we say.
Can you feature the pay you will receive in that day
and the office you may hold in that heavenly Gold?

* * *

FORGIVE

Please, God, forgive me this I ask,
Receive me into heaven at last.
Show me the task I need to do
Then I will try to be more true to You, dear Lord,
In more accord to Thy word as given through ages past.
I'll try to trust Thee until the last.

HURRICANE

The sky hung low, a menace, gray,
So still and hushed appeared the day,
As if the world's great pulse had stopped.
Then, one by one, the dry leaves dropped.

A breeze was stirring through the trees,
And then it was no more a breeze
But wind, its tendrils lashing o'er
The swaying trees and earthen floor.

It howled in fury overhead
As if a million eagles fled
From unseen dread, their wings abeat
In rapid tempo's onward sweep.

Then rain poured down in torrents strong,
A great crescendo to the song
Of Nature's own symphonic gale
That makes stout hearts grow small and pale.

Incessant wind and pounding rain,
A fanfare to the hurricane
That swept the earth 'til it was pure,
Then moved on to the sea once more.

The trees, now bare, stand in respect,
As all about the smashed and wrecked
Lie helpless 'neath God's mighty will.
Once more the earth and sky are still.

ECOLOGIST'S FAREWELL

Now, don't you think it's lovely?
Oh, isn't it just grand!
Across the road from my house
They're tearing up the land.

That useless field that lay for years
And sported naught but greenery,
Will soon bear condominiums
To brighten up the scenery.

Be gone, you birds and cottontails
And leave your nests and burrows.
Take wing! Make haste! Here come the trucks
And 'dozers digging forrows.

They'll plough the goldenrod and shrub
And push the thistle under.
Wild hyacinths will be no more,
They'll rip the trees asunder.

For, after all, who needs a field
When man needs space for dwelling?
But, why this lump within my throat?
What made these tears come welling?

What sadness strikes my heart and fills
My soul with deepest sorrow,
Each time I glance across the road
And think about tomorrow?

A WRITER'S PRAYER

God grant me knowledge to write words others
    can relate to
And help me share my talent with others.
God grant me the gift of help to help others
    through my thoughts and words.
And most of all, create in me a grateful
    heart to remember from whom my
    talent came.

* * *

AMERICA! OH, AMERICA!

America of the brave and free,
America, a home for you and me.
Its beauty reaches from heaven to sea
America is the place to be

Men have fought and died for our land,
But we are destroying it as fast as we can.
Values and morals are beginning to fail
And demonstrations and violence prevail.

Our intelligence and wisdom has grown,
But we are allowing the destruction of our home.
If we are to remain a whole nation and free,
We must restore America
And make it, once more, a great place to be!

MOTHER

From her heart flows a fountain of love;
From her mouth she speaks words of wisdom,
　　　guidance, discipline, and the distinction
　　　between right and wrong.
With her eyes and ears she looks and listens
　　　for danger;
With her arms she holds and comforts me
　　　through sickness and health;
With her feet she walks miles caring for me;
With her head she teaches and educates
　　　me for the future;
With love she nourished and carried me;
With love and travail, she gave me life.
Through birth she established a bond
　　　between mother and child that can
　　　never be broken:
Mother—the sweetest name on earth.

AFTERNOON LIGHT

The exquisite
Moment
Of memory
Comes into view . . .

I see him—
See
The young expectations
Rise
In his body . . .

I re-experience
The movement
Of his eyes
Shining
Intensely
On the scene . . .

I undress
Slowly,
Catching
The mirror's impression
Of my dark supple body,

And
My stillness
Becomes a dance,
Accompanied
By a symphony
Of afternoon light
Turning blue
Through
His faded curtains . . .

ON TAKING A TUB BATH

Thy bowl of limpid water,
Tepid, pure and effervescent,
Teeming with bubbling suds evanescent . . .
Take thee my naked body unto thine womb
And embrace me, Aquarius, with thy radiant lymph of the eons!

Mortal am I of this planetary sod,
Enslaved by the occupancy of existence,
I come to thee as a servant to desquamate the shield
And to expurgate the grime harvested of terrestrial toil.
Divest me, oh font of purity, with thy tranquil lavage
And rid me of the sludge and the eccentricities
That mire my being into degradation!

Thy lucent pool that immerses my body,
Fatigued with the residues of subsistence,
Possess me with thine arms of compassion
And let thy beneficent radiation
Permeate the abysmal recesses of the psyche
And liberate the odium and the obsessions
That pollute and misguide my earthly mission;
And reinvest me with thy affluence of pervading goodness,
And with thy love and faith, tolerance and direction
As ordained in the eternal laws of the Cosmos!

Oh living water that dissolves the detriments of existence,
Let me bequeath to thee a replica of the soil
Which rooted the flora that generated this corporeal being!
Let me rejoice with the naivete of creation, and give birth
To the gurgling, growling and grumbling debris
That reincarnates to posterity the fruits of my yield
Down the drain!

SAMUEL P. BURRE, M.D.

As I emerge shorn of the outer sheath
And resurrected with ablution in the edifying life before me,
I make my exit from the orbit of colluvial scum,
That adheres to the inner sanctum of the reservoir,
With reactivated nudity.

Heavenly bath that disrobes the residuum of yesterday
And transfuses me with the etherealization of vision,
Thank thee for communion with God
And for the renaissance of my protoplasmic abode.
Humble offspring fashioned in the image of the universe,
I kneel to thee for creating me worthy
To serve in betterment the realities of the morrow
With a conscience immaculate to match my integument!

ODE: SOUL MATE

(To you, my love: I dedicate the rest of my life)

Oh love! My hallow'd one!
Why hast thou come from thee?
Is it because you knew in your heart,
In your . . . soul
That I just want'd and truly need'd you
To be forever close to me?

     No, your physical body
I'll never again visibly see
     But even so
Your precious "love" and "spirit"
Are just as gratifying to me—

So on the wings of a dove,
Thou wast sent . . . and thus came forth to me
Right straight from heaven above—

     And for us
I know that there'll never ever be another love!

     Thy heart is true,
     Therefore I knowest
That I can'st always trust in you

My weaknesses, shame and doubt,
     Oh, my loving Angel!
Please continue to help me to cast them out!

"Peace on earth—goodwill to men;
I thank thee, heavenly Father, for all of my many
     blessings;
And I praise thee, oh Lord for my sweet, gentle,
     spiritual soulmate and friend! Se'lah

COSMIC SEASONS

(In honor of my deceased father,
            the beloved Reverend Ab Davis)

As Fall and Winter has
            or will soon come to town,
Most of us in some way or another
Will eventually find ourselves all burden'd down;
            But Thanksgiving's fiesta,
With family and lov'd ones all around—
Serves to inspire us more to pray
And to start looking forward to
            December;
Because Christ was born on . . . Christmas day—
Marveling in the fact that spring and summer,
            once again
        are on their merry
                way!

Well, spring is here now—
My very favorite time of the year!
And don't you just love to hear
            the cute little birdies
Sing their lovely spring cheer?

Colorful flowers have also begun to bloom
And for me—it's not happening a bit too soon
I like fall and winter, so-to-say;
It's just that after awhile
I'll start wishing that they'd hurry and go away
And I'll start looking forward to Easter day
            With all its beautiful
Bunnies of pink, yellow and blue—
Oh, merciful Savior of all mankind;
            black and white
            I love thee true!

And I'm so very, very sorry that they crucifi'd you!
Yes . . . spring with her April showers are here,
But summer is on his way again —
And oh, how I'll hate to see them end!
But looking on the bright side,
            perhaps you and I
Will make at least, one very good friend,
And may August of each succeeding year
Be heart-touchingly remember'd;
            because 'twas then,
That we lost the King of Rock 'n' Roll,
Who, to all of us, was so very, very dear!

CATHLEEN

Such a fairy elfin thing,
　　Like a bird just taking wing.
　　Something wonderful, divine,
　　　　Is this darling child of mine.

More than reddest rubies rare,
　　More than lilies white and fair,
　　More than Heaven's azure skies
　　　　Are her sparkling, laughing eyes.

Like a moth with gossamer wings,
　　Like an angel when she sings,
　　Like a veiling mist of moon,
　　　　Or a scented breath of June.

Do you wonder that I sigh,
　　And a tear drops from my eye,
　　As I muse what years will bring
　　　　Such a dainty, priceless thing.

* * *

MY FRIENDS

I do not choose my friends for fame,
Or for a grand old family name,
Nor look for mansion stately, tall,
With iron gate and garden wall . . .

Perhaps the house is strangely small,
With scarcely any room at all,
But there is always bound to be
A gracious hospitality.
With loving people living there
Who let you sit just anywhere,
And serve you with a cup of tea,
That is the kind of friend for me.

GRATITUDE

Though the winds of time change,
we can still hear your whispers
with every breeze.

And yes, it is apparent that you
have never left. Your spirits reach
on and on. Your love, tears, and pain
are felt in each reflection of the circling
ponds of life.

As it was your bond and duty to carry
your message on, it is ours to continue
to build on your hopes and dreams of a
better day; to be replenished by your
courage and strength.

We, your daughters and sons, thank you for
a heritage so great, for the love ever
precious, for the fight then yours, now
ours, which entwines us forever in a Quest
yet unanswered, but never lost.

LIFE EVERLASTING

Among us is the seed, the seed we will
nurture until it blooms bright, the
seed which will extend until out-of-sight.

    Pour forth the water
    Make moist the ground
    Until the earth
        EXPLODES!

And the seed is no longer a seed,
    It is here it lives.
    It is in you. It is in I.
    It is the Spirit!

JOURNEY TO ANOTHER LAND

Ferryman, take me to the other side,
Where clearest water runs without mere wave.
And love's sincere; emotions needn't hide.
Each moment there a golden treasure save.
The journey's easy; passage is by sleep.
I steer the course to find my fondest dream.
Each loving word and touch inside I keep.
Not even I can wreck my errant scheme.
The ferry's here. I can't return as yet.
I need total love to make me whole.
All sweet, no tears, no sad, no lover's debt.
Is love without pain my ultimate goal?
      Ferryman, come back for me while I will go!
      Utopian life makes passion much too slow.

* * *

ALL MINE

I, like Neptune, God of the Sea,
Maintain an invisible hold
On those who once loved me,
Though that love now flows cold.
I hold and I hold.

I sit on my throne with my subjects blind
And pretend each subject is all mine.
It is not my wrath they fear, I know.
It is just that they once loved me so.
So I hold, tighter, I hold.

153

ACROSS THE TRACKS!

A car rolls
Down a busy street
Garbage in a
Can very neat

Music song by
A record shop
As a car streaks
At a word called stop

Not a child
In the street playing
Not one piece
Of paper on
The ground laying

But as we
Cross the railroad tracks
There we saw
Large alley rats

Paper in the
Streets and garbage
Cans tumble
And even a street
Gang having a rumble

Large holes
In the street
And children
Crying for something
To eat

What can I say?
It goes on every day

One day they will
Move across the track
And push the white
People back.

* * *

IN THE EMPTY ROOM!

in the empty room
with old memories
behind her she stands there,

full with tears
in her eyes . . .
she cries to
the echoes of the room,

no one to hear
her cries . . .
cold, wet, and
lonely she is
in the empty room . . .

memories of mama
and papa together,
loving one another;

memories of laughter
and good times together . . .

then daddy died
and left me.

as time goes on
mama leaves
me here all alone
to sell her body
on the street
and leaving me
with nothing to eat . . .

in the empty room
where my cries echo
back at me,

cold, wet, and lonely,
I am only a child
in the empty room.

* * *

IN A DARK ALLEY BEFORE NINE!

A cry, a scream,
A dark alley,
A knife for a weapon
And a crime
Is committed.

In the morning
About nine
A body they find

Who cried for help,
But no one bothered
To take the step to help;
A cry, a scream
In a dark alley.

COME AND TAKE JESUS

If you're trapped and lost in the world around
And the name Jesus Christ is an unfamiliar sound,
Or your world right now hasn't much to offer
Lay down your sins and come to the altar.

Then stop and pause so you might see
How Christ our Lord can set you free
From sins and pain and hurt beneath
To the tree of life as one small leaf.

Don't pass Him up 'cause you feel ashamed
To stop and pray through His sweet name.
He died for the sins of all mankind
So that Joy Unspeakable you'd one day find.

If you feel you need help to understand
Look up to God and He'll lend a hand.
Just stop and ask to learn—He'll teach
If only for salvation you'll earnestly reach.

Don't put it off—for now is the time.
His door may close and you'll be left behind.
He's reaching out to help your needs
And can't you see He's begging? Please . . .

If He loved us that much to be willing to give
His life on the cross so that we might live,
What greater life could there possibly be
Than eternal Heaven for you and me?

A PSALM

I love Thee, oh Lord, with all of my heart,
And from Thee my path shall never depart.
Thou makest a path up mountains for me,
Thou sendest me light so that pathway I see.

Thou art my leader, my life and my all;
If Thou art with me, I never shall fall.
I will follow Thee from now to the end
For I know that Thou art my truest friend.

* * *

RELEASE

Honey, call me not again to this earthly life of pain;
Rejoice with me that I may go where I need not suffer so.
Though the path to thorns has grown since you travel it alone,
Bide it, Honey, bide a wee; then, my dear, you'll come to me.

When we meet beyond the river, in the land of the forever,
I will take your hand and say: "Come on, Honey, come this
      way";
We will pass a joyous spring, where the angels meet to sing,
The fountain and the tree of life, and a neighbor and his wife.

Then we'll reach our mansion fair, with its great big easy chair.
Honey, I came on to see where the finest things would be.
I'm so glad, my old sweetheart, that we nevermore shall part,
But will sing and dance and play in that wondrous land of day.

GIFTS

Oh! the hustle and rush of December
As we scurry here and there,
In search of a gift for a loved one
With a value beyond compare.

But remember, the love and devotion
That the Shepherds came to pay
Were as welcome as gold, and the great gifts
That the Wise Men took there that day.

So the best gift to give to a loved one
As we travel on LIFE'S WAY,
Is the love and the peace and the good will
That Christ came to bring on that day.

* * *

DAY AFTER CHRISTMAS

'Twas the day after Christmas, and girls and boys
Kept stumbling and falling o'er new Christmas toys.
First Donna fell down over Betty's new doll
To avoid stepping on Larry's little red ball;
Then Joycie ran out with rescuing hope
And got tangled up in John's lariat rope.

While Mother was trying to clear the room
She stumbled and fell over Joycie's toy broom.
Then Father, aroused by the cries and clatter
Came in to see just what was the matter.
He slid cross the floor on Billy's new gun —
And that was the end of the holiday fun.

NOBILITY OF PURPOSE

Wise men are great
Because of a spirit
Filled with content,
That flows freely
From a conscience
Crystal clear,
Knowing what he wants
And acquiring it with alacrity,
Linked with nobility of purpose.

* * *

LIFELINK

Knee-deep in the snow
of experience
We profit by its visit
Into our life's path,
And withdraw our boots
From the snowdrifts of life.

Recruit and salvage
The gems of talents and love
With active energy,
To create with steady gait
The gift of happiness,
Linked with good health.

LONELINESS

Is there a remedy?
When we isolate our mind
We stand alone under Heaven's sky-blue dome.
Loneliness? None will admit it.
Dreaming of memories, sorrows
And such, linked with power
To depress, till we shake
Our brains to see the
Many blessings we enjoy,
For which we should
Endeavor to be grateful—
To enjoy—and cast all
Anxiety into the winds of oblivion.
Then claim freedom from
Depression's prison.
Regain our wisdom's thinking;
Let the blinking sunlight of faith
Shine forth with joy and happiness
Instead of Loneliness.
Good-bye! Good-bye
Forever—Loneliness.

THE BEAUTY OF THE CREATION (GOD'S)

In so many things we can see God's handiworks and behold the
beauty of the creation! Yes, all over the nation!

We watch as corn is planted in the ground,
As it grows and its beauty shows, its crop becomes the talk
Of the town!

We watch as tiny buds turn to beautiful flowers; there's beauty
to be found in the summer showers!

A caterpillar may be an ugly sight to me, but when it
becomes a butterfly, it's a joy to see.

There is beauty in the creatures of the sea and in those on the
Land, but above all there is beauty in the highest creation—Man!

Beauty can be seen in many things if we'd stop! Look up! Look
    down!
Then we would see beauty all around.

Behold the stars as they lay in the sky!

Have you observed the birth of a baby? The doctor slaps him and
out comes his first cry! This miracle alone causes us to sigh!

God created a beautiful world, to admit this is a must!
Yes, He alone could make a Man from the dust.
We can hear sounds of beauty with ears;
Why some worship the beauty and not the Creator
Is what drives me to tears!

POETRY

What is poetry?
Is it simply an expression of thoughts in rhythmic, poetic words
    that incite emotional fascination? Is it something that
    embodies fancy imagination, finer emotion and a sense of
    incomparable beauty? Or something that represents the
    growth and shaping of the American spirit that momentarily
    captures lyric feeling, releases joyful laughter for sensuous
    moments of ecstasy and delight? Or, is it the art of writing
    poems that elicits reading pleasurable response when the
    quality of poetry is appropriate to the level and interest of
    the reader? Because of America's heritage, how can we
    define, and how can we elucidate what American poetry is?
    Could it be the pure essence of communication?

And why do we like poetry?
Because it can be more amusing, sad or romantic than any other
    kind of writing. It can portray the splendor of our
    imagination, our sensitive feeling of delight, our meaningful
    life and the world we live in through discreetly selected
    rhythmic words that will give us a series of meaningful
    thoughts through the lilting music of beautiful poetic words.

In the poems that follow you'll find reflections on life . . . some
    entertaining, some amusing that will be yours for reading
    pleasure. Give every poem a chance to speak to you in the
    language of poetry. Read slowly enough to appreciate the
    literary poetic quality penned by the poet, who expresses
    himself with imaginative power and beauty of thought.
    Hopefully you'll find in my selection, or in other selections
    by other poets, the true essence of poetry. Judge poetry by
    its character and quality.

Perhaps the best advice of all is in the following poem:

OF MUSIC

Not the tweetering songs
    Of robin on the treetop tall;
Not the rhythmic cadence
    Of drizzling rain on window panes;
Not the lilting tune
    Of my magic lyre,

Neither the ceaseless music
    Of the rippling stream;
Nor the whispering
    Of the whistling wind;
But your sweet voice, my dear,
    Is music to my ear.

* * *

SWEET MELODY

If I were a painter,
    I would portray the splendor
Of your delicate beauty,
    Elegance of movement . . .
Charming personality.

If I were a poet,
    I would write melody of poetry,
Of your gracefulness
    And incomparable beauty.

If I were a stream,
    I would ripple ceaselessly
In perpetual motion
    Till I joined the brimming river,
As men may come and men may go,
    But I go on forever.

If I were a composer,
    I would compose sweet melody
Just for you and me.

LOVE, ALMOST

I tried all I could but it wasn't enough;
You tried, too, but it was too much.
Someday the median we never found will be,
Though you may not be with me.

We'll be always, you know;
Unforgotten, unforgetting,
Iron memories of hopes made of sand.
As you stand, not understanding, unforgiving
I'll fall and reach for your hand —
But not far enough.

* * *

FATE

There's a perfect mate for everyone, they say,
and who am I to doubt?
Of course the girl was made that I can't live without.
She lived in Manitoba, in the back country
and was killed by a yellow pick-up when she was three.

* * *

MY LIBRARY

The ostentatious symbol of all I wish I knew:
Volumes I'm not so proud of go on the bottom shelves;
Titles enhancing my image of the moment are found at eye level.
Guests scan the shelves thinking they can tell a man's
true nature by what he reads.
They read my mask.
The real me is doodled on the paper marking page 37 of that
red-bound book I didn't finish.

LOUIS CARON

WHY I BELIEVE

I see a cloud up in the sky, a mass of vapor floating by;
    to wilting crops in sun-parched field where cattle
    low and stamp the ground.
In merciful bounty cloud does open, when sun retreats and
    drought is broken.
To drench the sun-scorched arid land and slake the thirst
    of beast and man.

                Who does these things?

I feel, I grieve for every living thing; the good, the
    bad, the rich, the poor, the very air we breathe.
For life is just a game of chance, devoid of rhyme and
    reason.
It's gambler's luck that calls the shots; we live not by
    method but madness.

Then faith prevails, life's not a whim; it does have rhyme
    and rhythm.
For only man does have a mind to think and act and reason;
    why he alone should rule the earth, and not the
    lowly bison.

When things go wrong, and doubt is strong, I ask myself
    these questions: is all by chance, or unseen hand,
    or planned with rhyme and reason?
To bring about a better plan for beast and man and season?

           I ask, myself, who does these things?

PHANTOMS

I heard a boy blow a cow horn
One clear, cold December morn.

The sound reminded me of my childhood dog
That used to follow me near foggy bogs.

The other day I rode near a live oak tree
Where Julie and I once parked on a moonlit night.·

Julie is dead.
And I remember some of the things we said.

The childhood dog is also gone,
And right after he died I was much alone.

Their memory and love will forever be
Free, as an eagle, and true to me.

Their memory and love will always last
For they are just phantoms of the past.

PEOPLE WHO SETTLED FOR LESS

Some of the people in Hart's Gap
Want to leave and see the world.
They will never go to Washington, D.C.
Or see the Smithsonian Institute
Or go to the top of the Washington Monument.
Or see where Paul Bunyan made the Grand Canyon.
Some will never see New York City
And what a pity.
Some will never see Oklahoma City,
They just sit home and put pennies in their kitty.

Some will never see Lake Pontchartrain
Or mystic New Orleans and the French Quarter,
O, what a pity;
They just sit home and put quarters
In their kitty.
O, what a shame.
Some spend their time with idle talk
And when it comes to growth or progress, they balk.
Some have a fear of being alone —
They want to get up and walk on.

Some sit in big cities on the same everyday bench
Seat, and it's no cinch.
Some spend their time with small talk, I guess,
And many are they who settled for less.

Those things that you always wanted to do —
Only you can make them come true.
Be as the bees in early spring, I see,
Do not be afraid to sail uncharted sea.
If you do you'll be surely blest,
And you won't be one of those people who
                    Settled for less.

THE TEMPLE

(For Barry)

Build me a monument to the greatest man on earth;
Set up a temple to tell me what he's worth;
Build it of gold, of which his heart is made;
Set it with a statue, that his likeness will not fade;
Scatter it with emeralds; that's the color of his eyes,
Deep, clear and flawless, they don't tell me any lies.
The gold that glints upon the walls is sunlight in his hair
To show the halo of an angel, who must have touched him there.
Fill the halls with music; that's the song he's touched me with;
Let the song play on forever, till it's legend and a myth.
You say you can't build me this temple? Not in forever and a
     day?
No matter what I promise you I would be willing to pay?
But you won't disappoint me, plunge me into dark despair.
This monument, I'll tell you, is already there.
It's here on earth already, and till I die it won't depart;
The secret to this is merely that it's here, within my heart.

WAVES

Gazing out upon the ocean late at night
The waves seem such a reassuring sight;
Like the waves of your hand
In rhythm with the band
As your imagination seeks its soaring flight.

Waves of compassion as you try so hard to find
Somebody who would seem "one of your kind."
Always groping for the answer
"Maybe that ballerina dancer,"
Never seeing, only searching with your mind.

Waves of love and waves of passion—
Neither of them was in fashion
But neither were forget-me-nots
Just macrame knots.
I really thought you needed some compassion.

Waves of tears I shouldn't cry
"It's just something in my eye";
I heard the wedding bells,
Staring at the shells
On the beach, and seeing the last wave good-bye.

HELLO, THERE!

Hello, there, sleepy people, what are you doin' tonight?
Are you sitting there in robe and slippers, and havin' yourself a
    bite?
Are you watchin' that ol' Boob Tube, while others are countin'
    sheep?
And laughin' your fool heads off, while others try to sleep?
They'll get you in the morning, after you've had your fun,
They'll be fryin' eggs and bacon, and letting the water run;
And they'll set the dog to barkin' when they open up the door,
And they'll invite the neighbors to listen to you snore;
And you won't be too darned happy to face the bright new day,
And if someone says, "Good morning," you'll say, "Ah, go
    away!"

* * *

CHILD OF THE HOLOCAUST

What evil star were you born under
That such a fate should have been yours,
When this mad world was torn asunder
By demons risen from the sewer?
The tragedy of your existence is a
Reflection of our time,
The awful things that did befall you
Were without reason —without rhyme.
Oh little Anne, child of disaster,
What anger rises in my breast,
That in these times, so very modern,
You should have suffered such a test.
It's too late now for retribution,
It's too late too for hopeless tears,
But when I read your little *Diary*,
My mind recalls those sad, sad years;
The days of Holocaust are over,
And they must never be again,
This is my prayer, Oh God in Heaven,
Make it come true, AMEN —AMEN!

171

DAVID CASPI

GOLDY

She walks with unsurpassed dignity,
She stands with great impact.
No one could touch her virginity,
That she is a sweetheart is a fact.

She frolics on all fours the whole day long
Ere she retires to bid day adieu.
My love for her remains so strong
As to last her lifetime through.

Goldy I am talking about.
A godly grace she possesses.
She has never given me reason to flout.
To me she's like one of those Barefoot Contessas.

Just look in her wide eyes and you can see
A world filled with faith, hope, and charity.
And now I will close the night
By beholding that beautiful young girl's sight.

* * *

MAJESTIC WONDERS

Blue-colored reflections, shent, watery eyes
Glare hazen truth from the sunlit red skies.
Lonely towers of virtue and spruce lurk sheer, unnoticed
By the advancing tide of waves belowhist.
Nature looks downward in scornful contempt
At those few slumber shadow-cast dim descent,
Whose worth lacks harmony, may not have been fortune spent
And blunder mars beauty heaven hath sent.
—From whom there is no answer—Time rushes on as if to say
"Farewell penitence, second chance, right of way."
Then cometh night, plus dawn to follow,
A vicious cycle spun of remorseful sorrow
For half-hearted beauties who weep a sigh of futility,
Crying unheard, "Look at me tomorrow, willingly!"

172

NATURE'S CHOSEN

High-flying eagles endowed demeaned renown
Play with the shrill fit a sad-hearted clown.
Frolicking deer, and of that variety
Wish pox on the evil gun-shooting society.
Foot-pounding growlers lay fast by the heels for their master;
All pray alarmed lest there fall nighttime disaster.
The hunter vanquishes a prevalent (not benevolent) air
Ere he retreats to retrace his steps elsewhere.
Despite taught hunger-stricken painstaking tasks to bear
Fettered, feathered furries languish, trapped by their inevitable
     lair.
Meanwhile, blighted servile human bondage by storm,
Domestic whelps felled with coats shaggy and warm
Tear wounded iron mold's brazen neglect,
Exhorting reason, assistance direct.
Nay a harkening heeded, nevertheless the tormenting
     endangerment strives
To test how tame and wild ones still persist,
Each fighting in desperate vain, until their lives
No more exist.

* * *

ERSTWHILE INCANDESCENCE IN ALASKA

The sea is fresh with salt water brine and fish
As I await on the shore bank for a catch.
The mist fills my hungry stomach and soul, wanting more
Than only a reel, bread, and hook can show for.
Jack London wrote about this time of year,
Ghostly pale and timidly appealing in October.
Suddenly it starts to rain—a harsh ending
To what was a promising summer's new beginning.
The call of the wild soundly beckons through the forest now,
A reminder of changing seasons soon to be laden with snow;
     Usufruct granted by God
     To all those who there dared trod.

173

DECADE'S LOG OF THE SEVENTIES

1970 — Riots at universities erupt, a decade's beginning.

1971 — Knapp Commission expose' of cops corrupt, Attica prison
        uprising.

1971 — President Nixon's trips to Russia and China, Israeli Olympians
        murdered by terrorist group El Fata.

1973 — End of Vietnam, comet Kohoutek, Watergate hearing.

1974 — Nixon resigns, Aaron passes Ruth, Patty Hearst kidnapping.

1975 — Job shortages, reduced budgets, cities' problems and neglect;
        "Jaws" had bitten.

1976 — A bicentennial and new president-elect; Roots was written.

1977 — New York has new mayor, Son of Sam struck, Concorde lande
        Groucho, Elvis, Bing and Guy die.

1978 — Two combatants win Nobel Peace Prize while we hear "Down
        with the Shah" and bid two popes good-bye.

1979 — Golda Meir and Nelson Rockefeller and . . . who knows what
        else is in store? Where do we go from here? Turn back the
        clock, start all over again, write a different history before
        the 80s come and dare bring us more pain, but let's hope
        more glory. That is my decade's log, yet another ten-year
        story.

THE QUESTIONS

WHAT is the demonstrative supposition whose assumption
    spawns the answer THAT, I DON'T KNOW, and WELL.
WHEN leads the asker to find out IF EVER, THEN, UNTIL and
    IS IT SO.
WHERE invites action, places, and directions HERE and
    THERE, COME and GO.
HOW might want to learn that which breeds understanding in
    order to determine WAY's rationale.
WHO stands for the estranged victim masked by his own
    personage, individuality or idiocy.
WHY inspires the all-begun, everything that exists,
    conventionally opening the transcendental door's key:
    FUTURE SHOCK, NIRVANA, and MODUS OPERANDI.
And back we go to whatever caused me to ask these questions in
    the first place, least to say answer them —(moot
    grammar)—I don't know, DO YOU?

* * *

THE WAY OF ALL MEN

Like the wind blows in many directions,
So people blend into different factions;
Power-hungry demons are thriving and flourishing
Only because we lent them strength;
Meek, homeless, innocent babes strive
Only for the bread and water on which they survive.
Yet several dangerous organizations continue
To vandalize and steal bleeding hearts of those glued
By the temerity-plagued pendulum of the time;
Each not sure why the other is committing
What to the One above must be deemed sinning.
Anyhow, we, blessed to live on this mortal earth
Yearn for more than deep drudgery and dearth,
And try to pass on the golden torch of existence
To those yet born who will chance
The way of all men.

175

DAVID CASPI

SEQUEL TO CLOCKWORK

Let us now attain what we have today
Else the world would lose its memory.
Tell the Lord He should LET CLOCKWORK BE!

Catch that spry, fleeting hour before it goes away—
Losing it can only lead to lots of sad dismay.
Only a watch can make time go so awry;
Check the minute hand before it steals your eye.
Keep the meaning and value bestowed upon its face
While looking for God's helping hand, leaving but a trace
Of the times we shared together, the happiness we knew,
Reliving those sweet days time can't let become untrue.
Keep, again, the beauty of the hour, expressed in this rhyme.

Before you lose all hope, before cometh the end of man's time,
Ending, may I say, ere all is said and done, LET CLOCKWORK
    BE!

THE TWINS

They were born in a hay field
    perhaps weeks ago;
Now there are two
    and run with their doe.
Two of a kind
    and wild and quick;
Ready to meet you
    and off with a lick.
Their tails wagging, too,
    and into the woods;
With a bound they go
    then back out and look.
Twin fawns they be
    and mother so sleek;
Proud as can be
    of her fawns this week.

THERE IS A FORCE

There is a force that chases me, and leads me, and embraces me.
Without it I could never be, could never see,
could never have climbed an apple tree.
Could never have held a crying child, or ascertain a smile so
mild.
I could not do the things I must, I could not love the souls I
trust.
I could not sleep a sleep of peace . . . could not enjoy a lovely
feast,
Or use the breath of life within, to help another day begin.
There is a force, where will it lead? It was there, I'm sure, in
Father's seed.
Throughout my life I've been aware, and I have to share its
presence there.
Where will it take me —I do not know . . . but I must go, it has
told me so.
In God's own way and in His own time,
He masters the talents of both reason and rhyme,
And I know He'll create some harmony,
ouf of this little old piece of clay . . . called me.

EDITH AND RALPH

God in His infinite wisdom selected Ralph to be my father,
    And I thank Him, because I like being me.
Out of a certain web of strength, authority, determination, and
    complexity
    God has woven all the fine and not so fine partitions of my
    life,
And I thank Him, for I could not be anyone else, you see.

God in His infinite wisdom selected Edith for my mother,
    And I thank Him, for she was just the mother for me.
Warm, tender, sensitive, meek, humble, understanding and
    forgiving,
    Which helps to balance the scale for living.
Both were a part of God's master plan, to help make me what I
    am,
    I am . . . Cezan.

THE VAGABOND

Squirrels dig deep for buried nuts,
Pigeons search the ground,
Hoping for their hungry mouths
Some crumbs will soon be found.

Lying on a lonely bench
Secluded from the town,
A weary soul is resting here;
He wears a furrowed frown.

It is the vagabond who seeks
His comfort in the park.
And no one seems to care his name;
When dogs go by, they bark.

If only someone cared enough
To give him human kindness;
Who knows the good he could produce
And show to us a bindness.

For vagabonds were human born
And somewhere along the line,
Received a very deepened wound,
Much worse than yours or mine.

* * *

BROKEN FRIENDSHIP

When darkness shadows o'er the heart
And friendship fades away,
'Tis better often just to part
Than try to hold your stay.

For pain to one, as you will find,
Is not the same to all;
And though your actions be so kind
Some never hear your call.

180

FIRST LOVE

with feeling, then,
not words
is how you came to me;
without compassion,
without promise,
like a peacock stirring
amidst the ashes . . .

* * *

REMEMBRANCE

roses, as i have
seen them fall . . .
i too have
felt
the pain . . .
(soon it will be time to go)

* * *

NIGHTFALL

               stillness . . .
a quiet
             time
stardust pirouettes on
         fine crystal
                and
you are there . . .

MOMENTS WITH YOU

Moments are precious and new
Moments that fly like a dove
Moments I've shared with you
Moments of our cherished love . . .

Moments when first we met
And said, "Yes, forever more."
Moments of watching the stars
From love's floating shore . . .

Moments of the future, written in the sand
Moments of holding that first tiny hand
Moments of a home filled with love and peace
Moments I pray that will never cease . . .

Moments of happiness and joy
Moments of sadness and tears
Moments of time turned to years
Moments I hold in my heart so dear
Moments I want to spend with you, forever near . . .

Moments when I needed you most
Moments when you were always there
Moments I didn't know what to do
Moments together we would share . . .

Moments I share with you will never die
So never weep, never cry
Moments of you and me
Are locked in my heart, for eternity . . .

TO FREEDOM

From facts related to time
In history's arduous grind,
Limited to what he perceives
Man translates from confusion
That which he believes.

Quality or quantity an essence to reckon
Thoughts of freedom forever beckon,
Dimly perception and organization
Meet confusion, illusion, and castration.

There is no form, just living
Returning to what was in the beginning,
Born of infinity existing in time
That bondage of reality however fine.

Pushed by history that guardian of slavery,
Shattered by caring, torn by thoughts of bravery
Man rushes in search of his own illusion
That nebulous essence born of confusion.

Of all qualities freedom to be
Most inhabits man's search into history,
Aided by reason, a questionable method of search,
Man finds confusion, form is left in lurch.

Those most enslaved and blind
Suppose freedom they find,
While those who glimpse freedom's serenity
Realize the absurdities of history.

There are times in the darkness of night
When all is calm, when all seems right,
Knowing man is only free
As he recognizes the nature of his slavery.

MY FUNNY LITTLE BUNNY

Nip came to me in a wild bunny rage,
and there was nothing I could do but lock
poor Nippy in a cage.

In his eye was a tear,
And somehow I felt in his heart there was fear.
But I'd do all I could to make poor Nip feel
the way he should.

From my duties I could not shirk,
And so each day I went to work.
It was fun coming home to Nip each day and I
cared for Nip in my very special way.

I watched Nip's coat dirty and loud
As it turned into one that really made Nippy
look proud.

Then one day at work,
Our boss called attention and a bunny show
was in mention. So, I thought I'd enter Nippy
too, like only a proud owner would do.

I took a seat till all bunnies did I greet.
Then I stepped outside, watching the show
and wondering if maybe Nip made the front row!

One by one the bunnies walked out and when
Nippy saw me he started to shout!
He walked proudly to me and he took a bow.
But Nippy really didn't know why or how he
was wearing the sign that read: "First Easter Bunny."

In bunny-talk he asked for a walk in the wood,
Like only a big-shot bunny should. We walked,
talked, ate, and got close to our gate, and then
I remember that sound, and when I turned around,
Nippy, Nippy, Nippy, I screamed, but Nippy, he
was gone, yes, my Nippy was gone. Yes, tears
choked inside me, but my Nip was gone.

But now don't feel forlorn, because I know somehow
that bunny had to be born. And by heck, just
you look at your bunny's neck. That "Happy Easter" sign —
Why, that's from me and Nippy, that funny little bunny
of mine.

THE FABLE OF THE TABLE

Joseph Edson built a table,
Doing the best that he was able,
And then concluded with a sigh
That he made the thing too high.
Now may I ask you, gentle neighbor,
In case you should, by patient labor,
A table build that was too high,
Would you then risk a second try,
Or would you do the same as Joe
And trim the legs an inch or so?
The table as Joe made it sat
Upon the floor entirely flat,
And for an amateur was good,
A solid job of sturdy wood;
So all that Joe now had to do
Was trim each leg an inch or two.
He laid the table on one side
And to the legs the saw applied,
Taking his measurements by sight
And trusting that his aim was right;
Soon with the sawdust there were four
Small blocks of wood upon the floor.
At this point almost anyone
Would reason that the job was done,
And Joe, convinced he had achieved
What he attempted, felt relieved,
So you can understand his shock
When now the legs began to rock.
It didn't take him long to see
That had he measured carefully
And cut from each an equal bit
He would have trimmed the legs to fit,
But now his task was to restore
The even legs he had before.
By this time Joe was well aware
That he would have to take good care
To find the shortest leg, and saw

The rest to fit without a flaw,
And this he undertook to do
With measurements he hoped were true.
He did his best, but strange to say
He simply couldn't trim away
From three unequal legs the bit
Which would have made all four legs fit,
And thus, as was the case before,
The table rocked upon the floor.
Needless to say, the crowning blow
Was that the table got too low,
But stil it rocked, and still Joe tried,
And still his efforts were defied,
Till he had taken all he could
And smashed it into kindling wood.
The moral of it, gentle neighbor,
Is that if you, by patient labor,
A table build and find it high,
And don't feel like a second try,
Then save yourself a lot of woe
And do not do the same as Joe.

* * *

AN UNKNOWN SOLDIER

He walked in life the common road
Trod by the millions through its span,
And toiled beneath a heavy load,
Toiled hard and bore it like a man.

He was a soldier of the ranks
Who fought with giants all his life,
Scarce conscious of the lack of thanks
And blood loss in the hopeless strife.

Through all his years of trial, still
He did not whimper or complain.
There was no bleat in him; his will
Subdued alike protest and pain.

No golden chances came his way;
His name was on no honored roll;
Continued drabness, day by day,
Walled in his life and chained his soul.

No bitterness his mind imbued,
No envy of a better fate;
He faced his lot with fortitude
And saw no worthy cause in hate.

Riches and fame, he was aware,
Are often given worthless men,
The captain who makes self his care,
The writer with the venal pen.

He knew that fair friends flit around
The shining bauble of success,
That noble grace is often found
Where it is easy to profess.

He saw that ofttimes men like him,
Who rise from dust to toil in dust,
Are playthings of ambition's whim
And pawns of greed and power-lust.

And still he realized full well
The imperfections of the world,
That wrong and rank injustice dwell
Under all banners yet unfurled.

The world's wrongs he would not condone,
Each was a thing man could avoid;
He saw relation to his own
And wished that all could be destroyed.

But just how this could be achieved
He did not know; the only way
That suited him, as he perceived,
Was still to do his best, and pray.

Despite all ills within his ken,
The scorn of snobs and friends' neglect,
He kept faith in his fellow man
And held on to his self-respect.

He welcomed from the cup of life
Such drafts of cheer as he could find;
Fond children and a faithful wife
Were proof that fortune could be kind.

And though he dwelt in poverty,
He still rejoiced to be alive;
He loved the zest of being free
And joyed in having strength to strive.

The consciousness of well-spent years
To him a consolation gave
Until his struggles and his fears
Were stilled at last within the grave.

THE MAIN HURDLE

Whenever you can
avoid burning the pan,
but if you should do so then clean it.
I learned this, you see,
at my dear mother's knee,
where she often would spank me and mean it.

We all make mistakes.
King Alfred burned the cakes
because he was preoccupied.
George misused his hatchet
and knew he would catch it
much more than he did if he lied.

It is not the wrong thing
we do that will bring
us grief if we try to correct it.
It is passing the buck
and hoping our luck
will be such that no one will detect it.

JUDY A. CROWELL

THE JUDGMENT

Beneath the waters deep
My eyes they cannot see.
The heart has stopped;
It is swallowed by the sea.

The waters are asleep;
My soul is forlorn.
The breath of life—
It is gone forevermore.

Am I, Dear Lord,
At your command
To show me your Kingdom
Where I shall stand?
Or doth the Flaming Sword
Below the sea
Stretch forth to take
My soul from me?

Then, without a doubt,
My soul it doth lift.
The mind feels lighter;
Lord, are you my gift?

But the Flaming Sword,
It pierces my skin,
And begins to lower my soul
To its chamber within.

Hear Ye, I beg you, Lord!
I fear of the Sword!
For I, a sinner,
Doth hold out my hand
To be swept up
Into the Promised Land.

My soul is confused;
My words, they are hollow.
I'm at your mercy, Lord;
But your decision I shall follow.

For my Lord
He doth know;
He is my Judge
As to which place I shall go.

* * *

THE MIND

The mind of man
Is always congested;
But the man with mind
Can always digest it.

* * *

A SOLEMN VOW

Lover, open thou mine heart to hear
And through thy love to me draw near;
Let me thy lover e'er pure retain,
Let me thy dearest and heir remain.

Then here will I today
A solemn vow make and say:
I will be true, for there is thee
Who trusteth me;
I will be pure, for there is a love
Who careth for me.

Lover, thou art mine forever.
Never suffer me to stray.
Let me in thy weakness
Never cast my solemn vow away.

AMANDA, ONCE AT SUNSET

Embers glowing on the hearth of dusk,
Passions following the flaming hills,
Down the valley purple magic stills
The burning storm alive in me.

Deepest blue and gold and crimson sea,
Passions riding on the sleeping crests.
Across the bay the lady rests
Upon her couch of misty green.

Islands lie adrift in yellow haze,
Passions cloaked, remote, never seen
By day, hidden fast, clasped between
Two worlds of light. One must give way.

Amanda, once at sunset we
Touched earth and sky and sea.

By the water, near the rocks we met,
Joined together just at day's flight.
Clasped together, between day and night,
Our hands once held a sunset dream.

The sky's fired beauty did not seem
To die at last. It lingered on
Your fingertips, and your lips. Alone
With painted sky and sea of blue,
Once I shared a sunset with you.

JOHN C. CURBOW

FOR YOU, AT DAWN

Stark arms of searching love
Rise against the hollow dawn,
Red upon the burnt black line
Of rock-strewn hills above.

In the stillness, cold and chill
Linger in the winter's
Subtle clutch close beside.
Darkness struggles dawn to fill,
But cannot halt the red tide
Of rushing morning sky.

No more will misty space and time
Or the dark and frigid mime
Of death capture your touch.

Burning in the seas of time,
Glowing in the cold depths until
False darkness fades at last,
Across the future and the past
Rolls your breaking, beating tide.

In memory and in hope of you,
Each dawn returns in love's soft hue.

ODE TO MY LATEST CRUSH

What can I say?
I have another crush
and this time it's on you
and there's nothin'you can do about it.
So there.

* * *

OUT OF SIGHT

he sure was good-looking
standing there waiting for the 7:25 muni;
his clothes pressed to a T
all the way from the beach to the ferry.
Lord have mercy, he was sharp,
every hair was in place,
even his trench coat was pressed —
yves saint laurent all the way.
uh-uh-uh what a fine-looking dude —
he even got off where i got off.

it would have been love at first sight
except i never saw him again.

LONELINESS

Have you ever been lonely and in despair
And asked yourself, "Does anyone care?"
Well, I'd like to think that someone does,
     for in the months ahead
It would make my heart feel lighter
     as I wearily go to bed.
And if you have been lonely you'll know just how I feel
For loneliness is a feeling that to me is very real;
The feeling to be wanted is one that we all share
So the same old nagging question: "Does anybody care?"
Now I've found someone who really cares
     and I found Him in a book,
And anyone can find Him if they will only look.
The Bible's the book of which I speak
     it says that God does care;
Just stop and look about you —his beauty's everywhere.
So no longer am I lonely or have a furrowed brow
I've found a good companion and He's always with me now.

* * *

HIS AND HERS

I often wonder why it is
That towels are labeled "hers" and "his."
A marriage is made so two can share —
No his and hers to divide the pair.
But I guess it's so the wife can see
Just how thoughtless her mate can be;
His is dirty, rumpled, used —
Hers is clean and unabused.

FROM MY WINDOWPANE

Someday when I muse about my memoirs
I'll think about God and His great outdoors.
Now I view a bit of the Lord's domain
Each day as I look from my windowpane.
In summer I may see a thrush;
The winter scene's changed by a frosty brush
As God paints the land in a blanket of white
So the earth may rest for a winter's night.
Each day new patterns appear in the snow,
The prints of a hare or maybe a doe;
And although I haven't seen the doe or hare
I know they exist —their tracks are there.
Just as I know there is a God —
His Son left imprints where He'd trod.

* * *

THEM OR US

This tale is about monkeys —harmless creatures —
And at a zoo they're a main feature.
They climb and they jump and through the air sail
And some are helped by a prehensile tail.
Through the fence you can hear them chatter,
It doesn't make sense but that doesn't matter;
They make children laugh and that's not so bad
It's what men do to men that is so sad.
Men kill men and wars cause a fuss,
So who are the monkeys —them or us?

RENEE

Hey,
     if I knew it would help
I'd stay.
But I see the pain in your eyes
     and I know you're crying inside,
So I think it best if I leave
     before I say something that
          I don't really mean.

Days
     have gone by and I know
you've prayed
In hope the feelings you have
     will be returned by my hand.
And I tried not to lead you on
     but what you read in my eyes
          was more than they said.

Renee,
     you have the prettiest face
I'd say.
But I have a real mixed-up life —
     I can't be stopped by a wife.

* * *

ODE TO A YOUNG BROTHER
(RUSSELL LYNN HIGGINS)
(1956-1974)

Some time has gone by
     since the day that you died
but the memory of your life continues on.
Your friends knew you well
     but I can tell
          that I hardly knew you at all.

Though you were my brother
    our lives weren't together
and we lived in worlds far apart.
But like some people I've found
    that with you not around
        life's not the same anymore.

But I should not complain
    because with this pain
there is a joy living deep inside.
You have a home up in heaven
    and I know by believing
        I'll see you there after I die.

* * *

IRON CELL

Bouncing off the walls are words
    that men spoke years before.
I hear the cries
    within their hearts
        and wished I heard no more.
All the hope drained from their soul
    their bodies dead and cold.
I'll join them soon
    this is my tomb
        like theirs many years before.

Oh, this place is dark and cold
    my mind hears words from old.
My time is short
    I care no more
        for I die like those before.

WHY ME?

Why is the world so hard on me?
Why can't people like me be free?
If not like wind, like a tree,
Just blowing endlessly.

I love mankind, but he hates me.
'Cause when I'm happy, he beats me,
Mentally more than physically,
Like he cuts down a tree.

I try to make it on my own.
I try to be independent.
I try to help people bare their hurts,
But they walk on me like dirt.

Society won't let things go right,
Day or night.
They tell me when you're seventeen
The world is very mean.
You can't do this and you can't do that
And let me say that's a fact.
When you get up, they slap you back.
Like a parent, to a kid, with a wisecrack.

My mother doesn't give a damn.
It's as if a door had slammed
Right in front of my face.
Meaning all my efforts *are* and *were* a waste,
Just like a horrible taste
That's in your mouth, you wash away,
That you hope is gone to stay.

Yes, I ask, why is the world so hard?
It keeps me constantly on my guard.
And it also leaves a scar;
On my brain it sticks like tar
And it won't go very far.

200

TO

To take any moment . . .
To hold it to the light
    And look close . . .
To touch anyone of those moments when
    I am thinking of you . . .
To discover just now how that moment
    Does shine so bright and nicely.
To discover at the same instant
    My moments melancholy:
        A separate dimension
            So grayly unsettled.
Perhaps it is best—that these moments
    Be varied; of both brilliant and
    Dimly rainbowed hues.
To take any one of those precious
    Moments . . . when I am thinking of you.
To miss you.
To forget you.
To care for you.
To be indifferent.
To love you . . . TO LOVE YOU.

Thank you for the moments
When you take me away to such delightful
Places as your pleasant conversation creates.
Because you are truly beautiful and truly
Beautiful to be.
Thank you for the moments.

SCULPTURE

Waters surge
In white foaming torrents,
Soon smooth to green
And swirl together
In places where
Water flows evenly again . . .

     Washing away small
         pieces of me . . .
     Leaving me smoothed
         and polished.
     My edges carefully
         measured, then worn,
     The holes of me filled
         with bits and pieces
         of so many others.

As waters flow here
With beautiful meaning

That we are
As much of one
As another

And are all the same
To even waters.

MOMENTS

Yes, the moments, yes, moments, that chase infinite time,
Soon catch up and leave quiet moments in mind.
Yet so good . . . but yet, last for not so long,
These moments forever remembered but never to be a song.

Clear as my feelings, the moments I can see,
Fulfilling yet valued, for they belong to me.
For as I stand—before me, moments focus into view,
My love, should I tell . . . It's all because of you.

I like to think with each moment that's passed,
Stir a desire that's promised to last.
For moments are few, precious, yet strong,
Moments we've shared are good; they shall never be wrong.

GALILEO

I think that Galileo, old and blind,
Must yet have walked in wonder and delight
For he still had the mem'ry in his mind
Of days that only waited for the night:
To see the awful mystery of things —
The planets plough their courses 'round the sun;
To grasp that matchless movement and the wings
Of time and space —infinity begun!
To be the first to know the cosmic law,
To sense just how this universe must be:
The spinning sun, the moon —all this he saw —
Slept under stars, ebbed with the mighty sea!
I think that Galileo's restless mind
Remembered much when he was old and blind.

* * *

FOREVERMORE

Oh never, never leave me, Love, until
The highest mountain topples in the sea;
Until the fir trees fall on this lone hill;
(How many times have you walked here with me.)
Oh, love me till the day the earth shall shake
And you and I find pieces of the sun
Upon the grass, and as we lie there take
A few and sadly say, "Now love is done."
Oh, do not go as long as you and I
Can speak together saying not a word,
Forgetting everything, content to lie
Upon the place where our first kiss occurred.
Each day the sun, each night the stars above —
They will not change. Oh, never leave me, Love!

BRAVING LAKE MICHIGAN

He took her out, though a bedraggled she,
with her life-giving, moody sails reefed.
Her booms had gaunt, unclothed, rude ends,
for the elements, maddened, roared for prey.

He started her through the protected harbour,
where old sailors placidly waited on Nature.
His spirit welcomed, trepidly, a contest dour
for his soul hated the confinements of flesh.

He met a fleeing yacht, splashed with spume,
and hailed, as they slid past "How is it?"
When "Keep off the lake" came back, he grinned,
for he was grimly set to know "just how bad."

His blood raced at sight of breakers set at naught,
but he hugged the shore and smiled ironically.
Some passengers commanded, some entreated "Turn back,"
for they saw awesome fury with feminine unnauticalness.

One passenger forgot any doubt and winked amusedly,
as he said "We're going out, shure, we're going out."
He nothing said, but took of the tiller a surer grip,
for death lurked within a drifting, deep, hundred feet.

At last among unchecked waves they violently tossed,
and the angry, surging, billows struck deadly blows.
But she rode over the froth with a saucy snub nose
for the fury of Nature is telegraphed to human cunning.

Athwart hills and dales of water the company danced
with the airy and watchful abandon of a cobra charmer.
The wind drove them safely onward and churned the Lake,
for science has force checkmate the same blind fury.

Fast upon her heels came another impudent sloop,

now a resting sea gull poised on a mountainous peak,
anon a submarine as the boat plunged into a trough.
Thus daring drew climactic scenes in a solitary waste.

He finally turned about for home in a long, epic tack
with the shore a wondrous, dark, velvet hinterland.
And the setting sun was a delicate orchid in the sky
to reward with infinite grandeur the determined explorers.

At last the vengeful wind lost the power to shriek
for a stern, fretful, disgusted, drooping lullaby.
So they sailed back into the harbour with reefs unfurled,
to prove the most insolent pride is that of a yachtsman.

Then the moon rose in wide-orbed, benedictional glory,
welcoming the mariners with the changing tints of chameleon,
Breathing ineffable peace with a strange, mesmeric power,
a divine elegy of rest that can only be known when earned.

* * *

REVOLUTIONISTS

Ofttimes I wonder, with brooding ache, why things are?
Things which revolt from closer sight as from afar.
Things of force with only claim to power in universalness,
A bastard extension atoning no iota of brutalness.

Things of commercial ambition, poverty, and riches inequity
Whose individual intensity silhouettes their social insanity.
And, wafted on the breezes, comes the sneer "Dead Sea
        Fruit" —
Sour grape evasion of culture, blind to social menacing plutes.

And, still aching, I turn to the world-acclaimed poets,
Surely futurist vision must rebel against human flesh marts.
To find D'Annunzio shrieking way to chorus of mob lungs,
Invoking primeval hate under a flag condoning civil wrong.

206

Anguished, I turn to the scientists of hefty brew serene,
Who neither dream nor idle, but seek the lowliest truth.
To find their greatest field is the mouldering past
And social justice too dynamic for a well-endowed last.

Despairing, I trek to uncultured depths and discover there
Souls who despise warring incentive and prize of commerce.
Uncouthly dressed beings who, reading the past as ruthless,
Do not sift it, scientific fashion, in truthless unmoral way.

Souls whom stern necessity does not bend to passing will,
But who, through sobering continuance, are revolutionists.
Passionate spirits who read history and reject the conclusion;
During souls who find right is might, despite past illusion.

* * *

WISE PARADOX

Wisdom comes with age and ennui,
To be sure is to be indifferent.
Then only the things eluding us
Keep alive a bored, pique interest.

Yet even wisdom has one paradox,
A thing assured without boredom,
Love attained is never eluding us
Since alight with iridescent fire.

REFUGE

Distance lends enchantment, it is said
by those whose eyelids are blasé.
A cynical paradox of their vices bold,
bred of fear at seduction of maritalism.

Out of sight is out of mind,
murmur the stagnating lizards.
A terse phrase expressing vacuity,
knowing no dreams of sweet memory.

Away from home is away from love,
is soft sighing of passioned life.
For home is the divinest refuge
kindly, deep souls seek from strife.

MY PRAYER

(Inspired after praying for
Divine Healing for Linda, my beloved niece)

Jesus, let me walk with Thee,
Now and through Eternity.
No doubt distress or fear will overcome me here,
For I feel and know you are near.
Dear Lord, please hold my hand,
As I journey through this earthly land,
Then and only then will I understand.

Whatever my cross may be, let me bear it willingly,
With courage, bravely unafraid, may I not fail,
Falter, stumble blindly, as one would do without you.
I know, you are closer than breathing, nearer
Than hands or feet, with you there is no defeat.
With firm steps I will go, and I know
Faith in you will make it so.

Dear Lord, lead me to a quiet place,
Give to me humility and your grace.
Flood my soul with expectancy, like was felt in Judea
Many years ago . . . the night you first appeared.
Kindle within me Holy Fires, as upon you I rely.
Heal me . . . touch me . . . take away my pain,
I pray, dear Lord, in your precious name.

May I radiate your abiding peace,
Which comes with forgiveness, bringing sweet release.
Give me eyes to see another's pain,
And render love in your Holy Name.
Then I pray: I may be a light along the way
To the Ones who have gone astray.
And each day know: "Lo, I am with you always."

SPELLBOUND BY THE ANCIENTS OF OLD

You can't begin to understand
My absolute intrigue,
In all creation 'round about
My mind does not fatigue.
Still not one scientific thing
Can my mind comprehend.
Yet I'm in awe of all these things
And I do not pretend.
I know not why I have this thing —
This total fascination.
I only know that I'm a part,
Of one of God's creations!

A tiny atom, a charm, a quark —
I know that I am just a spark!
I wish my mind was great like some.
Instead I'm just so plain and dumb,
The black holes, and a quasar
Are words of Greek to me,
And yet I cling to every word
Just like I knew. You see?
But God, I'd be so satisfied,
If my life could shine as bright
As one small speck of your universe,
Just one small tiny light.
Yet I'm in awe of all these things
And I do not pretend!
If I could come this way again
I'd like to be a scientist. Amen.

JUBILANT JOURNEY

I dreamed I flew across the fair skies
To foreign lands and the road to paradise;
What a journey! 'Twas truly great!
Never once was the jet plane late.

Saw Italy, Spain, France and Germany,
All the British Isles and Hungary,
Switzerland, Portugal, Syria and Iran,
Egypt, Russia, China and Japan.

Saw historic and unforgettable Greece,
Where once hung the Golden Fleece,
Guarded by a dragon until one day,
Jason and Argonaut took it away.

Visited the rugged Adriatic, Yugoslavia and Albania,
The deep waters of the Black Sea and Rumania,
Turkey, Bulgaria and the Balkan Mountains
And at Corinth saw elaborately graceful fountains.

Limestone mounts rose steeply from the shore of the Adriatic
Fringed with many islands 'twas most romantic,
Rocky hills descend in cliffs to the margin of the shore
Where little springs bubble up on the angry sea-floor.

Scattered towns and dry and barren soil—
The growth of which was reached by much turmoil;
Islets symbolize old but alien culture on the Dalmation coast,
And the Venetian lion adorned the buildings I liked most.

In Scandinavia museums gleamed like polished malachite.
There was the statue of handsome Balder, the Teutonic god of
        light,
And the goddess of fate at the foot of an ash tree by the road,
And Heimdall guarded the rainbow which led to the gods' abode.

Fountain shrines ever full of fascination
Were sacred during the Aegean civilization;
The most noted one was dedicated to Pyrene, the nymph;
Her tears represent the origin of the spring in myth.

When I went to see the marble Athenian Parthenon —
The most magnificent architecture ever done;
It was the great Pheidias I visualized from others apart
But I saddened when I saw the ruins of his noble art.

Saw Jerusalem, the holiest of Holy cities, peaceful and free,
Where clusters of rose-pink blossoms hung on a Judas tree.
'Twas the "City of Peace" in pre-Israelite days;
Its history goes back to the great Stone Age.

When I saw the Red Sea and the Nile River green,
And the Arabian Desert that stretched between —
'Twas a tranquil hour in golden sunlights
As I read in Arabic *The Thousand and One Nights.*

I called to mind a bird that lived five hundred years —
The lone Phoenix that consumed itself in fire, not fears;
Then rose renewed from its gray lava
To start another long life in the Sahara.

On the dusty Isle of Capri in Naples Bay
A nostalgic feeling overtook me that day;
I longed to go back to the Eternal City, Rome,
To gaze again at its grandeur before coming home.

Back to the Seven Hills of Rome at last!
'Twas then that I was in seventh heaven! Alas!
Secret thoughts were my own, and visions divine —
Of Jupiter's oldest temple that had stood on Capitaline.

Saw all those wonders and missed but few,
Again I'll go in nineteen eighty-two.

How good to be back to home and friends
Where life is serene and contentment never ends!

Oh JUBILANT JOURNEY! What precious memories you hold!
I dream of the work of Pheidias carved in ivory and gold;
Leonardo, Michaelangelo, Raphael, Virgil and Dante
May peace reign in your souls through all eternity.

* * *

AMERICAN SOCIETY OF ARTISTS

The American Society of Artists
        is a good place to be;
It has members from everywhere
        and some are good, believe me.

It has many exhibits a year
        in the sun and in the shade,
Where thousands of people go
        like a bright and exciting brigade.

They look at art and craft
        in every color scheme
And then they buy the works
        to hang where they are seen.

The gallery is a place
        where members' work is kept;
Where colors blend and glory reigns
        and nothing is ever inept.

Art patrons grow inspired
        when they walk into the place;
Reminiscence overwhelms them
        and they depart with steady grace.

213

Membership is ever growing
　　and we're now five hundred strong;
This must mean we are okay
　　and nothing can be very wrong.

When we reach a higher goal
　　we will know that we have won;
Our fond dreams shall not cease
　　till the setting of the sun.

The gallery is in the Merchandise Mart
　　in dear Chicago as you know;
Where the sky is ever-changing
　　and the lights are all aglow.

The Merchandise Mart is the best place
　　to stroll by on a starlit night;
Here is the fashion center of the city
　　where strollers are in divine delight.

The world is wide and has a place
　　for every kind of craft and art;
While some are good and others bad
　　they represent at least a start.

O, creative people! try again
　　and have faith, don't lose hope;
All things worthwhile take time,
　　don't feel you're at the end of your rope.

When a gallery draws people of every age
　　and their friendliness has unfurled;
You can bet the AMERICAN SOCIETY OF ARTISTS
　　is one of the best in the world.

TWO LITTLE BOYS

Noah and Asher, you are sweet and lovely boys!
I miss your tender smiles and bright eyes;
You amused me with your many pretty toys.
I'll see you again under the springtime skies.

What will you do when you become men?
I know! You'll have a palace of gold,
And a nice profession; you'll not be a "has-been."
To me, little friends, you can never be old.

MAIN LOVE

I've been wanting to tell you so long but i
couldn't find the right words to tell you.

The look in your eyes told me you knew
the feelings that i have for you.

So many times i try to hide the way i feel;
the feeling was so strong i couldn't.

Thoughts of you are spinning around and
around in my head.

I realize i couldn't ever have a life with
you; i will always feel the way i do for as
long as i live.

Seeing you makes my day.

* * *

NO MATTER WHAT

No matter what i may find,

No matter where i may be,

No matter when you need me i'll be there;

No matter what, i will always love you.

CLARICE DeVANNA

MY SON

When my dear son was only three, he used to climb
upon my knee, and say his little prayer each night;
His baby arms would hold me tight and I would
hold him gently, so, and sing him songs of long ago,
until his little head would bob and he'd slip off
to the land of nod.
But years go by, they cannot stay, and he is just
eighteen today; a handsome lad in sailor blue —
dear son, I am so proud of you. But now he's
putting out to sea, perhaps to die for you and me.
And so my son has gone away, I pray he will return
some day; he's gone to fight for you and me
to help protect our liberty.
And so to God with faith I cling, it always
helps to heal the sting; and when I wake at break of day
this little prayer I always say:
Dear God, take care of my son today,
keep his feet on the narrow way;
please mold his life and guide his hand
and keep my son a Christian man.

NOSTALGIA MENANDER ROD

Death is a prosperous time
Humanity, clay pigeons
God shot cheap black breath.
Lapis Lazuli like Emmett Till
Tall in the saddle.
Watch your tongue or
God will steal it.

* * *

NOSTALGIA MATADOR

The curtain opens, drowns a jealous wench
Once of consequence, Augustinian
In a sense. Only pernicious imitation riots;
Black obliques and circumstantial tomfoolery.
     Draft children
The vain succulence of angels angered
End to peaked resistant costume
O, odoriferous misogamist one wronged
Foxy commotion, mammoth in guilt.
     The female attains performance
Loins require love; love's great impeachment.
Dyed-red eruption and thick custom lenses.
     Dear Josef, my love so fraudulent
     I must suffer in aimless defenses.

DON'T WORRY

If my days were always sunny
And I never shed a tear,
Then I wouldn't need the God above —
I wouldn't need a prayer.

I wouldn't need that Man
Who died on Calvary;
I wouldn't need the blood
That was once shed for victory.

So I thank God for my troubles,
I thank Him for my pain;
It helps me to remember
Just why my Savior came.

He knew I'd have these burdens,
He knew the grief would hurt,
I know He carried that cross for me
When He fell down in the dirt.

Yes, I will always praise Him
And thank Him for His love;
I will accept my problems
And keep my eyes above.

NO NEED FOR FEAR

In this life we will have sorrow,
In this life we will have pain.
Christ has promised a brighter tomorrow
If we just trust and believe on His name.

Our bodies were not made to stay here,
Our souls are in His hands;
He's left His word to guide us
That we may reach that Promised Land.

So trust His Word and live it so
That when it comes your time to go
There will be no need for fear—
You can be sure He'll be right there.

* * *

I AM UNWORTHY

God knew when I was in my mother's womb
The life that I would live,
That I would lie and cheat
And take more than I would give.

Oh, it must have grieved him so
To see the places I would go,

The things that I would say,
The things that I would do.
Oh, Lord, forgive me—
How I must have hurt You.

I am so unworthy, Lord,
Of the great love for me You have shown.
Thank you, Lord, praise God
For wanting me as one of Your own.

'TWAS ONLY YESTERDAY

'Twas only yesterday, it seems, the foliage was green against a
    sky of blue. The drifting of fleecy clouds told a silent story
    of hastily passing time, from old to new. Every bush and
    tree and hedge provided shelter for feathered friends flitting
    along the garden ledge . . . warm earth gave up its food to
    nourish feathered birth.

God clothed the tree with cloak of coolest green . . . He sent the
    rain to keep the colors fresh until the Summer's end, and
    man no longer needed protection from the heat of Summer's
    sun . . . until fowls in southern flight no longer needed the
    shelter site for their chirping young . . . until ripened fruit is
    loosed from mother tree, and leaves her standing . . .
    lonely, but in dignity. 'Twas only yesterday it seems, man's
    foot trod the carpet green; and crickets sang a concert
    chorus all night long . . . a lullaby contentment song.

Was it only yesterday I saw a patch of red and golden hue
    against a sky of Autumn blue? The earth was halcyon and
    fair, as in life's autumn years, dwelt serenity there. 'Twas
    overnight the leaves turned brown and tens by tens they
    fluttered down, returning to the earth below, waiting for a
    cover of snow.

Yes, 'twas only yesterday God sent the snowflake blanket down,
    decorating housetop and tree. It lay snug on limb and
    ground, covering all the drab of dying year . . . making the
    winter-gray all sparkling clear.

Glancing back o'er the season's span, and holding close one's
    memories, only then can man perceive the flight of TIME.
    Near as swiftly as a cloud that passes o'er man's
    head . . . God takes the TIME and leaves His constant
    LOVE instead.

To Yesteryear I Bow;
        'Twas Only Yesterday;
            'Tis Now!

SPIRIT OF MY SOUL

Strange, sweet voices I hear
　　O Majesty of my soul;
Of mortal clay, I linger near
　　As You give me Your rites
Of an immersion in Holiness
Purged with an affectionate pierce,
　　Over and over soft, tender
Whispers flow in my ear
　　As some glorious melodious
Sounds of *Ave Maria* at vesper-bell time
Ringing out its voices and its Chimes.
We float out of the tunnel of Darkness
In fluent languages heighten to
　　More, More, More;
To an eternal light, its beam so bright
Flowing, flowing into my being, You
Permeate an immense warmth of a sacred love
That can only be given from above;
　　A pardon for all my scarlet sin.
Though toil and strife never ends
　　Glory to His Grace in this Holy place.
In quietness, We greet truth and peace from Thee
To brighter tomorrows, and in hope
　　We chase away all sorrows
As my eyes sparkle and my heart
　　Fills with laughter.
O Spirit of my soul, I give all
　　Honor to His splendor;
In perfect serenity I linger
　　Into the sweetness of Your arms
Sincerely, I surrender for . . .
　　More, More, More . . .

SPRING

Ten thousand green flashes
And a ruby-red ruff
A-dipping deep
To the honey —
sweet
sweet
sweet;
And scattering gold dust
Throughout the land.

A fleecy white cloud come
Down to Earth
Dancing, gamboling,
Bouncing, tumbling,
Cleating with mirth—
A being alive.
A whipped cream
Of cloud,
Of little gray smudges.

A trilling, a warbling, a rush—
A cascade of melody;
Joyous, plaintive,
Jubilant, rapturous!
Tutored by God—
Triumphant from love—
A twig becomes a mansion
And
A silk thread becomes a pillow.

ON RETURNING A BORROWED BOOK
TO ITS RIGHTFUL OWNER

Little book,
I borrowed you in all good faith
To have a look between your covers.
I meant to return you
But, like a wraith, you eluded my
Memory until now your owner looks at me
With doubtful eyes
And wonders if I mean to keep you.

Go home, little book; Godspeed, *Au revoir,*
Etc.
I've finished you now.
You gave me many pleasant hours.
Go home and nestle with your old friends,
And talk of the new ones you may have made
On your journey.

But before you go,
Please,
May I have one more look between your covers?

* * *

WELLINGTON SQUARE

A maiden fair sat by the tree
A-combing of her hair.
Fine youth passed by. "Halloo," he cried
"I'll meet thee 'neath the stair."

"Forsooth, false one, I saw you kiss
Plain Jane beside the well!
If you choose money instead of honey—
I give thee my farewell."

SECURITY

Dwell in Jesus and you shall abide
Under God's wings who is by thy side.
Testify to His abundant goodness,
Let the world know He's your fortress.

Even in facing danger you will not fear,
Rejoicing, praying to the Mighty One who is near.
Even in the darkest hour, you will shout,
As your Mighty Conqueror puts Satan to flight.

Many may you see fall as you go forward in His Name,
But no evil shall befall thee, no, not one.
Glorious heavenly angels shall be thy daily guide,
Sent direct from thy Master to encamp at thy side.

Thy foot shall never, never be moved,
For the Word of God has long been proved.
So hold fast to Jesus Christ, your ever-present King
And listen to the Voice He speaks to you within.

Victory is yours, so keep marching in step with Jesus,
'Til you reach the eternal assembly hall in heaven.
There you will reap everlasting joy untold,
And your special rewards the battles won through faith.

REV. CLYDROW J. DURBNEY

THE TEMPTER

He sleeps not, nor tires not,
Like a "roaring lion" he roams,
Going about where people are,
Trying to frustrate, worry or devour.
He takes special care to seek out the righteous,
Those who stand for Jesus and Godly living.
To them he suggests: "lower your moral standards . . .
Make more friends, a little wrong won't hurt.
Nor will a few white lies, when told to help someone."
Be on your guard, this comes from his deceptive evil spirit,
Accompanied by tricks, or changing into an angel of light.
Though he may threat by roaring, there is no need to fear him,
For he was defeated at the Cross of Calvary,
By Jesus who said to him three times: "It is written."
Like Jesus, we too can over come him,
By using the Word of God which is the Sword of the Spirit;
And by being fully clothed with God's armour;
Not a dart can penetrate and we stand successfuly against him.
Then we are more than conquerors over the tempter,
For he is put to flight . . .he runs away.

HELP ME LORD

Lord, Lord, look into my heart, and search me good.
See if there are things there that shouldn't be.
If you find anything that displeases Thee,
Convict with Thy Spirit and I'll bow in contrition.

Lord, let my tongue be touched and taught
By your hand of love, so I will speak as I ought.
Guide my feet daily to follow your example.
Let my ears hear you say: This is the way, walk ye in it."

Touch my eyes, open them wide, so I can see You better,
And more clearer the commanded paths of duty,
Paths that lead me to render selfless service to others.
Mold me completely Lord to do thy will and not my own.

LEAN ON

I took my pencil and prepared to write,
I thought I heard a Voice say to me: "LEAN ON.
LEAN ON, LEAN ON, AND ON" it said,
"Let not your heart be troubled, or be afraid.
Praise your King in Psalms and Songs,
Pray without ceasing and LEAN ON and On.
Trust in HIS Word and meditate too,
LEAN ON Jesus and HE'll take you through.
All dark clouds have vanished,
For the bright Light has appeared.
See the LIGHT . . . It is shining so clear. LEAN ON.
Jesus is the Light which brightens our way,
Just LEAN ON HIM and you'll never stray."
A thousand words could not convey my heart's meaning to you
So . . . just LEAN ON . . . LEAN ON JESUS.

ENCOURAGING ONE'S SELF IN THE LORD

I am happy to know that you are still looking to Jesus.
That is the right thing to do; don't give up but keep trusting.
I know many things have come up that tends to discourage you,
But GO FORWARD . . . TAKE COURAGE . . . The Lord is yet
    nigh thee.
He is overshadowing you now with His mighty wings.
What is an ocean to God, or a ship, or a bomb, or the might of
    men?
For thus saith the Lord: "Not my might not by power but by my
    Spirit."
Keep trusting . . . even if you do feel faint, don't give up hope.
Why go down in despair when all that you have need of is nigh
    thee.
Have you become so forgetful as to forget that Jesus is . . . ?
He is ever present, and is now at they side.
Know that: "He giveth power to the faith."
And "To those who have no might He increaseth strength."
Oh! you of little faith, take courage. "Be strong in the
    Lord . . ."
Do you think, that after such great deliverances you've had by
    Him,
He would forsake you now? No never. Fear not, hold fast to
    faith.
Mind not what man says or thinks of you,
"Wait on the Lord" Stand fast, you will make it.

STATUE IN THE PARK

An old man sits rigid in the soul of the park,
unshivering in the cold, turned to stone by circumstance.
He stares across snow-crushed footprints that mark the lane.

Stares, unfeeling, at a wino sprawled on another bench,
sandwiched between newspapers that proclaim in bold-faced type:
God is the World and the World is Dead.

Stares, unknowing, at the initials, carved not too long ago,
in the green paint just above the Obituary.
He has been here forever, seen many things; uncaring, has
      forgotten most.

But the old memories remain.
The sculptor's strokes were sure, the chisel sharp.
The memories remain, like the man, unmoving in the dark.

* * *

THE MONARCH

I saw a butterfly yesterday, sitting on a throne.
Pulsating with fragile life, resisting the inevitable,
arrogant, proud, regal,
he was magnificent.
His robe was sundown orange with bands of ebony
and across his shoulders he wore an ermine cape
with three diamonds sewn on each lapel.
His crown, twin spires of onyx.
He was a Monarch.
We stared, each in his own way at the other
until a sudden wind shift swept him
back into history.

WITH A MOTIONLESS FLOAT, I CRAWLED

When the leaves are red, falling,
and just after the birds sing,
fields full of brown seeds,
in my coat of nature
life has actually aged,
limited in time,
across the infinite wastes.

An old-fashioned scuffling of
autumn leaves;
Even the thistles
on the mangled dusty earth,
tunneled deep into the cold
of the dry riverbed.

The night breeze
tossed a cloud of dust
trying to tell me something,
often so loudly,
neither bark nor howl
could intensify the effort.

A pit in the sand,
A dark stairwell
in my little existence upon earth —
out of the primal waters
I crawled,
as the steel-blue flashbulbs
formed sunlight filtering among the spider webs.

GOD THROUGH TERRIBLE ACTS REMAINS GOOD

God hardened Pharoah's heart	Exod. 9:16
God drowned the Egyptians after the sea did depart.	Exod. 4:21
God caused Joseph as a slave to be sold.	Exod. 14:16-28
God caused Jonah to be swallowed by a big fish we are told.	Gen. 37:27
God let Satan to Job have his way.	Gen. 45:8
God let Jesus die on a cross one day.	Jonah 1:17
Respectful fear of God is in God's plan.	Job 2:6-12
We know the potter has power over the clay.	St. John 3:16
And if God's willing, we will fully understand some day.	Rom. 9:21
For as the Heavens are high above	
I know that God is good,	
For God is love.	I John 4:8

Note: Many times in the Bible, God is spoken of as being terrible fearful) because of the things He allows to happen, but God is always aware of the terrible (fearful) things that He allows to happen. However, the ultimate result is that the terrible things God allows show God's power and cause people to show a respectful, reverent fear of God, making God all powerful and majestic (Deut. 7:21—Ps. 66:3—Ps. 47:2—Prov. 9:10—Prov. 12:21—Prov. 14:26-27—Prov. 16:4—Ps. 34:8).

* * *

HEAVENLY MESSAGE

When each person takes time to be holy,	II Tim. 3:16
They take time to receive	II Peter 1:20:21
A message from Heaven	
As daily they read.	

GOD IS LOVE

For God is love.	I John 4:8
God gave the sun to shine by day.	Gen. 1:16
God gave the moon to shine by night.	Rom. 5:6
God gave His Son to strengthen our way.	
(Christ)	
God gave the stars for a dim light.	
God parted the sea for dry land.	Exod. 14:16
God gave a cloud to lead by day.	Exod. 31:18
God gave Moses the law by His hand.	Exod. 13:21
(God)	
God gave a fire to lead the way.	
God gave His son to die for us. (God)	St. John 3:16
(Christ)	
God gives an answer when we pray.	Matt. 21:22
God has mansions prepared for us.	I John 5:14
God's Son will come again one day. (Christ)	St. John 14:2
	I Thess. 4:16-17

* * *

LADDER OF FAITH

Faith is like a ladder	Rom. 1:17
Taking one step at a time.	Rom. 3:28 (first part)
If we slip it would matter	
But reading keeps us in line.	Rom. 10:17
Each step means only one more	
As faith ever upward we send.	Heb. 11
Many have climbed it before —	
It never comes to an end.	

EDWARD ECKHARD

NOVEMBER

Telephone poles like starched sentries
Stand their watch with the blunted sun,
Counting pine cones littering the land and
Faded needle beds stacked high with oak leaves
Like dead soldiers in khaki uniforms.
They see the blanched hillsides and fields
Empty but for wilted grass, cardboard-colored
Cornstalks, and dried out milkweed pods.
Angrily reading etched obscenities
On wooden benches and lonely fences.
Glaring at rusty barrels brimming
With bronze Budweiser bottles.
"Not like bleached and blushing Autumn,"
Sighed the nearest.
"Not like silver dusted Winter,"
Pined the other.
"Just brown," said the first,
"Yes, just brown."

* * *

MY OTHER WIFE

You mustn't be so bold.
Too quick you come with loving arms
Soothing my mind sick with sameness
As if no one could see.
My other wife suspects.
So often I'm gone, not to be touched,
Breathing a different fragrance,
Watering at different breasts,
Dreaming songs I dare not sing.
Why come to me, take me to you.
Sleep with me the deep sleep.

234

REFLECTIONS ON A SETTING SUN

At the water's edge, I see
The splendor of Nature's vitality
Blaze bright across amber skies,
As timid clouds blush beautified,
    Radiate life from a swelling sun,
    Above royal horizon pomps paragon.

Behold! the sublime of Heaven's grace,
Sparkles gold on waters embraced,
To bless profound thy mortal strife,
By love conferred, eternal life.
    In wonders proclaim my mind transcends
    Opinions of man to truth intend.

Mysteries seen through faith convey,
With contrite heart I kneel to pray
To Heaven's glory, then humbly bow,
And gaze upon an image shroud,
    In gilded light my likeness sees
    At the water's edge, thy humanity.

* * *

HUMAN NATURE

From my hand flow words of what
thoughts hold me captive.
Prisoner unrestrained, yet
Prisoner I remain.
A divided man bound to mankind,
Wandering within worlds
uncivilized.
Existing by systems and rules
based upon his talents.
For more his genius wanes,
from the heart and spirit of humanity,

Toward vanity waxed in his nature,
Where conditions dictate,
and desire acts
In academic tenor,
to advantages right and wrong.

* * *

UNREQUITED LOVE

Lonely thoughts are harsh to bear,
In mind and soul they dwell despair,
And to one's heart, lest of all, to spare,
A sorrowful pain of solitaire.

Oh! how burdening love does entrance,
        Upon a miracle's wish enhance,
        An inspiration to tender romance,
        A comely maiden of beauteous sight
        Who tinged my heart, such sweet delight
        As her eyes enchant a spell sincere,
        That rendered my soul, her image clear.

But to love unrequited comes suffering cause,
        With tears that say of love because
        I live in lonely thoughts of her,
        Who cast this shadow of love to aver,
        My grieving heart which now decries,
        The loneliness it must occupy,
In destitution of hope and prayer,
With no one to turn to but Pity's care.

MUSIC FROM THE HEART

On quiet somber nights, I dream
In innocence's passing shadow.
Where Orpheus' lyre lays silent,
Amidst pastoral meadows, sweet.

Fair wind of Eurydice,
Strumming softly upon weeping twine
In timeless refrain,
Till Eros dares to play it anew.

* * *

MEANINGS CONDUCT IN MANNERS CONVEY

A gesture is an actor
                of a thousand pictures.
A picture is a painter
                of a thousand words.
A word is an author
                of a thousand thoughts.
A thought is a philosopher
                of a thousand Wonders.
A Wonder is Love
                of Truth and Good,
                of Art and Life.
A wonder disclosed
Reveals God's light.

HISTORY

Reflections pass in thoughts discern
Manifest true the acts of man
Upon his conscious, intention due
In perspection's sense on faith concern.

A philosopher of civilized life,
Of suffered wisdom and compassionate heart
Inspiring those of righteous spirit
To edify truth amidst man's strife.

Social conduct marks sure his presence
In traditions cured from sources known;
Share in time thy creative spirit
To challenge with passion, fate's consequence.

History stands by the destiny of all
Counseling deeds of everyone born
To consult with justice, their nature true
So bear well thy matters upon his call!

LAST AUTUMN

I kissed you
Last autumn
When the lights
Were gold
And we drove down
Unfamiliar streets
And imagined the people
Who lived in the houses there.
We talked
Of going to Carmel,
Walking on the beach
And writing and painting
And I left my head on your shoulder
Where you kissed my forehead
When you thought I was asleep
And I wasn't.

But the winter took away
The gold lights and Carmel
As I awakened from my imagined sleep
And remembered your kiss and you
And a memory
That keeps me away from Carmel
And another love
Who might actually
Have taken me there.
How can I love you . . . still?

GOOD-BYE

I won't be
Coming back to you.
The dogwood
Will still bloom
On the hill
In spring
And the rock mountain
Will slowly
Be covered
With moss.

You loved me
When I was a child
Clinging to flowers
That bloomed on a tree;
Tiptoeing
Through the forest
From one season
To another,
Always afraid
Of losing something
That never was.

I've grown to the open now
In an autumn song
That blows away from you,
For the leaves that fell
From the tree
Can never turn green
Again.

I DON'T LOVE YOU ANYMORE

I don't love you anymore.
Not the golden spill
Of sunlight
In the summer
When we walked
Childlike
On the ochre road;
Not the rose-purple
Hues
That fell
On the water
Before the moon
Was yellow
In black crepe skies;
Not the chimes from
A chapel
At noonday
Or the leaf
From the tree where
We stood.
I stopped loving you when
The sunlight
Was gone; when
The sea could
Not hold
The sunset
And the moon
Shone
On the other side of
The earth.

I AM A RIVER RUNNING

I am a river
Running.
I will not say
Good-bye,
That I have changed,
Or that time
Replaces sorrow.
I will only tell you
I am a river
Running
In a valley
Between several mountains;
That I am as other rivers—
Afraid to stop
For one mountain,
One day,
One reflection of sunlight
Upon my waters.
I am a river
Running
To the sea,
Where turbulent waters
Will grow calm with mine
And there will be nowhere else
To run.

* * *

THE VINE

There is a vine
That grows along the fence
That bloomed last summer.
It stands against the brick
And sleeps and sheds its leaves
And waits for autumn.

A bird who sits upon its branches
Sees only the vine
That bloomed last summer,
But I who smelled its blossoms once
And watched its leaves turn brown,
Remember honeysuckle which now
Has turned to vine.

* * *

AUBURN

Auburn
Leaves on a frosty morn
Drifting slowly from somewhere —
Perhaps a tree that clung too closely to its foliage
In hope that it somehow might not die.

Auburn
A shadow of sunset at twilight
Spreading across the water
Lonely, forgotten, still.

* * *

MASQUERADE

It's a masquerade
Pretending to love —
Running through clover,
Freezing in the snow.
It's a party of people
Wearing faces,
Dancing to songs
They cannot sing;
It's a high
That's over

243

At midnight
When masks come off
And the music stops.

Just once
Let's be ourselves
Loving without frustrations,
Looking at each other
Without masks.
It's morning,
And the masquerade
Is over.

A MOTHER'S LOVE

Long suffering and patient,
Tempered like steel;
A rose in all its glory,
A sunshine that brightens the heart;
Ageless and flawless like time itself,
A crown of many jewels;
Each a symbol of God's love.
Her works give praise to Thee,
Her hands a tool in the vineyard of the Lord;
A love that will not let me go.

* * *

ODE TO OUR YOUNG

Oh, my child, as I stand gazing upon you in awe and joy
I see the gate swing wide into a new world;
One full of happiness, oh yes, my dear, pain also.
My heart and soul will always weigh with concern for you
As you tread along the many paths in life that will be yours.
Some you may stumble on and fall along the way, others you
        may not,
But always remember the hand of the Lord is there for you to
        grasp
So once again your pathway will be a brighter tomorrow.

245

THE BOOK OF BOOKS

When the Book of Books was written
It was meant to be our guide;
It was to be a friend to man
But never cast aside.

For everything is written there
Since its time begun;
Everything that has been
And everything to come.

It is a book, I am sure,
Where every word is true.
If you read if often
It seems to talk to you!

For every question there's an answer
In this book divine;
It will never hurt you—
It tells the truth, you'll find.

If you're sad or lonesome
It will comfort you.
In this Book of Books, you'll find
Every word is true!

LOVE'S SONG

Yesterday I felt a tingle in my heart; it
Created ripples that remind me of wind
Chimes in the air, unheard by those who
Were too deeply engrossed in their sorrows.
I saw an old man sitting with his head bent
But every now and then he lifted his head
And smiled in the direction of the wind;
In my heart I knew he smiled at things past.
Yet those that are young and think of past
Things, hardly ever smile.
But age is what brings wisdom and the soothing
Sound of love's song . . .

* * *

MEMORIES

A tear slid down her face, as old memories pushed
Themselves forward from the depths of her mind.
And with these memories came the soft sound of
His voice, like the warm gentle breeze that comes
With autumn winds. Gently his voice danced in
Her ears, soothing the need for his closeness.
As she closed her eyes to keep the tears from
Falling, his image appeared.
Tall and slender, with outer strengths so visible,
Eyes warm, gentle, a tender expression of love.
Then, as a mirage appears his image slips
Away; gone for now that image of strength
And so are her tears; sweet are the memories
Of all their fine years.

247

ONAWANATEKA

Sometime, just after the leaves turned brown, withered away,
    died, and fell to the ground, a Man came.
He commanded a way about the trees; He spoke, and they
    listened.
He came to take their spirits with Him for a while.
It was written in the law, that those that live a good and
    fruitful life shall help those that are less fortunate.
So He took their spirits, every year, just after they led a
    good and fruitful life.
To help those that needed help.
When He called to them, they followed.
They went to help, in a land where they were not just silent
    statues,
And He rewarded them,
He gave them a life and a meaning.
They were a people unto themselves there.
For when they came back, they were fresh, and new,
Alive with a spirit—
    His Spirit.
They helped those around them to try to feel His Spirit.
They, the trees, reflected His Spirit.
They had it together, what they did.
They worked to help, they had His Spirit.
Never did they fight among themselves.
They lived and grew next to each other.
They wait again for Him to call to them,
So they may follow, once again.
But they will leave their song behind,
The song the men hear singing through their branches.
They hear it.
It is the Man, Onawanateka.
They hear it, the men, and they say it is the voice of God.
It is Onawanateka calling,
Calling to His chosen ones.

CONQUEST FOR UNDERSTANDING

I stood all alone on the mountain crest,
    Just nature and I.
The wind whispering in the tall elms,
Sounded as though it were trying to help me
    make the decision of whether to jump, or not.
I didn't understand my father,
And he didn't even regard me as his son.
So, still and pondering, I sat,
Carefully weighing out my judgments.
The whispering in the elms turned to a murmur.
The sun was a disillusionment,
And the babbling brook nearby
Only interrupted me.
But finally, my thoughts gave way to nature.
I stood up and walked to the edge of the precipice.
Far off to the right was the scintillating blue of the lake,
    guarded by mountains.
Eight hundred feet below me
Was an empty space,
Abruptly ending in rocks, bare earth, and trees.
I took in an invigorating breath of cool mountain air,
Then leapt off into space.
All time stopped,
And I seemed to be suspended forever.
Inanimate and limp I hung.
Slowly I started floating down,
Gradually increasing speed,
The way gravity works on a raindrop.
Halfway down I reached a momentous decision.
It was not my father at fault—
All the time it had been me!
Oh, why did I have to jump?
Why couldn't I have a second chance?
To walk away from the crest,
Down the worn trail,
And go back to that lonely, little cabin,

To explain it was my fault?
But it's too late now,
Time wouldn't stop for a mere mortal.
Then I spotted something, lying on the ground below me:
It was father.

* * *

MORNING BEAUTY

Beneath stars of weeping sadness,
Shimmer silver leaves of isolation, gently waving in a gasping
    breath of wind.
Silhouetted forlornly, against an artist's sketch,
Painted disdainfully in the background, float crimson tears of
    rage on a blue amber sheet, the sky.
Far off, hanging on a thin gossamer thread of hope,
    is the horizon,
Suspended from a glowing silver-white peg
    that moves slowly across the zenith,
Pulling a different-hued blanket of tomorrow,
    over a coming lush greenness of pending beauty.
Geared and synchronized by coded signals,
    each character awaits his cue.

Springing lightly from behind a curtain of darkness,
Stand lonely silver leaves, turned green with life,
    Anew with feverish colors of beauty.
An orange spotlight signals its approval from overhead,
While rippling waters lazily careen off reflected rays,
Mirroring footlights, in a thousandfold effect.
Then, rushing lightly Heavenward, rises a lifting, shrouded,
    fog of hushed voices,
    As a quenching sigh of approval from the audience
    gently covers the land,
Like a fresh blanket of snow that falls during the night.

AUTUMN EYES OF YOUTH

The wind still blows . . .
And of whose hair to torment?
Heads will turn —
Eyes will look —
Yet how many will hear
The rampaging voice of love
That cries
        Loud as the October gales?

And who will see the colors,
Born to die in splendor,
That autumn eyes of youth
Long to hold,
Beyond the fluttering wind?

* * *

AUTUMN'S LAST WIND

Death unfurled from the grayed, silky curtains
That fluttered in the wind of the open window,
Crept over the patterns on the rug,
Stood up,
Sighed and stretched,
Bent over,
And touched the soft, young face.
It glowed,
Burned with fever,
Diminished,
Died out,
Snuffed out,
Stared, like the burnt coals of a fire,
Relit itself,
Then glowed again.
Death leaned over,

251

Kissed the warm cheek,
Then stood up,
Contemplating,
Turned,
Floated over to the open window,
And dispersed
With the waning sunshine.
The sun
Aha'd into the mountains,
And David Willoughby
Died in solemn grace.

* * *

LIFE—A NEW TRAIL

Lead me onward down the worn trail of life.
Through the forest of happenings,
Across the river of anxiety,
Into the underbrush of misery,
Ford the dismal swamp of depression,
Cross the "Lake of Tranquillity,"
Up the hill of soaring moods,
Down the other side on reflections of the past,
Sweating, puffing, heaving,
Step over the tortured log of death . . .
A new trail is in sight.

* * *

THE LAST SEASON
(As Hushed as the Buffalo)

In a line as hushed as the buffalo,
                  the sentinels roamed.
As still as the stars they held their position.

Into the first shades of night,
                the sentinels stood quiet and still,
            soldierly at attention.
Their uniforms bore the colors of another campaign,
And pastelled bands and groups into recognition.
                At the last light they were as solid as night,
            And only by the last light
                were they dismissed from sight,
But remained stonily solid
            and as straight as their shadows.
As statuesque as a reflective painting they posed,
        Colored by the ground on which they stood.
            And still,
        In a line as hushed as the buffalo,
                the sentinels,
                    the trees,
                roamed . . .
Into august season.

* * *

WINTER WHITE

Momma's breath,
        a mist upon the window pane, the tablecloth she's
        dropped before her eyes, a welcome table set for
        visiting visions as the sconce of snow defends her
        heart-head feelings of romanticized nostalgia in the
        glorious colors of winter that her eyes presuppose
        Woods might paint of a singular heart.
Her words,
        an archaic voice speaking the resemblance of the
        envisioned painting in her heart, only a foreign
        language to the children, whose remedy is shouts of
        glee and running past the three-dimensional paintings
        of winter white hung loosely about the house, the
        windows.
A lady's echo,

253

of bygone times and bygone words do not ring dormant
upon the ears of the old man in his restive corner,
who sits in years of lace, remembering the dusty visions
the archaic words can endorse, for the words,
and the visions might be archaic; of their times—but
the voice of love, forever rejuvenated with age,
sings changeless through the matrimony of centuries,
amidst the splendor of winter's ceremony, and winter
white love is painted by Momma's breath upon the
window pane.

* * *

ROSES IN RELIEF

A slice of lightning caught my eye this morning,
Wounded the sky,
And stilled the birds' cry.
The sky cried out in terror,
Or was it the song of the victor?
Rain flurries sequelled the early morning parish of tranquility,
Subdued a peace of nobility,
Leaving a kingdom ruled of omnificence,
Reigning tumultuously in the embryo of a new day.
Sparkled jewels strewn across the meadows,
Garnish beauty,
As in the eye of a dream.
Rain glistening, softened surrealism,
Harmonizes with the twill
        of the whippoorwill.
This day has approached me as a friend,
And I want to reckon with it as a friend.
Forgive me,
        For I go now to pursue this day . . .

SPEAK, MY COUNTRY

Calls for Spanish language equalization —
    Chicano, you're brown, you state;
    my country, my roots, my domain,
    My language, you claim, has degrees to rate
    Democracy, my government accept, don't strain.

Spanish language is history —
    Freedom, democracy, you claim
    Your form of government cannot rest.
    My language assets you rate in vain,
    Ethnically, linguistically, historically, the best.

Chicanos have responded and died —
    Brown, call me, I accept the test,
    Brown Chicano, in war, a life sacrifice;
    Brown, Mother Nature's roots, the best;
    Brown, in your honor my country dies.

Heritage acceptance, unity —
    Honor you, my country, it's my heaven.
    Accept me; I'm a branch, united a tree.
    My assets I offer, change and leaven,
    Freedom, united support, let's be free.

National unity of all ethnic groups —
    Love it or leave it, a coward's disgrace;
    Freedom, freedom for all, that's the test.
    Accept, accept cultural assets, that's the base;
    Change, change for unity, that's the best.

Cultural values have not been accepted; yet, support of
                              democracy —
          Brown, my country marches
          For your honor, my country suffers
          Acceptance; your government, vain latches
          Intelligence, my country, the Chicano offers.

THEME FOR IMAGINATION

It's great, yet it spoils a person. Hear that sax?
Purrs forth some sweet stuff, doesn't it? Drums in the
    background
And the accompaniment are too much for the adventurous ear.
I don't know where it comes from, but you'd think it was meant
For everyone. You start the day with such music and the rest
Of the day you're with that shadow, that star, new wonderful
Exaggerated feeling. For sure you'll never go away mad.
You've never had anything until you've had an excess of a little
Of that feeling. Creation must feel it. I know the music's
Almost over, yet when it's all over and gone that spark will
Stay awake. I guess the feeling that afterward you get to
Know so well, is just one of the sweet things in life.

I got that deluxe feeling now. That's why I want to roam . . .
Lost in search of a dream for something to climax the stirring
Inside of me, something for my heart's lifting, a desire yet
Undiscovered or understood.
You're with that shadow of a new, wonderful, exaggerated
    feeling.
The dreamy melody, it's on again, its promising pool of
Suspended notes demanding your appraisal. I want to sing, yet
Too enthralled! Can't you feel it? Everyone should feel it!
I want to wander down . . . down . . . down . . . into the
    hollow, and if I'm
Keensighted and do not have the ordinary blindness, I'll find
    what
Seems to be there. And when I find it, I'll transcribe and
Share this with all.

MY PRETTY TREE IN SUMMER

A tree rests by my window, in the evening, moaning low;
in the morning whispering so, to gentle breezes dancing to and
    fro.
The afternoon—it seems so free. The afternoon is left for me
and for the sun-dappled leaves of my favorite tree.

* * *

A VERY SAD POEM

A cross of stars, in the black of night,
A cross of stars, shining perfect light:
"Coo, coo," wails the mourning dove.
"Where, o where is the one I love?"
A windy whisper of leaves reply:
"Alas and alack, your loved one dies!"

Dawns a morn of palest gray . . .
Away flies the dove—away.

* * *

BURNISHED COPPER AND GOLD

Autumn arrives
with the whisper
    Of a falling leaf;
Melancholy and sad,
    Foreboding of winter
And bitterly cold,
    Waving farewell
To the summers of old.

Alas, with only
A hope of Spring,
    This life seems

Too much to bear . . .
Alas, with only
A faint hope of Spring;
Yet still remains
Your love, so fair.

OTHER SPRINGS

Seasons arrive
yet never quite the same;
the ones swept by have entered into
                    farce
like sunset's fan to evening grown quite
                    tall
while luminous things parade through
                    charted night;
our fantasies become as real as hope,
unhurried, until the morning's anxious scope
swift ride the thorn to a rose petal
to the cheek of time nestled in clover,
to the arm of the sea wearing thin circlets
                    of silver
like splattered slivers of distant pale moons
                    on a thundering shore.
I look again to evening's glance:
dark fringes of trees skirt the avenue,
long lashes from the sea curl up the beach
from some distant reach of knowing . . .
erased my tiny question mark.

OLYMPICS

O Olympic Victor of Old,
While tales of modern games are told,
What are you thinking about,
As the torch moves from Olympia out?
Do you see the fleeting runners and
              sinewy wrestlers,
And medals of gold, silver, and bronze
              on the victors?
Does that familiar half-smile on your face
Mean that you wish you were back in the race?
Surely, this sight must make you feel proud,
Seeing brotherhood and friendship among the crowd?

* * *

GROSSE POINTE

Grosse Pointe, jewel by the lake,
From whose life style all a lesson can take,
Where once the Indian freely did roam,
And the Frenchman called his home.
Today along tree-lined Courts, Lanes and Boulevards,
Are homes both gracious and historical to regard,
And beautiful Lake Shore Drive one must mention,
With its magnificent view and Canada on the horizon.
Finally, whether "On the Hill" or "In the Village,"
You can see Grosse Pointe presenting its grand image.

THE MALL

Village Common of Today: Consumer Center, Entertainment
    Enterprise, and Arena of Social Satisfaction,
Playing many roles in the present-day life of the nation.
Renewing the spirit of early America, as found in the village
    common or square.
Offering the citizenry goods, either to use or to wear.
Here you find literary luminaries, sports figures and entertainers,
Along with political figures hoping to increase the number of
    their supporters
A rendezvous for friends and business acquaintances,
As well as a meeting place for community audiences.
Here man can control the seasons by providing protection from
    the weather,
And by changes in displays and decorations can get you into the
    proper holiday fever.
Lights and music, hustle and bustle of the throng, cash registers
    ringing, conversations hearng,
The Mall—a microcosm of the community it is serving.

TIME

Time is parenthetical —
    Each end a semisphere
Within whose bounds
    man births and dies
    and counts his days
    beneath the skies
taut stretched to shield
    from questing eyes
God's great Beyond,
      that death's door prize,
Eternal NOW . . . Forever HERE.

TIME IS FULL

Time,
that strangely contoured vessel, was full—
    Full to the brim with the restlessness
        and avarice of those wedded to the dust;
Swelling full with knowledge
        and opportunity
           and desperate need;
Running over with nothingness and lostness,
        indifference and unbelief.
Time was full—
And, spilled over by the spilling hand of Jehovah,
Poured out ETERNITY HIMSELF
        into a woman's womb.

The Rivers of Time
    Again threaten its brim,
    Straining against containment.
Man and his greed and guile,
    His anger and his anguish
        is tossed stupidly
        in a million fractured guises
    On the full tide of time.
Inexorably the contents of that cup
        pile up against the brim—
No warning sounds above the noisy riders of the tide;
No hand deters the crazy flotsam;
No eye discovers the unbelievable beyond.

Time is full again—
    Ripe for the spilling hand of God.
The fullness of that odd-shaped cup
    will be drained into eternity,
Washing with great finality
    the silt that was humanity
        into the forever of God.

I SING TO GOD

I sing to god my song of HOPE,
    The Hope that fills my heart and mind;
That gives me nourishment to cope
    With trials that I leave behind.
Sweet Hope! What am I without you?
    Entwine yourself around my heart,
For there would be no joy in view
    For me—if you should ere depart!

I sing to God my song of LOVE,
    The Love that shines within my eyes;
That comes from Him who dwells above,
    Who tries to teach what man denies!
Sweet Love! What am I without you?
    Fill me! As long as there's a sun!
For without Love what would I do?
    I know that you and God are one!

I sing to God my song of CHARITY,
    The Charity that teaches giving;
With Love and Hope. you do make three—
    I need all of you for living!
Sweet Charity! What am I without you?
    Do come and fill my heart and soul,
I have Hope! Love! I need you, too,
    With joy! Do come and take control!

I sing to God my song of LOVE,
    HOPE and CHARITY! Yes, I sing
With voice that reaches high above
    The clouds. And with my songs I bring
A happy heart and laughing eyes.
    And I'm so glad my songs are three!
I'll raise my voice and fill the skies
    As I sing to God! His Majesty!

THE SPECTATOR

The people came from far and near,
　　To hear the preacher talk;
They hurried in through every door,
　　Some in a hurried walk
And some just came to look around
　　And stand around and gawk.
There were those who were excited
　　For the miracles to see,
And there were those with saddened eyes,
　　From demons would be free.
Some came and flung themselves in front
　　And cried on bended knee.
The hubbub could be heard around
　　At least a mile away;
And the talking, shouting voices
　　Sounded like a wild affray;
While the deaf and blind and crippled
　　Came in to weep and pray.

And when the preacher waved his arms
　　And pointed to the crowd,
A quiet hush just swept across
　　As if he'd dropped a shroud.
And even a child's breathing
　　Seemed coarse and very loud.

"Help me to make a miracle!"
　　His booming voice outcried;
"Raise your hand and make a covenant
　　To the Lord, who is sanctified!
Please! Give your hundred dollars, NOW!
　　Your soul I'll save and guide!"
A child, deaf, was led to him,
　　They heard her gentle squeal,
The blind and crippled stood in awe;
　　Some came forward to kneel.
The preacher touched them hard and cried,
　　"I say now, Heal! Heal! Heal!"

Through it all no one had noticed
    Him standing beside the door;
They'd shoved right past Him as they pushed
    Amid the babbling roar.
A quiet, gentle man, He was,
    So easy to ignore.
He shook His head, His gentle eyes
    Were very blurred and teared;
And His heart ached for all of them,
    His sheep were being sheared.
He wept, "This man comes in my name —
    His words are well-veneered!
Poor wandering sheep!" He cried in pain.
    "I told them there would be
Many who would preach my word
    And sound convincingly.
Poor lost sheep! For they follow men,
    Not Christ from Galilee."
He walked away so hurt and sad,
    Leaving them all behind;
His heavy heart was aching now
    For that mass of mankind.
He knew that all of them were deaf,
    And also they were blind!

A TURKEY NAMED MORRIS

Morris lives in a wooded park,
    With a small and wild flock;
And people know when he struts out
    That he is a Turkey-cock.
His pompous air and gaited strut
    Makes him quite a laughing stock.
"Morris! Morris!" Young David called,
    Then Morris came on the run;
And he saw visions in his head
    Of a nice sweet Sally-Lunn.
His tuft of hairlike feathers looked
    Golden-bronze and cinnamon.
Reaching David with open mouth,
    He ate all the sweetened bread,
Threw back his head with a guffaw,
    Then he stopped and proudly said,
"Gobble! Gobble! Hey! This is good,
    Now sir, I have breakfasted!"
As little Mary passed him by,
    Morris tried to peck her shoes;
Then screaming down the road she ran,
    Weeping tears that did accuse.
He couldn't understnd just why
    A small peck could so confuse.
Some of the people ran to see
    What the fuss was all about;
Then someone yelled, "That Turkey-cock
    Has a bill that's strong and stout!
He's swift of foot and ludicrous
    And he's MUCH A GADABOUT!"
So they called the park commissioner,
    All the mothers came out, too;
They called the Mayor and his aides,
    And—this mentions just a few—
"He follows kids and chases cars,
    Now, what do you say we do?"

"I say let's shoot him!" someone said,
    All the kids let out a howl;
The environmental leader
    Grunted with an angry scowl,
"Let's take him to another park
    Where he cannot run afoul!"
All the while Morris stood there,
    Listening to their silly talk;
Suddenly they ran to catch him,
    Morris yelled a raucous squawk.
And with a stately mien he fled,
    Leaving them to stare and gawk.
He ran into the wooded park
    Hid beneath the underbrush;
"People! I can't understand them!"
    He said to the missel-thrush.
"Nor I! Don't try!" the bird replied.
    Both sat in a quiet hush.
Now, at the clearing of the park,
    All the people had agreed
That they would try again next day,
    By spreading nuts, fruits and seed.
"We'll catch that Turkey!" they all yelled,
    "We shall try till we succeed!"
And Morris hunched behind the brush,
    He was wary of the crowd;
"They'll have to catch me first!" he screamed,
    "I am friendly—and unbowed!"
Chipmunk said in a quiet voice,
    "Friend Turkey, you are quite loud."
"My name is Morris!" he yelled back,
    And the wattles on his head
Changed hue—Chipmunk sat quietly
    With a mammoth piece of bread.
"Huh, you're still a turkey—Turkey,
    And I stick to what I said."
Meanwhile the papers screamed out loud,
    How a turkey from the wild;

Had been named "Morris" and was loved
    By every man, mom, and child.
And now they worried that he would
    Make all turkeys tame and mild.
Now, Morris being strong of wing,
    Spread his wings majestically;
Into the highest tree he flew,
    And gobble-gobbled gustily.
The Chipmunk shrugged and darted off,
    Feeling quite confusedly.
The last I'd heard the people were
    Setting up some clever plan,
They'd take him to another park
    Where he'd be away from man.
And Morris laughs as his big voice
    Shouts, "Come catch me if you can!"
Now Morris wanders through the woods,
    Loose of foot and fancy-free;
He talks to all the woodland creatures—
    Squirrels and moles and chickadee.
At times he feels a little sad
    As he gazes from his tree;
Because he has much time to think
    Of friendships with humankind,
He thinks of all the kids he knew
    And the joy he left behind.
His gentle heart—in spite of all—
    Is quite filled with LOVES that bind!

MORE ABOUT MORRIS
(Chapter 2)

Weeks have passed—the Daily paper
    Gave out some real good news,
"REPRIEVE FOR MORRIS!" In large print . . .
    After a state of muse—
They said they'd leave him quite alone,
    (That chased away the blues.)
There had been a great outpouring
    Of letters on his behalf;
Half a city had spoken out—
    (To Morris, I do quaff—)
Tip my glass to a gentle soul,
    He had the last, last laugh!
And now I hear he's wandering 'round
    Back in the neighborhood,
And everyone is hoping that
    He acts the way he should.
Are you list'ning, Morris? Don't chase kids!
    And just be Good! Good! Good!

ADVICE TO A VERY YOUNG LADY

I wanted you—and so you've come to stay,
    And I shall teach you, dear, from day to day,
The happy way to smile and romp around
    That I may show the world the joy I've found.
And I shall teach you how to love, you know;
    You must learn to love, my dear, as you grow,
And make your happiness and joy well-earned—
    But dear, your heart may break before you've learned.
You'll pick your way among the broken reeds,
    And your highest hopes grow among the weeds,
But always plant the kindest thoughts, dear heat,
    And pick the flower of *truth* as your sweetheart!

And soon 'twill be your turn to mold and teach,
    And you'll remember words that I did preach;
Your garden will be blooming all the year,
    Tending it with love—now and then a tear—
But darling, never stop! It's all worthwhile,
    Especially when you pick a charming smile!

THE YOUNG—AS OPPOSED TO THE OLD

In youth I thought of you with scorn,
My glowing body—young and strong;
My heart sang merrily every morn,
I hummed a tune or sang a song.
My young heart knew no bitter pain!
With great ambition it was filled;
At the touch of love it sang and trilled,
I laughed at you with cold disdain!
My skies were blue and lined with gold,
My body—flushed with love supreme!
In youth—HAPPINESS was mine to hold,
YOUTH held me in a radiant dream.
Ah! Love to me was eternity!
My heart knew no sorrowful stories
While I sought earth's pleasant glories—
OLD AGE! YOU! Were my enemy!

And now with age I'm old and gray,
No music fills my listening ear;
My eyes are dim and bring dismay,
My lonely heart is filled with fear.
More times than not I wear a frown,
Bifocals are my newest glasses;
My gait is truly like molasses—
I'm either looking up or down.
OLD AGE! YOU RASCAL! You have brought
A touch of wisdom with my age;
If in my youth you could have taught
I could have been a youthful sage!
At times I think my bones are rusting,
My body moves with spurts and lunging;
My spirits are forever plunging.
LOOK! OLD AGE! I'm not adjusting!

DIRGE

Tired body and aching heart,
　　Now thou sleepeth well;
Sleep and rest, rest and sleep,
　　Thou canst hear the knell.
Naught can ever break thy slumber,
　　Thy sweet peace and calm;
Sleep now, thy bed is made,
　　Thou canst hear the psalm.

Now thou hath gained another friend,
　　(Some gains bring a loss,)
Thy tired, weary body
　　Wilt gather soft moss.
Stillness doth soothe the atmosphere
　　And the cypress tree;
Sleep, tired weary one—
　　I would fain rest with thee!

* * *

THE NORTH WIND

The North Wind knocked on my window pane,
And shouted, "Come and play with me!"
He hissed and blew, like all winds do,
And he whistled and laughed with glee.
He huffed and puffed through my window sill,
And he shook his snow-covered hand
While his elves erected snow shelves
That they brought from the frozen land.
He blew the snow till it was tired,
He piled it ever so deep;
I turned in bed and sleepily said,
"Go away! And just let me sleep!"
The North Wind was fierce and angry,
And he moaned with a roaring sound,
He pushed his elves, tore down their shelves,
And piled them unto the ground.

He blew the snow against my door,
And blew some limbs off my tree;
Covered the street with ice and sleet,
And waited 'round the corner for me.
That's where I found him blowing squalls,
As I pushed through the deep, deep snow;
He whistled and blew as fierce winds do
And carried off my new chapeau.

He blew the snow 'round my neck and face,
Till my limbs just shook and quivered;
Nipped on my nose, tugged at my toes,
I shook —and shivered—and shivered! •
I mailed my letter—laughed at him,
And started back home on the run;
He yelled, "Come play!" I cried, "Go 'way!
I don't like your *frolicsome fun!*"

* * *

ODE TO DEATH

Death plays a lone and silent game,
It has no fear of wealth or fame.
Death has no pride, it goes within
All types of homes —in good —or sin . . .
And calls us from the highest plain
Without a thought of tears or pain.
Though we might weep from dusk till day,
Death takes our cherished ones away;
It leaves a sore and wounded spot—
Has no favorites—and spares us not!

A HAPPY ENDING FOR MORRIS THE TURKEY

The winter months have flown on wings,
　　The very worst was feared;
The DEC was very sure
　　Morris had disappeared.
When—lo! He came out of hiding
　　Still nervy and uncheered.
He had traveled fifty miles
　　Into another town;
Walked down the center of the road,
　　Just like a circus clown.
"Call the police!" a woman yelled,
　　As she grabbed and held him down.
"Can't arrest him!" Chief Hulbert said,
　　"I don't know what he's done."
"This turkey chases cars and kids!
　　He's Morris! On the run!"
"Well," Chief Hulbert said, "in this case
　　His career has just begun."
"Morris is a celebrity!"
　　A little boy cried out;
"He'll live with all the animals!
　　He'll never be without!
Hurrah! For Morris! One great turkey!
　　He's very brave and stout!"
Now—much loved and pampered—bagged off
　　To Lollipop Farm,
He talks to burros, deer and sheep,
　　(The chickens love his charm.)
"Long live MORRIS!" I shout with joy,
　　"May he never come to harm!"
On Sundays Morris struts around
　　He knows this is the day
That kids and other folks will come
　　To see the matinee.
And though the dogs and cats are loved,
　　Morris makes the gala day.

He's happy now because he knows,
        No more will he be chased,
He'll be well-fed and pampered, too,
        And never feel displaced.
And as he put it to the pig,
        "Miss Pig, I do have taste!"
The sheep looked up and just ba-ba'd,
        The deer was agitated;
The big brown hen kept on scratching
        For a worm she'd baited.
The burro said in his deep voice,
        "Friend, you're incarcerated!"
And Miss Pig just oinked and grunted,
        Duck continued wading;
And badger—in a nearby cage,
        Said, "I'm masquerading."
A dog who'd just come in that day,
        Said, "This's quite degrading!"
And Morris yelled, "I know all that!
        I'm smart and quite able
To figure out just where I am,
        I'm a bird that's stable!
And—better here, dear newfound friends,
        Than someone's dinner table!"

SNOW SCENE

The snow is gently drifting, falling,
    floating to the ground.
The multitude of flakes descend
    on tiptoe without sound.
Deeper, mounting, growing like
    tidal waves at crest,
The earth a blanket robed in white
    is nature's winter quest.
It's gleaming, glowing brightly,
    it scarcely blinds the eye,
Till sunshine breaks to reign supreme
    and melt it by and by.

* * *

DADDY WAS A COWBOY

Daddy was a cowboy
For ranches in the West.
The open range with starry sky
Was home to him, his nest.

His garb was wide-brimmed hat and chaps,
Bandanna, spurs and lasso,
High boots, with saddled horse nearby
And bedroll was his castle.

No night too dark or noon sun hot
Could make this bold man fret.
The cattle were his babes to guide
A job he'd ne'er regret.

Some men attempt to find themselves
On ships tossed 'round at sea,
But after his last cattle drive
Dad lasso'd mom and me.

Each night when I am tucked in bed
And darkness fills the sky,
I dream of stories I've been told
By Dad, my own cowboy.

NATURE'S WAY

The smell of the air and its fresh warm breeze,
The misty salt taste of the deep blue seas.
Flowers grow wild and trees reach high,
Trying to touch the sun as days go by.

While bees make their honey and birds make their nest,
Bears seek shelter for a place to rest.
Yet all through these things that man can see,
Life is but what he makes it to be.

The beautiful colors of a sun setting west,
Is a sight all in one and really the best;
Then night seems to be the darkness of day,
When we settle down to pass the evening away.

Frogs and toads croak in the dark,
As crickets chirp and firebugs spark;
The owls in the trees hoot and stare,
And bats fly through the midnight air.

And as we sleep all the night through,
Hoping to awake to a new morning dew,
We smell, see and hear all these that life brings;
But do we ever take time to thank God for these things?

* * *

ORDAINED

You cannot change the will of God,
    or the course of time;
But with sad regrets if they may be,
    you must have peace of mind.

SEE THE SILENCE

Silence is golden, some old folks say,
When peace to the ears makes your soul gay.
The wind blowing through the singing trees
Makes your heart pound to the rustling of leaves.
Experiencing life in such a quiet way
By walking with nature day by day.
    Noise, frustration, tension and fear
    Can bring about sadness and heartful tear.
    Anxiety, depression and loneliness, too,
    Will cause a person to think he is through.
But pride and conceit are dangers indeed,
To the inner forces of one's basic needs.
Don't give up hope nor faith nor love;
Put all your trust in God above.
He'll bring you back to the truth and the light,
He'll guide you straight and tell you what's right.
    Just remember what peace there may be,
    All wrapped up in a heart you can't see.
    Seek within your own soul and mind,
    Never stop loving nor cease to be kind.
    Maybe someday you'll tell what I've told,
    Silence is golden and oh, how quite old.

* * *

SHARING

Each holiday has a special thought, a certain joy and tear;
We celebrate these holidays throughout each winding year.
    There's one day when we think of snow and another when
    we think of spring;
    And as summer changes into fall we hear the bluebirds sing.
Giving gifts and showing love by every smiling ray;
But the real joy of the sharing is—the love on Easter Day.

FRIENDS

Good friends are but hard to find,
Especially ones like you;
You show you care and are concerned
In everything I do.

You're always there in time of need
To lend a helping hand;
And when it comes to having fun
You're the best in all the land.

So thank you for your honesty
And truthful, loving ways;
You'll always be a friend to me,
For many, many days.

* * *

REALITY

In finding friends of common wealth
and also of great pride,
We seem to lose an interest in the life
that we once strived.

To open up, express your thoughts,
and feel the things you feel,
May bring about an inner peace and
knowledge of things that are real.

So many times of loneliness,
so many times of fear,
When by yourself too long it seems
we shed the joker's tear.

Yes, friends are hard to find these days
and this I find to be true;
I am so glad that I have a friend
and this, of course, is you.

282

TWO POINTS OF VIEW

Plane flying low over Belgium
A boy and a girl holding hands—
He surveys the passing scene
And speaks "See, there is Antwerp
The forts a la Vauban—
They fell during the last war
The Holland-American shipyards,
Antwerp's a fine city, my dear"
But she had not heard him well
For she had been looking at the
Cathedral spire and the sun
Shining on the wide river
That seemed to flow into the sky.

* * *

SAINT DENIS (FRANCE)

Just then as the organ pounded,
Pounded through the Gothic arch
And the priest swung incense
Round the dark black casket
Lit with candles burning bright,
Just then I saw two figures of stone
On the tomb of St. Francis the First
Kneeling, hands together, praying.
It seemed as if they lived anew
And had returned to pray with us
For the new death. Amen.

GOSSIP

Who has said this, that I should suffer?
When that same thing was spoken
Without an origin from a word of mine,
And yet claimed to be my token.

Harsh tongue!
Bitter glare! Friendless stare! From out of nowhere,
Invented to cause me despair.

Despair? That is not honesty's wife.
Then I stand alone, unwed to this strife,
While cast upon me is that cover woven from threads
First made for friendship's cloak.

* * *

THE HOLY SPIRIT

There is a whispering in the wall
And a sounding in the board,
A time for hearing—discord.

There is a quiet in the carpet,
And a light in the blind,
A time for speaking—thoughts in your mind.

There is a softness in the grass
And a hardness in the street,
A time for knowing—what's come to pass.

There is a creaking in the steel
And a tension in the bricks,
A time for binding—the things we feel.

BIRD MIGRANTS

Up from the Gulf, the Argentinian plain,
They come, bird migrants seeking nests.
They cross the paths of giant liners on the main;
They cross subcontinents before they rest.
Tiny world travelers, to a northern spring
They bring the only tropic beauty that we see,
Brilliance of Southern bloom and sun, on fragile wing,
Colors of Bird of Paradise and inland sea.
Remembered watercourse and cataract the songs they sing,
Dawn chorus and the late-day splash of falling rain,
They of no fixed abode their distant winters bring
In haunting melodies of nostalgic pain.
These, who can fly from half a world away,
Bring tropic glory to our earthbound day.

WINTERSET

I stood high above the cliffs and watched a wintry sun sink into a
    sullen sea, a dull, red vanishing glow waning free . . . A
    flotilla of mushrooming clouds were drifting across the
    Milky Way, erasing the fading moonprints, blotting out the
    dying day . . . A cluster of lackluster moonbeams scudded
    on before the rising storm, darting behind a bank of angry
    clouds as in great alarm. A sudden slash of lightning scythed
    the sky and died in a thunderous roar, reverberating
    ominously out to sea and rumbling back along the
    shore . . . Surf churned the stretch of beaches and from out
    the deepening darkness rose the cry of a lost and threatened
    creature, a sea gull or a quail . . . The banshee shriek of
    mounting tempest sweeping in from storm-tortured seas
    hurled icy spume high into the gale-charged air. Surf
    buffetted the headwinds rolling in from out where the
    breakers ride the squall . . . Above the tumult, the roar, and
    the thunder, I faintly hear a dolphin's call . . . Lightning's
    gleam caught sheeted spray on roiling waters, setting the
    turbulence ablaze . . . I knew the signs and all the
    signals—a storm like this could go on ominously for days,
    or perhaps just deluge the thirsty earth with rain and pass
    within the hour, an icy winter shower . . . I turned to hurry
    homeward from this awesome, threatening, scene . . .
    Retraced my faltering footsteps down the slippery
    path with the force of a full-blown gale drumming its
    thunder in my brain . . . A light gleams in my window as I
    stumble through the rain. It's a beacon light of welcome
    with its promise of safety from the tempest's blast.

Illuminating the stygian rain-drenched night, dispelling an
enclosure of overcast . . . and later, much later and far into
the night I listened to the storm-made waterfall, that was an
hour ago the path . . . For hours I lay awake and pondered
the scourge of nature's wrath . . . Secure abed now, the
threat of danger past, I drift into a euphoria of warmth and
comfort . . . with a simple prayer of gratitude . . . I lapse
into a wispy kind of slumber that is stealing into my
head . . . I am just content to lie there now, and drowse
away in bed . . .

OF PRAYER

Prayer need not be repetitious sounds,
Restricted only to church grounds.
It can be guiding children at play,
Making those around you happy and gay,
The taking of time to admire God's wonder,
The rain, the lightning and the thunder,
The change of tides and the seasons,
Accepting life's crosses, asking no reasons.
Church must be attended, visits not too few,
But, remember, something else must be added, too,
A kind word, and some good deeds,
These are prayers; it's what man needs . . .

* * *

LITTLE MAN'S CONSCIENCE

Conscience, why do you follow me,
Open my eyes and force me to see
The things that I would rather not?
In humanity, I am just a tiny spot,
It means little what I choose to be.
If I close my eyes so as not to see,
I am only one in this world's many.
Of worldly plots, I don't have any.
Conscience, what do you say,
May I go on in my peaceful way?

Oh Conscience, I hear you loud and plain,
"Many spots together make a great stain!"

FRANCES M. FLORIO

INVISIBLE CHAINS

Oh fools, who think that only prisons lock up souls,
That only shackles keep people from their goals,
For few among the crowd walk unchained, free,
The rest are weighted by chains that eyes cannot see.
The heaviest chain is called by the name of Love,
Which tames fiery spirits to those of the docile dove,
And great are the clinging chains of loyalty,
Those bound will never know freedom's royalty.

For mothers, fathers and tenders of a family,
Of freedom's beauty they'll never see,
And of those who toil in business,
Of freedom's crop have even less,
And quiet are the thoughts of freedom's works,
If behind that mind a conscience lurks.
Clearly we see the chains of the old and the sick,
Of freedom's fruits they can not pick.

If there are a few souls who are truly free,
How small in number they must be . . .

* * *

THE WASTE OF TIME

Did you ever take a fraction of any hour
To admire the intricate beauty of a flower?
Or stop to feel the texture of a blade of grass?
Or watch some cloud in the sky about to pass?
Have you ever felt awed at the sight of some landscape?
Noticed that each tree has a different size and shape?
And if you have never basked in the warm sunshine,
You have indeed been wasting God's time . . .

NONA FOUSHEE

LOVE

The day seems lone and dreary,
One might say "quite contrary,"
As day turns to night,
I stand alone to fight
The loneliness that seems to come
Slowly and surely over one.

I wonder about tomorrow.
Will it be like yesterday,
Or will it be full of friends?
Will it be full of it, cans, and maybes?
Oh God! Please answer me.
What will tomorrow bring?

Ah! The day is upon me,
And what a day it is.
Must be rather early though,
For it is very, very light.
But when I take a second look I know
It's only the sun shining ever so bright.

It's true that I met her on this lovely day
On the corner over there.
She seemed so very gay,
Lighthearted in so many different ways,
That I soon began to bubble with laughter,
And then felt sorry right after.

All she did was smile,
And I was in a trance for awhile,
Though I soon began to wonder,
If I might wine and dine her.
Still I felt some fear,
But then she smiled and came very near.

That was some years ago,
Now there are only aches and pains from head to toe,
And little grandchildren running to and fro.
Yes, it's true—loneliness I once knew
But no longer—for I now have you.

* * *

PEOPLE

People are false and fickle—
You can tell them one thing
And it comes back to you a fable.

You can tell them about your life,
You can tell them about others,
You can talk about your own desires,
And yet when you hear it repeated to you,
    It's a story stretched into something sordid.

People are false and fickle—
You can tell them one thing
And it comes back to you a fable.

You can tell them about your transgressions,
You can tell them about your dreams,
You can tell them about your ideas,
And yet when you hear it repeated to you,
    It's a story stretched into something sordid.

People are false and fickle—
You can tell them one thing
And it comes back to you a fable.

You can argue with them about God,
You can argue with them about Hell,
You can discuss politics with them,
And yet when you hear it repeated to you,
    It's a story stretched into something sordid.

Ah yes, people are false and fickle—
You can tell them one thing
And it will come back to you as a fable.

* * *

NO MORE—NO MORE

The throbbing has started again—
Legs pierced with pain
And the stomach turned upside down
With the head screaming and pounding.
    God, how my heart throbs "no more—no more."

My life began with breath
And ended on a ?
Dreams of thousands continued
With only $10 earned—
    Disappointment again.

My life began with breath
And not a soul to love me—
My mother pawned me off
With aunts and uncles accepting and then rejecting—
    Disappointment again.

The throbbing has started again—
Legs pierced with pain
And the stomach turned upside down
With the head screaming and pounding
    God, how my heart throbs "No more—no more."

My life began with breath.
Marriage brought seemingly peace,
With a child—true joy—
But death wrought anger and hate
And divorce imminent—
    Disappointment again.

My life began with breath
And my love came from a man so strong and fine
He touched the inner part of me,
And taught me that I could.
We worked so very hard with no one to help us—
    Disappointment again.

My life began with breath
And ended on a ?
Dreams of thousands continued
With only $10 earned—
    Disappointment again.

Truly—life began with breath,
But after failure upon failure
    D-I-S-A-P-P-O-I-N-T-M-E-N-T—Again, again, and again.

The throbbing has started again—
Legs pierced with pain
And the stomach turned upside down
With the head screaming and pounding
    God, how my heart throbs "No more—no more."

TO A REVERED FRIEND

The hopes which are with us today,
    Are gone tomorrow;
So youth and beauty fade away,
    And cometh sorrow.
The fond deceit of time will dim,
    And lonely, leave us
To the wild vision it has weaved,
    Only to grieve us.

But in the sweet communion
    Of heart with heart,
There is a strength of union
    Nothing can part.

And this, dear friend, is ours; yes, here
    at rest
    Our hope remains;
And though perhaps it is mortal, it is
    the best
    Of earthly chains.
Yet, but a little while, and then we too
    Must go away;
But while we linger, let us still be true;
    And savor in our peculiar way
        Another precious, precarious day.

* * *

SPRING

The bud, the bloom
dream and fantasy
oh, blazed flower
obtrusive reality
gentle love, sweet humanity.

CAN WE?

A poesy molding one's thoughts in verse
is the blossom and fragrance
of all human knowledge; thoughts,
passions, and emotions which delight,
leaves are gathered one by one
in the anticipation of old age.
The trumpet winds have sounded:
humility is part of wisdom
when balanced on the scales of destiny
in search for peace and harmony.

Can we
enjoy the revitalized sense of values,
of prudence and compassion for one another,
rekindle our faith in thee
in the pyramid of time?
Can we aspire to be as beautiful in thoughts
and pursue the unpolluted joys,
musing about our thoughts
                    our ambitions
                    our inspiration
                    our illusions
                    our fidelity to truth
                    our destiny
in time of wonder and hope.
Can we?

DOLORES C. FULTON

INVITATION

Heaven sent an invitation
But I didn't want to go.

I knew they'd send another
—The Bible tells me so.

When that Jaguar came upon me
And the crowd began to gather

I could fancy I was lifted
And my wings were sweetly feathered.

But the nurse—though like an angel—
Said "You're still made of this earth."
   So I refused the invitation
   Sent me often since my birth!

* * *

CONVERSATION WITH A BIRD

Oh little boy with eyes of blue
You see the bird—its eyes on you!
"O, tell me, bird, where you abide.
I'd like you walking by my side!"
The bird sings back in high, high key
"I do not walk—I only sing
Come back and see me in the spring
Perhaps I'll learn to talk and walk."

MYSELF

When I want to talk to someone intelligent I talk to myself.
Nowhere have I found a more intelligent being than myself.
Myself contains all the glories of God. Myself contains the
kingdom of heaven with His everlasting words. All these
and more are contained within myself. Myself is open for
God to use me in a manner in which He sees fit, for the
good of the world. Myself is happy when I glimpse His
mighty and glorious kingdom. Myself jumps for joy when I
am able to see his word being manifested in each of my
brother's and sister's daily lives. I can truly say God lives
for He lives within myself. What about yourself?

* * *

BLACK HONOR

Whom do you honor? Do you honor the birds, trees, and
humankind? Or perhaps you just honor yourself. Honor.
Whom do you honor? We are all born with honor. Honor is
the strong force that has kept black folks, ask any elder.
Whom do you honor? Black folk honor all and all will honor
you. The world is your footstool with honor. Whom do you
honor?

* * *

BLACK WILLINGNESS

The will to give and forgive. The will to accept failure yet
keeping the will to try again. The willingness to love all is
the key to peace and happiness. Black Willingness.

* * *

VIRGIN THOUGHT

Smile, Trust, and Obey. It matters not what people say. You are
free from earth and harm. The great universal force will take
you in its arms. Smile, Trust, and Obey.

MEMORIES

So like the plant
that wilts in its pot,
is the forgotten
memory of the past.

Flashes of those times
reflect in the mirror
of your mind—
and then disappear,

to be brought back
like the flame
of a lighted candle,
in all its glory.

* * *

FATE

'Tis a black bear drenched in honey,
surrounded by a cloud of bees,
who scampers away to shelter.
A nose for trouble has she.

Quick to a hollow tree stump,
ah, 'tis a skunk snug inside;
fate holds no destiny, little bear,
for one thus prone to hide.

B. G.

LIKE YOU DO

I'd like to fiddle with you,
but I never learned
to put the bow to the strings,
and play beautiful music . . . like you do.

I'd like to be with you,
but I can't handle
being a puppet on a string,
and playing your games . . . like you do.

THE WAY

The huntress Diana;
miles I covered searching in forests
with no trees, no animals.
The arrows I carry are the rays of the sun.
My skies are forever, no ends and no beginnings,
AND,
in the nothing I hunt and find abundance.

* * *

HIKING

I walked around this planet
twice and thrice and maybe a million times;
I tire and sweat, cry and laugh, curse and pray.
Yesterday was, Now is, Tomorrow will be!
A catalyst holding together, mixing, creating and dismantling.
It is weird! It is weird!

* * *

CLASSIFIED

I touched the snow and froze.
Hugged the fire and burned.
Breathed the air and gasped for oxygen.
Stepped on water but sank.
I AM BLIND, you see—

LEAD ME, LORD

Let me do some good, dear Lord, to serve along life's road,
I want to be helpful along the way, so, Lord, lead me on today.
I want to aid a human wrong, so guide me, make me strong.
To cheer with a smile or song, lead me, show me, let it be so.
Let me ease one's burdens less to spread more happiness and
    signal S.O.S.

* * *

HEALING POWER

It seems so long ago when you walked beside me,
You're just as close as then, as memories don't fade away.
In faith, believing I know you still care, how can you forget so
    soon?
One day too late you'll try and squirm on back —when old,
    decrepit, wrinkled, and gray.
Then the healing test will shine through—this time no help—no
    loving care—no one.
You need to lift your heart in prayer—so ask the Lord not to go
    astray.

* * *

TO REMEMBER

Why is the world so distraught, dear Lord, why are there so
    many fears?
Shadows of doubt lurk behind each tear, no joy-peace-harmony
    around us . . .
All things good and right no longer exist for all—
All wonderful gifts from above vanished. Let's not forget to pray
So our answers may be heard and spread and come true—
To guide my feet, to light the way, shed a light, once more
    PEACE shine through.

LONG JOURNEY

I traveled far; was it wasted or will it in due time be a blessing?
Under pressure I was held captive by time. Now days grow
    shorter with evenings.
Even sunset isn't ablaze; my youth left me—so has he—and child
    to be alone.
Giving so much—no return payment due. Forgotten is key
    issue—'twas their gain.

* * *

PAPA AND MAMA

Dear Lord, why did they do—so much to see, feel and touch . . .
I miss you both—never a day gone by without a thought—WHY?
You both loved flowers—now you only see them on graves when
    I deliver from my garden.
Your daughter has not forgotten—gravesite I visit on a regular
    basis, wishing,
Wishing you were here—Please, Dear Lord, take care of me
    now—ALONE.

* * *

BEACH FEVER

I must go down the beach where the ocean breezes blow, sky blue,
    white clouds flying by;
The tide rushing in, spraying sea mist all around—white ermine
    sand underfoot—
Sea gulls crying out loud and sandpipers waltzing by—perfect
    tranquillity—Peace at last.

THE LITTLE THINGS

It's the little things we do and say, which mean so much as we
    go along our way;
One kind deed can lift a load from weary travelers treading the
    road,
A gentle smile, a big hello, can banish pain, ease our burdens as
    we roll along.
What joy, gladness, can spring from Little Things soothing to
    make a gain our way.

* * *

FRIENDS

It's fun to have friends as we go along life's road, journeying on
    through life.
I thank all my friends for all that they have done or said to ease
    it along.
A true-blue friend is a friend to the end—banishing doubt and
    strife.
How good it feels to find a gem sparkling brilliantly—a rare
    diamond indeed,
When troubles, doubts or worries brew—I know I can count on
    friends—so true.

JULIE M. GALAMBOS

PATTERN OF LIFE

Love, where is that ring of gold promised long ago? Remember
    me? I'm undone forever.
As I ponder I took to weeping, my love took off with
    another—and another—
At a distance from town he ran—no longer lament his loss in
    tears.
While time is healing damage done, weeding my thoughts
    through, I'm searching for truth.
Erasing the pain, I pause, realizing my catch was no prize
    package, a sour note.
Now I remain serene and calm and strong, for my guiding light is
    seeing me through—
I walk proudly, displaying my new life—With GOD how can I
    lose? My shepherd so true.

THIRD OF MARCH

Alone in this New England house
the third of March
in Michigan,
I am chilled past reason
by the sounds
of wind.
My spirits spring to nothing,
shivering veins.
The whole frame disappoints,
is witless.
Purposes goosepimple
and sneeze ideas away,
simple dust
settling on window sills.
The glass snaps cold
against the tap of branch ends,
a sky of old magnesium.
I poke up the fire,
drink tea,
take down a book of Lamb.
No use.
Out in that shifty, rasping wind,
my mind has left me,
and judges
down the chimney stone
all I am
and everything there is to be,
a day like this.

FREE FALL

Balancing the choices, here we are:
poor mariner collared with that reeking bird,

hopscotching, with the patches blurred. Envy things!
A larva in some wood, eating each day
to nothing, all devices,
and that final rest so plain: head
toward bark and wait for beetle's wings.

Pity the linnet who must strain to learn,
to get the rhythm right, the pitch,
before the sweetest energy may splash;
or some stray chaffinch gulled to fling
his alien night call, over huddled ferns.

We sing the lark?
No, better the pipit bird,
whose every single note is programmed right.
Never an off-beat muddled chirrup
through his tight winged dark. O!

Feather me round with berries
from a dozen days' October!

L. C. GALLION

THE BOUNDARY OF HATRED

There's a thin line between love and hate, like an imaginary
Line separating county from county, state from state, nation
From nation. Yet it's more dreadful, for it keeps apart those
Who would very much love to be together, but are afraid of
Being caught in a hurricane of suggestions that will never
Succeed. But the first step must be taken, just as with a baby
Who will only walk if he makes the first step.

Let us rid ourselves of such, sending those demons who now
Dance and rejoice upon that line that puts us into two different
Worlds, having the same aims and our goal such a short distance
From us, into another universe. Yet we'll never succeed as long
As hatred lies between us, not allowing one to touch the hand of
The other. It's a sickening line that brings forth tears unasked
For.

Let us not be as idols, closing our eyes that it be not seen,
Shutting our ears that we hear not the words, though like daggers
They put a pain in our heart, hard to bear, yet we must live with
It, or the paralyzing of the body that won't allow us to taste of
The true feelings within. Let us not let it be as such
For a long time lies ahead of us—
'Tis too precious to waste.

RUBY GARNER

TRUTH AND JUSTICE

Pilate knew Christ was an innocent man.
But Christ's cross was raised on Calvary's sand.
And there, He, Innocence was crucified.
Along with Holy Purity denied:
that same day, Truth and Justice also died.

The tomb could not hold Christ; He went away,
and now stands knocking at men's hearts, today.
Truth, also Justice, where do the two be?
    . . . They are still on the cross at Calvary.
They died there, on the cross at Calvary.

LOST ATLANTIS

Atlantis, where the sea is bright upon the courts of kings;
The men who swam the sea of time engulfed their minds with
   dreams;
About the world induced with pain eternal was the scene;
The men who fought the mighty kings lay tattered in the seas.

* * *

THE LAST MUTANTS

The world was at peace one day, till all of a sudden with a
mighty crash World War Three was here at last.
With the burning of cities and the bursting of towns the
children cried out from all around;
The radioactive material of waste spread forth vastly among
our race.
You see, radiation is a funny thing —it doesn't kill
everything;
It turns and twists and makes you strange so that you could
survive in the world of the slain.
Jona Blake crept up on all fours, and with a dying gasp he
cried "No! We won the war!"
With a squeal like a cat and a face to match he fell over
dead, dead at last.
The talker got up and spoke the howl of the clan to all that
could listen and heed his commands;
Could it possibly be there once was a race superior to we.
And they blew themselves up in a circle of hate, only to
produce an inferior race.

THE JASPER STONE

(Genesis 9:16) "And the bow shall be in the cloud;
and I will look upon it, that I may remember the
everlasting covenant between God and every living
creature of all flesh that is upon the earth."

BLACK is darkness, the void without a light;
GREY is ashes to ashes and to dust thou shall return;
BROWN is amber —phosphor PHOSPHOR (MORNING STAR)
    LIVING SOUL
RED is the rivers of waters of life He gave —(blood)
BLUE is the breath of life breathed in, His Living Soul;
YELLOW is an inner glowing reflection of His Majesty;
ORANGE is fiery, the spirit inspired by HIS WILL;
GREEN is the fruitful abundance of all flesh that he made;
PURPLE is Omnipotent Majesty, an AURA of
    TRANSFORMISM
WHITE is the whitest of all lights—purity of HIS SOUL
As is revealed in the CAMEO—A CARVED JASPER STONE.
        (Ultra violet Light)

(Revelations 4:3) "And he that sat was to look upon like
a jasper and a sardine stone; and there was a rainbow
round about the throne, in sight like an emerald."

A TWINKLE IN A DRIFT

The snow falls very softly.
The air smells crisp and clean.
The stars—they seem to twinkle with a sparkle and a gleam.
I sit here by the window
And watch the falling snow,
And dream of things that have to come
And things that have to go.

* * *

THE RIDDLE OF THE SPHINX?

Today I was born. Without a care.
Bare feet. My first pair of shoes.
To be old enough . . .

No longer am I a child. I am grown now.
In my mind, my body, and my soul.

I am old now. Less agile than in my youth.
People stare. Their looks answered by fear.

I say my good-byes to the world.
The fear is gone now.
Like a flower with no petals, I have withered.

* * *

UNTITLED

A lonely boy stands in the window.
Thoughts of the past follow like a shadow.
A puppy runs by.
Spirits fly.
"Can I keep him, Ma? Oh, Ma! Please, Ma!"
She fills a bowl with water. Tablescraps.
A dog and a man.

THE

I've been listening to the men of
wisdom
who answer no
although they will
to convey—
　　　the answer is lost in day of day.

They perceive all;
they have tried and have failed
but time of time must come
　　　and will come,
for none can stop
ideas of all—
others of not real
with colors of patterns have spoken,
　　　seeping water of tarnish gold sieves.

But ideas of screaming
nightmare
break into perception of lifting blocks,
for real is real only
if there is unreal,
which gives nothing of
　　　confronted mind in retreat.

We will be taken
        but will we leave?
never
if we fight the unreal which can never
        be of think.

You must understand:
        people live
in different color bags;
        some of paper
        some of plastic —
their faces most always
at the crumble where
pain must exist in order to reach
        the wind of winds —
the wind gives off scorching heat —
friction—
to stop any indifference.

Please
wrinkle at designated areas —
Beware:
the curative of the floating word has tentacles
which are always.

MY JESUS IS A FRIEND

So many friends,
So many people,
Some people don't have any friends,
    They don't have anybody.
My Jesus is a friend who will stand by
    You until the end.
Relationships begin, and all too soon
    They are over, but
My Jesus is a friend who will stand by
    You until the end.
Do you need a particular kind of friend?
One you can share your cares, troubles
    And woes with?
One who will love you in spite of all
Your weaknesses, frailties, and shortcomings?
My Jesus is a friend who will stand by
    You until the end.

* * *

SMILE

To smile costs you nothing,
    But merits you much.
A smile brings out the best
    Of yourself.
Give out a beautiful smile and
    Get one back in return.
God gave it to you to use, to
    Greet your neighbor with.
A smile is a frown turned upside
    Down, so I am told.
A smile is like the rays of the
    Sun, warm, friendly and welcoming.
Brighten up your day, and that of
    Your neighbor, by smiling your cares
    Away.

314

SIMPLE PLEASURE

It is he who rests with beauty,
    One who has a garden bench.
While he sits in silent pleasure,
    Wonder may his mind entrench.

It is he who has a little
    Piece of earth to call his own,
That can always reap contentment
    From the seeds which he has sown.

He needs no formal planting
    And no seats of lacy white;
Just a handmade, rustic bench
    Can afford a real delight.

There's no room for tribulation
    In this kind of peaceful place,
Here one finds his strength renewed,
    Any stress he now can face.

Breathes there man with no affinity
    For the growing things of earth?
He has missed the joy of knowing
    Nature's treasure and their worth!

Always keep your eyes wide open,
    Hold your head so very high,
Lest the wonders Earth produces
    Might, unnoticed, pass you by!

BETTER GIVE

Better to give than to receive
From those in sorrow or in need;
Open your heart and be kind,
That is what happiness you will find.

Better to give, than to receive,
Shoulder the burden of those in need.
Perhaps once they had, and lived well,
Once they too had a story to tell.

Better to give than to receive
And feel glad that you did your deed;
There is where love and understanding is bright—
By making other people's burden light.

Hold out your hand to those in need,
For a sister or brother, father or friend.
Don't hesitate but give and lend —
Better to give than to receive.

* * *

HAPPINESS

The sun, the moon and stars above
Are so many things we must love,
For it is a world of pleasure and bliss
To those who are willing to meet happiness.

Look back into the corner of life
Amid the darkness and the strife,
And put the sunshine in your heart
But never, never, let it part.

Let us rejoice and forever sing
With happiness in our heart, ever to ring
That there will be no more grief and sorrow
Just in looking ahead, into the morrow.

For happiness is right near by
If you would only look and try.
For the sun, the moon and stars above,
Are so many things that we must love.

* * *

MARRIAGE

Don't break that chain
That was tied into a knot
And forget the marriage ties
Which you almost forgot.

For you have everything
In life there is to claim:
A husband, children, sincerity
And his name.

Marriage is made on happiness
And bliss,
Which is the golden chain of happiness
And righteousness.

So hold it together like the band
Of a golden ring,
For marriage is the best of what
Happiness brings.

GOD HAS CALLED ALL TO ARMS

God has called, yes, called all to arms,
For the whole world to listen to His alarms,
As in this great test of all His people
To work to be good and give up evil.

For unity and strength, love and justice He spoke,
Though a great thick mist of fire and smoke.
Hold the great spiritual love now, one for all.
To listen with ear to the Almighty's call.

For in this great test, there is going to be
A great love and justice to keep us free.
While going through the test of air, land and sea
Regardless who the great or when, or what may be.

While the world is now being shaken forever from sin
There is a new world to look upon, a new life to begin,
And the soul that lived is the soul that gave
For their life will be brighter and worth to save.

And we will be more thankful to Almighty above
And give him thanks with all our love.
Then with outstretched wings the angels will sing
With the new world and liberty there to bring.

Yes, the road may be long, but it is never too late
To have love in our hearts and banish the hate.
By having new courage, and strength and great faith
As the old world goes, with a new world to embrace.

BETTY B. GREENBERG

A PENNY SAVED

A penny saved is a penny earned —
Can't the people ever learn?
Give to those who are needy,
Never you mind in being greedy.
Money was to have and spend —
Why not exchange and lend?
A rich man thinks a poor man gives,
Yet we all go on and live.
Let us all share the best we can
And try to help the hungry man.
We all are body, spirit, and soul.
Everyone has a story to be told,
And there is where life is to live
Is to help the needy and to give.
By helping others you help yourself
And that is God's greatest wealth.

GOD SHOWS IN YOUR FACE

You don't have to tell
How you live each day,
You don't have to say
If you work or play.

A tried and true barometer
Serves in the place,
However you live
Will show in your face.

The false, the deceit
That you bear in your heart
Will not stay inside
Where it first got a start.

For skin and blood
Are a thin veil of lace—
What you wear in your heart
You wear in your face.

If your life is unselfish,
If for others you live,
For not what you get
But how much can you give—

If you live close to God
In His infinite grace,
You don't have to tell it . . .
It shows in your face.

FLORENCE MARIE GREER

THE PRESENCE

Dear Jesus, you shed on Calvary the price for all our sins.
This includes me and mine and all my kin.
The ones I love the most, Dear Lord, so desperately need your
    help,
So in Your arms, Dear Saviour, so tender and kind I want them
    kept.
Out of Satan's reach and in Your loving care that not one of us
    can measure.
Your peace, I know, would be a positive cure.
For all the trials and pain that not just anyone could endure.
Oh, lift me, Lord, I pray to the sights that you have set for me,
And use me, please, as an instrument of Thy peace,
Because then, Jesus, even though here, in your presence I'd be.
I love you, Dear Saviour, and I know you're my friend,
'Cause in times of real trouble and need you are my only kin.
Watch me and hold me and help me, I pray,
Just to live with your help this minute, this hour—
Just for today!

FLOWERS OF GLORY

Flowers were put here from God's own hand;
He gathered these jewels from the angels' band!
And He spread them here and yonder and to and fro—
From His own hands the seeds He sowed.
He blessed their colors and made them bright
And caused them to bloom with dawn's early light.
They blossom and grow and our lives enrich
With a beauty so delicate and a fragrance that drifts
To kiss the honeybees in the morning sky
And brush the nose of a butterfly.
Flowers are lovely and here to stay
'Cause they're God's way of saying:
Have a beautiful day!

TREES

God gave me eyes that I may see the beauty of His creation.
The stately trees, tall, lofty, majestic in their elevation,
Resplendent in robes of brilliant hues, the High Priests of the
      nation,
Invoking songs of praise from myriad throats in pious adoration
Of Him. Trees! what greater manifestation of beauteous things
Can the eye discern? The royal splendor of their crusted barks
      brings
Significantly to mind the nature of the Deity; wrings
From the hearts of puny man the firm admission that nature
      clings
Not to the conventional modes of beauty through refinement,
But virile, vulgar, coarse in the treatment of her alignment,
She daubs masterfully; no tedious retouching. Her assignment
Embraces eternity. Trees! Trees!! no meager consignment
She allows to adorn the line of man's vision. In contour
They are matchless; remarkable, the minute details that score
Appraisal. Their shimmering leaves, dauntless and unafraid, lure
To thrilling trysts the vagrant wind. Do you not sometimes hear
      the roar
Of unmuffled kisses passionately spent 'gainst verdant cheeks,
      then soar
With elation into eternity? Then note with delight
Their din of chatter; the bold physical disarray that mar and
      blight
Their symmetrical composure as their roguish lover takes to
      flight.
Can you not see the virgin haste with which they set themselves
      aright?
Trees, beautiful trees, aristocrats of nature, scions of Time,
Oh may you always ever reign o'er man and birds and beasts
      sublime.

A SUMMER'S EVENING SYMPHONY

O dear robin redbreast,
from greenery to greenery,
from street treetop,
where locusts also sing,
to backyard grapevine
you keep an open line,
chirping back and forth in sweet evening song.
The message is yours alone.
Your notes, however, seem to come from the rainbow
across the eastern sky—
bars of reds, oranges, and blues
and the gold in the West
(a few hours ago a raging luzon)
now completes the symphony at its best,
playing the twilight overture.
Then quieter and quieter the music,
as the conductor gently lowers his golden baton
and the velvet curtain studded with a thousand
        twinkling stars descends.

* * *

JUST WHO WAS SHE?

A dear, sweet mamma in rocking chair and shawl,
I'm certain that you don't recall.
It was on Saturdays
while you were busy helping Daddy in the store,
and we kids, Dorothy and I, had to go up to Grandma's.
I guess that we always used "up" because Grandma lived on the
        second floor
and the street, Gravois, ran "up" from us.
Behind Grandma's was a potato chip factory
with pungent odors and 5 A.M. shifts.
Anyway, it was there that I remember this old lady—
well, she mightn't have been all that old.

324

It was just how she looked in red scarf, thin black coat,
which she wore even on warm days, and tennis shoes,
and what she did that made her look quite used, and us amused.
She looked the part of distrust.
And I was only about six or seven at the time.
I remember playing out on the back porch floor
and peering down through the wooden slats
when down the alley she came with bag and parcel,
picking from each can from which rodents ran any potato morsel
not fit to be fried, packed, and sold.
Now either she was a madam of thrift
or a victim of the times,
for it was during what I later learned were the Great Depression
    Days.
Now I think of them as the good times,
even though there were some scary times.
I am now in my late forties and remembering,
but why am I asking
as I embrace you in rocking chair and shawl
and Grandma's picture on the wall:
Just who was the old lady in red scarf, black thin coat, and tennis
    shoes?

* * *

THE ROSE REMAINS

Youth sees a rose thorn bare,
    it seems.
Middle-age some may appear
    to prick dreams.
After that they lay bare,
    but the rose is still there.

325

PATRICIA ANN GROSSIE

LOVE WISHES

I wish for you sunshine bright, to give you light,
and starlit nights to show your way;
I wish you peace like the gentle clouds and all the tales they say;
I wish for you a merry heart and the gift of the wind to whisper
     love's art.
I wish for you gray skies to heal hurts,
as raindrops come to soothe the earth;
I wish for you the sky so blue,
to make your world glow and look like new to you;
I wish for you the black of night,
that drifts from dark to stars so bright;
I wish for you sunlight's might,
to warm your heart and teach you right.
I wish for you the love of life
and friendly gifts of mind to share;
then the tale of the gentle soul can be
your gift of life to wear.

* * *

SOME THINGS OF LOVE

Clouds with silver linings and loving golden days are all within
     my view, when I remember loving you.
Oh, for a heart to dance in a sky of blue, for a dream of love and
     you!
If it would be for me to dance upon the wings of wind and bring
     my heart love's own song to sing,
I'd never ask to love you less, or quiet bells that ring.
But I'd ask that sun and wind would gently kiss you now and life
     teach you love's own way,
and bless you with love's song today.

HELEN L. GUENTHER

TWO BEST HOMES

Once upon a time a little boy
Went to his grandma's house.
"Your house is best," he said,
As quiet as a mouse.
"You have time to sit and read,
Or play a game with me,
And Grandpa swings me in the air,
Then sets me on his knee.
You don't complain when I make noise,
Or don't eat all my food.
You just make me happy,
I can't help being good."
When this same boy had stayed a week
He then was heard to say,
"I am so very happy,
I'm going home today!
I bet my folks have missed me,
And Sister must be sad,
I've had such fun but I can't wait
To see my Mom and Dad!"

* * *

CHILDHOOD

"Mommie, what makes flowers bloom,
And how do cats say 'meow'?
Do doggies cry, can babies talk?
I want to know right now!

"And Mommie, when I'm big as you
I want a girl like me.
Then as we work and talk and play
We'll have such fun, we three!"

THE FLYING GEESE

The Flying Geese are now at rest.
They were rated by the State with some of the best.
Those Flying Geese.

They dribbled, they passed, they shot with class.
They feinted and faked, they played the fast break.
They played man to man, when the opposition was in command.
Those Flying Geese.

They pivoted, they blocked, they maneuvered, and shot.
They stole the ball whenever they could.
They didn't howl when they were fouled.
They jumped with ease when they were in a squeeze.
It was amazing to see when the Geese got hot.
They would immediately stop and make the long shots.
Those Flying Geese.

They were as cunning as foxes and as agile as cats.
Soon the opposition recognized that.
They passed the ball with the speed of sound.
You should see them Geese pull those rebounds down.
They passed so fast the referees were aghast.
The opposition at times were indeed out-classed.
Those Flying Geese.

The Geese had a play called one, two, three.
To play it you had to be, as slick as an eel and busy as a bee.
They hustled and bustled, they schemed and pressed,
They left twenty-nine opponents in a heck of a mess.
Those Flying Geese.

To win the Sectionals you must have a good team.
The Super Sectional is more than a dream.
To participate you must use all of your steam,
On the way to winning a State title,
There is always a better team.
You scheme, you plan, you quicken your hands.
You want them ready at an instant command.
Those Flying Geese.

The Geese were anxious to dominate.
They ignored the changeable traits of Fate.
I settled for a Pansy, but I wanted a *Rose*.
And that is how this story goes.
Those Flying Geese.

No greater local aggregation was ever oganized
Than the Flying Geese of Wethersfield High.
The parents, the students, the faculty, working together.
They accomplished a *Feat*.
Their records will show they are hard to beat.
Those Flying Geese.

Their ambition is, "To do or die."
Their documental evidence of their accomplishments
Proves this quotation to be no *lie*.
So carry on, you Flying Geese,
Your record of 29-1 is indeed a treat.
Congratulations! You Magnificent Geese!

'TIS BUT A HOUSE

'Tis but a house, there it stands.
Guardian of time, sentinel of lands.
Mellowed with age as vintage wine
It sheltered me and all of mine.
These walls that once held joyous sound
Now are still in silence bound,
And memory's shadowed echoes hang
Where once young laughter pealed and rang.
No more a home both blest and dear—
'Tis but a house, a lonely bier.

* * *

KIND WORDS

Kind words are the jewels
In the crown of our thoughts,
Priceless when given and worthless when bought.
One hears them so seldom
Indeed they are rare;
Fortunate the ear that is privileged to share.

* * *

RAINDROPS

Where do little raindrops go when the sun is shining?
Do they find a fleecy cloud and nestle in the lining?
Or do they journey to the moon to watch the moonbeams play.
Or maybe catch a falling star or ride the Milky Way.
I do not know where raindrops go; I do not know, 'tis true,
I do not know, I do not know—I just pretend I do.

LOST LOVE

I loved but once and long ago.
I felt the warm and tender glow
Of loving arms that did caress me,
And joy of longing did possess me.
Ah, to remember! Ah, to capture
One sweet moment of that rapture!
That was love, this I know.
I loved but once and long ago.

* * *

I REMEMBER APRIL

I remember April, April in the spring
And that special fragrance only she can bring.
I remember orchards far as eye could see
And the budding blossoms clinging to each tree.
I remember riplets sparkling in the sun
Winding through the meadows, winding one by one.
I remember grasses greening by the brook
And the early violet peeping from her nook.
Time has dimmed this mind and memory of a thing
But I remember April, April in the spring.

* * *

PARTING

If I could speak a thousand tongues
And say good-bye in every one
The pain I feel could be no less
Whatever tongue I would address.
Every parting has its sorrow
And doubt uncertain of the morrow;
Give each good-bye its fullest measure:
We know not when t'will be forever.

331

I WISH I WERE YOU

I saw summer in visions of rocks.
It was peace unlocked.
the valleys, oh, so depressed;
And the mountains, so impressed.

The river boiled and swilled,
And fish pack and coiled
Newborn at play,
Sleeping mother's lay.

Lovers at rest,
Birds in the nest.
Clouds so blue,
Oh, how I wish I were you.

Starry, starry night,
Screech owls that gaze fright.
The moon so bright,
It must be night.

But here I lie,
In my grave behind the rocks.
Oh, so cold.
Oh, so dark.

DREAM DEMON

Whispering on the dust of
Dying into dimensions of voidless seas.
Reaching out with lust.
Hey, it's only me.

I am the Dream Demon of ages,
The winged hero of nightmare;
Seeking to gleam the world full of gold.
But, do I care?

Your mind is my playground,
Your vision of good is only my choice.
Am I kind?
It's your life to lose!

Molding in the wake of formless boil,
Never feeling the human cry;
Laughing at death.
Hey, I am not of the real.

After the game has been played
I sit in stillness.
Time calls my leaving.
But, I'll be back!

NIGHT STORM

Out of the raging heart of the night storm
I called to you,
With words unformed—
Lost in the roar of the sea,
The wind's howl,
        the wave's hurl,
The crashing, pounding, thundering
            sound of the sea . . .
I hear your silent heart answering me,
            answering me,
Above the pounding, thundering sound of the sea.

* * *

TODAY

Today the sun arose the same as yesterday,
And bathed the hills and glens in burnished gold:
The mountain brook went murmuring on its limpid way,
Touching my feet, then swirling past me out to
            the sea of old.

The children flew their kites . . . laughed, danced, sang;
And life went by me on the street, face after face—
Fragments of humanity—here a smile, a word,
            a sudden pang,
And then a swallowing up without a single trace.

Today—no, not the same as yesterday in any way:
The sun spun more gold,
    The brook swirled,
        and curled,
            and leapt more joyously to the sea.
The kites on high flew higher still today—
    the laughter, song and dance so free and gay;
And life came to me, soul on soul, to form
        the whole of me.

Oh, Love, the world has not turned from patterned time,
        I knew . . .
'Tis but MY world has changed because of YOU!

PAT HAMPTON

THE WELL-WORN THRESHOLD

The swamp grows colder
And darker. I call for help
Altho I know that no one cares
Nor speaks my language of despair.

(Oh God—I cry—what is Man
That Thou shouldst be mindful of him?)

No answer. I really did not believe
There might be one. But now I see
A tiny island in this dank morass
So I climb on it. I have found
A companion. He is only bones now
With ragged piece of cloth. So I
Will sit here as he sat, listening
To slithering snakes, the wild loon's call.

My surcease lies in this small bottle
With skull and crossbones. As I drink
It down, I see within his bony hand
A bottle such as I just drank.

Receive me now, whatever gods there be.
I have returned to that miasmic moil
Alone, except for him, my long-dead friend
Who'll share the feared Eternity with me.

DEFLATION

I had climbed to the top of my high hidden tower,
And my world was as large as the ant on the wall
Or the glowering peaks across seventy valleys . . .
There was no one to listen, to turn at my shouting,
So I yelled at the sky and the hills and the sun.

I was heavy with history and light as a shadow,
Defiant and humble, swayed by silence or sound . . .
The bass of Sibelius or the trebles of Brahms,
The challenge of Sousa or the heartbreak of Taps,
The scream of the comet, the pop of a pod.

I tore from each part of my sentient structure
The film of the present, the sludge of despair
And, when I was clean of the chains on my body
And, when I was free of the walls 'round my mind,
My contacts with animates pressed into diamonds.
I could hold in my hand, to inspect and admire . . .

    I came down from my tower,
    Again in perspective
    (We need only to trip on a phrase, poets know)
    And you said to me, "Dear,
    Could you write a nice couplet,
    Wishing the neighbors a 'Happy New Year'?"

SONG OF SAHUARO LAND

I did not mind the nomadic Navajo
Who fished my rivers, and grazed my broad expanse
With bleating bands, for he but little
Could disturb my rest. Before he came
Somnolent I spent long summers, windswept winters,
Centuries rolled across me, marked me not.
A minor irritation were the rails
Fast to my bosom, where the Chinese laborer
Monotonously swung his pick. Then came the train
Disgorging man and ironshod beasts
With plows to fret my features, mark me off
In squares and sections, sow my breast
With cotton ripened snowlike, merging to
My minor shadings. This disturbed me not
After a time, although the wheeled disk
Bit in my flesh—it could not always pain—
And if the worm that's man moved on
His aimless way, I straightway sent
Cactus reclaiming that which he had borrowed.
His gray-brown shacks, I tore at with the fingers
Of my unemcumbered winds. Those winds! They are
The artists in my power. How they work
With sand for oil, to blend and shape
Those alien buildings, sweeping joyously
Under the corners, chewing on the nails
My rare rains rusted, then, playfully,
With false surprise, touch gently
The weakened structure, 'til it falls!

. . .But now, these pygmies dare
To dam my river which, for long a lake
I kept to cover me, until it wished
To merge with other rivers, then,
(Indulgent as I am, and sluggard, too)
I let it work its way through solid rock
But slow and painful, as all great changes should be made.
My plaint is now these alien men
Who build in few short years the chains to hold
My muddy Colorado. I can foresee
Such tiny farms—much petty huckstering—
It angers me. I know that I have learned
To bide my time, for I am monarch of this land
But, gouging in my vitals with
Those snorting clams—bedaubing me
With concrete walls—daring to space
My mighty torso with their midget trails!
   . . .I feel me now, a mighty patriarch
Garish and painted with such silly pocking,
Each unimportant as a needled dot
On any tattooed giant . . . Ah,
I rouse myself and mutter through my teeth,
"My winds shall work again, but slowly, slyly,
And these usurpers of my flesh and bone
Shall vanish. Give me time—I SHALL NOT MISS!"

BATTLE OF THE SEA

Sea, with your maddened mouth,
Drink up your wine and men and ships,
Then belch them out again;
The splintered ghosts
That know no king,
The cast-off foam
That feels no pain.
Fight on. Wave your purple wrist
To burst the bonds abhorred.
Lose, your soul must bathe in salt,
Still bound to tide,
The weak one's Lord.
Ah, cannot you free yourself
From fault,
Penitent, a sober sea?
Is there nothing but echoes
In endless rhyme,
Crashing thru Eternity?

* * *

VISITATION

A feeling . . . or memory,
Stored between walls of filigree,
Rainbow'd
O'er my reverie.
Embodied silken spiderweb
Like
Skeins, acrobatic,
Pirouetted, ecstatic

CONTEMPLATION FOOD

True prayer is from the heart
No matter what physical position anyone takes:
Standing, sitiing, lying, or kneeling prone
It is the attitude that matters
And the sincere talk with our Creator.
He always listens when we converse with Him.

Yesterday is past and tomorrow is another day;
Today is as we live and talk with our Master
And makes yesterday a joy filled with happiness,
Every tomorrow filled with various visions
Of trust, faith, hope, charity and *love*.

Father God, the Creator of all within the *Universe,*
You and you alone understand us when we fall,
A helping hand *always,* we feel is there
To raise us up to try once again to *persevere*.

The quiet time is our rest and meditation;
Busy, buzzing work, our career;
However, silence is the best,
both for mental and physical *repair*
As it fills our minds with thoughts most dear.

Nearby the babbling of the brook's motion
without strife or commotion
Lovingly serving the needs of everyone
Goes onward, unswerving, bringing calmness and peace,
A true retreat, giving the quiet time of rest badly needed.

So let nothing in this world disturb you
As all things are passing away into nothingness;
People do change and only God is changeless.
He alone sufficeth to those who accept His way.
So as people tread the constructive pathway entered upon
It becomes to them a stairway that leads on and on 'til
They have reached the top —
                    Eternally . . .

* * *

CARE

To care is love for your fellow man;
It gives you fresh goals and unexpected ways
To share your life brotherhood with them.
So renew your faith and love in God;
To walk with Him hand in hand each day
You will find that care directs your pathways.

* * *

CHILDREN

Children are precious to all mankind
As their little faces shine with a love divine;
From the time they begin to crawl
They answer to their mothers' call.

They know the sternness of Dad's command
From the infant stage to the teenage drawl,
Yet love is implanted in each tiny heart
Because the great Jehovah really gave them their start.

KATHRYN G. HANSEN

THE CHILD'S DAY

Pitter-patter across the floor
Go the little feet to the door,
Curious to see who is there
They open wide the door.

There, outside, stand the four,
Just the ones they had been waiting for,
So out they run, shutting the door
Ready to begin their daily chore.

The four hold hands
Running and jumping in the sand,
They pick up trash upon the ground
Thus ending their daily round.

Looking up, they are startled to see
A beehive full of honey bees,
So together they agree to flee
Down the street to the Busy Bees.

All the four climb in
To find a seat where they can reside;
The first two children are the twins
Who settle down to read *Rin Tin Tin.*

The other two just sit and look
Out the window, rather than a book.
Soon they arrive at the school
Where before class they look at the pool.

Five hours the children spend
In reading and writing and using their pens,
Until the five hours are gone
Then they hear the dismissal gong.

THE CHILD'S YEAR

"Little Children, come and play,"
Said the Master with the tray.
From each vessel on the tray
Came transparent rays
Covered with all the colors of May.

The children looked in awesome glee
Wondering if this was only to see!
Or would they become a part of this beautiful stream
Where the Master stood awaiting their consent,
As the Spirit worked among them to agree.

"Come to me." He said, "for yours is the Kingdom of
    Heaven."
So the little ones came one by one, hopping and skipping,
Laughing with Joy—'til there were just eleven.
For the Master loveth His little ones,
protecting and loving them in all ways—now and eternally.

* * *

THANKFULNESS

The day is bright and balmy
The sun is shining all around,
Not a leaf is stirring or dropping to the ground.
Then, a bird begins its singing!

The sounds are heavenly notes
Which makes one feel the nearness
Of nature with all its different coats.
A butterfly doth wing its way aloft;

A child comes singing happily down the path;
Cannot we know from this that
God is very close—the beauty
Makes us wonder and gives us time for thought
We should all be thankful as time is passing on!

344

AUTUMN LOVE

Autumn leaves of red and gold,
Watching a love story unfold;

Lightly falling bright and gay,
bathing lovers all the day;

Piled deep beneath the trees,
softly sifting with the breeze;

Dusk arrives in crimson glory,
A lovely way to start a story.

* * *

I NEEDED, YOU GAVE

I need your love, I need your time,
My heart is blue, my eyes are cry'n;
Come to me now to rest my head,
My soul is hungry, must be fed;

You gave your love, you gave your time,
You warmed my heart and dried my eyes;
You came to me to rest my head,
My soul was hungry, so you fed.

THE SYMPHONY

While sitting in my pyramid this morning just at dawn,
    I heard the sound of music sing and felt like I were drawn.
All of the sounds that floated by became as one big note.
    I thought that I would share with you just what my heart has
    wrote.

The music that the birds do sing is full of love and joy.
    They sing of gladness for the day for every girl and boy,
And there is music of the cars as they go whizzing by.
    Some have loud vibrating sounds and others just a sigh.
The ocean roars and claims its right to join the symphony,
    And beat its drumstricks in the sand, or maybe just to be.
Another ocean that I heard while listening silently
    Was music whispering through the pines to fill all hearts
    with glee.

If you can sit still as I did and open wide your ears,
    And let the sounds of music flow so each part of you hears;
I guarantee a happening will take place and be true.
    You will merge with sound; you will become one—the
    Symphony is YOU!

THE ANT

Have you ever watched an ant as he struggles with his load
    In the dead heat of the day or the night so very cold?
Have you noticed that he never seems to let go of the fight,
    Even if it takes him many days and many nights?
He knows the road ahead is full of rocks and many stones,
    But he doesn't worry much 'cause he knows he is not alone.
As you are walking down this pathway and you come upon a hill
    Just remember that the ant may be back there struggling
    still.
And if that little insect, as small as he can be,
    keeps on keepin' on—then why, my friend, can't we?

* * *

FAITH AND ACCEPTANCE

You are walking down the road of life and find the way seems
    blocked,
    And everything you try to do seems like the doors are
    locked.
Don't be discouraged—don't give up—just keep on keeping on.
    Remember that the darkest part is just before the dawn.

The path you are on starts going up; you find you are breathing
    fast.
    The more you rush to reach the top the more you come in
    last.
You think you will never reach the end; you will wander on for
    years,
    So let me share this with you now to relieve all of your
    fears.

We go through these times in our lives to make us stop and be
    'Cause if we just kept running on we would never really see.
We have to find a power that is greater than we are,
    Something or someone we can trust to be our guiding star.

347

And then we let go and accept that He knows what is right.
Sometimes we have to act until we see the light.
Acceptance plays a great big part in living life today.
When we accept and do not fight we know we are on the
way.

There is something that walks hand in hand with just accepting
things.
It is what we call "belief" or "faith," our song of joy to
sing.
Faith is what comes when we accept the things we cannot
change.
The more we dare to try it out the less it will seem strange.

Acceptance and this thing called Faith are what we need to live.
We stop the fight—we act as if, and then we start to give.
We turn around and share with those that are with us on this
road;
If we will all hold hands and share we will lighten up the
load.
That is how we find acceptance; where faith can have a start;
If we will share with all mankind and have an open heart.

LIFE

What is life? We'd all like to know,
And what is it that helps us grow?
Life is really wonderful to live
You reap what you sow and receive what you give.

Is life a time or a space,
Or is it one big race?
No, life is none of the above
True life is living to Love.

Each life span is already made,
The reality of our dreams must never fade.
A law we must abide by is the law of giving,
Giving and loving are necessities for living.

Humans are the ones who don't live but survive;
The highest creature with the lowest drive.
Man has so much power he knows not
The true values of life he's got.

Live only the life style you dig
Whether that profile's small or big;
One thing you can be certain about life.
It was not made to be lived in strife.

UN PETIT MORTE

The window was open, before the storm
Before *un abeille*
Before *un petit morte.*
It rains gently, he removes his belt;
Cold hard metal would have ripped my skin.
He held me close, we love, it rains.
The trees are green, clean through the window,
The breeze cools us off, rains continue
Soft, gentle, like his love.
We felt emotion
We were in motion;
We heard the rain, I let out one tear —
Like the rain, it was fresh —no salt!
He licked the drop, we formed and shaped together,
The one time, time was not
Un petit morte.
Time stood still
against our will;
We could not move
Only hear the rain
That brought us here again
Un petie morte.
Amant, altesse
Amour, ami
Laisser
Un petit morte.

FLAMING BOW AND ARROW

Approaching August heat, it still could be July.
I walked along the beach with guitar in hand,
harmonica in mouth; I jammed with the
ocean rushing, beating the shore and the
seagulls gabbing daily bullshit.
I was serene and life seemed simple,
It clearly had a rhythm.
I looked for the sun to decipher the hour;
I decided days have been long lost for years.
I remembered Ronnie, how I felt,
how he felt, after night closed in on the circle
and how it could never quite stop,
just reopen the circle; time rejuvenated
with every new sun.
I feel like I'm crawling on a desert
like the classic "I need a drink" scene,
Sweating bullets, dying to be cool,
grasping for something that was not there.
He appeared on the jetty
Still in my dream, still harmonica in mouth
An oasis, An illusion. He stood
Flaming bow in hand, flaming arrow
Pointed toward the sun.
He did not see me; I stopped playing.
His bow and his arrow
Turned into a guitar . . .
I could only watch him play.

I NEVER REALLY NOTICED

I never really noticed
How love before me ran.
Running very swiftly
Holding out her hand.

I never really noticed
How she tried to show
That she was running from
The love she longed to know.

I never really noticed
That she always seemed to find
A chance to be caught waiting
For me to make her mine.

I never really noticed
And much to my dismay
Another found her heart—
And took my love away.

I STOLE A SMILE

I stole a smile from you today
And gave it to the sun.
He thanked me in his special way
And smiled on everyone.

I stole the twinkle of your eyes
And gave it to a star,
So its brilliance in the night
Could shine both near and far.

I stole the softness of our hair
And gave it to the wind.
He took it with him everywhere
Then brought it back again.

For he had seen your smile
The twinkle of your eyes—
And wanted nothing less
Than your greatest prize

So I went again to steal
The love within your heart—
But kept it only for myself
And gave him not a part.

For in your love I found
A beauty much more rare
Than any of your smiles
    . . . Or the softness of your hair.

LOVE

In the violet of your eyes,
garden portals of the earth flung open wide,
I stood amazed and wondered
just which way to go.
The spectrum of that violet
revealed the seven wonders of the world;
I stood in awe, tongue-tied,
and wondered what to say.
When heartbeats fused—
thunder, lightning, hurricanes,
four-corner winds enveloped me
and hurled
spinning across the galaxy—
and left me stranded
in the wondrous wonder of the universe.

* * *

THE NIGHT THROUGH MY WINDOW

Blue black
with silhouettes
halved, with faded blue and dotted
Loki's paradise with frantic cries
and eyes of vigilance gleam yellow.
Bolted doors and windows barred
against ingress,
yet, scenes enact,
of violence,
deaths, births,
fantasies strange or ordinary
and even love,
till blue black, chameleon,
transforms, transparent white.

BAY STREET

Scrolls and emblems, hieroglyphics,
dates and famous faces,
lions, relics
that belonged to you,
one by one have gone
devoured by the wrecking crew.
Now, smooth gleaming marble, tile,
ceramics, concrete slabs,
endless stretch of thick plate glass
soar dizzily to scrape the murky sky,
forboding and sinister
like Egypt's pyramids
against the setting sun;
your newborn children Bay Street
eerie and vertiginous,
obscure the sun.

* * *

SPRING FEVER

As the shoots of green begin to peep
in the rivulets of snow,
a craving comes a-creeping
from within
and seeps into each fiber of my being.
Excitement not yet born
exceeds the palpitations of my heart
and fantasies take flight
within my dormant brain.
Profound dreams frequent
so contrary to my capabilities,
almost virulent,
and conjure up the years gone by—
then youth is mine again.

355

AMERICAN BEAUTY

As I watch the bud of womanhood unfold;
The beauty of a little girl I behold.
A glimpse of childhood rare,
only a rosebud can compare.

Like the rose lifts its head for sun, demanding,
A young girl needs love and understanding.
In to gentle grace and womanhood repose
Like the beauty of a full-blown rose.

From womanhood on to a gracious age,
Long after her life is a record on a page
She is not unlike a rose.

After the petals from the bloom have gone,
a memory of her loveliness lingers on and on—

LOBLOLLY HILL

O, beautiful knoll; thou woodland gem
Nestled in these lovely mountains and hills
Where lofty rugged pine trees stem
And the thrush's music thrills.

Oft in sadness and in illness,
I have watched thy shadows bide
till the beauty of your stillness
Overflows me like a tide.

And in better hours and brighter,
When I saw thy shadows gleam
I have felt my heart beat lighter,
And Leap onward with a dream.

More than this thy name reminds me
Of loved ones, true and tried,
And thy name, like magic, binds me
Closer, closer to thy side.

THE SONG OF THE THRUSH

I woke at dawn
by the melody of her song;

the liquid notes that pour from her breast
Sets her apart from all the rest.

The splendor of a new day,
I seem to hear her say.
The glory of the sunrise—
Awake! and witness! she cries.

Stillness, then the soft whisper of a breeze.
Sunlight, and shadows dancing through the trees.
All the small woods' creatures

Join the chorus as they awake.
The stately oaks and the song of the
birds a cathedral make.

A day in harmony with GOD has begun.
Go forth, everyone. Find your place in the sun.

Tune yourselves to nature and gentle things,
is their morning song, through forest rings.
The exquisite music of their songs fade,
as they seek the woods and deep shade.

When sunset and deep shadows fall,
I find myself listening for her call.

In her song of benediction to her friends,
in the forest deep,
I seem to hear her say,"'tis time
for one and all to sleep".

As they go about their separate ways,
the melody of their song is in my heart to stay.

MARRIAGE

Marriage is when two of life's wanders join forces;
        and they—together in love—
        confront the harsh injustices
    and
        treasure the inexpressible joys
        of each day's unfolding.

* * *

LIFE

The mansion of life has in it many rooms—
each entrance leads to discovery,
        and experience is its exit.

* * *

FATHERHOOD

A luminary to every step taken
        and a navigator throughout life's voyage
is fatherhood—
        the guiding link to the future.

* * *

TOMORROW

Tomorrow is like a package
        of ceaseless wonder
    —carefully gift-wrapped—
            to delight anyone who anticipates it

359

LEIF A. HEGG

PEARL HARBOR

'Twas December the seventh in '41
The treacherous dastardly deed was done.
Peace they proclaimed as war was planned,
Our fleet lay idle, no guns were manned.

'Twas Sunday morning just about eight,
When the Japs sought to seal our Navy's fate.
Bombs and torpedoes they dropped with care;
They knew each position of ships that were there.

Hickam Field blazing, their planes were hit
But Taylor and Welch got into the thick of it.
Between them they flamed eight of the Nips
Twenty-one downed by ack-ack from land and ships.

A sailor stood alone on a Navy dock
Tears in his eyes for deep was his shock.
He longed for his ship and all the crew
For at general quarters his place he knew.

He felt some guilt, a little shame
He'd been ashore when the attack it came
No one was guilty, no one was shamed;
Lethargy, pacifism, apathy—a nation was blamed.

Pearl Harbor, its men and battleship row
A good part of the Navy sunk by the foe;
Roosevelt spoke and to the nation did say
That infamy was the deed that day.

On the *Arizona* a plaque, a flag doth wave
For the crews and ships, the lives they gave.
Ships and crews sank 'neath the sea,
They fought for the land of the brave and free.

Most of our ships again rose to the sea
And went on to pursue the enemy;
Kimmel and Short the blame they shared
In truth 'twas a nation caught napping and unprepared.

Let us as a nation pause to pray
And remember the infamy wrought this day.
Remember Pearl Harbor and those who sleep
May our country eternal vigilance keep.

* * *

FOR ONE DEARLY BELOVED

God took you from a world of care
So you could grace His mansion fair.
He left your image in our hearts
So we in life would love impart.

I'll love you till the world doth end
And rainbows no more to earth do bend.
Time to me shall mean no more
Till we meet upon the golden shore.

And when I go to eternal rest
I come to you at His behest.
Let my epitaph plain and simple be.
I lived my life because of thee.

LEIF A. HEGG

TO MY CHILDREN

I bequeath to my daughters and my son
A heart full of love and goals to be won.
I leave you the Bible, its proverbs and psalms;
Embrace God's words and have no qualms.

I taught you to be always steadfast and true
To love God and country and mankind, too.
Just live for today and pray for tomorrow
Whether it brings you joy or sorrow.

God sends each day His gift of love
Remember His ransom that came from above;
Use not your brethren as stepping stone
Whate'er thou doest, you one day atone.

Down life's byway you must e'er go—
Be careful then of the seed you sow;
Keep His commandments one thru ten
Give thanks in your prayers again 'n again.

Rise above the temptations of life
No matter the load of burden or strife;
Remember Calvary, the way of the cross
You'll know His glory and suffer no loss.

THE BEACHCOMBER

How I have longed to be in Hawaii,
Where palm trees throw deep shadows
In a quiet sea.
Long have I sighed for Hawaii and you,
For moon-drenched beaches on a bay of blue.
For flushed lips and the feel of velvet breast,
Beneath a tawny sky, far to the East, the West.
Where sleek white arms would cradle my impetuous desires,
Aflame beneath the crest of Kona's magic fires.
And as we lay on Hawaii's moon-drenched sand,
We watched the foam-tipped breakers wash this lost,
    enchanted land,
Somehow we knew, this beauty was made for us two,
A thousand million years ago they thought of me and you!
We were alone and lost in one vast open void,
And Nature, in its own wise way, was simply overjoyed.
Like the glassy waves that beat the snow-white shore
Our hearts did beat; our fervent hands explore!
Two ardent arms went tense, as willing bodies kissed,
While our lovely world went reeling in a blood-red mist!
We broke our hearts that night, by Kona's lazy sea,
When both of us made promises we knew could never be.
If I have gone from you forever then never let me know,
While Hawaii's sands are pale and white and tropic
    blossoms blow.
        Oh me!
If I could only be in Hawaii
And place gaudy, crimson flowers in the hair
Of one I love.

THE TALKING DRUM

Once life was sweet as springtime,
    waking up like a beautiful dawn.
Once love was a thrill of happiness,
    O where, O where have you gone?
O to feel once more like a singing bird,
    sailing on widespread wings.
To know that life is an endless joy,
    a package of happy things!
Summer came, with its flowery mood,
    painting the perfumed air.
While we were caught in love's sticky net,
    showering kisses everywhere.
The trees wore new coats of baby green,
    over their leaves of tender lace,
Through which the rays of sunlight
    poured on my shadow-spotted face.
Each of us were filled with dreams
    of times that were yet to come,
When we would walk life's battered stage
    and beat its talking drum!
Today I feel a restless urge, I'm a wave
    flying over a roaring ocean.
There are undiscovered worlds within me,
    I'm a river of violent emotion!
So turn back the clock to that other day,
    that enchanted tick in time,
When love was a tiger, stalking the earth,
    and life had reason and rhyme!

PEACE ON EARTH
(A CHRISTMAS MESSAGE)

Still with the passing of the years;
The beauty of that night appears
    With its resplendent glory.
A night when earth with strife was torn
And Christ, the Prince of Peace was born,
    And shepherds heard the story.

Still do our ancient woes survive,
And men for peace do fiercely strive,
    Their efforts unavailing.
The Christ whose birth glad tidings brought,
As then, is now, by men unsought;
    And thus their cause of failing.

O earth, earth, earth, of mournful plight,
Thine only hope—The Christ that night
    Who came to earth so lowly.
Now find in Him the peace He wills
To those His Holy Spirit fills,
    And joy that's pure and holy.

STRANGER'S ARMS

The radio blurs that familiar song,
Teardrops light her deep blue eyes.
He's been gone much too long,
Where the sun touches western skies.

She yearns to leave that familiar home,
And run to where the bright lights are.
But settles for blasé existence,
Knowing that he's gone too far.

Sacrificing a much nobler life,
Days now nearly all the same.
Fantasies of husband and wife,
She hears him whispering her name.

Tears trickle slowly down her pale white face,
Like an icicle touching spring's first light.
She dreamt of times spent loving together,
Knowing he wouldn't be home tonight.

Only a minute of an endless night,
Overwhelmed by his subtle charms.
You can't stop her incessive plight,
Lying in a stranger's arms.

just like that!

just like that, you walked into my life
without any bangs . . .

just like that, you held me in your arms,
kissed me, and told me nothing at all . . .
just like that, i kissed you and we met . . .

just like that, you said good-bye and left;
i didn't hear from you again.

just like that, you knocked on my door again,
called me, and we talked . . .
what am i to say to you if you do not respond?
just like that, i loved you . . . didn't you know?
i loved you . . .

* * *

you don't have to be anybody at all!

you don't have to be anybody at all
to do something in this world . . .

you can be a somebody and do nothing at all in this world.

you don't have to be anybody at all
to write letters and protest and comment
about the slums in a city . . .
you can offer to help the old, the young,
the poor, the dumb . . . you can offer to pain,
to drive, to meditate, to fight.

you don't have to be anybody at all to do something.
you can be wealthy and be an alcoholic or
dope addict.
you can be a somebody and steal and lie,
and perhaps this is why there are so many
who prefer drinking and doping and stealing
because it pays . . . you can be a somebody and
be an alcoholic and be a dope addict.
better to take medicine for your ailments . . .
better to eat a well-balanced diet and rest—
but there is no money in being decent.

you don't have to be anybody at all.

* * *

KOTOBUKI 1054

soon there will be an election . . .
a presidential election
soon kotobuki will emerge for what it is.
in all its beauty, it stands . . . architecturally perfect,
the backdrop for a city . . . in the midst of urban decay.

if you think you're right, you're not!
if you think it's all right to live in decay and hurt others,
       it's not!
if you think you're right to drink too much, to eat too much,
       to swear too much; you're not!
if you think you're right to bear babies when you've no money,
       you're not!

if you think we can live on nothing, you're wrong!

Kotobuki . . . brown, black, moss creeping
       to you i'll return when i'm tired
       to you i'll return and write about . . .

THE OLD SCHOOL TIE

The shades of Homer, the lab the book,
The sounds of music in the shady nook;
The Red Man's arrows, the tomahawk,
The honeysuckles, the apple crops, the brook;
The Western Front where once troubled nations shook,
The Victory Medal, Harvard,
The surge of the mighty oceans,
The plain, the mountain tarn, the sky:
Cato at Carthage and Cato at Phillippi,
Job's sad suffering and Isaiah's seraphic cry,
Will's dark lady and the puzzle of malachi,
Devon's rocks and where Killarneys lie:
Are all part of me,
And are embedded in the old school tie.

* * *

THE WHITE CROSSES

When I perceived the white crosses, row on row,
The shaven lawns, the flags drooping,
In the windless sky—then:
For these young men I could only ask
To what purpose their once existence;
And then the sunset gun, the flags descending
And in the fiery red of the sunset's afterglow
The dead seemed to answer me—the white crosses, row on row.

* * *

AN OCTOGENARIAN CHANT

Where have all the young girls gone, gone from the clover?
And will they e'er be back? No, they will ne'er be back;
For where old girls adorn tea parties on the lawn,
And gossip fore'er and yon, and on, and on, and on:
That's where young girls have gone—forever gone.

369

WHERE STRUMS THE OLD BANJO

Where strums the old banjo, night vista falling;
And o'er the mighty lake, the daylight palling:
There burly oarsmen row
To a safe harbor.
And where strums the old banjo,
There wavelike shadows flow
From the scenic watery world;
And ebb into the undertow
Of old sol's afterglow;
In dark red hues of gold
to a safe harbor.
And now when day is done
Hear Truth's matchless voice from somewhere in the sky:
Know, man, your God is One; know, man, your God is One.
As strums the old banjo
One one! two two! one one!
One one! two two! one one!
As burly oarsmen row to God's safe harbor.
And now while strums the old banjo
And while burly oarsmen row to a safe harbor:
There too my skiff I row,
As blustery breezes blow,
In October's dark-hued glow,
To God's safe harbor.
As strums the old banjo
One! two! two two! one! one!
One! two! two two! one! one!
Do, re, mi, fa, one! one!
Sol, la, te, do, one, one!

THE WATCH IN THE SCHOOLHOUSE DOOR

The cloud that rose upon the nation's natal day,
Which frightened Jefferson and trouble long forbode;
At last had extended to the dusty road:
Where it found old men,
Gossiping before the country store;
A historian standing in a schoolhouse door,
Mindful of the cloud's import
And the ominous tidings that it bore—
Watching young men
Their blue coats glistening in the road's brown dust,
Hurrying down the dusty road to war.

* * *

FATE'S FINGER

The finger points,
Whether to fame or doom, it matters not;
The finger points to Gettysburg:
Along roads by some unknown surveyor mapped,
Where all roads leading there to,
Have converged, crossed over and collapsed.

Along these selfsame roads,
Once came Lee's army and Meade's army:
And left there a ruined orchard, broken caissons,
A trampled corn field, the dead:
And an awesome warning to a once sundered nation,
That to this day calls upon His name.

DON'T LET IT RAIN ON YOUR BALLGAME

We rang the bell, and knocked on the door
And even in your half sleep you tread lightly.
We did not hear you cross the floor and sofly let us in.
You mentioned something about a cup of coffee;
I said I had some before,
Couldn't handle anymore.
Your sweaty face, uncombed hair,
Filled up ashtrays, empty beer cans everywhere . . .

We managed some small talk as we stood in the smoke-stale air.
I keenly felt your misery and despair.
Maybe even then I knew it would soon cease.
Oh, proud spirit and generous heart,
Why were you and joy so far apart?
Why were your days so full of hurt?
And as I turned to go, God, I didn't know,
I thought that even by a look I might wound this gentle soul.

I think you kind of knew
I was hurting, too,
And then you were hurled
Into the breathless beauty of eternity—
And you climbed and climbed
So far,
But now I can look.
Because how could a look hurt
A rising star?

A NEW DAY

When I awake to watch the mystery of night merge into day,
And in that almost reverent time,
When night lifts its mantle to embrace the maiden light,
For they are soft and gentle in their rendezvous—
Oh, how much like lovers are these two.

* * *

ALWAYS SUMMER

The June, that knew no September.
That rich spring, and last summer that are in time forever still—
You didn't feel the winters' cold, or piercing winds chill—
That heart that knew no sorrow or dispair
But dwells in its own paradise—
Forever captured there.

How could life retain any joy,
Even in a most secret place,
That he could not seek out and make his own.
And that chalice that contained the heart and mind
Would not grow in worldly ways of any kind,
The youth that knew no age
The morning that knew no afternoon
For its flight, was so swift, so soon.

PEACE

The dove, who flew into the canyon, that is life.
And the edges of that canyon are sharp and jagged.
And deep in the breast of the dove, they found their marks.
Of he, who only wanted to wipe away the hate with love,
And bind them all together with peace.
And that clear blue sky above
Where he could soar and herald his song of love.
Or lay mortally wounded on the canyon floor . . .

MY MAN'S A FIREFIGHTER
Dedicated to My Son—And to Firefighters Everywhere

A firefighter is a special breed of man
For he gives his all in doing what he can.
He answers the call day or night
And you can do your thing all right
By not giving fire a chance to start
By not smoking in bed and using your head.
It is plain old common sense, so have a heart.
My man's a firefighter, a man of all seasons,
Doing his thing in your neighborhood
When you gamble with your loved ones' lives.
With heartache and injury and sometimes death
So it's up to you to do your part.
If you value your loved ones' lives
Then don't give fire a chance to start.
O careless one where is your sting?
It's when we hear the fire siren zing!

GIFT OF THE SENSES

When your lips explode with pleasure
from the nectar's sweetened flavor,
Do not in haste devour,
but take time in which to savor.

When you behold the wonder of the sun's descent from sight,
And linger to await the star-pierced
blackness of the night;
and as you watch this awesome miracle unfold,
do you know that you have witnessed
what can ne'er be weighed in gold?

When you lie your head upon
the smooth and warm embracing sand,
and close your eyes and listen
to the oceans meet the land,
and well-spaced sea gull sounds
break the silent interludes,
do you marvel as you listen
or let some mundane noise intrude?

Have you ever lifted up a rose
to inhale its sweet display,
and smelt the earth and trees
and grass when rain has gone away?
And known the lure of kitchen smells
when hunger pains are strong?
With life's gift of senses
does this olfactory sense belong.

Have you ever held your hands outstretched
to touch someone you love?
and through that touch such joy abounds
as if directed from above,
a gentle stroke of hair or cheek
few pleasures can compare.
But the greatest gift of all these gifts,
is that you are aware.

wayfarer

At Thy shining gate I fall . . .
Thou art God and Lord of all;
a wayfarer of earth I come
to my home at rise of sun . . .
weary miles and sore I trod
seeking for Thy land, my God . . .
my journeying is over now;
at Thy wounded feet I bow . . .
content at last and evermore
Thee to worship and adore;
at Thy shining gate I fall;
Thou art God and Lord of all!

* * *

signposts

to the Eternal Throne I'll come
to God my home when night is done;
signposts strange mark my way . . .
donkey, sheep, oxen, hay . . .
a wooden cross against the sky;
His empty tomb to light me by . . .

* * *

solitude

across the fragrant floor I'm bound to go
where silence walks on needles soft and deep,
and folly's gone and clamor far away
and thoughts like trees stand quietly;
where shafted light falls downward like the rain
and nestlings rock on gently swaying boughs,
and bright-eyed chipmunks have their secret home;
where smallness has no part and man grows tall
and solitude like thunder thrills the soul.

IRONIC

She was so young and beautiful!
A callow youth's bewitching dream;
But so exalted by her wealth,
So high above his social rank,
She would not dare accept his love,
But met his every overture
With haughty word and cool disdain.

In time their fortunes were reversed:
He now walks on the dizzy heights,
While she, with friends and fortune gone,
Walks lonely valleys of despair
Rueing the day she turned away
A youth whose only lack was in
His lack of wealth and social rank.

Then, one June night, athirst for love,
She came to him with faltering steps
To place her trembling hands in his;
But time and gold had long contrived
To bind him bridegroom to Success,
The fires of his early love
Dead on the altar of his heart.

Rejected with a cool disdain
That chilled her like an autumn wind,
She left him in the pale moonlight
And sadly went her lonely way.
He watched her go, then coolly went
His chosen way, seeking the warmth
From fires of consuming greed.

THE OCEAN

The ocean, the ocean, time set in motion,
overlapping its seams, building new hopes
and dreams.
Giving its beauty, sharing its grace, it
gives something to all, each and every new
face.
It gives solidarity and unendless pleasure,
treat it always as a newfound treasure.
Come one, come all, see its vastness and
style. It reflects its peace with each
and every mile.
It will endure all seasons, all passing
of time, it will outlast us all, this
thing so refined.

* * *

PIANO MAN

Play my song, piano man,
        the song of life
On which my dreams are planned.
Fill me with the memories of love lost—
        give me the courage
To continue to love at all cost.
Love is the essence of life, it's true,
        win or lose
I'll always have my memories of you.
Life is a symbol of what love is,
        for without love
One's life is . . . not.
Play it again, piano man,
        the song of life
on which my dreams are planned . . .

FLOWERS ON THE WOODED PATH

Flowers on the wooded path
In heat of sun or stormy wrath,
Your loveliness can come but now
With sweet perfume while farmers plow.

Lover on the wooded path
Forget the reading, writing, math,
And lend your thoughts to one so dear
Who needs to overcome a tear.

Joys in beauty fill your heart
With lover's love e'er new to start,
Sometime twixt daylight sun and set
Our love will say: we have met.

* * *

THE LEAFY JEWEL BOX

Who lives in the leafy jewel box?
Finch or fly or a fish or fox?
In Cypress Swamp on tree-top towers
red orchids know such an answer well;
But while they while away the hours
They will never, never tell.
I stopped near an angel's wings to ask,
A sea gull said, "Tis a seaman's task,
I'll decipher all alone
The secrets of the alphabet cone.
Lion's paws and bleeding tooth,
Please tell us now, what is the truth?
Who lives in the leafy jewel box?
A living mollusk who *is* the jewel box.

JUST BY YOUR EYES

No one will ever know of this
    poem I write for you, to let
you know how I feel about the things
    you don't let show.

In your eyes I see the love that only one can see;
It's the love of happiness and longing to be free.

I see you as a cool calm sea,
    a rolling, bubbling brook, or
a multicolored rainbow.
    If only you could let it show.

I knew down in my heart that all of the hatred
    and meanness you show isn't really you.
You try too hard to be yourself, and *who* are
    you pretending to be if you have to try?

I bet you never knew, just looking in your eyes,
I could see all this, but it's there to see if only
you'd open up and let it go for others to see.

Don't mistake me and change your ways.
    I like you now, the way you are,
I like right now, having it to myself,
    so I can engulf myself with all this joy.

So, now I've said it, and now you know,
So why not open up and let it show?

Also now—before you begin—
there is something—one more thing:

In the life ahead of you, waiting in the sun,
    I want to wish you happiness and love and joy and fun.

But most of all for days right now,
    I wish for love throughout your day.

ESCAPING

I'm slipping away to a land far away where nothing is real and
        nothing
will be. It is all so familiar, I've traveled this way before. I
leave my senses and come here quite often to escape from reality
        and search
for my soul.

I close my eyes and ears on the world and somehow fall asleep,
        and I'm
at the root of all my problems or the source of my pains. I look
        through
the eyes of another man's face and see me as others do and find
the answers to all the questions yet unasked.

* * *

FIRST EXPRESSIONS

The first time I saw you
I felt my heart expand,
making room to hold your love.

My heart is being held captive now,
live and open wide,
Open for a person who is locking in their love,
afraid to let it go.

JILL HEATHER HORN

A JOURNEY WITH TIME

I will follow in your footsteps
to trace the patterns of your life,
To become as much a part of you as I possibly can.
I will speak to you with all my heart in every
word I let my lips release.

A REPUBLICAN CANDIDATE

Thomas E. Dewey!—And don't you dare say phooey!
A mighty fine candidate, and the Republicans can hardly wait;
To see him walk through the White House gate,
And take his chair before its too late.
Too late for what?
How dare you ask a Republican that!
When the Democrats have taken all of the fat,
For twelve long years and not a spat
Toward lending a pat
To the little Republican's back.
Large, thin, medium and small,
Be sure to vote one and all,
And don't let Dewey fall.
Join in the emergency call,
For it is time for the Republicans' ball,
And the Democrats must make a haul.
Vote straight Republican.
See the post-war conditions wane;
No more waiting in vain,
And the return of your loving man
With everything well in hand,
After the defeat over Japan.

* * *

ALONE

Alone and no one hears me. Alone and no one fears me;
Alone and no one seized me. Alone and no one can see me;
But alone.
Alone and no one wants me. Alone and no one taunts me;
Alone and no one has haunted me;
But alone.

385

DISCOVERY

Close your eyes and listen to
The colors of your mind,
As the vividness of the spectrum
Begins to swirl and then unwind.
Hear the roaring whispers
Of each speaker's point of view
Until the endless chatter heard
Reveals the wonder of you . . .

* * *

MOONBEAM

A moonbeam danced into my room last night.
It journeyed along in most unusual flight
Aimlessly frolicking off the curtain with ease
It jumped on the floor, acting just like a tease.

Then up from the floor radian moonbeam arose
Dancing as though a pair of slippers with toes
Next landing upon a raincoat neatly hung
There was no doubt in mind of the evident fun.

Leaping at last to the edge of the bed
Winking its eye and nodding its head,
The wee little moonbeam launched into the night
For running behind it chased morning daylight.

SOMEONE ELSE

I tried to climb a mountain
but the mountain was too high
And then I tried to be a bird
But I found I couldn't fly.
And then I tried to swim the sea
The waves were far too rough.
And then I tried to touch the sun
But my arms weren't long enough.
I tried to cross the desert
It was too vast and hot,
And then I tried to race the wind
Sore feet was all I got.
I tried to face the question
As to what I'm tryin' to do—
Maybe if someone gave me answers
Then I'd be able to say I knew.

* * *

LOVE'S FOUNDER

The great sea is deep and the high cliff is steep;
The great plains low and the running waters slow.
The great blue lake which God did make
He made with love—a great white dove
Who found the sea and you and me.

* * *

MY SURENESS OF YOU

When you take my hand
You make me feel so grand
You make me feel secure
My love for you is sure.
(For my monkey, Wayne)

LOVE LOST

The weeping willow swaying gently in the breeze.
The murmur of a stream's endless flow,
Soft fragrance of the air, stars peeping through the trees
Return the love we shared not long ago.

I held you in my arms, your lips pressed close to mine,
The magic of your charm was like intoxicating wine.
I thought we'd never part, but I was wrong, I guess;
So with all my aching heart, I wish you every happiness.

* * *

SONG TO A CARDINAL

Oh, bird of radiant hue,
You perch upon my clothesline
High above the morning dew
As on a round worm you dine.

Your crown you wear with dignity;
Your soul into a song you pour.
My soul fills with humility;
For you never will be a bore!

THE BAND DIRECTOR

He has a bearing military.
To the awkward boys he's so unkind
As he fights, leads, shouts himself hoarse
To inspire them with perfection.

Straighten up!
Forward march!
Watch those toes!
They should be in line with your nose!

Shoulders up!
Stomachs in!
Hide that grin!
Agony—it's time to begin.

* * *

TO A HAMSTER

You wee powder puff of humanity
You cling to life with a tenacity
Unbelievable. And at me you gaze
Your small, beady eyes enormous with rage!

Why? Because you may not roam the house free
But forever confined and caged must be.
After my touch, you scrub and scrub your fur,
'Til I say, "thinks she, I polluted her."

Up and down all around you climb
And climb. You are still in your prime.
I envy you your carefeee life,
Completely free of any strife.

389

LIFE NEEDS COMMITMENT

Life without commitment
    Is empty;
        Void of meaning . . .
Goals need to be made;
    Covenants kept;
        And trust in God developed.

* * *

CAN YOU IMAGINE?

I wonder what reaction
    Our Lord would have, if He saw
        Every mortal on this earth
            Scurrying around,
                Trying to undo all their wrongs . . .
Can you imagome the chatter
    It would create in Heaven,
        If god and the angels could view
            Our "switch-around"?

ANNA M. HOY

GOD HAS NEEDS, TOO!

God has needs, too!
As a Person in His own right,
    God could naturally weary
        Of continual demands . . .
        Especially without so much as a ''thank-you''
        From many of His receivers.
It is time we realize:
God has needs of His own, too!
He needs our love;
    Our willing service;
        Our submissiveness;
            And our gratefulness.
When we
    Actually put God first
        In our heart, and deeds . . .
Then with joy,
    God gives,
        Out of the abundance
            Of His cares.

A SPECIAL GIFT OF FAITH

Faith
  Cannot be received, just by wanting it!
It is a gift from God,
    When we have performed goodness
      Without expecting anything in return.
Faith is given to us
    When we give, or when we have shared
      Whatever we have . . .
        Especially when we feel we can't afford to do so . . .
      Whether our gift
        Is time, or money, or energy,
          Or just showing another we care . . .
      And by giving that portion of us,
        When it is needed or wanted.
Having faith, is a by-product
    Of "going out on a limb" for the Lord,
      And trusting in Him . . .
        No matter what.
It is loving and fearing Him so much
    That we willingly perform frightening tasks . . .
      Because fear of turning away from God
        Is greater than fear of the task itself!
But assurance comes,
    When God's desires and commands have been catered to,
      Ahead of our personal wishes . . .
Then when God's timing is right,
    We discover:
      Faith has been given to us!

TO WALK WITH GOD

I must learn to walk with God,
 Or to follow Him . . .
  And not walk ahead of Him.
For if I go my own way,
 Without first consulting God,
  There will be places I may go,
   That He may not like . . .
 And He may disappear
  Without me knowing He has gone.
 When suddenly I realize
  I missed God's companionship,
   It would be more difficult to find Him.
Whereas: If God walks alongside of me,
 Then I can better see He is there . . .
 But I must take time to look at Him . . .
 And must not do all the talking,
  Because God may have something to say, too!
  And I must really listen to what He has to say . . .
   Lest He wearies of my idle quest,
    And leaves toward more interesting places.
It is good to follow God . . .
For when He is ahead of me,
 I can more easily see He is there!
So if, for some reason,
 God would decide it was time to go elsewhere,
  I would have a better chance
   To see the direction He was going . . .
I may then be able to continually follow Him,
 Keeping Him within my sight . . .
  In all my steps ahead.

ERLING MILTON HOYER

POTENTIAL MIGHT

No man who walks upon the face of Earth,
May say, "I'm not as other men have been."
For no man really knows his worth;
'Til balanced 'gainst the worth of other men!

Potentials are but dormant, lifeless things,
When left in pools of stagnant thought;
While might-of-mind, and all success it brings,
Unheeded, brings us not the worth it ought.

Don't underestimate this Power that is yours,
Nor pass it by without at least a try.
A pessimistic outlook now may close the doors
Against a *strength* you cannot buy.

What right have you to say to us,
"Come what may, let fate take care of me."?
The Power-that-Creates has never meant it thus;
But gave a MIND to guide our course to be!

You need not ask of any man the right
To perform, when you KNOW the skill you have.
Doubt not that you possess the KEY OF MIGHT;
Fear is a "wound." . . . confidence . . . the "salve."

Anything you feel is worth achieving,
Is really worth the effort to sustain.
Instead of time that's spent in "grieving,"
USE that moment TRYING to attain!

Doubt. and ALL the World shall doubt YOU!
Fear, and "they" shall "Trample on your Soul!"
Be *the* One all men may proudly look to;
Confidence shall guide you to that goal!

Set a "Standard" . . . not by others' ways of doing;
But what YOU know, that you ALONE can DO!
And retiring, leave behind, what man reviewing,
May set their "course," and plan their future to.

* * *

THE SUN IS A WOMAN

I can smile, feel just fine
Always know the Sun will shine
Never find a day that's "bum."
I can laugh, and hear the lark;
See the Sun shine, through the dark.
I'm the kind of man you'd like!
My Life's "adventure," not a "hike."
But, alone, I'm not this way . . .
Everything is Dark and Gray.
I'm a pessimistic "cuss;"
Always "crabbing," full of "fuss!"

So . . . Don't give any praise to me,
If this happy man you see.
Give it all, instead to Her . . .
"She" is why my doubts defer . . .
"She" is what's behind this man.
"She" is *when* his life began.
And so, I'll cherish all my life . . .
This lovely Dream . . . My Dearest Wife!

Erling Milton Hoyer

ADVICE TO FRIENDS

When one loves you you are immensely happy,
Yet whom you love nobody is able to say.
All my sweet dreams of spring night end in smoke,
All pretty flowers withered and fallen over the way.
Living miserably in a melancholy hell-like world,
One becomes a victim of fear, grief, and at bay.
Should you consider gain and loss vanishing cloud,
You are in paradise enjoying felicity day after day.

Why wandering at the cross road?
Why not give up vanities, be philosophical and gay?
Why madly seek fame, profit, and put self first?
Why look for a needle in a bundle of hay?
Real immortality lies in love and sympathy;
Do away with warfare and hatred, for peace daily pray.
A great ego means oneness of self and universe,
And with courage on the step of sage tread.

* * *

TO LEADERS OF NATIONS

Boundless is the miraculous space,
    Endless is the marvelous time.
Interplanetary travel in a space age
    Like visiting a neighbor once in a while.
It behooves us to regard all nations
    As a living body of mine.
No grounds whatsoever for hating others.
    Why revenge and fight? Why not love and smile?

396

WINTER'S GOING! SPRING IS COMING!

Winter's going! Spring is coming!
Can't you smell it in the air?
Snow is melting! Streamlets running!
Green and browns are everywhere.

Sun is shining! Birds are singing
Joyful songs of newborn spring.
Flower bells of spring are ringing
Nature's children forth to sing.

Winter's going! Spring is coming!
Zephyrs play the pipes of Pan.
Buds are bursting! Beauties waking!
Wordland paths are free again.

* * *

THE CHRISTMAS TREE

Tinsel and a candy cane.
Jack Frost on the window pane.
Christmas tree balls all alight
Making the Christmas tree so bright.

Presents under the Christmas tree
Fill our hearts full of glee.
I make a wish as I shed a tear
To keep the Christmas tree all year.

THIRST FOR LOVE

Entertain me for awhile.
let me pour into your thoughts
my point of view;
let's merge minds and exist as one
just for a moment . . .
share my sorrows
enjoy my good times
wear my pleasures . . .
try to realize
that everyone needs someone to lean on . . .
pull me from this world of loneliness
and let my heart quench its thirst for love
in your tender eyes.

* * *

THE SHINING STAR

Once I saw a shining star
that somehow did not seem so far,
so I reached out toward its light
to try and steal it from the night,
but the dawning of the sun
came around and it was gone.

MEMORIES OF DAYS GONE BY

Memories of days gone by
are like stars up in the sky.
diamonds, rubies, chains of gold
we can see but cannot hold.

Some are jewels within our mind,
as experience that we find in the rough roads that we pass
through the turns that takes our path.

But to dwell among the stones
that were thrown to break our bones
makes us miss, along the way,
all the treasures of today.

* * *

MY PLOT

I request a lonely spot
with many trees to mark my plot,
on a hill where I could rest
among the gift of nature's best;
a cool wind from the east shall blow
toward the valley down below
and up above the sun will shine,
the birds will sing, their songs are mine—
but if in doubt, my place to dwell
can't be in heaven or in hell . . .
I pray the Lord denies me not
that lonely spot that marks my plot.

EARTH RHYTHM

Richard, oh Richard, where are you?
in the orchard? say something.
I hear a sound, I hear you, I'm
going all around.

Yes, I know I'm high, high in the ground.

* * *

A FLOWER

A flower is ever a lovely thing, never
to say good-bye to, and the teardrops of
mankind are fewer.

* * *

REST

When everything that you
caress becomes a mess, rest
is the best for a real bless.

* * *

FLOWERS

Without a flower there
would be no life tower,
everything would be sour,
flour would be meaningless
and the hour doom.

SIDEWALK

Concrete poured
Sidewalk born yesterday
Today hurt by a footprint
That it will never forget.
It wrinkles from age
Lies quietly
Knowing that it is losing ground
Feelin' the earth move.
Its nerves trembles with fear
Skin stretching;
It raises in pain
Remains in terror
Until
Time heals
But leaves the scar
Of
A footprint . . .

* * *

EATING TRUTH

Saw you last night driving your 240Z
In the car, behind, saw you weren't alone.
Blew the horn, you didn't know it was me.
I recalled the argument on the phone.
As you went up the road, I stopped to eat.
Watched you leave me, I a shadow of your past.
Picked up my food, slowly taking a seat.
Time, space—how could I expect it to last?
Still had food left, I put it in the bag.
Love sometimes easy to lose, hard to find.
Love sometimes easy to lose, hard to find.
I walked to my car, trying not to gag.
You drove up, her secure with what was mine.
You looked at me with those brown classy eyes.
I knew then your truth had been all your lies.

401

BARBARA JACKSON

AN UNWRAPPED GIFT

Must I ever
be myself?
Should I love
someone forever?
Perhaps love is in me,
to feel and give
so freely.
Could someone turn down
such a precious gift,
of all I have, and need,
just enough with out greed?

* * *

THE TRIP OF GROWING OLD

When I grow old I'll be the
Coolest, baldest, faded, figured, wrinkled,
Slow-walking, squinting old lady you've ever seen.
I'll hustle and do the bump, or whatever takes their place;
I'll style in the latest fashions and
Exercise to keep in shape.
I'll still play basketball
And wear my black and white Adidas;
They'll match what is left of my salt and pepper hair.
At the end of the day
I'll sit in my contempory pad
And listen to my stereo
Until
Young couple, down the hall, complains about the noise.

GHETTO CHILD

If he thought it would make him free, to the
devil he would sell his soul.
Darkness,
Loneliness,
and cold
is the plight of the Ghetto Child. With pangs
of hunger, his little body folds.
Fears,
Angers,
and anxieties
show his tenacious clinging to life. His life-
long battle remains untold.

* * *

COLOR WHEEL FANTASY

Color Wheel Fantasy,
A dream of all dreams,
How very real and vivid it seems.
Distorting my mind
A delusion of all illusions,
Until I'm bent to the edge of extremes.
Prismatic spectrum,
Patchwork of all colors,
Trickling in circular streams—
Splishing and splashing
Mixing of all pigments,
And blending of colorful creams.

RAIN, WIND, AND YOU

I walk in the rain
Sloughing down a lane;
I walk in the wind
Blowin' round the bend,
And who do I find
As on my way I wind?
Why, I find you—
Wonderful, wonderful
You.

* * *

THE STARS GO DRIFTING BY

As I sit 'neath the branch of an old oak tree
All was quiet, all was still on hill and on lea.

I looked up dreamily to the sky
And watched the stars go drifting by.

O beautiful moonlit night serene
On tree, rock and bush there lies a sheen—

A sheen from the moon and stars in the sky
While the flickering stars go drifting by.

WINGING HOME

As dusk sets in at evening tide
Off to their nests the birds do hie;
Hushed now the world in quiet keeping
Little white stars above start peeping;
When day is done, the sun goes down
Evening shades their mantle spread around.
You will find that indeed they do
Yes, everything wings away home, 'tis true.

THE DRAMA OF SUNSET
OR THE PAINTED DESERT AND THE PETRIFIED FOREST

There is a mysterious significance
In the luminous glow of the sun descending
The desert sky. Great tongues of flame
Blaze the pathway of the Solar Monarch as he
Rises and sets in seas of sepia and crimson.

The western vault of heaven leaps forth
Clothed in scarlet as our smoldering sphere
Dips to his evening repose. The painted pumice
Draws nearer as we are bathed in rosy warmth
Against the coolness of the approaching night.

The sun-worshippers, once lordly connifers, lie
Petrified in glorified agate and quartz,
Doing homage to their supernal god, as he
Sheds his effulgent glory down.

What invisible power hovers over this scene?
A power more fascinating than a Japanese garden
Where clouds of peach azalea blossoms send forth
Their delicate petals as messengers of peace
On the briefly twilit ait.

These are all Nature's representatives revealed
Against the sunset sky, holding fast to the
Ancient promise: "While the Earth remaineth,
Seedtime and harvest, cold and heat, summer
And winter, day and night shall not cease."

BECOMING

No more a child,
I could feel the skirts of immaturity
Being pulled from my grasp.
No longer able to hide behind them,
I stood naked
To bear the punishment of my own sins.

In a twinkling
The magic of adulthood came,
Ripping away the shield of my mother's love
And I was no longer protected,
So naked I stood
To suffer the sorrow of my own mistakes.

And suddenly
The day of adolescence died
Taking with it the light of my father's wisdom.
And left without guidance
I was naked
In the dark of my own misunderstanding.

And yet
I have not broken under punishment;
Sorrow has not yet torn apart my soul
And the tiny light of my own wisdom
Grows brighter with each new experience.

MY GARDEN

When the sun of reality finally rose,
I hurried to my untended garden.
But the seeds of Doubt had been sown
And the weeds of Despair flourished
Chocking the flowers of Hope and Faith.
The price of experience
And knowledge
Is high.

* * *

MEMORIES

Once your small world passed close to mine.
You reached out from your world
And I from mine.
For one, brief, beautiful moment
Our fingers touched.
Then your world slipped on by
In the Universe of Time
But the memories of you
Still linger . . .
Precious memories.

KALEIDOSCOPE

My life is an eternally deep, green, green emerald
Without a fiery ruby near.
Is a cocoon all it will ever be?

It is the thousand shades of green inside early Spring's frozen
    pond,
And Spring's first red blossom not yet in sight.
And where is the butterfly they promised me?

And when Summer does come, will she find the emerald
    shattered,
The pond dry, the cocoon crushed?
And never is the butterfly they promised me.

* * *

I LOVE YOU

I love you.
Because I love you
I do not judge your past.
Your past, after all,
Has shaped you into what you are today.
I do not ask change of you.
I love you for what you are
Not for what I believe you could be.
I do not question the future
For I trust you
And your reactions to whatever Fate may bring.
I love you.

SEARCH WE MUST

Some men search for a lifetime
And never find that which they seek;
Challenge is sought for by those who are strong
And safety by those who are weak.

The strong seek challenge and danger
And finding it, conquer or die;
The weak seek for safety and refuge
And finding it, they cease to try.

The strong must conquer and gain control
Tho in winning they lose, by reaching their goal.
The weak seek safety, through doubt and fear
And finding it, worry that its loss is near.

Some seek wealth, some wisdom,
Some seek for knowledge and power,
Some seek fame and the world's acclaim;
I seek after perfection, for one bright shining hour.

To live, to love, to seek, to find,
To seek unfinding, as a man gone blind,
This is our glory, our fate, our doom.
To search for life, to find a tomb.

Yet search we must, without goal or prize,
For it's in the search that our destiny lies.
To seek, to struggle, to strive, to grow,
To learn at last what we need to know.

LOOK FOR ME

Look for me, my darling,
When spring shall warm the air;
I will be here if I live
To claim my lady fair.

And if spring comes and I do not
Then you shall know I died,
And neither love, nor will, nor thought
Could bring me to your side.

But know this truth, my darling,
Mark it down and mark it well—
If I live, I'll come for you
Tho I must come through hell.

* * *

TRY

There is no sin in life but one.
To be less than God meant you to be.
To settle for less is an insult
To your God, to yourself and to me.

You dishonor your father and mother,
You dishonor the race of man;
You dishonor the God that made you
When you try to be less than you can.

COMING HOME

The fog was swan's wings over the mountains—
God keep me to the end,
In the minds of those I knew,
That I could call my friends.

And let not the hurry I cannot leave,
Pull me away from a dream
Of the snow and the rocks of a day I climbed,
Of the sounds of a geyser's steam.

For I've never seen the stars that way,
The lake and the rocks of Earth,
Or felt anymore a part of them,
Or risen to a higher birth.

So let me remember how hard I worked
To reach the things I knew,
That the glory I got was the comrade's share,
And the things they said were true.

And it is my prayer that they'll think of me
At night when they build their fire,
As they tell their dreams to the moon till dawn,
When they wake to the cold creek's choir.

God bless them all, in the woods they've earned,
And send them a laugh all day,
So never they lose their love,
So they always find their way.

RATTLING THE CHAIN OF EVENTS

Whenever I stumble on a little cold cash
Off to a fool's market I then heatedly dash.
Wheeling a squealing cart, I spendthriftily stash
Cancerous condiments, and other tasteless trash.
Beef prices "Butcher" me, "Rustling" my pocketbook;
Somewhere in the middle, "Hides" a "Meat Hustling" crook,
Skinning beef carcasses, and the poor public, too.
The law needs "Beefing Up" to protect me and you.
Away down in Brazil, coffee grown on a hill
Has "Perked" its price way up, and "Perking" higher still.
As our leaders "Bleed" us, they swing "High" as a king
Champagning their ladies, on free fling after fling.
For brunch they "Punch" "Jim Crow," "Sheeting Up" for his
        "Roast,"
Then "Butter Up" their roles, with Toast after Toast.
Brandying up their bellies, they bid a crass adieu
To our "Liberty Belle" whose Pride they've perjured, too.
"Statutory Rapists" voting to dine and dance
Away the high esteem we deem our gift from France.
Let's beseech a Preacher to teach us a new prayer
Asking God to exhale, and Sanctify the air
That taints some Congressmen, as Secretaries "Bare"
"Pay for Play" positions, that are "Headlining" there.
We'd hear no more about an "Energy Crisis."
Could we share the "Hot Air"? Congress compromises;
Cast your votes to elect Candidates who reject
Leaving "God" and "Country" in a "State" of neglect.

BONNY BILLY BONNEY'S BOTTLE

While digging for old bottles, in a "Ghost Town" dump one day
My spade refused to invade a hard hostile clump of clay.
Coaxing the clay to submit, to my fain surprise there lay
"Billy the Kid's" own bottle, "Sprite Sprits of Yesterday."
I thirstily clasped that flask, "Eyeballing" it carefully,
To "Drink In" the "Ambrosia" left aging within for me.
"Puckered Palate Poised to Quaff," booze "Slumbered" to
    perfection
Sweet "Hibernating Honey," snoozing sans mans detection.
I "Thumbed Out" the crumbling cork, "Tossing a toast" to the
    "Kid,"
Right then I forgave "Billy" for all the bad things he did.
His name was on the label, his picture "Plastered" there, too,
He must have "Bottled" his sins, to "Mellow" them in his brew.
After toasting my dead host, I drank to dread Billy's fame.
Mt "Pie-Eyed Adam's Apple" pumped "Spit" to put out the
    flame.
Whatever he had "Embalmed" in that ancient fire flask
Would sure as "Hades" have made "Billy's" an easier task.
"Fanning" dead his fearsome foes in the "Hot" towns he went
    through,
Had he "Shot"'them with a "Tot" of his "Mickey Finning
    Brew,"
He could have "Up-Staged" them all, avoiding a bloody brawl,
"Whiskey-ing" those "Bad Actors" to their "Final Curtain
    Call."
I drank no more to the pranks of "Bonny Billy the Kid,"
Spilling that "Swill" on the ground, I disdainfully got rid
Of that "Liver-Leeching Lye," disavowing any claim
To this "Gut-Rotting Poison," whereupon he "Notched" his
    name.
His hate of honest people, fermented for a century
In a "Vial" of "Vile" bile, that "Worked" its fell fury free
To "Float" down my thirsting throat, "Cauldroning" its way in
    glee,
So "Billy" could "Sate" his "Hate" on poor "Bottle Digging
    Me."

DOROTHY JOHNSON

FALL

Fall came and summer bowed her head
And closed her eyes of green,
Her hands to fold while earth beholds
The colors to be seen.

The blue sky turns to shades of gray
While the warm brooks, they get cold;
Fall's chilly breeze fades summer's trees
Into shades of gold.

The fields of wheat now flourish;
The cattails stand so tall;
The old oak tree, she stands so free
To let her acorns fall.

The green grass now is covered
With pedals of the rose,
While the pumpkins lay upon the hay
For a child to hold.

Now the earth is swirled in colors
From sea to shining sea,
For when time calls, fall is all
That summer cannot be.

SHE TOUCHED MY ARM

A little girl I know
    Went past me in a crowd
And said hello
    And touched my arm,
And now I am a slave.

EARTH GODS

Giants ten feet tall,
We meet them now and then,
Not of Earth at all,
Nor things that might have been.
Deific they are;
Immortal bits of clay,
Man's own borrowed stars
To walk his wavering way.
Christ was one of these
Who breathed our immortality
From His cross of Peace
While deathless death became
        Eternity.

* * *

GOOD-BYE

There's a word of grief, the sounding token;
There's a word so filled with human tears—
The saddest word fond lips have ever spoken—
A little word that breaks the chain of years.
Its utterance must ever bring emotion;
The memory it crystals cannot die—
'Tis known on every land, on every ocean
'Tis called "Good-bye."

RANDOM THOUGHTS

In the evening of our lives
We are assailed by doubts and fears;
We slowed our inner drive,
We think of many wasted years.

We know the end is near
No matter what we do;
We must not live in fear
Of something old and true.

Our night must arrive,
It is nature's way;
We must hope and strive
To be healthy and gay.

Our loved ones will ride
The same old road;
We will step aside,
Let them carry their own load.

* * *

FATE

What is fate? The eternal riddle.
The brave, they laugh at it.
The weak, they blame it.
The brave, they control it,
The weak, they bemoan it.

When it strikes suddenly,
The brave, they wither and die;
The weak, they die again.

Who can foresee the blows of fate?
Who is so wise to avoid them?
Who is so strong to conquer them?

Be humble, ye mortal.
Fate plays tricks on you;
You are weak and fragile,
In the hands of fate.

* * *

UPWARD, EVER UPWARD

Up and down the winding road of life
Man marched on in struggle and strife.
A long road it was, covered with blood
    and tears
A tortuous road it was, haunted by
    dread and fears.

But upward, ever upward in his weary
    climb
By a purpose driven on to reach the
    high and the sublime,
And out of the mire of ignoble strife
He slowly attained a beatific life.

But lo, out of the dark, spirits of
    evil appear
To fill his world with deadly fear,
To crush his spirit and befog his mind
And bring utter destruction to human-
    kind.

But from countrysides far and wide
Men of courage, stalwart and tried,
Rise and gather in legions great
To hurl defiance to all hate.

Arise ye men, true and brave!
Death unto the villain and the knave!
Struggle onward for a world of honor
    and mirth
For peace and happiness for the land
    of our birth.

WORLD AFLAME

In a world aflame
We move about like ghosts;
In dishonor and shame
We watch the marching hosts.

Death from the sky
Death from the sea
Murder from on high
Murder of you and me.

Cries out a mother's voice:
"Children of men, are you stark mad?
Have you no other choice
Is nothing else to be had?

"In my humble woman's breast
There glows a holy light.
I am in eternal quest
For the noble and the right.

"My life I gladly give
A new life to create,
A life made to love, to live,
And not to die and to hate.

"I'll gladly work and slave
Human lives to help and save.
War, hate and disease I shall ever fight.
Peace, love and good will, my eternal light.

"Children of men—wake up and hear
A woman's mournful plea.
Gather from far and from near
From the mountains and over the sea.

"One people in fair and foul weather
The welfare of all—there lies our wealth,
Stand united—work together
For peace for life and for health."

PAST FUTURE

Up and down the eternal road of life,
Man marched on in struggle and strife;
A long road, it is covered with blood and tears;
A tortuous road it is, and haunted by worry and fears.

But upward, ever upward man continued to climb,
Driven by purpose to reach high and the sublime;
And out of the mire of ignoble strife,
He slowly climbed to a new and beautiful life.

But out of the dark evil spirits appear,
To fill the world with deadly fear;
To crush man's spirit and mind,
And bring death to all humankind.

* * *

A WOMAN

Nurtured on man's finest creations,
Absorbing the culture of many nations;
Yet a lonely soul in the world of motion,
One of the millions tossed on a stormy ocean.

Alone, yet firm as a rock,
A woman, yet fearless, daring and strong;
Accurate and exacting as a clock,
Yet tender and soft as a nightingale's song.

* * *

VERSE FOR DEBORAH DINNER

Give us peace, we all pray,
Good will to men, we all say;
Let us bring back the joy of life,
For we are weary of bloodshed and strife.

But peace—it flies away,
It grows dimmer every day;
For the hearts of men are filled with hate
Driving them downward to their eternal fate.

Hatred and envy bring ruin and death,
They poison and choke our every breath;
If peace and life is our goal
We must first bring love into our soul.

* * *

VERSE FOR DEBORAH DINNER —
CLOSING REMARKS

Out of the dim and distant past
Emerged this creature called man;
His climb was furious and fast,
He conquered all—this being called man.

The savage in him still lives,
The beast is still in his heart;
On conquests he still thrives,
And murder is still his part.

But slowly the noble of men they arise,
Human and kindly, Godlike and true;
Tested by life and wordly-wise,
They call us our faith to renew.

Our faith in the goodness of life,
Our hope in man's nature divine;
Our dream for the ending of all strife,
Our faith in all that is noble and fine.

Together we must march on our way,
Soldiers of humanity one and all;
Together we must firmly say,
All for one and one for all.

FUTUREWORLD

Life may be hard and dreary
We may be tired and weary;
But strange as it may seem
There is always a new dream.

New hopes and dreams stir our souls
We see new horizons, new goals;
Man's surge upward cannot be contained
His soul cannot be chained.

To hate and to slay
Cannot be the human way;
Some day we will end all strife
And show the way to a new life.

Though humanity is writhing in pain
Though millions have been murdered and slain;
Yet hope must eternally rise
For a world saner and wise.

Though life may be hard and dreary
Though we may be tired and weary;
Yet strange as it may seem
There is always a new dream.

ISRAEL KATZ

REBIRTH

Firm as a rock we stand,
To defend the true and the right;
Solemnly we raise our right hand
And pledge our means and our might.

To live, to love, and be free
To give, to help, and be kind;
Our hearts as open as the wide sea,
Our fears left far behind.

We face the rising sun,
We want a world of peace;
Our work has just begun,
Our task must never cease.

Out of the ashes of a world
Torn with strife and consumed by hate,
We'll create a new world
Pulsating with life—marching to a great fate.

HE IS A FRIEND OF MINE

I want nothing of him,
He wants nothing of me;
But I'll do all for him,
And he'll do all for me.

He is a friend of mine.

I like the color of his tie,
I like the twinkle of his eye;
I like his frown and his smile,
To me it is all worthwhile.

For he is a friend of mine.

Life flows on from day to day,
New friends come —old ones go away;
This world would be a lonesome place,
Without a friend's smiling face.

Wealth, fame and success—it comes and it goes,
Like a river it sometimes dries up and
                    sometimes overflows;
But your true friends are always around;
When you need them, they are to be found.

TO OUR PATIENTS

Be brave and of good cheer,
Good times are on the way;
Let us banish all fear,
Tonight let us be happy and gay.

New hope for today,
Good health for tomorrow,
We hope and we pray
This is the end of all your sorrow.

* * *

LIFE IS

You have written a moving page,
In a world torn by strife;
Bruised and battered in this tragic age
You retained your zest for life.

Carry on and do not despair,
This silly world will see the light;
Soon it will be clear and fair
And day will banish the light.

This just a thought and a wish.

* * *

TO EVE ON HER FORTY-FIFTH BIRTHDAY

Here is to you at forty-five,
Beautiful and lovely and very much alive.

May you continue your life
As a sweet mother and wife.

May you continue to bring cheer
To those who live in fear.

May you continue a long life
And avoid trouble and strife.

These are my heartfelt wishes to you,
To a sweet lady who knows who is who.

* * *

THE YOUNG AND THE OLD

We want to live long,
We hope to do much;
We plan when we are young,
The top of life to touch.

We get old and weak,
The struggle was hard and tough,
We are worried and we are sick,
And we think enough is enough.

* * *

EPILOGUE

In the autumn of my life
I sit and think of the past;
The years of struggle and strife,
The years which passed so fast.

I loved my fellow men,
I tried to help the poor and the sick;
I never argued the which and the when,
When help had to come on the quick.

So now I am old and tired,
Let the young come to the scene,
Let them be ready and fired,
A better world to build and to win.

THE HILL

In my youth I climbed to the top of the Hill,
      and surveyed the scene below:
"I'll own all of this some day
      I want every one to know."

In my middle years I climbed to the top of the Hill,
      and surveyed the domain below;
"There is beauty here and history, too;
      I'll own you before I get through."

Now in my old age I climb the Hill,
      and survey the scene below:
"I'll never own you," I say,
      "but I will always love you so."

* * *

A FARAWAY WAR

I went far away and fought a foreign war,
      and the enemy's blood was red,
His cries and yells were very real,
      and will always resound in my head.

His language was strange, and his color was, too,
      and his idea was to make me dead.
My talk made no sense to him,
      so I talked with bullets instead.

If we could have met somewhere else in time,
      and seen each other face to face,
I am sure that we would not
      ever have fought in this place.

CYNICAL, CARESSING, UNION

Heart, cynical at times,
yet can be rhythmical and finessed as a connoisseur with wines.
Heavy debates at its cause,
Beginning from a dawn of realizations,
and ending at present with many revelations.
Persons try with little success
the endless task of a heart's cynical regress.
Persons relate with unknown cosmos,
Many which are drawn to caress?
This bondage of unquestionable heart,
draws the union of two never to part.
So in the face of aridity and disenchantment
don't be cynical of heart, for it shall come your way.

FOR J.W.H.

Slowly the tide recedes
The sand dries.
Stranded sealife gasps for renewal.
Seaweed lies like motionless serpents
Shell-encrusted.
Like a drying beach my stranded life
Lies gasping for resurgence,
And memories serpents—
Grief-encrusted—
Await a non returning tide.
You were my tide.

* * *

WHERE THE HUNGRY LIVE

Ask not the untouched to soothe your grief
Nor the sound to dress your wound,
But go where pain is a shard of glass
That pierces and scrapes and rasps and tears
And movement a gasp of ice.
A heart will rise to share your ache
And solace will drip in the gash
Of the raw red cut and the gaping hole
That you never can close alone.

Where the hungry live, go ask for bread,
Reach out and touch a life.
Walk where gaunt-eyed patience stares
And swollen bodies shame your need.
A hand will lift to share a crust
And the bitter taste is gone
From the tear-salted meal and the acid rind
That you tried to eat alone.

KNICKERBOCKER BOY

She fell in love on a dance floor,
And knew she'd see him some more.
The Knickerbocker Boy kissed her on the arm.
Then he kissed her again with a smile of charm.

He came from a land far away.
They both knew he would come and stay.
Life pulled these two lovers in many a way
But they're still together day by day.

God works His miracles for all of us
As he is always fair and just.
Love is a good force in Life.
Especially for the Knickerbocker Boy and his wife.

* * *

THE BREEZE AND I

The breeze and I are friends
My body and soul are on the mend.
When we look out to sea
You think God is with me.
Gently it will tangle your hair,
Then you think, forgotten is all the bad affair.

TORNADO

The rain was slapping harder,
harder, against my pane.
The flapping and the clapping,
were driving me insane,
Waking me from napping,
with its endless sort of rapping,
sapping and entrapping,
encroaching on my domain.

The wind was howling louder,
screaming in my ears,
with the chilling of its drilling,
amplifying fears.
The cacophony of spilling,
in not a moment milling,
with the shrilling and the swilling,
conjuring evil to appear.

And there it was I saw,
with the horror of discerning,
in the crashing and the slashng,
as everything was turning.
The window pane, then smashing,
cutting with the flashing,
in the crashing and the slashing,
everything was churning.

The room was gone in moments,
nothing to stem the tide,
no bracing in the chasing,
there was nothing on my side.
Everything was racing,
a gigantic finger tracing,
displacing and erasing;
it was then I died.

I AM LOVE

I am the warmth of wanting.
I am the peacefulness of holding,
and the passion pressing too hard.
I am hurt in the solitude of losing.
I am scars, healed helping.
I am a new friendly feeling through a moonlit night,
and arm and arm advancing in a new world.
I am passion still pressing but learning.
I am success.
I am a new life living longer as the backstop of anger.
I am the helping hands of understanding,
of hope and need of life.
I am patience practiced.
I am love.

DOUBLE HELIX

You are my friend, and
I love your soul as my own.
Your joys are mine:
Your life a mirror to image my own.

We are different,
Yet the same:
A balanced duality of oneness
that reaches into the fields of divine nature.

* * *

WORSHIP

Why worship a mythical god I cannot see
when I can worship the divinity within
the soul of my friend?

* * *

WIND

The wind sighs with despair,
stirred by the vacuum
of your absence.

Rain falls swiftly
from a weary sky,
and seeks to mask my lonely tears.

My affections are distilled
in the flask of your being.
Why aren't you here?

EVENT OF THE CENTURY

An intangible mystery of God's creation in Space;
In our time, man has begun to explore.
The celestial bodies are in prearranged place;
Man, in amazement, strives to understand more.

A giant step was the "Moon Walk" by man.
We people on earth could hardly believe!
God unveiled knowledge, guiding hearts and hands.
His power the Astronauts have received.

Americans have survived and worked in space
As they observed astronomy, the sciences of life;
Cosmonauts from Russia have joined the race.
Knowledge, united, still fails to suffice.

Stars shining in order, so sure and serene,
God smiles, as rockets cut deep through the night;
Space earthlings are bewildered by sights unseen;
Beauty so boundless in magnificence and might.

The brains of our universe try to comprehend;
Space unending, no accurate measure;
God's vibrations to mankind He sends;
Someday, more discoveries of unlimited treasures.

Giants of science make history in concentration,
Americans and our government do their part;
Astronauts are ever dedicated to this nation,
God's combined efforts; our minds hands and hearts.

Regions of the unknown beyond the sun and stars;
Astronauts are aware of lofty harmonies in space.
God now reveals fringe areas, the mystery is afar;
In eternal futures, each heart will have a place.

AVE SOL! (Martyr's Song)

The hour has come —I have to die,
I, child of King, condemned to death,
Though innocent, accused by mob.
Messiah, Saviour, be merciful till end!

Soon comes the Judgment Day of God
For criminals of His eternal Sinai Law,
On stone the only script of God to men!
They'll answer then for every deed and word . . .

The Judge is at the door—beware—
To prounce the verdict of Eternal Court,
As once to Sodom and Gomorrah
And millions perished in Deluge . . .

No sacrifice of the best of saints
Can wash away a single stain of sin,
But blood and righteousness of Christ alone,
Who died to atone all sins of everyone!

Not forever mercy last, alas!
Unrepenting sinners will be lost!
Jesus justifies, imputing and imparting His righteousness
To repenting —by faith, only while probation lasts . . .

The rays of sun and stars and silver moon
Go out and die in clouds of thunderstorm;
Never Thy love, nor mine:
It's sealed forever by immortal hand.

Sun of Worlds, Thou, God of love!
Praise to Thee for all wonders of Thy grace!
Thine forever are my heart and soul and spirit
And with roses last my greeting "*Ave Sol!*"

SUMMERSONG

I have listened to the song of the summer breeze
Blowing warm wisps of its coolness,
Brushing across my face in tenderness.
When it's not there, I miss it,
When it comes, I welcome it.
It brushes reverently—it whipers to me softly —
No summer night would be complete without a breeze.

* * *

GREEN VELVET

Green the trees, breezes within
Gently blowing leaves of all the trees
Soft your kisses under the trees . . .
Caressingly, I touch your lips and the leaves
Being close and loving too—all things green
Drinking in its cleanliness—nature, and you.

* * *

AFFINITY

Moonlight cast the shadow of your body over mine;
Lying there beside you, I slowly let my fingers fondle through
     your hair.
I let my lips kiss your forehead, I hold you tightly,
tenderly and lovingly to let you know I care,
And in the morning when the sun peeps through,
Gently kissing our bodies with its warmth from above,
I'll lean over—awakening you with more love.

VELA P. KINGSLEY

DEFINITION

The dictionary calls it fondness
A liking or desire for something;
Songs are written, words are written,
But nothing describes the merry-go-round of love.

The dictionary says affection, benevolence,
Devoted attachment for sex;
Birds sing of it, lovers express it,
But nothing describes the merry-go-round of love.

QUERIDO

Dearest—
Be my sweetheart, be my woman, be my wife;
Be the only girl in the world for me,
Delight of my life.
Be today and be tomorrow,
Be my joy and be my sorrow,
Be my happiness and moment of surprise.

Yes, my darling, you are beauty,
You are love, and you are duty,
You're a song within my heart that will not die:
You are life, you are creation;
Lovely Circe of temptation,
The rarest mystery on earth, dear, lights your eyes.

You're my pretty, you're my pleasure,
You're my wonder and my treasure;
There's a secret in your heart, love—
              You are mine.

DEDICATION

With a thousand years for learning
   the path his feet must trod;
After he learns to be human,
   then he can learn to be God.
When man dies no more forever,
   from death his hand set free;
The gift of all creation
   is the gift of humanity.

Death is only for dying,
   but doesn't need to be so;
Life itself does not wear out—
   from eternity bestowed.

It is only the body that crumbles
   with time's unyielding woe,
And this is the business of science:
   to conquer the mortal foe.
We are given voices for singing,
   our eyes for seeing it so;
The mind is the tool of eternity,
   the promise of man behold.

HOME

There is
A touch of loneliness
About the house now.

Gray are the windows,
The tree is still there;
But the birds are more at ease.

* * *

GRAVEYARD

A black tree,
Motionless;
Silhouetted against a winter sky
Of icy gray.
A lonely crow
Snarling the sounds of death,
Bringing yonder closer.

* * *

ETERNITY

Hot air trembling,
An impassible southern sun
Burning intensely
On Provencal mountains.

Does it matter anyhow
That you,
Living thing
Between busted stones and dry bushes,
Are there,
Too?

　　　　　　　　　DONNA S. KUERSTEINER

ANCIENT ELM

The skeleton of
An Ancient Elm
On the Hillside Stood.

Once the King
And Lord or Realm,
Now a tower of wood.

One wonders what
the tree beheld
beneath its spreading branches,

If caravans of
Gypsies dwelled
casting spells and trances,

Providing shade
in heat of day
for the weak and weary?

Offering cover
in damp delay
When weather there was dreary?

No more the tree
of sweeping Grace
And fountained Regal bearing,
But a mere monument
to what years erase
time etching on and wearing . . .

SLIP AWAY

To me, you know . . .
you were Michelangelo's ''David'' . . .
you were Crosby, Stills, Nash and Young . . .
you were all of the songs . . .
left in the world . . .
yet to be sung . . .
too young, they kept saying . . . he's too young . . .
a misty veil clouds my eyes, the world fades away . . .
but here comes the sun . . .for a moment or two . . .
while I was thinking of you . . .then . . .
slip away, slip away . . .
love is hiding behind another cloudy day . . .

* * *

CHANGING OF THE GUARD

Winter slides down the mountain . . .
in gushes of slush . . .
only to swing into the most beautiful . . .
fountains of Spring
on the lower slopes, where the grass has become green . . .
and the Earth wears a few early flowers in her hair . . .
. . . to witness . . . a day so fair . . .
. . . is very rare . . .
the changing of the guard . . .
from white to green . . .
a deeply moving and lovely scene . . .

PRISONERS . . . ALL!

What is a prisoner?
Need he be surrounded by walls, gates
And bars to be a prisoner?
No . . . Man can make himself a prisoner;
A prisoner of his own thoughts,
Creator of his own private prison,
Entrapped, imprisoned by his own choosing
In a situation that he seems to be chained to.
And so I say to you:
Although your body may be confined,
Never imprison your heart, your soul,
Or your mind.

* * *

DREAM ON

Don't let people belittle your dreams,
For dreams become thoughts and
Thoughts become things.

* * *

LOVE

Nourish the flower,
The plant called love
Or it will slowly die;
Before your eyes its leaves
Will gradually wither and dry

TRUST SILENCE

Trust silence, for in silence you will find yourself.
Do not fear silence, for silence can be beautiful.
Listen to the inner sound, which is your soul, speaking to you;
It's the real you, the you that really matters.
In your deepest silence there is true sound, a voice from within;
Listen, listen, LISTEN! to this powerful, strengthening, soothing,
Comforting, wise, beautiful voice from within.
It's the voice that knows everything about you.
Part of the inner sound is what you have created
Through your thoughts . . .
Stronger than what you have created through your thoughts is
The voice of god already within you, reaching out to you with
His loving, understanding arms.
So do not fear silence. Do not hate silence. Cherish these
        moments,
Because in the stillness you can communicate with God,
And will hear your own soul speaking to you.

From the seed you planted with your thoughts and deeds,
You will see, hear and feel the blossom of its results.
Do not fear silence; listen, see, feel, hear your inner being.
So many answers are there within you, so do not run
From the inner you; do not loudly block out your inner voice
By losing yourself so wildly in the physical world.
When you truly hear and communicate with your inner being,
You will not so desperately need all the sound, the noise of the
Outer world; you will no longer need to run away from yourself!
You will find peace, tranquility and all that matters within you.
You will gain new strength, new power, a new, more joyful life.
All weeds that surround you will die; lovely flowers will bloom.
Whether the sky is blue or black, you will see and feel beauty.
Through all the noise that surrounds you and through
All your restlessness, you are searching for peace; LISTEN . . .
In stillness and silence you will find it . . . waiting within you.
Learn to trust silence.

(I dedicate the above poem to the many people I know and care
    for who are afraid to be alone with their thoughts.)

MOON SPELL

I am bewitched when moonbeams softly shine,
And make a silv'ry path across the sea;
It's then the strangest, magic spell is mine,
Away from earth is where I long to be.

I'll walk into the moonbeams' gleaming way,
And to enchanted lands the path I'll take;
In moonlight's magic kingdom, there I'll stay,
I'll find a moonbeam home beside a lake.

Bewitched in silver, I'll forever dwell,
I'll dance with moonbeams, sing the moonbeam song;
I'll never wish to break this wondrous spell,
No longer to the earth will I belong.

If you would be bewitched by silver light,
Come to the sea! Come on a moonlit night!

* * *

OCEAN'S EDGE

I sit at ocean's edge,
And here I sort out my thoughts,
The troubled ones I cast
Far out to sea;

The peaceful ones
I keep within me
Where they, in time of need,
Will rise like brightest waves,
Refreshing me,
Restoring me;

What better place to sort my thoughts
Than here at ocean's edge,
INFINITYS RIM!

MERMAID MAGIC

The mermaids live in deepest caves of sea,
They sing their haunting songs the livelong day;
No one who hears their songs shall ere be free,
To doom they bring the ships that sail their way.

And as they sit and comb their golden hair,
And sing their spells to lure men to their caves;
None can resist their music, magic rare,
That mingles with the lovely sound of waves.

There was a ship, a gallant ship was she,
It sailed one day too close where mermaids dwell;
It sank in ocean's depths, and now must be
A captive held forever in their spell —

So, Sailors! Ships! And all at sea, beware
The songs the mermaids sing: *Take care! Take care!*

* * *

WEDDING ANNIVERSARY

Wedding Anniversary —
Without you;
To what far realm
Have you gone?
I cannot see you, touch you,
Feel your loving presence;

Death is so silent,
But if I am quiet, *very* quiet,
I can hear you calling me,
Telling me,
"We are not apart, EVER,
For Love is the great bridge
That spans ETERNITY!

447

FRUIT OF THE EARTH

The Curse.
What's worse —
the source of War!
So far,
It ain't up to par . . .
the Earth!
The spoils and toils
of war is a land
or a band with a hand,
A King with a ring,
A turf,
The fruit of the Earth! —Let's not spoil the fruit!

* * *

TO BE WITHOUT!

A friend.
To be with
A companion,
To build a foundation
of . . . understanding.
To understand the purpose
of the foundation.
And if understanding is *true*
Love will come.
To be without understanding is
to be without
Love!

SADNESS

I know that I love you,
And not in an ordinary way,
Never shall I know this again,
Will we ever be together, like today?

No, probably not,
Things aren't what they seem,
The way they should be,
But I'll still dream.

What will happen to me?
Will I live forever in sadness?
I don't know anymore,
But I'll survive this.

Time is a laughing man,
Laughing from dusk to dawn,
But he's giving me this moment
To linger on.

ANN F. LANNOM

SEVENTEEN

Every day is all brand new when you are Seventeen;
One day you are a princess, the next day a queen.
Love flows all around you, so near, so far;
God shines His light upon you as you reach out for your star.
Winds that kiss your fingertips, sunbeams shine for you,
You wonder where your love is, each day is all brand new.
So climb your highest mountain, reach for the furthest star,
Don't be afraid to travel to Jupiter, to Mars,
For you only have one chance at life, so live it while you may,
Put your dreams into tomorrow and think good of yesterday.

* * *

SHARON

May you use your unique beauty
    to separate wrong from right;
May you love so deeply
    with a feeling that's out of sight;
May you love so warmly
    by flowers and candlelight;
May you love so abundantly
    that your light will always shine;
And may you treasure this moment
    and the ones you leave behind.

ODE TO SNOW

Snow manifests a sense of purity;
    so white it appears
without a tiny spot dirty.

Snow displays a feeling of serenity;
    so calm it reposes
like a sleeping beauty.

Snow represents a symbol of equity;
    so thoroughly it embraces
all in its entirety.

Snow shows a look of beauty;
    so exquisitely it radiates
joy in plenty.

* * *

MISSISSIPPI

mississippi, the mighty artery of our nation:
it supplies our sources of irrigation;
it flows as a waterway for transportation;
it provides us many varieties of water fowl and fish
for our provisions of nutrition;
it helps our industrialization;
it also furnishes us with scenic spots and beaches
for our leisure pleasure and recreation.
Perhaps just seeing the river
we may feel a sense of relaxation,
and even a little reflection and meditation
by the great river's inspiration.
All in all, the magnificent river is Mother Nature's creation.

AURELIA I. LEIGH

HEAVEN AND EARTH

Among God's beauties that I shall hate to leave:
Flowering Cherry, pink and white; Red Maples,
Dogwood dressed in white, Red Bud with its purple hue,
Azaleas tall of many, varied colors,
Lilacs, and my Violet patch, Crab Apple, Elephant Ears
Broad and tall, and stately, tiny Lily of the Valley —
You can see I'm attached to God's beautiful world
And will dislike dragging myself away at the Trumpet's call,
Unless, God, you have saved some for Your Heaven.
Golden streets don't entice me, but Oh, the trees!

* * *

WHAT A DAY BRINGS

"Construction Ahead" reads the sign!
Powerful machines cut a path in a thickly wooded plot
Where trees already are giving way, dying a violent,
Sudden death, to make way for those "savers" of life,
In a hospital to rise where now the logs pile high.
Progress through destruction? The forest gives
Its life for you and me.

CREATION CONTINUED

The earth and all therein
Is constantly being renewed.
Tiny seeds, within a span of years
To big trees grow.
Spring experiences new birth
With tiny, beautiful offspring
Replenishing the earth.
Baby birds with rainbow plumage,
Kittens, puppies galore —
Man's mind, too, demands its renewing,
Whetted constantly by new ideas and challenges
Until it creates a more understanding you,
Continuing God's creation in His world of great
And small—perfection at its best.

* * *

APPRECIATION

Give some thought before it fades, to the wonders
Of a bird's song, seeing a loved one's face,
Walking on two good feet, enjoying the taste of
Good food, feeling the delicate skin of a child—
The things we take for granted and miss the most
When we can no longer use the senses formerly possessed.
Before it's too late, make happy memories, not bitter.

453

GODDESS

Goddess means: I Love You
You are more transcendent . . . than the
Heavens and the Seas
You are prettier than the flowers . . . and
more erect than the Trees
You have a smile that is perpetual . . .
and it lights up Christmas trees
You are considerate and thoughtful . . . more
than the angels above . . .
You have a look of serenity . . . that imparts
tranquility of thought . . .
Goddess means: That the world revolves around you and in
your presence . . .
I bubble with Love . . .

Thank You, God

THE PRINCESS

She is just a little Lady,
Sent from above . . .
She has a smiling Heart
Full of love . . .
She tries to please
With all her Might . . .
To achieve Perfection,
To fulfill her Life.
She has things to say,
And Things to do . . .
That makes her Unique
From any view . . .
She perceives Life's Pleasures and
Joys and
Knows she is only passing through . . .
Thank You, God

A TRIBUTE TO *ROOTS*
(WE ARE ALL AMERICANS)

From the sunny shores of Africa
Came our parent's great-great-grands,
Big and sturdy black men
To work in this strange land.

White traders rough and ready
Aboard the dark slave ship;
They whipped and tortured all alike
To hold a strong, firm grip.

The African, so proud and noble,
Knew nothing of this threat;
He gagged and wept and trembled,
Bound with chains around his neck.

Yes, black men and their women,
Young maidens pure and true,
Were forced to act their sacred vows
In shame, but did subdue.

The masters—deep in ignorance—
Thought Nothing of this deed,
Not realizing what they had done
While mixing up our breed.

The only thought the traders had
Was to safely land ashore
And sell the slaves at highest bid—
His greed was nothing more.

The slave ship landed one bright morn
With quite a few slaves left;
The ones that didn't make it here
Were thrown into the depth.

The African worked hard and long,
They hoped and prayed each day
That soon they'd be returning
To their homeland far away.

Two hundred years have passed us by—
The black man did advance—
He toiled and struggled and soon found out
He could conquer, had he the chance.

Quite true, we are all Americans
And so we hope and dream
That all of us will be regarded
And held in high esteem.

ETERNAL BEAUTY
(Dedicated to my Mother)

My soul aches with the beauty of the night—moonlit—
　　More exquisite than I can stand!
Why is this priceless beauty poured out so,
　　In this bright flood, with such a lavish hand?

The question trembles through the silent world;
　　The treetops quiver with the night's deep sigh;
The moon draws down a fragile lacy veil,
　　And my heart stills to hear the hushed reply.

This beauty—ageless through the changing years—
　　A sweep of glory, spread from pole to pole,
Is unsurpassed except for this, alone:
　　The living beauty of a lovely soul.

* * *

MARCH

March, with a lushy shout swoops into
　　town,
Cavorting rampageously up hill and
　　down:
Whooping and romping from bare tree
　　to tree,
Shaking their branches with mischievous
　　glee.

Dizzily whirling, she swings down the
　　street,
Recklessly scattering snow, rain and
　　sleet;
Snatching our hats with a boisterous
　　screech,
Impishly rolling them just out of reach!

458

Suddenly pausing, she stops her wild
   mirth,
And tenderly, warmly caresses the earth.
Winsomely smiling, now, sweetly she
   sings,
Her soft voice attuned to the whirring
   of wings.

March is a rascal—a rowdy—an imp!
Her whirlwind assaults leave us breathless and limp!
But we can forgive her for having her
   fling,
For March brings us crocuses, robins
   and spring!

* * *

HOME FOR CHRISTMAS

Ah! This is Christmas! here where festive throngs
Send ringing laughter through the frosty air;
While straying snowflakes, drifting softly, form
Their fragile lacy patterns everywhere.
The streets are gay with wreaths and candlelight,
And here and there a wide-flung door reveals
A radiant tree aglow with fairy bloom,
And children laughing with delighted squeals
Oh! happy joyous sight for homesick eyes!
Reality too wondrous to believe—
To be *at home* in this dear land of mine,
Upon this merry, merry Christmas Eve!
A hush falls now across the snowy night,
And through the dark the church bells softly chime
The old familiar carols that we love.
This is, indeed, the blessed Christmas-time.
My singing heart repeats the glad refrain
The angels sang that first blest Christmastide:
May Glory in the highest be to God,
And everlasting peace with men abide.

Do you see another baby,
Little Jesus, warm and sweet,
With the shepherds and the wise men
Laying treasures at His feet?
In a humble little stable,
Where the gentle cattle rest,
Flooded with a radiant glory
By his holy presence blest?

Do your quick ears hear the music
Of the angel choirs on high
And its echoes, soft and tender,
In His mother's lullaby?
Keep your joyous heart, oh, baby!
Keep the laughter in your soul!
May God give you grace and wisdom
With a body strong and whole!

May you see the angel's message,
When all hate and war shall cease,
Reach its glorious fulfillment,
And all nations walk in peace.

* * *

PREVIEW OF AUTUMN

(On finding a brilliantly colored "autumn" leaf on a New
                England village street early in August)

Oh! Little vagrant visitor from Autumn's cool retreat,
What brought you through the golden haze of high midsummer heat,
        heat,
When youthful August hastens after July's flying feet?

Oh! little restless wanderer, what impulse, wild and sweet,
Possessed you to remove your coat of green, so cool and neat,
And set off for gay adventure down this quiet village street?

460

Oh! little venturous spirit, in flight so light and fleet,
What eager wind could hold you, or what artist's brush repeat
This lovely flame of color, jewel-brilliant at my feet?

* * *

FASHIONS OF THE DAY

Day wakened sweetly from her night's repose,
And for her morning negligee she chose
A dainty robe of turquoise blue and rose.

Her dinner gown was styled from colors bold:
Cerise and purple with brocaded gold,
While palest yellow showed beneath a fold.

Black velvet gowned, with veils of misty white,
And silver sequins twinking in the light,
She steps out shyly now to meet the night.

OCTOBER

I saw you smile, October,
As you came flashing by,
Trailing veils of heavenly blue
Across a quiet sky.

I heard you sing, October,
As —dancing on the breeze —
You sent your merry lilting tunes
Through all the waiting trees.

I watched you work, October,
With colors bright and bold:
With strokes of orange, brilliant red,
Bronze and flaming gold.

I heard you laugh, October,
In tones of sheer delight,
To see the trees' ecstatic dance
In garments gay and bright.

I heard you sigh October,
As you stepped gravely down,
To meet sedate November.
Garbed in robes of sober brown.

* * *

MY MAGIC WISH

If I could gather all the wishes
Made since time was new,
I'd put them in a bundle, dear,
And give them all to you.

I'd wrap them in a fleecy cloud,
Tied with rainbows bright;
Fastened with a twinkling star
And cords of soft moonlight.

462

Inside I'd put one red, red rose,
Forget-me-nots of blue,
A feather from a bluebird's wing:
My magic wish for you.

* * *

WANING MOON AND STAR

A slim white moon hung, luminous,
Above the darkened doorway of the morning,
Suspended by a cord invisible
From one clear jewel, set for her adorning.

A slim white moon hung, radiant,
The fairest light of heaven's vast array;
A softly glowing lantern hung out by the night
To light the first timid steps of day.

* * *

LINES TO A LAUGHING BABY AT CHRISTMAS TIME

Tell me, little laughing baby,
What bright pictures do you see?
Do you have enchanting visions
That are hidden deep from me?
Do you see the Christmas fairies?
Do you guard their secrets well?
Do you hear a little pixie
Laughing in a Christmas bell?

Do you see the Christmas candles
Lighted by your mother's hand
While her thankful heart rejoices
For the freedom of this land?
Blessed land! Where little children
Freely play, out in the light,
And where loving mothers tuck them
Into safe warm beds at night!

463

THE SCIENTIFIC MEANING OF EASTER DISCLOSED

Easter — the joyous Resurrection!
So few people understand!
We could if we would —
It would do so much good,
Throughout this and every land.

The cruel crucifixion was
Endured by our Blessed Lord.
He could escape
Any such fate —
But he wished to fulfill God's Word.

He wanted to prove that man is of Spirit,
And not subjected to flesh!
So He rose again
From the body of pain
Which held Him as in a mesh.

Then he appeared to His disciples,
And then disappeared from their sight!
So, the flesh, He proved,
Can be removed
By a Law of Spiritual Might!

Jesus practiced a science unknown
When He raised the vibrations of flesh;
So the flesh disappeared
And then reappeared,
When the vibrations He lowered became flesh!

Astronauts of present-day fame
Would do well to look into this science —
There'd be no more trips,
In mechanical ships
But in etheric bodies, they'd place reliance!

O, Blessed Easter, how little we know!
The Bible states: "Get understanding." —(Prov. 4)
So let's get to work
And no longer shirk —
Of ourselves we must be demanding.

* * *

AN ODIOUS HAZARD

How can anyone be so vile
As to smoke smelly cigarettes all the while?
Blowing the vile smoke into nonsmokers' faces—
Causing us to make peculiar grimaces!

Good manners is something they know nothing of
As they don't care if we choke, rub our eyes and cough!
We hope someone soon will come up with a trick
To banish this bad habit that makes us all sick.

And as they don't care that for fresh air we yearn,
Let's dump all those mean smokers in a furnace and let 'em
    burn!
I don't mean they should burn just *because* they smoke,
But because they brazenly harm us. It's no joke!

They don't seem to care that their own health is at stake!
The smell of tobacco always makes my head ache.
And if they must smoke, I'd say: "Go right ahead —
But don't smoke around me —I'd rather be dead!"

THE HAND OF GOD

Beyond the blue of the distant mountain peak,
Back of the yellow loveliness of autumn leaf . . .
Beneath all things of air, or sea, or sod
There is a Creator's hand . . . the Hand of God.

For every throb upon the bed of pain,
For every tortured brow by fever slain,
For every ache of those who through pain must plod,
There is a Physician's hand . . . the Hand of God.

For every temptation along the way,
That allures, that entices to lead astray,
There is a means of defense . . . a battering rod . . .
A hand to check; it is the Hand of God.

For the grief that bows the bereaved heart,
For the sorrow that comes when loved ones part,
For the hidden woes of the trails untrod,
There is a hand to solace . . . the Hand of God.

Back of life begun in the hush of dawn
Or of that ended as shades are drawn,
Or of life flourishing, as an opening pod
There is a hand that sways . . . the Hand of God.

To the heights of joy through a service of love,
To a reward all deserving in Heaven above,
That we may tread the streets the saints have trod
There is a hand to welcome . . . it is the Hand of God.

FRIENDSHIP

Friendship is like music on dark waters,
Like sighing pines as the wind passes by,
Like pearls fresh from the deep ocean,
Like stars sprinkling the sky . . .

* * *

AT SUNSET

At Sunset —
      What is your thought?
Is it of God —or of what *you* have wrought
For gain of this world's pleasure?
Or is it placed on Heavenly Treasure?
      Is it a day nearer the brink
      Of war? oh, what do you think
            At Sunset?

At Sunset —
      Do you forgive the wrongs
Done by the individual or the throngs?
Or do you give them harbor through the night
To launch again in the morning light?
      Is it a day of forgetting the Lord?
      Is it a day of rejecting His Word?
            At Sunset?

At Sunset —
      let it be faith, and joy, and peace,
Faith in god and man, let it not cease!
Joy in service of our Lord and King,
Working through love —true in everything.
      Let it be peace! Peace of the Soul,
      Free from all sin, by Christ made whole
            At Sunset!

467

I'M SORRY

I'm sorry in this world so blue,
Where the sun shines,
Where the shadows of gloom appear,
Where winds blow heavy silence all
around us
Where your love is smiling down
from a cloud to say I'm happy.

I'm happy to live in the house of
light,
So, my love, Smile, do not cry,
so could it lead you astray
for I will melt into shining light.

* * *

IF COULD BE, LET BE
(QUESTION)

If I could fly high, I would and leave
My dreams behind like they do in the
Movies.
Over the sea, sailing high on the wind,
Only wish I could go walking to the sunset
In my bare feet, feeling the mud between my
Toes.
How I wish I were home in the valleys
where the lilies hang low.
Watch out for the man in the moon or
he will catch you and you'll be a MOON BEAM.
A star not far, a soul no more,
Nature all around.
Close one eye, then two, in time you'll see none.
Music I hear, dandelions dance, forget-me-not,
In the night I will come unto thee.

468

what are you

what are you
you're life and dream
trying to fuse
what are you
a lens setting clear
distorting too

it is through you
there was a way
that led me on
so could it lead you astray
what are you
you're a hold holding on too

what am i
a matter of fact
cynical lie
what am i
dreamingly analyzing
and always knowing why

i am aggressive antiviolent
fighting you
then asking you why
what am i
strong a man
self-piteous sigh

altruistically self-centered
schizophrenic
freakishly sly
what am i
your fairy king
your open eye

so what are we
singing our songs
dreaming our dreams
what are we
in our little ship
fighting the world's fleet

romancing on in love so deep
quarreling away
our sleep
so what are we
well it's us
it's you and me

(This poem is from the book titled *Words to Unpublished Songs,
    Poems by Harald Long,* published by H. Klingel Edition,
    P.O. Box 2878, D 2000 HAMBURG, 19, WEST
    GERMANY.)

STEVEN AT THE BAT

Eyes that twinkle at fairy tales told
A heart so pure with love that unfolds.
A cute smile with crooked teeth —
Could it be a little boy at my feet?
Uncombed hair, and dirty jeans
What are the makings of your dreams?
Strike you're out!! They called out!
And away he walks all drawn out.
He tries to pretend, oh! that was fun
But deep down inside he wished he won.

* * *

OH HONEY, WHAT DID YOU DO?

Your words are empty, meaningless,
You can't even define
What my heart wants to find.
My heart was true
But you made me blue,
Oh honey, what did you do?
You took me by surprise
Only opened up my eyes,
To see how you really are despised . . .
Now comes the time
When the old church bell rings,
And well! I've gotten back
Into the swing of things.

CREATION
(Genesis Chapters 1 & 2)

Before man or beast was ever formed
This earth a mass of darkness lay:
No moon or stars to shine by night . . .
No sun to bring forth light of day.

"Let there be light!" God's great command!
And light shone forth and beamed the earth;
Thus darkness fled and light appeared . . .
Like a newborn babe springs from its birth.

The darkest night turns bright and gay
By millions of twinkling stars on high,
The big round moon sheds brilliant light
Like God's great "flashlight" in the sky.

Green turf of grass that clothes the earth,
Tall towering trees for shade,
Sweet-scented flowers in various colors arrayed,
Add beauty and splendor everywhere.

He made fishes and whales to inhabit the ocean,
The birds of the air He gave the trees for home;
The gopher and such like choose to burrow underground,
While the beasts on land they do roam.

Thus everything was made at god's command —but man.
God took His time to form a man,
And from man's rib a woman He made,
For that was a part of His own divine plan.

In His own image made He them,
Male and female to worship Him;
Oh, let us exalt His marvelous name!
For He alone doth cleanse from sin.

M. MAY LOVELACE

EMBEZZLEMENT OF TIME

God created man and then commanded:
"Have dominion over fish, and fowl, and beast."
Man obeyed, went ahead and traveled land far and near.
He explores the depth of the ocean, and still farther on he goes,
He travels through air at highest speed, and then he strays off
    course.
He skillfully and safely invades air space, and daringly lands on
    the Moon.

"How great an accomplishment!" we declare, and really, that's a
    fact!
But restless man in his discontent places no bounds to his
    experiment.
His eyes probeth the sun in the high heavens above,
Then back to earth he studies the clock; he queries the matter,
    then
declares: "Not right! 'TIME' should later be."
He dares not, he cannot interfere with the untouchable sun,
So the clock he doth tamper with to match.

We clap in glee, we work and play, we eat and drink,
For "time" we say, "is all behind. Instead of seven, we'll make
    that
eight. And then we call it, 'DAYLIGHT SAVINGS TIME.' "

If men in business here indulge in practice such as this:
And falsify accounts to match —that sure would be a crime!
Then why should we interfere with the course which God
    Himself has
planned?
To do such things, my eardrum sings: EMBEZZLEMENT OF
    TIME!

And so, on forged time man travels along,
Happily and gaily with not even a sigh!
But birds and beasts they pay no heed;
Content they lie while man rushes by.

M. MAY LOVELACE

S.O.S. TO HEAVEN

S.O.S. to Heaven: Lord, have mercy on my soul!
The cares of life have pressed me sore and breaks my very heart;
My sin-tossed soul can find no rest, it cries out in despair,
This evil, wicked, sinful world, is tearing me apart.

S.O.S. to Heaven —God's Holy Word declares:
That evil men shall wax worse and worse in this last day and
     age:
Deceiters, traitors, covetous; blasphemers, truce breakers, proud;
My eyes doth see, my ears heareth, and my whole being sags,
     adage!

S.O.S. to Heaven —gross darkness covers the land!
Busy people everywhere—traveling to and fro;
But through earth's thunderous, boisterous scene I still can hear
Him say:
"Though your sins be scarlet red, I'll make them white as
     snow."

S.O.S. to Heaven: Lord, I fall on bended knees,
In humble, lowly, contrite heart I bow before Thy throne.
Oh, help me, Savior, how I need Thy cleansing power:
Save me, wash me, heal me, Lord, and accept me as Thy very
     own.

S.O.S. to Heaven: I thank Thee, Lord, for answered prayer,
My heart is bubbling over with joy, my soul hath found its rest.
And now in Thee, without a doubt, I'm completely satisfied,
I'll have no cause for worry or regret, for I know this is the
best.

"Cast your burden upon the Lord, and He shall sustain thee."
                              (Ps. 55:22)

473

ADAM AND EVE

And God said, Let us make men in Our image, after Our likeness . . . So God created man in His own image, in the image of God
created He him. And the Lord God said, It is not good that the man
should be alone; I will make ham an help meet for him. And the Lord
God caused a deep sleep to fall upon Adam, and he slept: and He took
one of his ribs, and closed up the flesh instead therof; And the rib,
which the Lord God had taken from man, made He a woman, and
brought her unto the man. And Adam said, This is now bone of my
bones, and flesh of my flesh: she shall be called Woman, because she
was taken out of Man. Therefore shall a man leave his father and his
mother, and shall cleave unto his wife: and they shall be one flesh.
(Gen. 1:26,27; 2:18, 21-24).

* * *

LONELINESS

Loneliness! Oh, what sad endurance!
E'en though one may possess much wealth
and home;
For, said the Creator in the beginning:
"Not good that man should live alone."

The lonely heart cries out for love,
Amidst turmoil, cries out in fear;
It reaches out in deepest need,
And sometimes gives up in despair.

Oh, pitiful soul that has never been loved!
Nor has never loved as well:
For how can one give that he has never received?
The worth! The fulfillment! How can he ever tell?

There is hope from above for all who will look up
And accept what is freely offered to all;
For with Christ one need never be lonely,
He is ever present to answer each call.

ANONYMOUS WRITER

I sought not for fame or world reknown
When I took up my pen to make this known.
Oh, no, not fame —fortune, maybe,
And to share my experience with all, you see.

So if you have been helped by what you've read,
I am glad you received it before you're dead.
Just look and see if there's someone around,
And pass on the good news of what you have found.

I passed it on to you —no bones about that!
Now, all you're doing is just yak-e-ti-yak!!
But while you are there with your hacking cough,
I just sit here at home and have a good laugh.

I am not a hermit as some of you think,
Just a normal being, sometimes even on the rink.
And quite often, unknowingly in everyone's view,
I am usually right there staring at you.

* * *

OLD MOTHER HEN

Once I was a chicken,
Now a mother hen.
Once a brood I followed,
Now the brood I tend.

Once carefree I wandered
While Mama gave to me,
Now I have to hustle
As busy as a bee.

No fun to scratch in search of food
From dawn till setting sun.
And if a little rest I take,
The brood sets off a-run.

I have to go in swift pursuit
In search of my little flock,
And if nowhere in sight they be,
I just give a loud "cluck! cluck!!"

They all come running back to me
As fast as they can make it,
And then I start all over again
To satisfy their craving.

But that makes them grow much faster —
That I can clearly see.
Soon I will chase them all away:
Mama did that to me.

* * *

BUM, HOBO, AND TRAMP

Bum, Hobo, and Tramp —those are my three dogs,
Oh, boy, how they like to be on the run!
Why did I give them such weird names?
Ah, well I'd simply say, just for fun.

Truly, Bum isn't a bum as bums really are,
He's so smart and really likes to be on the go:
He brings in the papers, and takes out the trash,
And wags his tail always to both friend and foe.

Hobo, the next, he follows the same trail,
Every morning, as a rule, he gets up at six.
And if ever he looks around and finds nothing to do,
Oh, boy! that sure gets him in a fix.

He'll bark and he'll jiggle, and pull your coat, too,
And naught can you do to quiet him down.
But he'll settle for less if you'll just say to him:
"Now, you go and roll over on the ground!"

476

Tramp—he's a tramp all right as tramps are indeed,
For he's never around —he wanders day by day.
He prowls and he travels from one place to another,
And quite often he leads the others astray.

One morning quite early I got out of bed,
But none of the three was anywhere in sight.
I thought and I wondered—I looked here and there;
"They are somewhere a-hiding! I hope I am right!"

I traveled and searched for those three little brats,
I crossed streets and alleys till I reached under the ramp.
By chance I looked up into six eyes staring down at me:
If you guessed whose they were, you're right! Bum, Hobo,
and Tramp! (What do ya know!)

EVENING IN THE VALLEY

Slowly, and with precision,
   Each star comes into view,
And slow but sure the village windows
   Bring forth their lights anew.
Just before the sunset
   We heard the last bird's song,
And we step outdoors to enjoy the silence
   And feel that nothing is wrong.
When you want to receive a blessing
   Drink in this peace serene,
Breathe in deeper and close your eyes
   And you'll feel God has washed you clean.
The Power of God's Presence is rich indeed,
   It will bring to your life all that you need.
Ask the Lord for forgiveness, forgive all others, too,
   Then your mistakes and harsh words
     Will be forgiven you.
   Give thanks for your blessings,
     Past and present too,
And if you give thanks in advance for things,
   You'll be surprised what God will do.

* * *

THE MIND OF CHRIST

Thank You, Jesus, for dying for me
   On the Cross of Calvary.
Now forgive me of my sins,
   Let me feel Your love and power within.
My faith in You I now confess . . .
   To Your Will I say a definite, "Yes!"
I praise You for rising from the dead
   You took my burden of sin and died in my stead.
I'm thankful the Kingdom of God is within
   Come reign in my heart and keep me from sin.
The Mind of Christ I now adopt.
   My carnal thinking now is stopped.

I accept You as my Saviour
  And Your promise of eternal life,
And with joy I turn away from this world of strife.
  Help me, Jesus, to never stray,
I want to always walk in the Way,
  The Truth, and the Life.
Thank You for showing me the Light.
  I'll try to serve You all my life.
I believe You are Divine. I am Yours and You are mine.
  I love You and You love me . . .
I belive in the Holy Trinity.
  Thank you, God, for answer to prayer,
I feel safe when I know You're here, there, and everywhere.
  In the Name of the Father, and of the Son,
And of the Holy Spirit . . . Amen.

* * *

POETRY AND MUSIC

Poetry is music of a softer tone
First heard by the inner ear,
The voices of angels exchanging their views
That men may rise, if they'll hear.
The glory of God in the dawning
Is like the poet's rapturous thrill,
As he pens the words they are giving
That men may read and be filled.
Do a lot of deep breathing
In a quiet, restful pose,
Then health and wonders of the higher planes
To you will be disclosed.
So many inspiring lessons
Are given in angels' talks,
We mortals have but to meditate
To join their celestial walks.
Yea, volumes of poems and music
And prose of the highest type,
Go floating off in ether
If we don't get up and write.

HAROLD P. LUCY

THIS WAS MY COUNTRY

Yes, it was a brave and shining land,
fathered by demigods. For even though
the teachers of my early youth did never
call them demigods, they later did
refer to mud-slinging historians
possessing shabby taste and treasonous
propensity to show some smudges on
the shining coats of armor flaunted by
the fathers. It was the land of the free and home
of the brave. This meant, the land belonged to the free,
not to the slaves. And patriotic mobs
were tools, and symbols, and the very substance
of democracy in my childish view;
ideas that are like the adolescent
views of modern youths. "My country, right
or wrong, but my country." Brave and tinseled words,
unlike the syllables of modern youths.
In youth I worshiped the revolutionaries
of earlier times. But modern youths, who worship
nothing but themselves, adore their own
cute images as revolutionaries,
condemning this, or that, or anything,
or, perfunctorily, everything.
My country was all-powerful, all-right,
possessing boundless resources. But today
I see it thwarted in, and by, a little
nation on the far side of the world,
its mineral resources largely gone,
and its dependences on foreign sources
flourishing apace, and yet with fools
reviling those who urge our change of habits
that are the most destructive ever seen.
In swine-sight they proclaim, "As long as any
substance lasts let's use it up. Let coming
generations deal with absence of
our mined resources. ——After us the drought!"
And yet, such fools have always blocked our progress.

I look about and see democracy
in neither local, state, nor federal law.
But, thanks to the recorders of mud, I know
we never had democracy. Our land
is not now going to the dogs, for it
has always been surrounded by the dogs.
Our people never had the vision and
the fortitude to try democracy.
We never had proportioned presences
in Congress. We never had a government
respecting human rights; states' rights and other
will-'o-the-wisps have always superseded.
We never had a system of justice, owning
only a system of lawyer-advantaged laws,
the cretin child of a bastard trial by combat.
So, the muddied histories have served
us well. A realistic view of yore
tends strongly to relieve despondent views
of now and morrow. Just as mobs are not
the method or the fact of democracy
today, they also never were in the past.

There's room for a trial stance of optimism.

But in this dubious euphoria
two nagging questions stand: Is our resource
in vision, understanding, expertise
in democratic process better now
remarkably than it was yesterday?
Can a people such as we, so madly
infatuated with the hedonistic
myth of irresponsibility,
sometime acquire the wisdom and the guts
to love the only freedom that exists,
complete and glad responsibility?

EARLY MORNING

The day is new. A fresh start.
Yesterday's problems look different.
Some are bigger, some lesser.
Who shall say what should be first?
One's conscience, being rested, must
    settle all this.
The world is waiting for greatness:
Not the greatness of office
Nor pompous greatness,
But a big heart and spirit
That leaves itself behind
To help others, to have right,
To speak experience, do more.
Time will sort us out.

* * *

IOWA INFINITE

Bisons, coyotes, cougars, prairie hens
Flourished in wilds around the Sioux and Sac.
Came wagon trains with all that they could pack.
Then white men drove them from their native dens.
School, churches, farms with animals in pens,
A burgeoning culture came along the track,
So Easterners never did go back.
Thus wild animals forsook their dens.

Today the highways, industries and schools
Provide technology, fine arts, athletics, too.
Super-developments keep coming in to stay.

Our state now has the quality, the brains, the tools
To build, replenish, refurbish and renew.
Today the highways, industries and schools
Provide techniques, fine arts, athletics, too.
Iowa's ascendancy has come to stay.

HAD YOU HEARD?

The thing is incredible, but it must be true.
It was on TV out in full view.
And did you see what the paper said?
I wouldn't believe it until I had read.
The speaker today in his final remark
Had something I thought should be kept in the dark.
Though I dare not tell some things that I know
They surely would make a wonderful show.

ELNA MCBEE

LIVE FOR OTHERS—TODAY

We only pass this way one time,
   it's but a span so brief;
so what our God has blessed us with
   it is not ours to keep!
Our kindness we're to give away,
   the warmth of our bright smile,
forgiving one another NOW—
   TODAY—Don't wait a while!

It's in caring and in sharing,
   in our laughter and our tears,
as we live we're touching others
   through the days and through the years.
Our lives are like a vapor here . . .
   we vanish—soon—away—
let's give each other happiness
   while we enjoy TODAY.

Look for the best in everyone
   there's good in every life;
live peacably within—without—
   and free from doubt and strife;
unselfish in our attitudes
   and careful what we say,
don't hurt or hinder anyone . . .
   help—lovingly—TODAY.

BEYOND THE STARS

When the arms of the night
Close around the trees,
And a mysterious aura
Lends itself to the earth;
While the stars sparkle and tease,
I look out and wonder
About the daylight's worth;
The day brings noise, confusion,
And a running pace;
The glare of the sun
Makes all seem sordid,
As we race to beat time
Rushing past a stranger's face.
The night offers an alternative—
When we can look into our souls,
For, in the darkness
We're in a timeless state
Where we can plan
What may be extolled.
The inspiration of the night is endless
Like the black depth overhead,
And beyond the stars
We may look and find bliss
And answers to the questions
The day has made.
So let the arms of the night
Enclose, embrace you;
Forget the confusion—shadow the glare
And do look up—beyond the stars:
The answers are there.

PERILOUS JOURNEY

Somewhere in the middle of nowhere
  Flying high through the clouds they go,
Soaring their way toward the north lands
  Along the air lane where wild rivers flow.

Gentle winds plead, "Give them safe passage,
  'Cause the perils of their journey are great,"
Down through the ages they pass timely—
  Not heading—destiny will guide their fate.

Why do they make the perilous journey
  To nest by the silent, cold, arctic sea,
Who knows why the wild geese go farther—
  Do winds whisper, "Go where the world is free."

Listen, my friends—wild geese are honkin',
  The familiar formation is passing o'er,
They tell the world, "Our babes are with us,"
  The winds tell the world, "They made it once more."

* * *

WHERE TIME STANDS STILL

Come sit with us and rest, old pardner,
  In the shade of this rugged pine tree,
Mountain winds whisper strains of long ago
  As though Mozart was playing softly.

We can watch the clouds go floating along
  Like a white swan out on the lake,
Or listen to a few concerts by the crickets
  As they wait for all the world to awake.

486

We'll wait for the deer that wander down
    To graze close where the brook is flowing,
Where the lone eagle soars o'er the rocky cliffs
    And purple columbines are always growing.

This place is truly, "Where Time Stands Still,"
    A paradise carved by the ages of time—
Pardner—there's no need to hurry 'round here,
    Just linger on—in this grandeur sublime.

ARTIE NETTLES McCOY

DRAMA OF A NIGHT

Gleaming in the north's winter white,
   Frosty diamonds in the moon's eerie light;
A wolf's shadowy form with head bent low,
   Follows man-made tracks in the snow.
Stealthy in the shadows the creature keeps.
   As nearer to the man's cabin it creeps;
Watches the weary man bent beneath a load;
   Watches him enter his humble abode.

The man stirs to bank the fire,
   A good night's sleep his one desire;
Feels pressing in the solitude,
   Awakening more the lonely mood.
Gladly would he escape into slumber,
   The dreary thoughts that encumber;
He sees not the woodland diamond set,
   But counts the pelts he has net.

Pelts from creatures wild and free
   That roamed the wooded fearie;
Lapped water from a crystal brook;
   Played with their young in a sunny nook;
Searched for food by sense of smell,
   Communed by keen sense as well.
To live in their natural habitat,
   They asked naught of man than that.

The lone wolf, in search of his mate,
   Links the man with the she-wolf's fate;
Lifts his head skyward, lamenting woes,
   And from the hills his voice echoes;
From the dark trees is joined by others
   For a wolf pack, yet are brothers.
The howling reaches the sleeper's ears,
   And his dreams interpret what he hears.

Dreaming he stands at hell's open door,
   Hearing the wailing of those gone before;
The devil is signing newcomers in,
   Directing, he says: "I want this one's skin."
The man leaps up awake, hears a dozen or more
   Howling wolves outside his door;
Gropes to light the lantern on the wall,
   Sees from each object its shadow fall.

He throws open wide the door,
   His shadow, like a spirit, goes before.
The wolf knows not, nor cares not why,
   He lifted his head heavenward to cry.
The pack had lent their voices to his own,
   And by sharing, some solace is known;
Somberly, he trots away in the night,
   The others slink into shadows out of sight.

Alone in the northwood, cold and still,
   The man cries accusingly to the silent hills;
"Demons of loneliness, harborers of woe!"
   The hills sling back the mad echo.
He sees shining forth the morning star;
   Thinks of the wise men that traveled afar;
Wonders if God knows or cares for such as he,
   With starving soul, he prays on bended knee.

"Why, oh spirit of man, doubt you so long?"
   Came the answer, his heart leaped with song.
Soaring, his spirit is touched, strength given,
   He weeps that he knew not reason for living;
Weeps for the wasted years, prepares to depart;
   Leaves the north wood with joyful heart,
And the awesome silence in the minutes after,
   Is broken by an owl's exuberant laughter.

LORD, GUIDE HIS FOOTSTEPS HOMEWARD

Lord of all creation,
Dispenser of goodness and mercy,
Look down today in Thy infinite mercy
Upon the storm-tossed life of one we love.

Help him to see the intentions of others,
And know that they only wish to be kind.
Reach down, Oh Lord, and sustain him,
Let not his feet go astray;
Heal the wounds of lost hope and endeavors
Renew his faith today.

Wherever he is, Dear Father,
Let him know that someone cares,
Guide his wandering footsteps homeward
Where weary hearts will understand.

VIRGINIA IV

I never thought
     we
Would share a
     windy
Midnight beach. Nothing
     between
Us but gentle
     foam
And glowing sea-sparks.
     Your
Hand tells me
     you
Love me —a
     message
Timeless as the
     waves
Which whisper to
     us
Now. The passing
     years
Cannot erase love
     touched
By foam and
     sea-sparks
On a midnight
     beach.

PAUL

Serious brown eyes.
                My
Friend. Hair blowing
                over
His ears. A
                smile
When I return
                home
Is his silent
                greeting.
Tickles his brother
                and
Laughs.

* * *

ALAN

Hamsters and cookies.
                Pure
Joy and celebration
                of
Life. Laughter and
                song.
He is my
                son.

ADRIENNE D. MCGILLICUDDY

UNITED
(An Anthem)

United States of America!
United! United! We stand for thee!
One nation of allegiance and equality.
One way of life and liberty.
The land of a country.
The blood of a people.
The love undivided
Under Heaven above!

United States of America!
All mighty! A fortress of the free!
One Constitution equanimity.
One Bill of Rights for eternity.
The house of a person.
The community at large.
The rights individual
In America I love!

United States of America!
United! United! We sing to thee!
One leader by election, will, infinity.
One Congress by selection of ability.

The choice of the many.
The consideration free.
The glory in the banner
Of United States beloved!

STARLIT

Have you ever crossed the river
On a swinging bridge
In the dark of the night?
With only little fireflies
For a light?
They are diamonds in the night,
Lighting the way
Like the stars light the Milky Way.

* * *

EQUINOX

Pretty yellow rose,
Growing by the garden wall.
Soon your beauty will fade and fall
And I'll forget you,
Till I hear a robin sing.
And once again it's Spring—
With pretty yellow roses
Growing by the garden wall.

* * *

SWEET SONG

Little songbird, winging through the sky.
Stop at my window on your way by
And sing a pretty song
To cheer me all day long.
Before you journey on,
You will find sweet cherries
In the top of the tree
All for your kindness to me.
Bye-bye, little songbird,
winging through the sky.
Stop again as you pass by.

494

MY PLACE

Wandering near the old mill pond
The stranger stopped to rest,
His weary legs had walked all day,
His feet had done thier best.

The loose-fitting coat was not his size,
The sleeves hung over his hands,
The baggy pants were patched and worn,
They had trailed across many lands.

He sat on a rock at the water's edge
Brushing the dust from his clothes,
The battered shoes he rubbed with care
As if he were proud of those.

An old top hat sat on his head,
Almost touching his ears,
The tattered brim clearly showed,
It had seen some better years.

A soft gentle breeze cooled his brow,
A smile showed on his face,
He settled back and then he said,
"I think I have found my place."

THE VILLAGE

The American small town on a Saturday afternoon is the
locale of many scenes. On various street corners groups of
ten or fifteen men may be seen leaning against all available
uprights and calmly rehashing the week's events. An
occasional fat cheek denotes an extra large "chaw" of
tobacco running the gauntlet of bicuspids.
Busily engaged in dodging the expectorations of these men
may be a dog or even a cat that has been abandoned by
some poverty stricken family.
In contrast to these shabby street corner philosophers,
occasionally a young lady, done well in pink or blue and
apparantly aloof from it all, might be observed stolling along
the avenue. However, if one were to notice closely, a look
of disgust might become discernible, for one of the men in
the group is probably her father.

THE WAITING ROOM GAME

'Tis a game we women play,
    sad to say most every day.
Waiting for that plumber to
    come and fix the sink.
And where the heck is the
    garbage man?
I sure don't like the stink!
The maid I've had for years
    and years
Has worked from dawn 'til dusk.
My kids are waiting,
wanting Gram to read
to them—
or sing or dance a few.
If I've become a "doormat"—
and that hated word
    applies—
I might as well admit it,
And dry my tearful eyes.

LOOK AT DEME

It seems as if it were only yesterday,
When I heard my baby cry—
Look at Deme,
She's a big girl now.
I held her in my arms and
Thanked God for His blessings—
Look at Deme,
She's a big girl now.

I've felt the pains of growing—
The laughter and tears,
Just looking at my little girl
I just don't see the years.
Look at Deme,
She's a big girl now.
She soon will be eight then nine and ten,
Before I know it
She will be a grown lady and then . . .
Look at deme,
She's a big girl now.
I love her now and I'll love her then
Because she's my little girl;
Look at Deme,
She's a big girl now.

MOM

Mom didn't have to keep us,
Mom didn't have to care.
But when we were all frightenend
Well, Mom was always there.
She started with the nine of us,
She did it all alone,
No matter what we said or did
We always had our home.
Through all the years of ups and downs
She somehow got two more.
She took them in and loved them
And Mom was always sure
She had the same love for them
And to spare, well . . . she had more.
So remember when you're mad at her
And you don't come around,
Mom didn't have to keep us—
She could have turned us down.

MEASURE MY LOVE IN DREAMS

If I could measure my love
with a spoon,
With one small sifting
I'd reach for the moon.

If I could capture the song
of the hummingbird,
I'd sing them to you
without a word.

I'd listen to his melody
so sweet and so true,
And with my pen
I'd write the words for you.

If the beauty of a rose could
never fade, and its fragrance
remain true,
Then I'd capture the sweet smell
of the raindrops
and save them for you.

TIME TO THINK

In early morn
I seek this time to think
Upon the beauties of the earth
And the whitecaps of the sea,
And pray for wisdom
To meet the duties of the oncoming day
And the strength to endure.
Then give thanks for the fulfillment
And the closing of another day.

In early morn
I seek this time
To go about the duties I must perform,
As quickly and quietly as the unfolding
Of the primrose on a warm summer day.

In early morn
I seek this time to walk
Down the winding path
That passes by the primrose,
As I listen to the morning song
Of the meadowlark not too far away.

In early morn
I seek this time to think
About my faithful friends,
The kindnesses they have performed,
The constant care,
The time they spent to release me
From my loneliness.

In early morn
I seek this time
To watch the rising sun,
And to feel the warmth that inspires
All forms of life to grow.
In early morn I set aside
This time to think.

501

REMEMBERING

Remembering well my childhood days
Were filled, more so as I grew older,
The need of me, I thought
To help some form of life or other.

Did you ever, while walking in the park,
Down by the pond, stop to help
A nonswimmer in distress, like a beetle or a bee?
You threw it a leaf or a twig of a tree,
Then pondered about the man
Who walked upon the sea.
And the spider that's skipping on top
Of the water just in front of thee.

As I walked along the winding path
How hard I tried one day
To help a butterfly
To lift its wings and try to fly.
Little I knew,
For I was much too young to understand
Its days of life were gone.
Little I knew
About the life of a butterfly.

Very gently
I placed it in my hand,
So beautiful, yet so delicate
I dared not touch it more.

There before my very eyes
Its life expired.
I wondered: why
A thing so beautiful
Had to die.

Carefully I placed it between two leaves
Sad as I could be,
I showed it to my mother;
Soon I was much the wiser
From the story that was told to me
About the life of a butterfly.

* * *

SEARCHING

My daily walks
Upon the sand along the shore,
And listening to the tragic stories
Of the singing shells, and the driftwood
From the sinking ship, far out at sea,
Makes no happy moments
While walking on the sand, for me.

The moon's effect upon the sea
Brings the restless waters to my feet
That carries the stories of the deep.

I gaze far out upon the sea
And hear the cries of tragedy,
And the roaring waves that pound the shore,
That never cease.

On my daily walks along the shore
Upon the shifting sands,
As I gathered up the seashells
I found a silver bell.
It tolled about the wedding
And the tragedy
That happened on the sinking ship
Miles far out at sea.
In the twirling waves the ship
was broken into two,
The bride lost the bridegroom,
The ring and the tiara, too.

503

I held the silvery bell
Close to my beating heart.
It told me that I'd find
The bridgroom and the ring
Upon an island in the sea.
I, being the bride,
Searched, and searched, in time I found
The sacred vow, the ring
Still clutched within his hand.

MEDITATION

Cathedral set among the pines,
Wind whispering a message from the Divine.
Sitting for a moment to meditate,
Radiantly surrounded as he relates,
Feeling the vibrations in my body move,
He changed my aspirations and every mood.
A lovely light shone in my heart,
Lingering shortly, as if never to part.
As I arose to complete my day
I knew he was there never to stray,
Leading me more to enlightening ways
Enjoying perfect moments of solitude,
Giving me strength and fortitude.

* * *

TEA PARTY

The East India Company was about to succumb;
Appealing to its government for additional funds
Parliament passed a duty-free bill,
Refunding to the company the tea tax frills
It made the colonies want to fell.
'Cause East India Company could undersell.
Fear of affecting other commodities besides tea,
Colonial merchants wanted to disregard the fee.
The Sons of Liberty could not heed,
When told what the Governor had decreed.
Sound of war whoops and the cries were loud,
Boarding the ships—the roaring crowd—
Tea chests were thrown overboard into Boston Harbor,
Destroying much of the British Charter.
The King's efforts to punish the patriots' move,
Led to the war that eventually grew.

505

LIFE'S MUSICIANS

A lover's laments keep time to a country fiddle,
While love's celebrations are scored with violins.
A nasal twang complains and bitches,
The melodious tune praises and thanks.
Would all my life be scored with full orchestration
With never a country beat
Oh, that I could hear only the lovely music
No matter the life's musician's I meet

* * *

TO BE FREE

When will I be free?
Free to be me and do and feel
Only for me and to know
What and who I am.

The pull by others chokes and binds
My expression and realization of self,
And leaves me too exhausted
to discover mine.

When will I learn to wisely choose,
To not deal with what us not for me
In this road's toad to growth,
And at last come into my own?

A POEM IS MY EXPRESSION

A poem is my expression
Of my innermost heart's thoughts,
A way to say what I'm feeling
In words, in rhyme, in prose.

Poems lend themselves to saying
What lies within my heart,
In form that is clear and terse and short.

So get into my poems I pour my heart,
    I set down my life's thoughts.
And on the paper upon which I write,
Is my life both dark and bright.

* * *

VALUE THIS JOURNEY

I exit in nothingness
My head empty—my heart canceled out—
Days are dreary and blank,
Like is dead-ended.
Stir up the happenings,
Jazz up for living
Go—do—move—reach out
Grab each moment—reject emptiness—
Value this journey.

507

WASTEFUL WISTFULLNESS

I dwell again the elusive land of imagination
Resplendent with precarious dreams and poetic fantasies
And life is dazzling and filled with rich emotions.
My lyrical script is borne up with joy and hope,
And I am met with vivid, overflowing happiness.
I revel in rapture that is complete and abiding,
And desires are fulfilled that are noble and enduring.
I yearn to stay forever in this blissful contentment,
But melancholy mourning seeps into my joyous journey,
And I return to the familiar chasm between fantasy and reality
Neither proceeding nor retreating.
I sink once more into wasteful wistfulness.

ECKANKAR, A WAY OF LIFE

Through ECKANKAR we can find out who we are,
Where we're from where we're going
And what we'll do when we get there.
We can find out about the world we live in
And the myriads of worlds beyond the physical—
Exploring their unfathomable magnitude.
We do this through contemplation and initiations.
CONTEMPLATION gives us momentum,
Deepens our inspiration, crystallizes our plans
And increases our awareness or understanding.
INITIATIONS are the means to reactivate
The sacred forces within the individual—
Increasing the awareness of the spiritual life.
The goals of ECKANKAR are Self-Realization,
God-Realization and BEING a co-worker with God.

* * *

I LOVE LIFE

I love life. I love life.
The very thought of it
Sends me into flights of awe,
Untinged with fear
At its stupendous magnitude.

To be a part of it
Is the supreme privilege
For which I am eternally grateful—
KNOWING that without God's love
I wouldn't BE.

"SOUL EXISTS BECAUSE OF GOD'S LOVE FOR IT."

(The desires and love expressed in the following songs
Seem almost sensual in nature, until one remembers
That they are addressed to God. The words and music
Were written by [Sri Darwin Gross,] the Mahanta,
The Living ECK Master [record or tape IT JUST IS].)

* * *

IT JUST IS

Thank you with love. It just is for you alone.
The walks we took among the stars.
The words were few as we sailed through the cosmic sea.
With the clasp of our hands we became one
Where the foot of man has never trod
And only Soul can journey.
I'm thankful for these moments you shared with me this night.
Your unselfishness goes beyond time and space.
For we have sailed the cosmic sea of life. For it just is.

WITH ECKANKAR

To understand the Master's words
Let the Spirit of ECK flow through.
It must be free to flow through you,
To share Its wisdom from the heavens above.
The fruits of the Spirit, the gifts of God.
Most Souls are seeking peace, health,
Love, you, and prosperity,
The timid never find true love and happiness,
But the bold do.
Kneel before the Spirit in true humbleness,
And say, "I surrender my will to You, O Lord.
Do what you will with me."
Let your mind dwell in the sea of Spirit
To be lifted above your daily problems.
Then you are in this world, but not of it.
Once grasp the Great Form without form
And you roam where you will,
With no evil to fear,
Calm, peaceful, and at ease with ECKANKAR.

AT THE GRASS ROOTS

I'd like to pass on the feeling
Of great joy I've found in ECKANKAR
For those who have ears to hear.
For I too have had a longing deep inside,
Never knowing where to hide,
For one day up, the next day down.
No longer am I tied to this earth world,
Its troubles or woe.
I have no fear of death no more
Since on the path of ECK (Spirit).
Greater is he that ruleth his own Spirit
Than taketh a city, for inward rulership
Is the mast'ry of the Masters.
This too can be yours.
For those at the grass roots
And those in doubt who just don't understand,
Let your ears hear these few words:
Give no thought of where you are
For the Master is always with you,
For in Soul you can be free.

* * *

OH, HOW I LOVE THEE, BLESSED SUGMAD (God)

Oh, how I love Thee, Blessed SUGMAD,
With all my heart, Soul, mind and strength.

I'M SITTING ON TOP OF THE WORLD

I'm sitting on top of the world,
Sailing the cosmic sea of life.
In this world, but not of it,
Living in the Ocean of Love and Mercy—
The very heart of God, the SUGMAD.

I'm a cell in ITS body, a drop
In ITS Ocean of Love and Mercy—
The living truth that IT IS.
The blessings IT pours on me are:
Merciful love, protection and guidance.

ITS voice is a luminous musical wave
Guiding me, in melodious strains,
Back to my true home again—
The kingdom of Heaven—
As a co-worker with God.

ITS pillars are LIGHT and SOUND.
I look and see the Light, which is knowledge,
Illuminating the way for me to see the pitfalls
And to recognize the many ways I can serve IT
NOW in this lifetime and throughout eternity.

I listen and I hear the Sound, ITS melodious voice,
Telling me ITS abode is within my heart.
ITS presence is as close as my breath and heartbeat.
IT is in me and I am in IT—
The all-embracing God, the SUGMAD.

Oh, how I thank Thee for Thy Presence,
For I know Thou art always with me.
For I thank Thee for Thy Light and Sound
To lead me homeward bound.
I'd be like a fallen leaf you see,
Just bouncing all around.

For the love I have for SUGMAD
Goes forth a radiant HU,
For I've come a long, long way
From home, it's true.
Oh, how I thank Thee, Blessed SUGMAD,
For Thy true words, the Shabda Sound.

* * *

YOU CAN MOVE MOUNTAINS [Sri Darwin Gross]

You can move mountains with ECK at your side.
You can go anywhere that you decide.
There is no stopping those who know the ECK (Spirit).
Life of an ECKist is of a new spiritual freedom.
It is this special attitude of balancing the mind,
To dwell upon the great Divine.
This Light within you when chanted HU
Brings forth the knowledge that's given to you.
No one can tell you what you should eat or do.
Life of an ECKist is of a new spiritual culture.

* * *

I LOVE TO HU [Sri Darwin Gross]

I love to HU. I love to HU.
I love to HU the whole day through.
If you just HU the whole day through,
You'll find your days just pass away—
For I love to HU.
I love to love you each moment of the day.
In every blessed way.
Just with the Divine HU.
I love to love you within the Light and Sound,
Which is a HU as seen and heard through the HU.

(NOTE: HU is the universal name for God. HU is the highest vibrational
sound. HU is the original word current— the source of all motions,
forces, lights, sounds and elements. Human=Godman.)

MAN'S APPEAL TO GOD

Paul Twitchell tells us in **The Far Country** that
"Man is a god clothed in rags, he is a
Master of the universe going about
Begging a crust of bread. He is a king
Prostrated before his own servants,
A prisoner walled in by his own ignorance.
He could be free. He has only to
Walk out of his self-constructed prison,
For none holds him there but himself."
In the Flute of God, he says:
"Man's appeal to God is: 'How can I become
A channel for thy great work?' The answer is simple.
Think, Feel and Act. That is all there is to it,
When combined with Beauty, Love and Wisdom."
So, if all our thoughts are uplifting,
Our feelings motivated by love,
And our actions tempered with wisdom;
We will be a clear channel
For God to pour ITS love into the world.

(NOTE: For information on ECKANKAR write: ECKANKAR, P.O.
Box 3100, Menlo Park, CA 94025.)

MY LIFE

My life I see as a fallen tree,
　　its roots left barren,
　　its limbs left free.

　　My life I see,
　as a withered flower,
　　left to die,
　at noonday hour.

* * *

A GENTLE BREEZE

I caught it in a gentle breeze,
　though times, like seasons fade,
and clash against a darkened sky,
　　I bid it on its way.

On summer nights I sit and rest,
　　beneath a starry sky,
　and listen to it howl away,
　　until the morning rise.

Often do I see it dance,
　across a trembling sea,
and often do I hear her voice,
　echo soft to me

A WORM'S VIEW

One evening I walked through a dark alley
And spotted a large earthworm crawling
Upon the rough surface of asphalt.
I stopped to observe its slow accordionlike body
Extending and retracting over loose pebbles,
Inching toward a turf of damp grass.
A wet wave of fascination splashed against me,
Allowing me to observe the lumbricus
At a tongue's distance.

A rubber head coiled outward,
And a fleshy slit of a mouth
Took shape from the pulpy mass and spoke.
My eardrums were opened,
And a voice scarcelly audible penetrated my ears.
The words formed within my head reading:
Young man, Consider the worm in its season.
It will speak of a new world,
And the destruction of the old earth.
Look at the air surrounding you, and the people
Who talk like parrots.
These will be the days when missiles blaze close to houses
Starked with heat, diffusing atoms,
Numbing the air with pastelike acid.
Radiation will cluster the sky a yellowish-orange,
And the earth will yield an acrid stench of scorched humans,
Whose lungs will be permeated
With cobalt-60.

WE AGE

We watch the days grow cold and gray
Birds slip through wind like fluttering leaves
Mist and rain soak the ground
A sponge for men to suck the sound—
Of mumbling people tired and old
Chewing the thoughts of death and age;
Stale gum and breath mints
Coat our throats
With a corduroy sweetness,
And you cry because my jeans are old,
Patched and torn with soil and mold.

Fret not at my crusty pants,
They march through time without the thought
Of growing cold or gray.

* * *

ANGER

I saw your anger gallop.
Hoofs clacking against asphalt,
Crushing red ants.
Your steel shoes
Ground pebbles into fine sand.
You approached a high wall
And your face lit up like a torch.
You leaped into the air like a Titan missile
And exploded.

MY DEAREST GIRLS:

Yesterday I wandered down the lane
And thought of when you walked with me
Down that very selfsame path
And laughed at all there was to see—
The peach tree still has in the crotch
The old and rusty horse's shoe;
The horse is in the field next door,
And every time I pass he asks of you—
At least I really think he does.
I know he's asking something, that I do.
He always leans across the fence,
I'm sure he's asking me of you.

I saw the other day he needed shoes.
If he knew a shoe grew in the tree
I'll bet he'd try to dig it out,
And then he'd need to find just three.
He doesn't know what else I know;
That one's nailed o'er the tile-house door.
If he found that, he'd then have two,
That's not enough, he'd still need more.
Should I tell him something else I know?
Perhaps I should have told before.
Deep buried in a box inside
He'd find enough to make his four.

I'd better think about it deep and long
For winter's not far off, and so
When he next hangs across the fence
I'll tell him everything I know.
Of course, I'll have to learn horse talk
But trying hard—oh my good land,
With horse sense and a lot of luck
I think he'll hear and understand—
There's so much to tell these autumn days
Of haze and color, sound and smell—
So now I'll close with all my love
And write you later when there's more to tell.

519   Grandpa

THE COBWEB

As I rode along the countryside
A cobweb floated out of space.
It, gently moving, drifted down,
And wrapped itself around my face.
Its shimmering iridescent strand
So seeming frail, yet still so strong,
Wrapped itself across my eyes.
Did nature seek to hide a wrong?
Had someone in a pitch of folly
Marred the beauty of the earth and sky?
Did nature seek to close my vision
Until I passed that black spot by?
Perhaps the cobweb warned of danger.
Life is complex and with danger pent.
I broke the cobweb and went on,
Wondering what it meant.

MARIGOLDS, YOU'RE A CELEBRITY

I sit beneath the maple tree, the winds of June
    they comfort me. The flowers are
swaying in the breeze while the leaves are
    fluttering through the trees. Now
what was that the marigolds said to the
    beautiful rose, who gently bowed
its head? "Your fragrance filled the early morn.
    Gee, aren't you glad that you were
born?" "Oh, marigolds, please stand erect. And
    lift your head, now what the heck!
You're as pretty a flower as there ever could be—
    why, marigolds, you're a celebrity!
The buckeye folks they love you so, with your
    beautiful color of yellow-gold.
So stand erect and lift your head, for your
    beauty surrounds this whole
flower bed. Marigolds, you're a Celebrity!"

* * *

A TASTY DISH

I walk beside a lovely brook. I have no line,
    I have no hook. The fish are swimming
there within, they flip their tails, and work their
    fins. My, what a beautiful, lovely
brook. I am glad I have no line nor hook.
    I guess I should be on my way
and leave the fish alone today before I get the
    urge to fish. They sure would make:

A TASTY DISH

IN OUR YOUNGER DAYS, OLD FRIEND

Old friend, in our younger days, we could
Race down this path, through these woods,
Heels flung high, muscles astrain,
Around the redbud tree and back again.
We'd run even through the misty rain,
Through sputtering snow, wind-tossed,
Through autumn leaves, crisp with frost,
And then sit upon the log to rest
Where the wild rabbit had her nest.
And then, not on any given day,
We just did not care to race,
But ambled along at a leisurely pace,
Paused to listen to the catbird's song,
The scolding of the Blue Jay,
And watched the feisty squirrels at play.
Sometimes we'd walk in bright moonglow
Where lacy shadows cast strange forms.
The gurgle of the creek's swift flow
Blended with the scurring of little feet
Of some wild creature we chanced to meet.

Oftimes you'd sit, your head upon my knee,
Your warm brown eyes aplead with me
For one short romp, but I could not go
For rheum-age had a grip of me.
Age dimmed your eyes with a cloudy haze,
And you no longer heard me call your name,
And white crept into your all-black hair,
And your legs became so stiff and lame.
And we only walked on sunshine days.
For sixteen years we walked this lane
Down to the redbud tree, and back again.
The redbud tree is gone, felled by an icy storm,
And now you are gone. Old age took you today.
This morning I found your cold still form;
Sometime in the night you just slept away.
Old friend, my heart is heavy with sorrow,
For I will walk alone, come tomorrow.
But I can remember how we used to run
On strong young legs, just for fun,
Down to and around the redbud tree,
A very young dog and a younger me.

THE INLET TIDE

From far, far out, to the inlet inside,
    From sand to sand was a low, low tide.
As fixed as the shoreline and unmoving grass,
    No wind to churn it, 'twas smooth 'n' fast.
No life at the edges, nor stir in the deep,
    Like a body less soul, how still it did sleep.

As weak as mortal, so wet from th' womb,
    No flow, no drift, yet to come soon.
A gentle swell, in the surface of glass,
    Meant life to th' water, and movement at last.
So slow at the first, yet surely it came;
    The flood was born from the vast domain.

Far in the east beamed the first dawn of light,
    As the rising fire turned th' purple to white.
With a whisper of wind ripples are born,
    And roll endlessly by in the infant morn.
Like days of youth they drift away,
    To vanish forever, in eternity to stay.

On, on came the surge faster the current flow,
    Stronger grows the flux, sand yields to winning foe.
In, in drove the swell, with all design of power,
    Filling the role to surely full, at the appointed hour.
Higher, higher it rises, as man nearing prime
    So able to overcome in the allotted time.

O how the ocean main did press, from sound below the sky!
    a western draft against th' flow, an' how the foam did fly!
With torrid heat from high aloft, th' gait intensified,
    'Til whitecaps on the surface danced, 'n' began to multiply.
'Twas white on top from sand to sand, with just a tinge of gray,
    As mortal man with crown above, in the latter day.

The tireless tide a-waxing deep, seemed to never cease,
Yet breaking chops whane to roll, 'twas a glint of peace.
As tho, the sand in glass were down, th' run began to ease,
A hint th' briny blue did slow against the gusty breeze.
Th' weary mass did litle drift, as tho' it needed rest,
Like flesh that's pulled the double watch in the upper nest.

'Twas full high tide from bar to beach, no motion, rise or fall,
Th' crest had marked the upper sand; th' sea had done its all.
all.
While shades of eastward clouds on high turned th' blue to gray,
A breath of floating seaweed refused to go away.
O' how the reach did fall asleep, with snoring th' surf;
Th' resting mass was waxing strong, to give th'ebb its birth.

Then by signal far away, the gulf begins to slide,
Bit by bit it slips to east, a-trying to decide.
Like liquid cane upon the ice, how slow it edged away,
Had two glass turns more to go than when it came today.
The doubt to part ere long had gone, th' ebb began its train,
As seamen who have sailed their full, surely fade and waine.

O' how the ocean main did draw 'n' begin to take its toll,
The western wind kept its pace, th' ebb did fully roll
Th' sea had turned 'n' pulled away, th' shore held its own,
As victor in a battle scene, the beach stood alone.
With current swift the waters raced as though t' hide way,
Like fire a-sinkin in the west, past the noon of day.

The water flowed from higher flats against the inlet force,
An eddy marked the undercut as foam piled at the source.
Upon the shoals afar ouside, the ground swells build and grow,
And vanish in th' deeper veins, never again to show.
The billows break and wash th' slopes, and quickly slide afar,
While riptides down the shoreline run and cut inside th' bar.
The swells rolled on across the reef to pound the coast away,
Like hounds of hell, they'll never stop until th' final day.

When unseen time secured its fare th' ebb began t' lag.
 As flesh 'n' bones in the stretch, start to slowly drag.
The wind was fading to a breath, old Sol a-cooling down,
 Th' waters turned to grayish green, with fog beyond the
 sound.
The inlet chops lost their crowns, the flow did surely pine,
 Like top of man in age matured, loses frost to shine.

The western hue blushed to red, then faded blue to black,
 A blanket o' mist hid the span when air a' fully slacked
From groaning of th' bar t' shore, whisper demons of th' deep,
 "We'll be back along ere dawn, th' sand's not yours to
 keep."
A murmur of th' surf to sand, "I'll grind you mortally fine;
 You'll flatten down an' waste away; all I need is time."
Said spirit of wind to shifting sand, "Thou shall abide,
 For I will never cease to be; in age I'm like the tide."

As though th' sands of glass were down an' nothing left to go,
 Th' ebb was drained of life itself; no movement to or fro.
The run did fade in th' great abyss which once gave it to birth,
 As soul of man returns t' God, the One who made it first.
As th' ebb flowed into eternity the time seemed to cease,
 Like mortal giv'n up the ghost, it sleeps in serene peace.
Only stars, like the eyes of God, watched the fathomless deep,
 As flesh less flowing blood, th' vast was dead asleep.

With drawing force from har on high th' pull begins to tell,
 A sleeping tide springs to life, th' waters start to swell.
Like mortal turned immortal, the tide is truly raised,
 As man born again, his soul forever to praise.
The tide will live as long as earth across the sky does trod,
 Second only to souls in glory, with the Son of God.

526

THE FIREPLACE

'Twas midnight ere Christmas
    As I sat all alone;
My spouse was in glory,
    The children all grown.

I gazed at the fire
    And the light it did give!
Three score and ten
    were the years I had lived.

As the logs turned to dust
    in the midst of the flame,
I saw in my life
    where time does the same.

The glow of the wood,
    The room it did fill;
Gave peace to my soul,
    For me to be still.

The invisible heat
    that warmed my skin,
Was as the Spirit of God
    That abides within.

The seasons rolled by
    And much did I give;
'Twas when I met Christ
    That I started to live.

As the fire fades away
    And dim grows the light;
My faith in the Son
    makes all things bright.

The sparks soar upward
    And in space disappear;
So shall I,
    With the absence of fear.

Through the flickering flames,
    In eternity I see—
A place with God
    Where I'll be free.

I GRIMACE A TERMINATION TO MY WRITING

I grimace a termination to the writing that I've done,
Concerning poems I've written this month, it adds to only one.
I prefer to have completed two, three, or maybe four,
But I've only one solitude poem: I believe I do need more.

Now if I place a conjunction with my thoughts and with my
        mood,
A token of wonder may follow and a poem may interlude.
If I add a touch of wisdom, it may help to keep the pace,
And words of wise with wisely words may follow into place.

The two verses above are a very possible sign
I'm in the process of poetry, and I've written another line.
Oh my! I'm so excited, think I'll scream but instead I'll shout,
Isn't it a wonder how writing poems can come about?

At one time there was a grimace at words that need come from
        my thumb
But now my poem is over, and in other words: I'm done.

* * *

THE CHIP

There once was a fellow named Skip
Who invented the potato chip
When asked how he did it,
He politely admitted,
"I had salt, but nothing to dip."

A SPRING DAY

Birds start to chirp and sing
Calling —now the time is Spring—
Putting aside all winter harm
The trees, flowers, and all birds regain their charm.
Watching the morning bees
As I wander through flowers and trees,
Bees, hummingbirds, chirps fill the air;
Tulips popping up and happiness is everywhere.

* * *

A SUMMER DAY

Summer has gone; it's here no more.
Sea gulls whistle on the shore.
A lonely beach— No one but me—
I watch, I listen to the sea.
It seems sad summer has gone,
I should cry; I should mourn.
Alone I wander at low tide—
The ripples are wide; the summer has died.

* * *

AN AUTUMN DAY

We walked through the park that sunny day
Below the leaves flying away.
The branches bare, the tree stood tall,
Soft and gentle the leaves when they fall.
We know summer had gone by;
Looking up we could see the sky.
Autumn moves mountains and hills:
All the wonderful sounds of summer are still.

FALL

I like the snow
Because it comes and goes;
It is very white
When it is shiny and bright.

I like the spring
Because that's when the birds sing.
When the flowers grow there is no more snow.

Then comes fall—
When the leaves big and small
Make the tree look tall—
Then you know it's fall.

* * *

WINTER OF 1976

All night a strong East wind has moved the snow
With blinding force, slowing man's effort to go.
Strong arms against the stormy night are seen,
Humans and machinery are struggling together as a team.
Young and old, weak and bold,
Bracing against this country's fiercest cold.
To remove the mountain of snow we must,
Counting our trapped survivors a plus.

ALIVE!

I am me, alive in body and spirit,
Sharing in a world where I grow and learn
Of life and deat. Bit by bit,
From day to day, I pursue the fulfillment for which I yearn.

My purpose . . . I feel it . . . deep down inside.
My happiness will come from that of others
When my mind, heart, and hand reach out as the tide
To improve this world—the lives of my sisters and brothers.

And death won't rob me, of that I do not fear,
For I will be in those with whom my love I've shared.
I hope for life with my God; if not, I won't shed a tear,
For my reward will be that men know—I cared.

I see reality: the happiness and sorrow.
My joy will be what I do.
And as time passes quickly to tomorrow,
I will follow in its shadow and try to touch you.

* * *

UNIVERSITY OF VERMONT

. . . Within the vastness of creation,
There is a place I know of
Where an elemental congregation
Is moved by a spirit of love.

Earth and water, air and fire—
Where beings called human
Share the desire
To find themselves and understand.

In one of its corners, I see
Rolling green mountains and running clear streams;
A rich unity
Of natural schemes.

And there in that matter,
Some men come to be,
To learn of their world and each other,
As a university.

JOYOUS ENCOUNTER

From peaceful plateaus of dreamless sleep
I awaken to a symphony of sound,
No more to weep, no more to weep.
    The answer now is found.
Before this day, and on this day, and after this day is o'er,
He'll be with us, for He's come with us to dwell.
And He will leave us nevermore.
    On, sing Noel! Oh, sing Noel!

* * *

CHRISTMAS MORN

Dear Lord, let me find a way
To make an extension of this day—
This glorious day that means so much
Pass as swiftly as an angel's touch.
Tomorrow and all the days that are to be
Let me know my kinship unto thee,
That kinship that will never cease,
Leading on through paths of peace.
Till full circle comes again that morn
That holy day when You were born.
I need to know no more than this.
I kneel to greet You with a kiss.

THE PLEDGE OF A KISS

How can I put into words the way I felt
At the mere thought of our lips meeting?
Panicky clung together as two hungry objects
Shriveled into one;
The only kiss that revealed to me the true meaning of love,
And a complete understanding that I was free to love
for life.
No imagination beforehand could possibly give me
A taste of the willing of pure joy that came with it,
No other kiss holds such promise
As the one that's a pledge of love and fate,
Given before God for the whole world to see;
No meeting of lips is ever quite like the one
That meet on your wedding day, so full of meaning,
Given with such sincerity and truth,
As the one of your beloved,
The only girl who's changed in a few moments' time,
From girl to woman, from sweetheart to wife.

EYES' REPLY

Bright eyes!
        Can't you smile through each and every line?
        How shall I know the tame and tawdry from the fine
           Unless your seeing sanctions mine?

        How know the poem is true
           Until
        Your touch is found?

           Most infinitely delicate
           Quest for the whole and round?

"Follow . . ."
        I seem to hear you say
"Till all is crowned . . .

        "The witchery of word and Wonder-sound."

INTERIOR NAVIGATION

Have tied my fate to the tail of a kite.

However I flap in gust and gale
Or whiplash the wind,
With a bright, air-worthy lead—I sail!

When I come into port in the thick of night,
I'll hurl the umbilical rope afar
And tether somehow by some indrawn sight
This battered bark to a star.

Though I wake in the cave of the troglodyte,
Or the underground vault of the safely dead,
Like a vapor I'll rise, or a flaming sprite,
To moor my ship overhead . . .

Then drop anchor
        By some secret sleight of mind
Up in the midnight sea

And wait on the deep for the marvelous Light

        That guides solitarily.

I HEAR YOU PRAYING

I heard you pray for me today
　　Entreating God to guide my way;
You pray so devoutly, my dear,
　　Your voice, I'm sure, He likes to hear.

I heard you pray in Heaven above
　　Beautiful, consoling words of love;
You were so kind, gentle and sincere—
　　It's very lonely without you here.

Keep on praying for me each day
　　Guiding, directing my earthly way,
Until once more I am with you
　　Embraced in love, forever secure.

SUE M. MORELAND

THE CARDINAL TREE

I looked out my window and beauty I did see,
God's creative majesty in a maple tree;
The trunks and boughs cloaked in soft snow,
Crimson splotches making them glow;
One, two, three, four in symmetry,
Like Christmas ornaments but more beautiful, these.
Oh, gorgeous cardinals, you're a message to me,
Thank God for my vision to view this special tree!

DRY FOUNTAIN

The night was slowly melting into morn
As she slipped softly into lasting sleep;
Where she would wake into a timeless dawn,
While I was numb, and could not even weep.
Yet from that moment I have sadly known
A barren spot down deep within me lies,
Which she had filled with love and overflown.
But now, the fountain gone, the water dries.

* * *

MOTHER ELIZABETH SETON

The whole world now proclaims her praise,
As she stands forth in glorious rays;
A moment of grace and she became
Sister of Charity, Woman of Fame.
The land she nurtured, the youthful mind,
With love of God and of all mankind;
A loving mother, a perfect nun,
"Flower of Sanctity"; Sainthood was won.

* * *

SUSTENANCE

The day may be dark and dreary,
The night may be cold and wet;
With you in my soul to guide me,
There's nothing that can't be met.
The world may have turned against me,
And failure have come my way,
With you in my soul to lean on
What more can I want this day.
There may be times that I'll question
The why and the how of things,
With you in my soul to answer—
I'm richer by far than kings.

REMEMBRANCE

In the garden of remembrance
We planted yesterday,
Children's laughter filled the air
We were young and gay.

Now summer's sun has faded,
Winter's wind chills the air;
Gone is the laughter of children
Only memories linger there.

Let's drink a toast

To the days of our youth
When we were gay—
To friends and lovers
We met on the way—
To fortunes amassed
And dreams gone astray—
Let's drink to remembrance,
The wine of yesterday.

THE COMING OF NIGHT

The sunset fades from the forest glen
And shadows fall on the trees, but then
The glowing moon peeps o'er the hill
And floods the valley quiet and still.

Then once again can the eye behold
The objects there all bathed in gold;
Creatures move within your sight,
Boldened by the streams of light.

The scene has changed, both far and near
From day to night but do not fear;
God has not left His wondrous world,
Only changed it some and then unfurled

More beauty still, to touch our hearts . . .
There is no place which He departs.
No time or space He does not know,
No land so far He cannot go.

I feel His presence ever there
In darkness or when skies are fair;
Oh God, you cannot hide, you see!
Your love reveals you, still, to me.

THE PUSHER MAN

I started to take dope
With life I couldn't cope.
Soon I was addicted,
Something everyone predicted.
Then I was a Pusher Man
Driving my Caddy sedan.
I had friends and money
All the whores called me "Honey."
    Good things must end—
I did something I couldn't mend.
I sold stuff to a cop
And they put me to a stop.
    I got railroaded and busted—
    I was very disgusted.
    Here I waste in jail
    Sittin' on a high bail.
    I was too stupid and bold;
    When I get out I'll be old.
Thinking of all those years
I start shedding tears,
So take heed of my plea
Or wind up like me.
Go straight and be well—
Instead of this hell.

CASSANDRA M. MULLEN

LANCER LUNACY

I went to a school where the faculty oinked, and the
principal hee-hawed.
The stallions barked, and the girls were pawed.
Where the musical director was an undoubted cluck,
And the choir tuned up to the siren of a fire truck.

But we were treated well, and never kicked,
And when we were good, we were even licked.
What a miraculous institution to find in this age,
Every comfort of home . . . even a clean cage.
I had only one gripe, or call it a wish:
They never did personalize my dish.

* * *

ODE TO A GREASE MONKEY

Endless Sundays of slicing ham, and watching you in
your pretty Grand Am.
It all came true, and it's been better than great,
all that coffee and grease—you're a hell of a date.

I must confess, I'm sorry you're not Prince Charming on
a big white horse;
On second thought, the smell would kill me and we'd
probably divorce.

So, dear grease monkey, I'll keep your Fords and your
Pontiacs.
What must be, must be,
But you gotta read my books and my dumb poetry.

544

JOURNEY

Engulfed by that salty, sinister mass . . .
it seeps into me, as I am swept through the fathoms of its depth.
Beautiful as we see it, evil as we know it,
it contains the origins of life—primitive to contemporary.

Picked at by assorted scavengers, I view the colors and
abundance of various forms.
I am swayed to and fro in the midst of the mindless,
instructed only by its irregular motion.

Shapeless and passive, pleasurable yet destructive,
needless yet needed, I sink into the murky abyss.
Like an enormous sable-feathered condor, I continue to
drift, lost from civilization as I had known it to be.

A beauty more splendid than imaginable, a murderer more
cruel than conceivable.
A burial ground for riches . . . a safe with no lock,
guarded only by terror and uncertainty.
Only matter, its elements enjoy a repast . . .
one nibbles at my eye, and another consumes a limb.

It is so natural to them, yet fiendish and grotesque to
me.
I have reached pitch darkness; all of its radiance has
vanished and I am entangled in slime and twine.
With no visual salvation, it is repulsive . . .
Cold . . . dismembered . . . I surrender.

TWINS

My soul wanders, not yet at peace,
Oh, the misery of bondage, destined never to be released.
I am so very tired, in search of the soft poppy field,
and the assimilationist to fuse the two.
But all I can behold is evidence of nomads through
  scorching
sands, with no sign of you.

The intense rays of the sun beat savagely on the earth,
spreading their sabotage, but they shall never touch me.
I have donated my thoughts to fantasy, where pain is
in true, and reality offers no plea;
Where hostility sheds no tears, deceit's obituary was
born, and where no man possesses fear.

There is no competitive force, no stipulations, and
no jurors,
It is as passive as the sea with no denials nor remorse,
but what pleasure can be derived from this?
Tranquil, yes, but can fulfillment prevail solely upon bliss?

There is no risk, no gain, no doubt, and no physical
salvation,
And for these, there is no compensation.
For the mind that wanders is led blindly through the
sluggish darkness, picking up no companions,
Wandering listlessly through the fathoms of its own
fraudulence—never witnessing daylight, condemned to the
monotony of bleak canyons.

How did it come to be that I am here and you are not?
You were as flexible as a young sapling, not I . . .
and yet we were straws selected from the same lot.

SUGAR PLANTATION SUGAR

I was born dark as the night
On an island far from all sight.
Having no control over this situation
I grew up on a sugar plantation.
I grew and grew to become a man,
Now look! look on the scars on my hands.

Was it by choice that breakfast, lunch and dinner was rice?
Or is it because of this man Christ?
Ho no! my Lord—he is not to be blamed.
It is you and you who should be ashamed.

Look at my bones, peeping through my skin
Or is it the mark from the bull's whip?
I would rather not think.

Sugar is sweet, and so are you.
The crack from the bull's whip would make you cry, too.
I am crying, crying! Why am I crying?
This question often ask.
Have you ever been on a sugar plantation?
Ho no, my Lord, you would rather die.
However, we need the sugar.
Sugar plantation, sugar.
Sugar plantation, sugar.

MAN IS BODY, SOUL, AND SPIRIT, THE BIBLE SAID, BUT WHERE ARE THE DEAD?

To Pastors, Elders, Ministers, Mothers, Saints and Friends:
At the first resurrection of Christ, for Christians death will end.
A few words of comfort to the bereaved today:
Our bodies where we live are only houses of clay.
Yes, they put the bodies in the graves
But the spirit goes back to the God that gave.
(Find this in ECCLESIASTES 12:7)
In Jesus' resurrection He took the saints who had died,
from Abel to Christ to heaven.
(1 Peter 3:18, 19) the Bible tells
That Jesus descended down to hell.
He has conquered death, He has paid the price.
Now, the dead saints are no longer down in Paradise.
Now here is a little illustration:
Jesus talked to Elias and Moses on the Mount of Transfiguration.
The spirits can be heard, and are not always seen.
The soul is immortal, and looks like a human being.
Jesus will come as a thief in the night, in the sky.
The living saints will be changed in the twinkling of an eye.
The dead bodies will be resurrected, and with Him, the Bible
     told,
Because He has already resurrected the souls.
The body is the house for the indwelling of spirit and soul.
The soul is that which feels, and the spirit is that which knows.
(The 16th chapter of St. Luke) The rich man died, his body, the
     Bible did
not tell,
But he lifted up his eyes in hell.
(In Matthew Chapter 28 and Verse 10) Those that kill the body
     are not
to be feared
But fear Him which is able to destroy body and soul in hell.
The soul and spirit has a form and shape exactly like the outer
     man;
The inner man wears clothes, rest, eats, drinks; they can,
Because it is like the outer man.

Men, women, sons and daughters—
The spirit and soul are immortals.
They seem to be one, as you search the Bible through,
Although they differ in the things that they do.
This is true, that I must tell—
When unsaved people die, their soul goes straight to hell.
And when the dead in Christ dies
Their soul goes straight to Paradise.
They will stay in hell to torment
Until the Great White Throne of Judgment.
It will be sad, they did not try;
Death and hell will be put into the lake of fire . . .
Will they burn up? No, never!
They will be tormented forever and ever.
The atmospheric heaven and this earth will be burned up, and there
    will be no more sea.
The Holy City, New Jerusalem, will come down from God out of
    heaven, and
there is where the resurrected saints will be.
The Glory of God from New Jerusalem will give light to Paradise
    earth;
The chosen people of Israel and saved nations will inherit it. Oh!
    what
mirth!
How long will this last?
Forever, and we will not remember the past.
Eternity is not the ending of time,
But the continuation of endless time.
Eternity is the transfiguration of time.

JOHN PATRICK MURPHY

STORY OF A MAXIMUM SECURITY WARD

I awoke in my sleep,
Thinking of my past.
It's hard to sit in group therapy most of the day.
I saw someone get mad over his medication.
Laughter, comedy, funny joke, being here.
Saw someone almost kill someone.
Some sick, some do life here.
Some die!
Some lie!
Some leer!
Some learn!
Some never understand who they are or where they're at or
Where they should be.
Life goes on, in a dark way.
Not much life here.
Thinking of Christ, but all I hear is pill call.
The person who almost got killed was I.
Tell me—is there a god?

SHY FRIEND

I am a rabbit, kind of shy.
I am
  Always
    On
      The
      Run.
You're a mouse, kind of cute.
I though I saw you dance around.
But then I am always on the run.
So
  I
    Guess
     She
      Passed
      Me
       By.

JOHN PATRICK MURPHY

THOUGHTS OF LOVE

Thoughts about you must
Linger on through the days.
Oh! I would like to pray.
Thoughts about you, of love,
Unfold.
Thoughts about you are a thousand
Days old.
Thoughts of love and laughter,
and a word untold.
Thoughts of the way you walk and talk.
Thoughts of you when you cry.
Thoughts of you when you smile.
Thoughts of summer and thoughts
Of spring.
With a word of truth and a
Last good-bye,
Until the day's end.
I love you . . .

THE FOUNDER OF THE EMPTY HOUSE

As I sit at the table by the window with a
weird feeling of emptiness as dreary
as the weather, my thought is of
myself. How lonely I am, wanting some
one to love me with sincerity. I live
alone with my four walls, no one to
talk to, only my beloved, where charity
and love prevail. With sadness that
crushes the pain of my eyes I think of
no tomorrow, only of the days and minutes
I spend with reget. I am determined to
allow myself fundamental reason to live
affectionately, with anticipation about my
very own salvation. From the depth of my
heart I cry out for peace in my empty
house, where charity and love prevail.
All that is seen and unseen will not be
forgotten. I stand in the room like a
pit of fire. I feel the beating of my
heart. I am begining to realize why
I am here. My heart overflows. I cry
out! Oh, heart of mine! I know the one who
dwells in the shelter of the most high will
be my refuge. I will have no vengeance in
my heart; I will not be rejected any more.
My fulfillment is much greater than I thought;
My house is a house of depreciation with the
qualification of love, where charity and
love prevail.

TIME

You don't have time, you say, my friend,
To help the neighbor down the road?
He's out of work, his wife is ill,
He carries a heavy load.

You don't have time? Can this be true,
As you hurry through your day,
Or have you grown so callous now
You let no one in your way?

You don't have time, you told your child,
When she asked to share your day.
You must rush out and make a buck,
Instead of stop and play.

To say you don't have time, dear friend,
Are the saddest words I know.
For in the end it isn't time,
As time will stay—we go!

* * *

DEAR GOD

I walked about in Your world today
And marveled at its worth.
Your majestic mountains, Your valleys green,
Your oceans wide and deep.
I wondered how Your plan, Dear Lord,
Could include someone like me.
And yet, I felt Your Presence there
With the sunbeam through the tree.
Somehow, I know, when tomorrow dawns,
I will walk with Thee.

THE APPLE SEED

Count the seeds in the apple,
before it is opened please?

No!
We don't have the answer—
for only God knows and sees.

We praise its appearance
how beautiful indeed,
through this miracle, the apple,
God speaks to you and me.

Think of all the wisdom
in a tiny little seed—
think of the wondrous secret
that only it and God must see.

Thank the Lord for His blessings,
He supplies your every need,
and pray
He keeps you in his bosom
like the tiny apple seed.

COME TO ME

Come to Me through the beauty of a rose,
Through the cuddly softness of a baby lamb as it grows,
Through the caress of your child so dear,
Through the protective love of your helpmate near.

Come to Me through the quietness in a forest of glen,
Through the whisper in the treetops of what has been,
Through the aloneness on a mountaintop so high,
Through the feeling of blending in with the sky.

Come to Me through the beauty of a sunset in the west,
Through the quietness when most creatures rest,
Through the stillness of a big moon so high,
Through the lacy silhouettes it makes of treetops in the sky.

Come to Me through the lilting beauty of the song of a bird,
Through the total quietness when nothing is heard,
Through the exactness of the toll of time,
Through the rhythm of the universe sublime.

Come to Me through the simple basic beauties of life,
Through unknown strength one uses during strife,
Through the depth of sorrow and despair,
Through the knowing *I* am always there.

Yes, Come to Me through the total plan
of the Universe of God and Man.

LOIS NICHOLSON

DREAMS

As the day begins thoughts
upon thoughts, dreams upon dreams
run through my mind:
    Thoughts about the past,
    Thoughts about the future, as
the day passes on.

As I gaze out the window
dreams appear:
    Dreams about being famous,
    Dreams about being successful,
as the day draws to an end.

Thoughts and dreams come to
a close,
    Night sets in and all is quiet
    As I close my eyes to rest in peace.

K. M. NIKAIDO

SEPTEMBER MORN

Lo, how the year has passed on,
Suddenly it is drawing to a close.
This morning dawned with
A clear blue sky and the glow of the
Morning sun reflected in the
Clouds hovering over Mount Tamalpais.
How beautiful the glowing clouds,
As they slowly move over the face
Of the majestic mountain, so bright
In coloration, like the tinted clouds
In the Eastern skies that
Herald the dawn of another day.
Morning after morning the eternal skies
Hold the promise of a better day, or the
Storm clouds that becloud our
Lives in sorrow or deep gloom.
Deep in the September of our years we
Look back to other years that have
Marched past in splendor or disarray.
We now look forward to more years of
Accomplishment or durance to things
That have kept us apart from the reality
Of the true meaning of this life:
Now approaching the final years
That may still reveal in a flash—or in
Sequence—what this life is all about.

GRADUATION

Heave O! Heave O! anchors aweigh,
    Voice these "Little Barques"
        To their first voyage.
Ready to venture where duty calls
    What matter the stars give light
        Or the course be an uncharted flight.
No fear the winds or the ocean's wides
    The boisterous waves
        Nor the tumbling tides
They are keel'd to compass life's tempestous sweep.

Their builders and makers now standing by,
    Their eyes dimmed with tears
        And hearts filled with pride,
They have viewed each step
    in molding the hulls
        And with a touch of affection
To the trim of each beam
        To echo the songs of the tides.
Now sealed with a prayer
    Their benediction to bestow—
        So be it with these "Little Barques,"
    As in the infinite venture of man
        The helm to steer all destinies
God holds within His hand.

Yes, years will come
        And years will go
            As tales that are told,
    And silver threads will mingle
        Among those strands of gold.
            And voices whisper in soft worn tones
    As they turn to the homeward stretch.
        Like the tumbling tides that ebb to flow
            Filled with the pride and joys of their years,
    Ready their anchors to hold
        In that harbor of rest,
            And list the refraining echoes
    Of the waves gently calling: "Come back,
        Come back,
            Come back to the sea . . ."

FOO DOGS AND SHIH TZUS

I am crazy about those horrible dogs
    One sees down in Chinatown;
You can see them all over my place
    Wherever you turn around.

One day in June a magazine came
    With a Foo dog at the top.
Under this they showed Shih Tzus—
    For a Shih Tzu I did shop.

From Georgia came my first Shih Tzu
    A lovely golden brindle.
After buying Gold Ray of Davaar
    My, how my money did dwindle!

There are those who say I'm foolish
    Over these things, but who cares?
Foo dogs and Shih Tzus aren't money,
    But I'm a millionaire!

* * *

MY SHIH TZUS

Oh, vagabonds with all your flare,
    You shall wear ribbons in your hair.
All through the day early dawn till
    You are my lovable vagabonds.

561

GABBY

I always said you would be around
    When I was dead and gone.
You are gone and I am here—
    Seems that I was wrong.
I miss your hello and good-bye
    When I go in and out,
You are my lovely mynah bird,
    And I miss you about.

You always let me know
    When someone was around;
I relied on your good judgment
    And you never let me down.
Remember when Helen put raw meat
    In the bottom of your cage?
It frightened you so bad
    You went into a rage.

Ynez telling you to shut up
    And you screamed all the more,
Then you gave her the razzberry
    Just to even up the score.
Telling Jessie you are a pretty bird
    She said, "No, a dirty bird."
After that a dirty bird was the only kind
    As I remember I ever heard.

Remember when Linda and I
    Took you to the vet?
When he said you couldn't live
    We shed tears of regret.
I couldn't throw you in the garbage can
    Like you were so much trash.
I buried you under the lemon tree
    Where the earth is free of ash.

WINTER LILIES

I stood in fields of lilies at Christmas,
Beautiful lilies, fields of massive white.
All I saw for miles and miles around me
Were fields of lilies, such a lovely sight.
I gazed in awe, it was late December,
Yet there upon the fields were lilies white,
Fields and fields of white, white growing lilies
To me they looked like snow, those lilies bright.

* * *

HAIKU

Distant lights moving
In far off hills at midnight
Fills me with wonder.

* * *

SENRYU

Our obscured vision
prevents our comprehension
of reality.

* * *

TANKA

Love embraces all
wherever it is welcome
to visit and share,
if but a crumb of stale bread
or a fragment of ourselves.

OLE MAN

I give you so much love each day,
Ole man, you gotta believe in me.
I have so much I wanta say,
Ole man, you gotta make me free.
To feel love, in a special way,
Ole man, you gotta stand by me.
So lonely days will stay away,
Ole man, you gotta make me see
Your love, while by you I lay.
Ole man, you gotta always be
A friend of mine, from day to day.
Ole man, you gotta let me be
When we have nothing much to say.
Ole man, you gotta never leave,
I can't think of another way.
Ole man, you gotta make me free
To feel love in a special way;
Ole man, you mean so much to me.

* * *

WHAT IS LOVE?

People moving in infinite directions,
Just to gain their own perfections—
Is love a means of altering confusion?
Peace of mind, two sharing one illusion?
What is love?
To possess or obtain for mind inflation,
The desire for man's greatest physical temptation
To some personality difference is mind aggression;
Yet, can love last on mere impression?
The giving, the taking, the loving, and sharing,
Hoping and wishing, yet freedom of leaving.

GOLDEN MOUNDS

Beneath the towering golden trees
I raked a mound of golden leaves,
Piled them high, then gathered more,
Making mounds two, three, and four.
Somehow I just could not ignite
Those golden mounds. To my delight
Within an hour a golden child
Came racing to me, diving wild
Into my mounds. The gold was scattered,
His golden hair with leaves was splattered.
All the leaves became alive—
Tossed to the wind. Oh, sweet boy of five,
Dive in my leaves, I will not scold,
Peek out at me through tresses gold.
Leaves are for scattering. Fling them high
Over your head like rain from the sky.
After this day, in my golden dreams
This scene will remain. I will hear the screams
Of a little boy (Oh, such golden sounds)
Coming out of my golden mounds.

* * *

DRIFTWOOD

There, upon the lonely beach
just a yard within my reach
lay a twisted mass of wood
battered, bleached, no longer good.
Like a lonely derelict—
tossed by waves, by footsteps kicked.
Just a place for gulls to perch;
that is, until I went in search
of Driftwood.

G. JOY OSTROM

THE SAME DESIRES

I remember playing and eating with my pet,
The desires we shared are hard to forget.
Sharing the warmth of the sun, the need to sleep,
Both enjoying splashing of water on hot tired feet.
Do you know wildlife is now in despair?
Too many have forgotten how to share.
The lost fawn whose mother was shot;
The poor animal caught in a trap lock;
The car that kept going after hitting a dog;
The newborn seals that are clubbed with a log;
The animals killed for greedy desires of fur and horn;
Horses, birds, and turtles have rights after they're born.
The dolphin, porpoise and whale just want to live—
Can't you be humane, with more kindness to give?

THE ONE DAY OF THE YEAR

The one day of the year which to me is so dear,
The sparkle of the tree and the gifts underneath
Raises all our spirits, even my grandson Keith.
They eagerly tear open their gifts with eyes gleaming,
Then hugs of joy and pleasure start tears streaming.
All the turkey they consume, and even the pie
But all too soon the time comes to say good-bye.
The one day of the year the family is here
With all good sharing of love and cheer;
Now the glamor and brightness of the tree seems gone,
Only quietness reins after laughter and Christmas songs.
The little ones are growing so fast—
I hope their sweetness will always last.
The wonderful time we had Christmas Day
I will cherish while they are away
Until next Christmas, when we will let our love out,
And together find out what Christmas is all about.

ARE YOU REALLY SERIOUS?

I heard you were in great demand
People are eager to push their fancy schemes on you.
You're kind and you listen,
Despite the fact that you're on the other side of
the fence.
You've been that scene before.
You know what that got you?
Still you ask for more.
They don't take it seriously,
Because you don't seem to have any lasting values.

You're never one person for very long.
You change like the breeze.
You do what you please.
But can you actually find meaning in your words?
What you said yesterday might not hold after you and it.

You can say I go along chasing rainbows.
You ask where it leads me?
I've found gold many a time.
That wasn't enough for me;
I'll always need more.

I'm just like you in that way.
In another way,
No one has even begun to know me.
They haven't shown me anything I haven't seen already.
Yet I'm different, my values are strong,
I know what I want out of life!

You say you have the truths of the world in the palm
of your hand?
If there is truth in this world I'll find it myself.
I don't need you to tell me about trust.
I even trust you,
When it comes down to the truth.

MY DATE, ON HALLOWEEN, AT MIDNIGHT

Complexions started to fade,
He became a lighter and lighter shade
Until all at once he was gone,
Yet something was holding my hand
Or was it someone terribly strong?
Was it a ghost?
He led me by the hand;
Into the haunted house we ran.
The lighting was eerie,
Lights of black and red,
Over the door a sign read:
"WELCOME ALL, ESPECIALLY THE DEAD."
Musical instruments floated in the air.
One wall was lined with chairs.
A skeleton couple were having punch,
The Headless Horseman and Ichabod Crane were doing
        a dance they called the "Crunch."
At the refreshment table
There were all matters of delicacies:
There were spider legs,
Even wings of bats,
All guaranteed not to make you fat.
When the party was over
I must admit, I felt so sad,
That experience wasn't the least bit bad.
I thanked the werewolves for having us there,
Told them it was a lovely affair.
I was standing on a grave
When a hand from the grave did wave,
A VOICE SAID: "I'LL BE WAITING HERE FOR NEXT
        YEAR."

YESTERDAY'S DOLLS

They sit in a cardboad box,
Cobwebs dangling from their rooted hair,
Long-forgotten since the days of my childhood.
Some are losing their hair,
And one has a broken finger,
But I still would not part with them,
Even now.

As a child
I pretended to be a housewife and mother,
And my dolls made of vinyl
Were real babies to me.
I would dress them in pretty clothes so tenderly,
And talk to them as if they were listening.
There was a special magic in their plastic eyes
That only children could understand.

It seems so long ago,
And yet it was just yesterday
That my dolls made me feel
I knew all about motherhood.
And today, with a baby of my own,
I realize that Yesterday's Dolls
Will one day be loved again by tiny hands.

INTIMACIES

the smile of the woman
on the boardwalk bench
attaches itself to my eyes;
tells me she knows—
has always known—
will always know
the smile feeds my mind,
and I walk on
filled with us;
her silent laughter
rings after my blush
but I choose to misunderstand,
imagining intimacies
from the wordless greeting
of a smile . . .

DON'T LOOK NOW

Little Johnny
has hatcheted
Little Sarah to death;

perhaps the result
of a TV show,
a newscast,
something seen in the subway,
in the parents' bed—

or perhaps a quality
or quantity
so deeply embedded
in the brain,
so forcefully rushing
through the veins,
it can only be removed by:

tear up all the nasty pictures
erase the words
pulverize the mind . . .

Little Johnny,
daily hatcheting Little Sarah,
perhaps the result . . .

SUSAN PACKIE

DIVISIONS

We live on the south side of town,
surely an advantage
for upward mobility.
The real estate agent told us
when we purchased this house
that land values would double
by the end of the decade.
We prided ourselves
on our intelligent selection.

When the plague struck our town
it wiped out the houses and people
of the north side, as if an invisible hand
had drawn a clear line of demarcation.
God was on our side.
All was right with the world.

The high school is gone now,
the butcher, the baker, the candlestick maker—
lower class types,
if you know what I mean.

We live on the south side of town,
cold and hungry and slightly illiterate,
but moving up in the world.

New people are moving in
directly to the south,
but for now,
we live on the south side of town.

BUILDER OF THE GREAT PYRAMID SURVEYING THE COMPLETED WORK OF CHEOPS

Timeless, but born of time and science you shall stand forever,
    my handiwork.
Has ever a mason been found with greater ambition,
Or monarch more demanding of his servants' accomplishments
In designs, grown monument in scale?

Sands shall storm your gate but Pyramid shall stand
against greater perils than of thieving men.
Your pale skin—will it remain fair as the queens,
Or stripp'd, shall you appear as a simpleton
Exercise in giant cubism?

What extraordinary weight in granite-limestone blocks have
    floated
      over Nile,
Been budged up packed ramps inclined to your staggering height:
All to what purpose?
For Pharaoh's vanity? He is mortal, but Pyramid is everlasting.
First and last to endure
All of the histories of history and more.

What conquerors will try to know your secrets?
What royal lovers seek your shadows?
What God will find your sanctuary?
What progeny shall you embarrass by brilliant concept
Or rival in your simple beauty?
You shall outlive all and sundry visitors,
Regal, romantic and scholastic with their impoverished goals
Compared with the riches of your pile's invention.

Grains of sand in time's desert will not erode
Your substance any more than river's torrent
Will be effectual in swallowing up your stones.

Asunder?
When chaos reigns at earth's end.
I built you with a string and my mind —
An unrivaled achievement that will stand the lengthy
Burden of days.

* * *

HASTINGS REVISITED

KNIGHT:
I shall not soon forget fair Lorette
In the corner tower where we made our bower
Before the affair went sour, at unseemly hour.
Prior to that our worlds were one.

One funny, happy hour we knew
Together the transports of joyous surrender
That grew fast upon a chance bender,
Which sent us on a separate way,
All within that single sorry day.

Still soft is the memory of moments in fulsome carouse
Until that hateful bell sounded battle's arouse.
I left on mournful note, hot,
Without taking my lined fur.
Our horses sped 'cross the field
Yet my mind refused to yield . . .
To the wrench'd embrace.

Under snow I found her grave on my return.
Our agape turned to sad, solitary sojourn.
I was to remember often again haunting fair Lorette
On chill spring mornings since.
She sleeps in my coat,
Thirty-five springs past.

PARIS: PLACE DE LA REVOLUTION, OCTOBER 16, 1793

Marie Antoinette:
My husband, poor Louis, has climbed these stairs before me.
That very blade glinting in this morning's sunlight, last winter
Made a mince of the man whom Destiny united with me
In proxy. Ultimately we mingled our royalties.

Oh, my poor children! Shortly they will be orphans, much
    abused,
As were their princely parents by hateful beasts
Who make worst of the best; by what right?
I leave them so little—it was to be the throne of France
For Louis Petit;

What thrones might his sisters claim?
Will there be thrones enough left for them? Or shall
Our lot be visited on their innocent heads? *Mais non.*

My hair? What devil-mercy that I am granted no mirror.
Beautifully coiffed, scented, powdered, transformed by crude
    snips now
Into this peasant shock is my glory flaxen to prison drab.

Were it not for my children—jewels—I could welcome my life's
    end.
Those months have been infernal, despised.
Those dour, sober days are at end. Lovely autumn air, yet I
    shiver.
My bravery falters here in this noisome rabble. What is it?

Citizen executioner, do you handle your Queen thus rudely?
Must this heathen crowd behold breasts bared
Which have suckled a royal family? Remove your
Bloody hands from Marie Antoinette! Hold your slanderous
     tongue!

Father-priest, make suitable prayers as I exit this chaos;
Pray your lips blistered. remember constant and long
This tragic household in solemn requiems.
Forgive this widowed mother who alone pleads for our new
     young king,
My son, his noble sisters, and their devoted father; our sad
     family.

Demon guillotine, do your awful work well.
How does regicide exist?

Trinity Divine, look to my penitent soul.

Mother!

ROBERT PARRY

POEMS OF CANADA:
TYRANT OF THE NORTH

Once again the winter strides
    down from the icy arctic tundra,
Shrieking its unrestrained wrath
    upon the deserted apprehensive prairie.
Then sits back with unashamed delight,
    locking in its frozen grip wooded
        sloughs and streams.
Poplar and birch beautified by hoar frosting
    sparkle in crystallized air.
Dark evergreens draped in mantle white
    unimpressed by winter's rage,
Seduced each fall to shed its barbarous coat,
    Resisted,
And stands to remind us all
    That spring and summer warm,
Will rule with gentler hand.

POEMS OF CANADA:
SOLITARY HOMECOMING

Silently, the bark canoe
Rippled the emerald lake,
The air hung heavy with scented pine,
Soft rain left in its wake.

Slowly the paddle rose and fell,
The traveler cast his eye
To the bush along the shore,
Bright! in the moonlit sky.

A northern pike rose from the deep
Then with a splash was gone,
An owl hooted through the dusk
To warn the Buck and Fawn.

The craft eased in among the reeds,
The boatman then looked back,
Took out his knife and buckskin coat,
And headed up the tracks.

Amid the trees his long home stood
Deep in the forest green,
A cabin mellowed by the years,
Ten summers it had seen.

Once inside, the blue smoke rose
Round game upon the spit,
With tranquil gaze he watched the flame
Dance from the blazing pit.

The day was drawing to an end,
A night chill made him stir.
He closed the door, lay on his bunk,
And drew up snug, his fur.

SON OF THE SOIL

Here is no common man,
No ordinary man of toil,
But a true Son of the Soil.
See him bending low
Over the never-ending rows,
Superb muscles flowing rhythmically, evenly.
Year after year he labours
Beneath brilliant burning suns,
Skin gleaming like rich mahogany,
Sinewy shoulders heaving,
Lithe waist twisting, turning.
This is his world, this lush green world,
His Garden Paradise—
Product of his strife
Against Nature who would claim
The land and make it hers.

Watch him as he pauses, keen eye alert.
Search his face: brown, wrinkled, dried.
No signs you find of prejudice or greed,
In his humility, no defeat.
Rather more plain virtues override
Pretension and conceit.
To be patient, kind, loyal:
This is his creed.

You question his content and sense
The secret of his toil,
His inborn self-respect . . .
The Soil . . . the Soil.

SHORTCUT

Have you wondered as you wait in vain
Whether he is on the way
From school or been detained?
Considered some dark fate that might await
His homecoming? Confirmed in your belief
That this is so,
Suddenly you're relieved
To see your Joe.
Whistling or humming, as the mood suits,
Kicking clods of dirt with his new boots.
"Oh," you sigh, "how can you be so late?"
And Joe replies, completely innocent
Of his offense.
"But I took the shortcut."
You listen, and as Joe describes
His path you realize
The magic of a broken fence,
A swinging gate.
No ordinary walk from school
Can quite compare
To a private talk with pirates rare
Or floating chips on a lazy pool.
And so you skip the lecture you prepared
And with a warm embrace you remonstrate,
"Hurry a little faster, *please!*"

YOUNG LOVE

Oh, for the hillside of our youth . . .
Sweet spring flowers in profusion.
Garlands we made of the blossoms fair;
You wound them playfully in my hair.

A few years passed and we wandered by
Hand in hand, reserved and shy . . .
Then love came whispering on the air
And we swore eternal kinship there.

It was long ago but I recall
The secret wonder of it all,
As though it were only yesterday
We made our vow and you went away.

Duty beckoned and we must bide.
We little guessed as you left my side
Though the hillside bloomed perenially . . .
The love we pledged was not to be.

* * *

REGRET

The unkind word that is spoken in haste,
A startled look on a guileless face.
A smile arrested before it lights
Like a vivid butterfly poised for flight
Impaled by the collector's pin . . .
How harshly I reprimanded him!
Would that I might once again
See the wonder and not the pain;
But I can only endure regret
And hope my little one soon forgets.

GOING FISHIN'

Another day is dawning,
The sky is clear and blue;
The birds are sweetly singing
A good mornin' to me and you.

There's a spot down by the river bank
Where I long to be,
Where God smiles down from Heaven
And the world seems right to me.

The catfish all are jumpin'
And saying, "Come on down
For another day of fishin'
And don't forget your hound."

The sun is brightly shining
And lights the world aglow
With the beauty of its golden beams,
So off to the river I go.

I'll take along some fishin' bait
And old Sad Eyes too,
With a small bag of munchies
And my favorite pair of shoes.

I'll say good-bye to Mom and Dad
And then I'll go on down,
And there I'll stay till supper time—
Just me and my old hound.

CATHY SMITH PATTON

ROSES IN DECEMBER

Roses in December
A glorious sight would be,
Amid the snow and icicles
For all the world to see.

* * *

MOONLIGHT REVERIE

In the moonlight first I saw her
As she walked along the shore,
A goddess of great beauty
From the portal of Heaven's door.

For hours it seemed I watched her
As she strolled so leisurely,
In the splendor of that moment
Just her, the sand, and sea.

Her hair cascaded freely
Long and raven black,
Not one small ounce of beauty
Did the goddess lack.

She stopped but for a moment
And frolicked in the sand,
A beautiful Cinderella,
The fairest in the land.

My heart stilled within me,
Bewitched by the sight
Of such an exquisite creature
On a moonlit summer's night.

I dared not approach her
Lest she turn and run away,
But how I longed to hold her
Till forever and a day.

Silhouetted in the moonlight
A picture-perfect scene,
A fairytale princess
From the pages of my dream.

* * *

MY LOVE

My love is like a merchant ship
That sails upon the sea,
Bearing jewels and costly pearls
He brings them all to me.

My love is the fairest of them all,
In him no spot or blemish found.
With kisses as sweet as honeycomb
And eyes so deep and brown.

My love is as sweet as ambrosia
And as strong as the cedar tree,
As warm as a ray of sunshine,
And spreads his love o'er me.

A seal he has placed upon my heart
And together we'll forever be,
Till the silver cord be loosened
And in death I am set free.

CATHY SMITH PATTON

SPRING IN BLOOM

Daffodils of yellow
With stems of forest green,
Herald departure of winter
And all the earth is set free:

From the grip of frosty freezing air
And blankets of glistening white;
From long hours of darkness
To the blessed springtime sight;

Of vast arrays of tulips
Growing 'neath my window sill,
Vanishing winter's blahs
Cure all for winter's ills.

The pallor of the napping earth
Gives way to colors gay
That fill the world with sunshine
And brighten up my day.

THE QUESTION OF CHRISTMAS

What do you think of Christmas?
Is it just another day of the year?
Or is it a time for celebrating
And spreading a little cheer?

Is Christmas when you go to church
And try to act your best?
Then the rest of the year you take it easy
And just sit back and rest.

What do you think of Christmas time
After all the glow is gone?
Is it just another holiday
On which you partied much too long?

What do you think of Christmas time
When you see the manger scene?
Do you see all its beauty
And feel its peace serene?

What do you think of Christmas time?
Is it just presents and lots of fun?
Or is it a time to honor Jesus,
God's only begotten son?

What do you think of Christmas time
Is Christ to be honored but once a year?
Or will you honor Him daily,
And serve Him with reverence and fear?

Christmas time is a joyous time
Filled with love and cheer,
But what you think of Christmas
Will depend on what you've been all year!

BE MY VALENTINE

Sentiments put into words
On a painted pretty card
Can never tell how I feel—
The language seems lacking and hard.

Some things just can't be expressed
Even though they're felt within,
So I'll just say I love you
As I've told you time and again.

Today is a special day
So I pause to let you know
How much you mean to me.
Be my Valentine; I love you so.

* * *

GOD IS ALWAYS WITH US

God is always with us
Wherever we may go,
Whether on the highest mountain
Or in the valley low.

There has never been a place to go
Where His eyes couldn't see,
And there's not a way to separate us
From His love for you and me.

So when passing through pain and heartache
Remember this and know:
God is always with us
Wherever we may go.

MY PEOPLE

(I dedicate this poem to the nicest people in Flushing,
Samuel and Miriam Tikulsky)

I'm searching for my people,
My people—I search;
Sunshine faces, stretch
Embraces, and exalted phrases.
I visit every old spot,
The house where I lived,
House where I worshipped
On the street by the nook—
By the fen and the brook.
People, where are you?
You give me courage in despair,
Please, believe the words I say,
Your wishes I like to obey;
Through all the world I shall trace,
I'll never find the place . . .
Like the place I have near you,
Because, people, I love you.

ME AND MIDNIGHT

The neatly manicured lawn feels cool against my skin,
So unlike the warm, comforting breeze that caresses my face and
    tousles my crop of disarranged hair.
It is easy to experience such simple sensations, for a blanket of
    darkness has put the village to bed.

Midnight is upon me, being a small black feline that playfully
    scratches my chest and purrs.
This idling motor is the only sound and beams from starry
    headlights above the only vision.
Midnight reminds me that it is nearly twelve by rubbing her thick
    fur against my torso and darting her tail playfully through
    my fingers.
Thoughts come of midnight being the witching hour and my own
    Midnight being a witch's black cat.

The intention of this nightly mission had been desiring to speak
    with God.
Midnight continues to distract my thoughts with her subtle
    movements and subdued sounds.
Suspicion arises that she may indeed be on a witch's mission,
So I push her away and gaze intently at the spirals of light
    originating so far above my head.

A sensation of loneliness sweeps my unsuspecting body and I
    shiver involuntarily.
Staring deep into the vast, dark emptiness of space, I feel
    nothingness funneling from the wide speckled sky into my
    entranced eyes.
Joined spiritually with God, I feel sudden bigness, in possession
    of something special, not alone.
God, the Creator of nights, has given me exhilaration with
    calming peace—indeed, a rare creation.

Midnight is once again scratching my chest.
This time the suspicion has fled.
Midnight is a beautiful creation of God and should not be
    misunderstood.

NEW HORIZON

Let us say, dear,
That a new horizon is near,
One, darling, to view forever;
And let the past drift away
Into the mist of yesterday
To become an ember forever.
Sweetheart, can all of this be,
Or be just a beautiful memory
Lasting long after forever?

* * *

WHEN I'M AWAY FROM YOU

No sail is on the sea
Today, bringing gladness to me
When I'm away from you.
My heart is held by emptiness
Which speaks of only loneliness
When I'm away from you.
The sun has not its golden glow
To mellow the madness of the show
When I'm away from you.

* * *

LET US IN THIS MOMENT STAY

Eternal sleep can never dim
The days that once were ours,
For they lie on the crimson rim
Of the horizon with no hours.

So let our thoughts dwell on tomorrow—
No, let us in this moment stay
And from it ever borrow;
Then today will never fade away.

591

MY IDEAL

Your soothing and honest replies,
Your body tender and fair,
The baby stare in your eyes,
The look of innocence there
Blur out my surroundings;
I see only you, my Ideal.
Now divine music is playing,
Heaven seems ever close to me,
And angels singing are saying:
"Love is a longing, truly
Beyond our reason to explain;
For something or for someone—we
Lift the veil of love in vain."

* * *

ETERNALLY YOUR KISS

To hold you with my hands,
To caress you or to crush you
As the occasion demands,
To caress your lovely face
In a lingering embrace,
To crush your beautiful bosom
To my breast and spoil your lace.
Night and day can't take me away
From this: I await
Eternally your kiss.

* * *

IN THE GLOAMING

The future once was in the gloaming,
The stars that float on the sea;
But now the sea is sad and foaming
And has swallowed up the stars—and me.

SHE TOOK ME BY THE HAND

She took me by the hand and led me far
From stoic peace into a land afire
With joy and love, that bright eternal star
That twinkles o'er the lands afar, that lyre
In hands of sirens fair. If only I
Might find my way back to the earth again
And end this dreaming, dreaming in the sky;
But why waste words in etching with my pen,
For here I am, ah yes, I'm here to stay;
Unless I should forget her breast so fair,
Her eyes like nights at rest in fields of gray,
Her voice that sings and laughs without a care.
Now all this leading didn't lead to play:
She led me to the altar of Despair.

* * *

IN SLEEP

In sleep I kiss my darling o'er and o'er—
Her kiss so warm and sweet I feel in dreams;
We row in bliss together on the streams
Of happiness till we perceive a shore
On which we hear the foaming breakers roar;
Way high upon its bank a light there gleams—
A light of home where dwell exquisite dreams.
I would that I might sleep forevermore,
But no—the day must dawn to bring me back
To life in which there are no streams to see,
No happiness, no home; there is a shack
In which I dwell alone; then comes to me
By day those thoughts of grief so cold and black;
Then I'm a rolling derelict at sea.

TO PAULINE

You are a symbol of Spring, Dear;
You make sweet memories reappear;
And when the shadows of night
　　Dark moments bring,
You make all this disappear.

* * *

THE ROSE ILLUSION

No rose will ever bloom
With such radiant glory
As the rose of my joy and gloom.
If this rose were mine to guard,
I'd place her down inside my heart
And let her there remain interred;
The fire of my heart would melt this rose
And send her surging through my veins;
Then we as one would e'er repose;
Here I'd have her for my only
Bride and sweetheart always
And ne'er again be blue and lonely.
And when old Death swings high his scythe
With one swing of his craggy arms
And brings to end my physical life,
Grim Death won't ever know
That one life will never feel
The pain of his angry blow.
Two seas can blend into one sea;
Two lives can live as one,
Here and in Eternity.

A BUDDY

A crimson sun faded out
On the fateful day of a buddy.
A gray sky, serene and nonchalant,
Gazed down on the scene
Of one who died for duty.
His thoughts were near and far
As he knelt o'er the grave
Of one daring, gallant, and brave.
Tomorrow amother's heart
Will be breaking for her departed
Valiant son, he thought,
As he wept o'er the grave of
A buddy.

* * *

LOOK UP

Look up.
Then
The party cup becomes
A Chalice.
Look up
And
Your ring will be,
Not for a moment,
But eternally.
So
Look up
And accept His Love
To seal your lvoe.
Yes,
Look up!

BYRLE PAYNE

THIS PICTURE OF YOU

Before a window I stood enraptured
    Yet viewed with alarm;
For I saw that a camera had captured
    Youth, beauty and charm.

It seemed that art took on a new yearning
    With this picture of you—
Just like a beautiful sunset burning,
    Blushing away a sky of blue.

* * *

TO A HULA DANCER

She danced along the stage last night
As fairies do in works of art.
She waked within my soul delight;
She seemed to dance along my heart.

* * *

THE TRANSFIGURATION

With three of His disciples Jesus walked
Into the mountains—there to pray. His face
And robe were bright. Then Time turned back the clock
As Moses and Elias steps retraced.
These two appearing on the scene, the sky
Lit up all brilliantly. They talked with Christ
About His coming death—yet death defying
By His resurrection—Lordly Tryst.
"Let's build three tabernacles," Peter said—
A splendid light illumed a Sung landscape;
In mist the mountains disappeared ahead.
Out of a cloud—and loud—a voice then spake:
"This is My Son beloved. Hear Him!" Then a
Transcendent light did blank out all but Jesus.

NEVER OR FOREVER

Please don't be kind to me
Unless you don't mind to be
        Mine forever,
And never give your heart to me
But to depart from me forever.
No, Darling, it must be
        Never or forever.

* * *

MY LAST LOVE

When you said, "It might have been!"
Then I knew that love had passed me by —
The magic touch, the golden lure,
The quickened pulse, the lover's sigh—
All this for me was in the by and by;
For, Sweetheart, in life and death
You are my last love and happiness.

* * *

THE EMERALD'S SONG

Look within my depth, you Unbelievers,
And read the mystery of life.
You think I am beautiful;
Yet I am old. I was born
On earth before life began.
I saw its beginning
And I reflect its meaning;
But you are too young
On earth to understand.
From my gleaming, if you could read,
You would see its meaning—
Unbelievers, my green rays
Point the way to Paradise.

597

JOHN HOWARD PAYNE

SYMPATHY

Now that the quiet hours have come
And the silence of a voice that once you knew
Is like an empty chasm, deep and wide—
Words seem so helpless to express
    My Sympathy
To assuage your overwhelming grief.

But the touch of a kindly hand
The telepathic message from a sympathetic eye
Or the warmth of a friendly smile—
All give you confidence and assurance
    From My Heart
That you are not neglected and alone.

These simple unspoken sympathies are stronger yet
Than an oration or an exhortation not to grieve—
When nothing seems to ease your broken heart
These small but subtle actions of human kindness
    Convey My Understanding
And help to bridge the chasm of your grief.

FALL

Fall is happiness.
In fall leaves fall to the ground.
It's a lovely sound.

* * *

RAINY DAY

A rainy day is a gloomy one,
Then you wish you could see the sun.
But the rain is good for the crops and trees,
It especially washes the wind and breeze.

Rain is good for the air,
It makes it clean and fresh.
When you take a whiff of it
Your troubles don't matter a bit.

When you sit down
And take a little nap,
You wake up that day
And smell the sweet smell of sap.

When you go to sleep tonight,
You'll go to your bed and lie down.
Then you will dream of being a king
Wearing a golden crown.

RODNEY DEANE PAYNE

TORNADO

One day when Mom was making dough,
I heard the sound of a tornado.
Then I ran out the door,
Down to the basement floor.

It was safe in the basement
But there was nothing to do.
All I did was sit there
And listen to the wind while it blew.

When the wind got quiet,
I climbed out to see what would happen.
I looked at the house out in the yard,
Then it started a-crackin'.

When I turned back around,
The house fell to the ground.
It's funny, because it didn't make a sound,
But the house fell to the ground.

Now what would I do!
Mom and Dad were trapped in the basement.
Now I was all alone.
Then I wanted to moan.

I started walking around.
I tripped and fell on the ground.
Then a tree fell on me,
And there was nothing left of we.

VIGNETTE
(*La Femme Au Naturelle*)

Dusk was diffusing the colors of day,
(the end of my journey a few hours away)
when suddenly, against the background
of twilight's purple haze, just ahead
the lowering sky outlined her silhouette.
A figure to entrance—perfectly defined—
she stood in regal stance at the edge of
the wood, impervious to the maze of traffic,
raucous noise and noxious gas, motorized
humanity zooming past.
As lanes of traffic began to slow,
strident medley of horns began to blow—
my reflexes trigger-ready, I nudged my
brake just so—my adrenalin flow was
heady—split the second—quick the eye
in momentary gaze, I waved at her hello—
good-bye—to stop, I wasn't brave . . .
Who the hell was she—why was she there—
it was a mystery—uncanny, I swear,
evoking sensation suffusingly rare—
it was no illusion, I know she's for real,
else how to explain excitement I feel—
mile after mile, not the least weary,
remembering her form so lovely—so clearly . . .

SEQUENCE TO SUICIDE

Little I care that love is gone—
it matters little—tears are dry—
little I care the dream went wrong—
it matters little—the last good-bye . . .

    Little I care to scheme again,
    it matters little to win or lose—
    little I care (not one little damn)
    it matters little I pay the dues . . .

Little I care that love is past—
it matters little to rail at Fate—
little I care the die is cast—
I care little—Johnny come late . . .

    Little I care the play is over—
    it matters little to laugh or cry—
    little I care to run for cover—
    it matters little, a lover's lie . . .

Little I care that flesh is prone,
catatonic—indistinct—
it matters little that heart is stone
inert as the kitchen sink . . .

    Little I care when dawn will break—
    it matters little when night must fall—
    I care little that Spring is late—
    and love—love matters least of all . . .

ALONE

I am alone without you—
You whom I have not found,
And while I eat and drink,
Read and think,
Inveigle and connive,
Live and share with those about me,
And even in a crowd
I am alone.

* * *

DESIRE

You are so close
And yet so far,
The light I see
Yet as a star
To only see
And know you are,
Yet not to touch
And not to share
And take together
Whatever their:

* * *

GOVERNMENT

Of government it's hard to say
They're only men, pliable beings
Molded by hidden hands and finished
In gold and glitter.
Occasionally a true one appears,
Only to be tarnished and swallowed
By the acid atmosphere.

603

MOTHER

O Lovely Lady, I'm so glad
To know that you are here,
To cheer me up when I am sad
And brush away each tear.
To perk me up when I am low
And comfort me when I'm scared,
To wake up every morning and know
That someone's waiting there.
To know that you will always be
Near if I should need you,
To help or watch or counsel me
In every thing I do.
O Lovely Lady, I'm so glad
It's you and not another
That God, with all His love, thus bade
Me to call—Mother.

GREEN DREAMS

Green dreams in dark nights
Light a path to higher spheres—
Swelling the heart with new-spun joy,
Lacing adverse events together
To form life's pattern,
A beauty too close to be seen.

* * *

WATER

Water, my pedigree of calibrated life,
An encore of unfathomable profusion,
Found blue-quilted and ripple-waved
Squirting, spouting, splashing, springing
Under rainbow-smiles of gods above.

River-gushing rapids tickle the banks
Making the mountains rise in laughter;
Frothy nebulous drops spume
Through gutter-drain sewers;
Incandescent sweat drops in hot Turkish baths
And green-emeralds of the leprechaun
Lie forgotten on chilled clover fields;
Honorable Surf, we cheer you.

THE RISING OF THE MOON

Before the moon begins to glow
The night is filled with sound,
The world a tuneful background.
Music comes from the earth below,
Winds across the pine tree blow,
Turbulent, tumbling rivers flow;
Before the moon begins to glow
The night is filled with sound.

The far distant call of the crow!
Churring of the night jar abound,
Crying of the curlew aground,
These are the symphony so slow;
Before the moon begins to glow.

* * *

FRIENDS

Friends are ever present with me;
Some live close by and some far away,
Several are telephone visitors,
Others are pen pals, whom I've never met,
While dear ones welcomed me on the day of my birth.
Sympathetic ones came to me during sorrow,
Merry ones came to my house when I was entertaining,
Business ones come to me from all walks of life.
I dearly prize my old friends—
And am always ready to make new ones.

A HINT FOR KEEPING HEALTHY

If you would desire
to balance your nerve and wit,
get in the frame of mind
for keeping physically fit.

If you have good health
and your clear mind want to keep,
try going to bed
to get your share of sleep.

Then you'll wake up in the morning
with a jolly bit of song,
feeling gay and cheerful
and whistling all day long.

* * *

DO YOU WONDER ABOUT CLOUDS?

Do you stop and wish to gather
those spongy clouds on high?
and wish to touch the clinging raindrops,
while they are tossed in the sky?

When the earth is parched and dusty,
so thirsty is the grain—
The world's refreshed by the spraying
of the cooling, pelting rains.

BELONG TO YOU

Between body and soul,
That is Love
For you and me . . .
Receding from us at the speed of life
I can feel my heart broken . . .
I belong with you.
Today I look at you,
Temporarily, until the solstice
of Love and Hate . . .

* * *

LOOK AT YOU

While listening to the wind
I heard you come
Into my mind and touch me . . .
I long for you, sweet man of my soul,
Sweet man, I long for you . . .
You—who are bits and pieces of my mind.
Your eyes were made to reflect, to speak softly to me . . .
I am here to look at you;
Look at me—I am here . . .
Come to me—let my mouth surround you with feeling.
My arms were made to hold you close . . .
Come to me and let me bring you joy;
Come to me and let me bring you peace;
My love, I love you . . .

THE REUNION

I wish I could have been there to see
The reunion of Elvis, his mother, and brother Jesse.
What a happy time that must of been, Elvis getting to meet his
    twin.
His mother must have jumped with joy to once again be with her
    baby boy.
Elvis loved his mother with all his heart,
And he took it very hard when they had to part.
From the beginning she taught him about God, good manners,
And to love and respect everyone.
This he never forgot, and has always done.
She was a perfect mother, and he was proud to be her son.
While Elvis was here with us
God put him through many tests and, as always, he did his very
    best.
Now he is free from pressure, heartache, and pain.
His death is our loss, but heaven's gain.
Mrs. Presley liked nothing better than to hear Elvis sing,
And now she can listen forever to the king.
Like the black man, he had natural rhythm, plus a lot of soul,
And every song he recorded turned into gold.
He achieved riches and fame, and everyone in the world knew
    his name.
Although our hearts are broken,
We should be happy that Elvis was granted his only wish,
Which was to talk to his mother, whom he really missed.
Maybe now Elvis will be able to rest, since he is no longer under
    stress.
I know he is happy, because he is with God, his mother,
And his brother Jesse, and for him there is no better company.
Yes, I really wish I could have been there to see
The reunion of Elvis, Mama, and Jesse . . .

A VERY SPECIAL FRIEND

The loss of my idol was hard for me to bear,
But it was made easier by someone who really cared.
Not many people would have taken time to listen to a boy of ten,
But Mr. Homer M. Gilleland did, and today he's my best friend.
He knew my idol for many years, so he understood the pain of my
    tears.
He was Elvis Presley's personal barber, and Elvis loved him like
    a father.
For Christmas he gave me a lock of my idol's hair,
And that's just one example of how much he cares.
I appreciate his phone calls, and the letters and gifts that he
    sends,
For you see I'm often sick, and they help me to mend.
I also enjoy the stories that he tells; believe me, they're really swell.
    swell.
Wouldn't it be wonderful if everyone had a friend like Mr.
    Gilleland?
The world would definitely be a better place,
Because everyone couldn't help but walk around with a happy,
    smiling face.

* * *

LOVE IS

Love is having a family.
Love is a little baby.
Love is a smile from a little boy.
Love is joy.
Love is a hug and kiss from a little girl.
Love is the happiest feeling in the world.
Love is having a true friend.
Love is being with God in the end.

BABIES

Babies are the Angels of the World.
Babies are Love.
Babies are as delicate and pure as a white Dove.
Babies are a Beautiful Miracle from the Lord above.

* * *

MOTHERS, GRANDMOTHERS AND
GREAT-GRANDMOTHERS

Mothers are very special in every way;
They spend all their time making sure our day is perfect,
So we will always be happy and gay.
They never take time out for themselves,
Because they are too busy cooking meals and getting us ready for
     school bells.
Sometimes mothers are ten different people in one day.
They are chauffeurs, maids, nurses, tutors, and cooks, to name a
     few.
It's amazing how they accomplish all the things they must do.
Mothers know when things are going wrong,
So they sit with you and talk, and sometimes even sing a song.
You can depend on them night and day, to make everything
     okay.
Grandmothers and great-grandmothers are extra special, too.
They always have lots of love and hugs and kisses for you.
They spoil you and give you your way, and never scold you
     when you get dirty at play.
Mothers and grandmothers are a gift from above that we should
     cherish and love.
They teach us to pray, and see to it that we do it every day.
Mothers and grandmothers are beautiful, thoughtful, and kind,
And I thank God every day for mine!

MORNING PRAYER

Thank you, Guardian Angel, for watching over me through the
    night.
My sleep was very restful, and my morning is already bright.
I'll try very hard to make the best of this sunny day,
And if I'm lucky, I'll spread joy along my way.
I think I'll start by calling my grandmother, and wish her a happy
    day.

* * *

FATHERS, GRANDFATHERS AND
GREAT-GRANDFATHERS

Fathers are strong men who want their sons to grow up to be just
    like them.
They teach us to be rough and tough, and how to handle
    problems without making a fuss.
They teach us how to ride a bike, and are fun on hikes.
They teach us how to play baseball, and when we lose, how to
    stand tall.
Fathers tell us to always be honest, and to do the best we can,
Because when we grow up, that's what will make us a man.
Grandfathers and great-grandfathers are a pleasure and privilege
    to have and love,
And are just as important as the Almighty God above.
Because of their years they are wise with knowledge,
And listening to them is like going to college.
Grandfathers add that special touch, which means so much,
And to a boy of eleven, this is heaven.
Fathers, grandfathers, and great-grandfathers, today love to you I
    send,
And God, I am very thankful to you for each one of them.

THE MANY THINGS I ASK OF GOD

Each morning as soon as I rise, I ask God to walk by my side.
I ask that He hold my hand, when I become weak and cannot
    stand.
I ask that He fill my mind with good thoughts about everyone.
I ask that He keep my eyes open, so that I can continue to see
    the light.
I ask that He touch my lips with His Blessed fingertips.
I ask that He fill my heart with more love for Him.
I ask that He warm my body with His precious sun.
I ask that He guide my feet, so I will walk the proper street.
I ask that He wrap His arms around me, whenever He is free.
I ask that He help me to be the child He knows I can be.
I ask that He bless me with peaceful rest when the day is done.
I ask that He also stand close to everyone.

* * *

THE WORLD

The world is a gift from the Lord above, and we should fill it
    with love.
The Lord created many beautiful things for us to see,
And they can be found wherever you may be.
There are many different countries, each with its own culture and
    race,
Which makes the world a very interesting place.
It's a shame we don't appreciate and enjoy all that we have,
Instead we spend our time hating and starting wars; how sad.
Every person, regardless of his race, creed, or color, from
    chocolate to vanilla,
Is the same under the skin.
We are all brothers and sisters, and when we fight, no one wins!
Extend your hand to your fellow man to show that you
    understand,
And prove you want peace and harmony throughout the land.

If you can't speak your brother's tongue,
Smile—that's the one thing that is understood by everyone.
Share the beauty of the flowers and the trees, and the wonders of
    the rivers and seas.
That's the way the Lord meant it to be, when He created the
    world for you and me.

* * *

LIFE

Life begins and ends as fast as a flick of light in the night,
So don't waste a minute of it by using a drug kit, and being a
    misfit.
It's a sin to waste precious time,
And besides, the world needs the help of every man's mind.
Life can sometimes be mean, but usually things are never as bad
    as they may seem.
It's perfectly normal to have a bad day; just don't let it affect you
    in a negative way.
Life is definitely worth the fight, so don't let problems put out
    your pilot light.
We wouldn't be able to appreciate the sunshine, if we didn't have
    rain.
So it's through Life's problems that we benefit and gain.
Make the most of every precious minute of your life,
Because it begins and ends as fast as a flick of light in the night.

A. LEON PINES

THE FAILURE OF SUCCESS

Extension—

Higher yields result in profits,
and these in turn bring fame.
Do there not exist some limits
to this materialistic game?

Means Versus Ends—

What is our goal, we ask,
and with what tools to implement?
The former is the *task,*
while the latter is the *instrument*!

Education—

Teacher, liberate the learner,
and help create a mind!
One who queries as a scholar
will then the answers find.

Extension Education—

A richer farmer with no mind,
a success in the extension tale;
But "education" of this kind,
in succeeding we did fail.

FROM THIS DAY FORWARD

From this day forward
I do accept thee as my husband,
To love, to hold, and to cherish.

From this day forward
I will try to bring much happiness
        to us in the coming years ahead.

From this day forward
I will be a friend to you;
I will understand when you need
        understanding;
I will be a guide to you when you
        need guidance.

From this day forward
I do but pledge all my love to you—
my heart, my soul, and my life.

From this day forward
I will satisfy you to the fullest,
Only thinking about pleasing you,
        caressing you, and loving you.

From this day forward
I will give to you all of me,
All the warmth and love that
        lies within

From this day forward
I will stay by your side,
go with you wherever time may take us.

If there were eight days from this day
        forward
I would only love you deeper and longer,
more intense, and with a mounting
desire to love you more and more,
to hold you closer and closer, till
we were one—sharing more and more
every day, every hour, every minute . . .
I Love You From this Day Forward.

FOR YOU AND ME

Softly, the grass is swaying,
Quietly, a flower is praying;
If such can be—and so close be
It makes you stop, and wonder why
It came to be
For you and me.

Slowly, a tree grows tall,
Feasting, from spring to fall
If such can be—from God's good earth,
Deep in the ground, which gave it birth,
It came to be
For you and me.

Proudly, the flowers are growing,
Suddenly, the prize is showing;
If such can be—from trodden lands,
To stir our minds and fill our hands,
It came to be
                For you and me.

* * *

TAKE TIME

Take time for children and their play,
And for the sick and old,
To pick a flower on the way,
Its treasures to behold.

And when you bask in happiness
Take time for just a word,
Don't let another day go by,
Just say "Oh! thank you, Lord."

A TINY FLOWER

My love for you is like a tiny flower;
Thinking of just you through every hour;
But if from you, my love you should dispose,
This tiny flower would bow its head and close.

The silken petals represent each thought
Of love, where sin has touched it not.
But to enter your heart, another person would try;
These tiny petals would bow their heads and die.

The stamen and the pistil represent love's growth;
Where love each day will write a new oath.
But if someone should ever break this token,
The stamen and pistil would die, with their hearts broken.

The stem holds all the love I ever knew,
And that is love this flower holds for you.
But if this stem someone should ever break,
A new flower my heart would have to make.

So let this flower, just as it is, be ours,
And let it be a flower of all flowers,
Let no one ever break this stem apart
But keep this flower whole, forever, in my heart.

JOHN M. POLLARD, SR.

THE WORTH OF CHILDREN

When children are born, they are additions to this
world
And most fathers would want a boy, but would
settle for a girl.
As long as they're wanted, it really doesn't
matter
And brought into the world normal, making plenty
of chatter.
Some babies are born with no such luck,
And with birth diseases they are unfortunately
struck.
They go through life with a problem from birth
Not really knowing what their lives are worth.
All children born should really be wanted
So they won't look at the world as if it's
haunted.
Unwanted children are generally ill,
Their bodies move, but some of their minds
stay still.
With this illness they can't help themselves
So they wind up statistics, on medical book
shelves.
People should be more concerned than they really are,
Because they are not excluded from this tragedy,
by far.
This has been a problem that has been
handed down
And it can happen to any family around.
So I would like to appeal to all husbands
and wives:
If you're having children, plan healthy lives.
Have all your children out of love,
And say a prayer to the Man above
That all your children are normal from birth,
And get out of life what they are really worth.

THE WHISTLE OF A FAR-OFF TRAIN

Whatever means the whistle of a far-off train?
The echo long repeats its noisy words.
Like a precious memory we wish it to remain;
Nothing comparable has ever been heard.
All other sounds are pictured as snow, wind and rain,
In likeness we describe, time, morning, noon and night.
The whistle is the difference twixt both joy and pain
When its sound pulls the curtain to darkness and light.
Thoughts seem yet ever homeward to find a way again,
Though the whistle tells the story of a faraway place,
The sensation is exciting: hear the whistle of the far-off train.
To some it is joy in the evening of a well-spent day,
The happiness of meeting friend or loved one, and then—
Who can describe, in words, the loud rending sound?
To some 'tis farewell as valued time grows wane.
The whole world over, nostalgia in like manner is found,
Whenever blows the whistle of a far-off train.

* * *

THE WINDMILL WHEEL

Close out the present to turn back the time,
To be down on the farm and the wind at high gale.
Ah, precious memories much finer than gold,
It's turning! it's turning! The Windmill Wheel!
Hear the water splashing, the sparkling drops
Quenching thirst of both man and beast.
Let's pass the shiny tin cup, its cold surface feel,
It's turning! it's turning! The Windmill Wheel!

GOING HOME

My orders came through today,
I'll soon be homeward bound;
But a thought of sadness strikes me
As I pause and gaze around.

I look toward the hillside
Where the sun is streaming bright,
And firmly staked in the ground
Are crosses glistening white.

Now, underneath each cross there rests
For all mankind a story
Of how a soldier in battle died
And now has passed to Glory.

Heroes they, yes, every man
That lies beneath that sod,
Lay down and gave their very lives
To their country and their God.

THE COAST OF CALIFORNIA

Longer than the length of days—
Forged before an eye could see—
The gulls fly free.
The crystal caps that break against
The cold and placid sand,
The jagged rocks,
The golden hues of the sunsets,
The lonely cranes—
A rugged remnant of beauty and peace
to stretch the length of the coast of California . . .

* * *

WHERE IS THE WISE MAN?

Where is the wise man who mourns not
what he can not change—or wiser still—
and has nothing to mourn?
Where is the wise man
who knows why he was born,
who sees the sunset and knows
its place as he knows his own?
Where is the wise man whose life
has been found in giving to others of
a mind firm and sound?
Who knows how to laugh and cry
and when and why?
Who knows that to be free
is the key?
Who waits for each tomorrow
devoid of sorrow?
A new day to pursue,
bold and true.

HOPE OF THE HEART

Don't talk to me of love, dear,
For I have felt the crushing blow,
Felt the sickening hurt of winter
When I cried amid the snow.

Don't talk to me of love, dear,
For sometimes I still cry
When I watch the birds wing southward
Across a blazing sky.

But just as sure as April flowers
Follow winter's stormy blast,
I know a new tomorrow
Will come to me, at last

                              Rita Pyles

* * *

FAIRYLAND

Come, my child, and tell me
Where the fireflies sleep at dawn,
Where the fairies dance at evening,
Where the leprechauns have gone.

Let me with you tiptoe softly
Through the meadows' dew-dipped grass,
By the sleeping daffodils
Lest we wake them as we pass.

Help me see through eyes of wonder
That world of yesterday.
Come, my child, and show me,
For my heart has lost the way.

                          Linda Edwards

lovesong

a letter from Briarcliff Manor

There comes a time
in everyone's life when they find it
necessary
to break down the old
to make way for the new;
I have come to that time.
Today my heart was troubled,
my heart and eyes were crying all day.
I took a walk
and the sun's smile did dry a million tears,
so clearly I saw—
I saw myself,
a minute speck in this glorious world
and I thought how funny, yet how true those clichés had
     become
"Who am I?" "Where am I going?"
I walked on . . .
I came to the lake,
I stopped,
I saw myself . . . so clearly . . .
the reflection of the dark green water
so still and peaceful.
I thought of the time
you and I were here,
you casting stones into the water.
I saw my life as that stone
gliding through the air.
I thought:
"Life is thrown away . . . just like that . . . "
it goes just as fast . . .

some stones make a bigger splash
yet the rippling water is so soon forgotten.
I want to be a big stone
with a big splash,
not to sit back and take
but take a chance and . . . give.
my eyes . . . they have been opened to the world,
but today I learned to see further by having looked into myself
and the beauty is so deep . . . so close . . .
since I have found you—
of the trees
of the wind
of the leaves . . . of the rippling water . . .
in the lake
I saw your reflection, too,
as still and peaceful
as your causes and words . . .
you are so very special . . . yes . . .
well . . . that promise
to make way for the new
once seemed so frightening,
but as you said some time ago
as we watched the ripples borne of a cast stone

    " . . . no promise is better
    than the promise in yourself . . . "

               * * *

FRIEND

. . . the first friend you'll ever have is yourself . . .

and the very next
is the one who lets you be yourself . . .

changes

Yesterday is yesterday and all that it's left me
is this faded photograph of you and your smile;
you look so familiar
but I guess I don't know you—
you just remind me of someone
I knew for a while.

changes bring changes that won't last forever;
guess this is that lesson we should learn while we can,
but feeling those feelings
that kept us together
means more than some photograph
of me and my friend.

    Like time turning pages
    in a book that never ends,
    we've been through the stages
    once strangers . . . once friends . . .
    like faces and seasons
    whose changes never bring
    the rhyme or the reason
    or the lovesong to sing.
    but yet time in time changes
    and some lovesongs may never fade,
    so the promises I'm keeping
    are the promises we made.

yesterday is yesterday; the change and the sorrow
is hid in a photograph of you and your smile.
you look so familiar
but I guess I don't know you—
you just reminded me of someone
that I loved for a while.

DELIGHTFUL DAY

This delightful day, the lovely honeysuckle
With sweet scented lips—hummingbirds yield to kiss,
My pensive thoughts to solitude retire:
What more could I desire?
Nature's works of art are clearly seen . . .
The craggy towering mountains, so steep and high!
Where the golden eagles fly . . .
In the depths of the azure sea
Schools of fish dive-play.
In cavern and crystal caves,
Mermaids play and swim under waves.
Deep in the ocean, where mysterious creatures dwell
In cavern and crystal caves,
Mermaids play and swim under waves.
Deep in the ocean, where mysterious creatures dwell
Coral gardens adorned with lovely blooms.
At dawn, the sun-kissed water of the sea—
Sparkles like a thousand mirrors
Floating and bouncing like silver dollars,
Kindling sound and cry by the wild ocean waves . . .
The last ray of the sun shines on sea's brow—
A fiery fire—a large Red Flame.

* * *

JUNE

June, the month of lovely roses:
The month of matrimony! Lovers' delight!
Love calls and mating and pleasant sights,
The fragrant scent of the flowering vine,
Dressed in gorgeous summer hues.
I breathe with ecstasy the sweet perfume
And kiss the ruby lips and drink the honey dew.
From the high bower the nightingale outsings the lark;

Moonlight, roses and nightingales make
A bit of Eden—hidden—yonder woodbine—
All night and day insects make music.
Now let the jasmine and sunflower
With golden buttercups, and bright-eyed narcissus bloom
On woodland, valley and meadow;
I'm the loveliest flower of June!

* * *

PATH OF LIFE

Show me the path of life, dear God,
Help me to imbibe Thy Holy Spirit.
Grant me Thy healing touch that I heal another,
Help me to subdue the desires of world and flesh.
Thy light illume my path—that I follow footsteps of Christ
With meekness, humility, and love.
Help me to radiate Thy infinite light
And do what is pleasing in Thy sight!

THE CITY IN '76

Cars in contrast with the homes
The city life is strife
With people moving to and from
In haste of something nice.

The disco scene
To dark, to lonesome
People searching for their self
Though some to be denied
And satisfaction brought.

A shout was cried, confused,
As shots stilled petty crimes
And babies weeping lonely
Just another Friday night.

And for some Friday's delight
Did fade by morning's light
As some awoke in jail
With others seeking bail.

But others hard at work
As someone missed their bus
And dealers dealing fast
The desperate cannot last.

While children play on hardened streets
And others do their chores or eat
As lovers sleep to noonday's light
Though some from bodies—heads to tight

And youth roaming restless
Whose blade reflected bright—
Some child lay bleeding, desperate,
As others ran in fright.

The music challenged laughter
The down folks feeling good
As some preferred unnoticed
There's danger in a flirt.

One's guilt was an assumption,
For rookie cops in fear
Reacted to one's manhood
As some folks stood and stared.

And political in nature
A bicentennial celebration
In search of long-lost fame . . .

THE LOVER OF MORAL BEAUTY

The lover of moral beauty
will have no need for a religious shrine;
Nor will he require a God to keep his
    morals in order;
Nor will he commit a worldly crime!

The lover of moral beauty has no need for
    rules,
Or man-made laws.
He constantly seeks moral perfection,
Eliminating all its flaws!

* * *

CHARACTER—YOUR TRUE VALUE

Your true value, your character,
Can be likened to a violin's musical tone!
It is the only true value you do own.

Your material wealth or your education
May cause you socially to sail
Like the musical note of the violin
Up or down on the musical scale.
But the true wealth you do own
Is still your character, your tone.

But in spite
Of the changes in customs, or the changes
    in style
That often defile,
True character will soar.
It will continue to live forevermore.

IN JUST SPRING

I, smiling child with brown and tangled hair,
Stand beside my broken tricycle on a worn and
Weathered cobblestone street, looking into the
Cold, gray stillness of an autumn afternoon.

Long and tedious shadows of blue-black weaving
Whisper to weeping willows and goldenrods, as
Tiny petals poke their snubbed little noses from
Beneath trampled logs of silver birches' green,
And then nestle snugly among bogs of withered
Branches.

The wind is wounded in gooseflesh, and sparrow riots
Swell and echo in the damp wood. But I am ablaze with
Wonder as my dreams dance in the mist.

MAN'S LOT

Man searches for something, he knows not what;
he tries to envision what is to be his lot;
sometimes he is beset by mixed emotions,
he cannot fix his beliefs, his notions.

Sometimes he is troubled, his paths are a maze;
he can find nothing of value to appraise;
he searches his wisdom for a way
and if he finds it, it is his for a day.

Come dawn, a new day, and he opens his eyes;
he knows out there somewhere his fate lies;
he will pursue the ways which form his lot,
through life's endless paths, toward he knows not what . . .

* * *

UNWANTEDNESS

Pity the unwanted old man who sits alone,
waiting for the touch of death to come along,
hearing whispers from his own, in darkness of night,
feeling their irritation, sensing their spite.

Hearing their whispered discussion, of old age homes,
their muted whispers and giggles o'er the telephone;
feeling the unwantedness of each passing day,
until the old man wishes death would shorten his stay.

FIRE

You started a fire inside of me—
Struck up a match and lit up a corner of my heart.
You fed the flame with yourself, a little at first, then furiously
    later.
Soon the fire spread from my heart,
My whole body became engulfed in flames.
I was on fire, totally consumed by you.
Then one day, you stopped feeding the fire and the flame started
    to die.
You were gone, but you forgot to extinguish the blaze.
You burned me, and a burn takes a long time to heal.

* * *

MISSING

What is that little extra part of you that I miss?
Is it your smile, your manner of speech, the tilt of your head?
Is it the way you walk, your hair, eyes, your physique?
No, I think not.

I miss the man who is hidden away,
The rare creature you have hidden from the world so well.
The sensitive genius of you, the brilliant poet, the vulnerable
man you did not share with anyone but me.

CHANCES

A stolen moment here and there,
Hiding feelings of joy.
It is not easy caring like this; fear is a constant companion.
Voices whisper in the night, "Be careful, be careful."
Dare I take those chances?
Dare I think that I can see you again?
Yes, you are worth taking the stolen moment.
I shall ignore the voices whispering in the night;
I shall see you again and again and again.

SHARING

Come walk with me through golden fields
With trees of green, 'neath sky of blue.
We'll drop our barriers, walls, and shields,
And speak of all things, old and new.

We'll share the fragrance of many a flower
And caress the soft, billowy breeze.
We'll dance in the coolness of a summer shower,
And together find our release.

* * *

METAMORPHOSIS

If I, like the eagle, could fly;
Could soar, float, and glide—
I'd find a mountain, majestic and tall,
And live high above away from it all.

If I, like the dolphin, could swim;
So shiny, silver, sleek, and trim—
I'd go to Atlantis where the world makes no sound,
And live down below where I'd never be found.

If I, like the cheetah, could run;
Swift as the wind 'neath a golden sun—
I'd find a valley, so vast and so green,
And live within its walls, never to be seen.

But I'm neither cheetah nor dolphin nor eagle,
Just a common soul, not majestic or regal.
Still, the valley, Atlantis, and the mountain are mine—
For my heart has been there a thousand times.

MEDITATION OF A POET

I felt that I must write today
   From deep within my soul;
Perhaps I'll write of things just past
   Or maybe centuries old.

For a poet does never know
   What lies beyond the mind,
But he releases himself to search
   That a treasure he might find.

Through the silence of the night
   His searching will not cease
Until at last he has found the key—
   And the treasure then released.

So, great poetry, live on,
   From the earth you'll never fall,
For poets will always write
   Until they search no more at all.

A SHORT STORY

The Great Designer of the starry firmament
Put His image into the monument;
His Light is lit into the cloister close,
Of Him to know
It is enough, with our wit.
He is behind the screen which covers sort of stages
For the past ages, not all to be seen.
By His great will for the noble deed
Grows the seed oughtn't to kill.
The subject to decay puts its shows,
The tempest blows to the last day.
The unequal creature of heaven's kingdom
Got the wisdom to grasp the picture;
And its heart aches, when in display
The disarray ends in ashes.
Language is the instrument of the magical spell;
It is the ringing bell at the top of the monument.
All together, the human beings want to fix things,
Even the weather.
And through the air are heard the tones
Of lovely songs to peace on earth.

* * *

RESUME

With glancing pupils the castle's guest,
On quicksand, loses the feet
To tread toward the spectral fleet,
And in time unfixed, ends the quest.

EXHIBITION PICTURES

—the end

of making pictures is never in sight; the tease
of reality in how the West was won must stand
in the way of any but fictional treatment; the same
goes for Custer's relapses which gained him the name "Yellow
     Hair";
the Maricosa situation, the name
it gave us in France, but pictures can give the air
to any situation, and cover the truth
or reveal it, whatever may be required; the scene
in heavy-water Norway is what the sleuth
would call an example; it gave us Bohr, he came clean
to our side of the fence, and what the outcome of that
was we may never know, except that now
we are safe for a while, and hope that our secrets stay flat
and secure, and escape the charge of occultism's row
and contention, and be a source of strength and not
of weakness, which may be true, because everywhere we look
there is camouflage, and in unity of thought
and coalition there is precedence and the book,
or conservatism, as we say, with Hess
and his four-nation guard, the raving maniac
is not to be considered a friend in need; yes,
we need to be strongly organized . . .

ELAINE ROBERTS

TO DEAR SANTA CLAUS

What do all the reindeer do
When Santa has gone and all is through?
Where has all the music gone,
The merry voices, the friendly horns?
What did Mrs. Santa say
At the end of Santa's day?

Does Santa work all day and night,
And wait till all the fields are white?
Then come out and say "Ho, Ho,"
To find his reindeer in the snow
And harness them to the sleigh,
And get his bag all filled with gifts?
In summer, fall, or spring,
Does anyone think of him
After Christmas Day?

* * *

LITTLE LEAVES ON THE TREE

Dear little leaves, stay on, don't fall.
I tried to tie you on, each one.
The day has been so long, but now
I have only one to do; the tree is very high
And I am very small.
The thread is getting shorter, too.

One of them fell to the ground
But I've got it now, and I can rest.
You see, I heard them say that when
The leaves begin to fall, she will
Not be here at all, but now
I know she'll stay, that's all.

CORONATION

Just a tiny needle with a length of thread
From a spool of blue, yellow, mossy green or red.

Stitches on silk or satin, a drawing of the thread,
The only way to make a robe when all is done or said!

Yes, it is but a needle straight and made of steel,
Yet it holds the power over just how people feel.

For did you ever stop to think the gown of richest gold
Would fall apart before our eyes unless the stitches hold?

The Queen in her Royal Robe could never take the throne,
If the stitches fall apart, and leave the cloth alone!

* * *

SPRINGTIME

There is a bud to open in the spring,
There is a bird, his song to sing.
There is a brook to babble on and on,
There is a clock to tick the hours away.
There is a road that takes us many miles,
There is a lamp to light the way.
But all these things in life so sweet,
Cannot without you, be complete.

ORISON

Remove the scales from my eyes, O Lord,
That I may see Thy wondrous workings.
Let my eyes behold, my breath inhale,
Thy Spirit pervasive and essence rare;
Wafted on wings of air and fragrance pure.
How beautiful Thy dwellings, O God;
The dewy morn, the flower redolent,
The wooded grove, the Hart therein.
All proclaim a Spirit unseen.

In Thine image createst thou Man;
From his vitals didst fashion woman;
How beauteous in form, flawless in shape,
As Thy symmetry, as Thy image.
And, yet, how pales the sight of mortal,
When the crushed petals of a rose are seen.
For with Thine image endow'dst thou Man;
But with Thy Spirit the down-trod rose.
All proclaim a Spirit unseen.

Let my soul absorb, then, that which my
Form can ne'er compensate for. Verily,
Thy image have I; Thy Spirit not.
Vive some sacred flame to remove the dross
From me. Let my hollow Spirit nurse
On the smell of a rose, a crushed rose;
On the sight of a star-studded sky;
On the virginal verdure of sun-beat leas.
For all proclaim a Spirit unseen.

YOU HAVE FALLEN, MY LEADER
ODE TO JOHN FITZGERALD KENNEDY

You have fallen, my leader,
Never to rise again; untimely
Departed from our midst;
Removed from us too soon, too soon.
Cut down in the street by an
Assassin's bullet, in a moment;
Your candle's glow sputtered, but
Briefly, in that moment; and, as life
Ebbed, the glow became a light eternal.

You have fallen, my leader;
Not by ballot, nor vote of the people,
Has your mantle been lifted;
Your voice has been forever stilled
In the privy chambers of world councils.
Not by debate, nor rhetoric, have you
Been downed. No longer shall you trod
The world stage. Instead, a hush descends,
Long before the final act has played.

You have fallen, my leader,
And a great void exists. Forever
Gone is that smile, which was the
Mirror of your soul; the quick,
Tousled nod of your head; the vibrant
Wave and handclasp; the ready wit
And warmth. Instead, an ocean of
Emptiness remains; an agonal moment
Has impaled history and transfixed time.

You have fallen, my leader,
Prey to a higher order of things;
Fair game, it would seem, to a
Wanton deed. But, in accord with
That Grand Design, it matters not
How a man dies; nor, how cheated by death.
Only how he has lived, is what counts.
And you, beloved leader, have become
A teardrop on the conscience of history.

THE PROUD KING

The distinction of a king is noble and distant,
As the kindliest peons of life contemplate,
Each day's silence as obscure and resistant,
Yet fluorescently glistening with inhumanities' hate,
In composing the servants and all their gaping,
At magnificent ladies of alluring grace,
Emerging the victor, yet quietly shaping,
That which befalls creature's of earth's race,
Bruised by the beatings of laborous hesitation,
No longer knowing what kindness should mean,
Left to smolder in the cauldrons of isolation,
Touched and summoned to approach each scene,
Bowing in fury and kneeling in rage,
To thrones of passion beseeching the stress,
Destroying the fervor of all who disengage
Their minds and souls from nobility's disdainfulness.

* * *

THE POETIC SOLITUDE

How shall I hold my head in pride?
Where shall my love and I abide?
I would gladly seek to know.
Lost in the era of contemporary expression,
Remote in humanity is the total suppression
Of emotion and feelings one must surely show,
Yet of myself and worth, there is no denial
That these depths are merely an isolating trial,
Of the plight wrought by the ingratitude,
That forever leaves the countenance downcast,
As the world had done for endless years past.
Yet in a poem shall I find solitude.

SONNET I

My step is slow upon the path; I'm old;
I walk alone; it was not always so.
I walked with my two sons; my step was bold;
those who see my now will never know.
On either side of me my sons sould cry
with laughter and delight at games we played.
How can the echo of their laughter die
or memory of their upturned faces fade?
Within me is the woman who was I—
a younger woman, one no one can see—
the one who, smiling, twice would say good-bye,
as time moved on, to let her child go free.
Now, as I walk, my heart holds tiny hands,
still clasping mine, across so many lands.

* * *

SONNET II

I think of thee, Rome, city far way,
The phantom forms of Caesars of the past;
Ghostly gold chariots on thy Appian Way
Keep casting that same spell as once was cast.
I would embrace thy sun, thy wind, thy rain,
And walk upon the paths where Caesars walked,
Mingling with theirs my footsteps, once again
Among the graceful monuments time mocked.
Although my spirit and my heart thou knowest
I will not see thee more before I die,
Yet only dying will I let thee go.
My death will close the door on thee, not I.
How oft I speak thy name, beloved Rome—
If wish were grace, it is to thee I'd come.

MAHLA'S PRAYER

Oh Lord! Give me the strength to face my critics without
malice, my tomorrows without fear, and my past mistakes
without remorse. May my enemies become my friends
because I may wish it to be so, and may my friends
who have passed on add substance to my life.
May my tomorrows be an improvement over
my past, and may the beauty of life
forever enrich my humble soul.
AMEN

I WALKED WITH GOD

The burdens of my weary heart
Were lost in one short day,
Along a shaded country lane
Where lay the new-mown hay.

I walked by clover-scented fields
With birdsong on the wing . . .
The music of their happiness
My heart kept echoing.

There all the world was at peace,
Kissed by the sun and wind;
Touched by the hand of love divine
Where Nature was my friend.

Along a shaded country land
Where purple daisies nod . . .
I lost the cares of yesterday
And walked again with God.

* * *

SPRING SONG

He sang with the dawn from the apple tree;
Sang to awaken the flowers and me.
Over his head the eternal sky
Throbbed with his song as the wind passed by.
Lifting his song to heaven above . . .
Sang of the springtime mating and love:
Again he sang and again I heard
The whispering wind and the singing bird.

EVERYONE'S GIRL

Everyone's Girl—
That's what I seem to be . . .
Doesn't anyone care for
only just me?
I'm good for the parties,
I come with the laughs—
If they only knew
How they break my heart in half.
I listen to their problems
I open my heart,
I make love to them and
then they depart.
Their lives go on
They return to their homes;
My dreams go on and
I write my poems.

* * *

ONE WEEK OF LOVE

One Week of Love
I was not to be saved
From the routine of bars,
Dull, boring men.
He was exciting
But it suddenly came to an end.
It takes so long to find someone
who means more than just a date.
One Week of Love—
That was to be my fate.
I really wanted this love to last—
One Week of Love—
and now it's past!

648

ANOTHER WOMAN'S MAN

Collectively my thoughts narrow down to you;
no space remains to distract me away.
Outrageous dreams continue through the night
and day, till once again—together we are one.
Registering only that I need you, I love you,
and most important of all, you care back
(imagine that, you really care!)
Creating a turbulence that cannot be controlled,
I cannot fight, I must flow with the tide
(only time can measure what is lost).
Ignoring all signals that warn me to "beware,"
Knowing only my mind, my body needs you,
Outweighing the happiness against the hurt,
Which one will finish first? Does it really matter . . .
(does it matter at all)?
Nevertheless, I am here, I am yours, until you
walk away, until you have had your fill—until
Eternity has reached its destination.

* * *

IN MEMORY OF ELVIS

Another year slipped right on by
While a Babe is born
And then destined to die.

This year a man was taken from me
One who will go down in history.
He was generous, well-mannered,
a little boy and a clown,
But to his friends remained true.
Still he was insecure and needed love
The same as me and you.
He gave so much but we wanted more,

He could not walk the streets,
At his clothes they tore.

No entertainer had so many fans:
They still come in droves
From all over the land
To pay their respects
For he died not in vain—
His spirit and music
Throughout the years will remain.

Now he lies in peace by his mother's
side—no longer alone—
Behind no gates must he hide.

In memory therefore
Remember the reason why we are here:
To comfort those in need
And let them know that we care.

For life passes quickly
And it's hard to explain why
A Babe is born
And then destined to die!

REACHING OUT

Now, friends, for a few moments,
let us share the pain that is in our hearts.
Let us try to gather some strength to endure
the heavy burden and let us bring comfort to the
children of our beloved Corgie.

This is a moment to reflect: 'What
is it all about, where
do we come from, where
do we go?'' Certainly to suggest
that birth is *the beginning,*
and death is *the end*
is not even worthy of consideration.
Birth is a *local beginning.*
Death is a *local end.*
But above it all, there is a *quality*
which is infinite in scope.
And it is from that *quality*
that all of us emerge
and to which all of us return.
Only faith can enter the realm
of that infinity.
But then, to what purpose
does such faith serve?

The answer, I believe, is quite simple.
The *raison d'être*—justification—
for such faith is to imbue us
with the will and desire
to do the very best possible
in this world, as Corgie did all the time.

A wise man named Hillel once said,
"If I am not for myself, who would be,
and if I am only for myself, what am I,
and if not now, when?"
Now, there are those who only consider

the first part of that sentence.
"If I am not for myself, who would be?"
They try desperately to get hold
of the whole universe,
drag it down,
pull it down,
slice it up,
cut it up,
squeeze the particles into their ego,
fill their ego with it,
and fill it some more,
until finally they are nothing
but a mass of selfish obesity.

Then there are the few beautiful ones,
like our beloved Corgie,
who consider the whole sentence.
Rather than down the universe,
they reach out toward it
and by this very act
become stronger and grow taller.
And, indeed, Corgie did reach out,
grew stronger, became taller.
Having done that, she was
thus in a position to help others.
That she did!

This is her legacy to us.
By emulating and implementing it,
we, too, will become stronger and grow taller.
As long as we do that,
our beloved Corgie
will be in our midst forever.

                              Professor Max Janowski

SOUNDS OF SILENCE
(Dedicated to the ever-present memory of CORGIE BERREND)

I promised you a poem, Corgie.
Some may say it's a little late
But you know it's not
And, after all,
I'm writing it for you.

Sunshine splashed faces
And flowers
And trees and grass today,
Much as it did
The morning you left for work.

You were confident then, that you would see it
Nestle in the evening sky,
But the swift hand of death scooped you up instead
And your sunshine shone
From the other side of life.

YOU ARE STILL HERE
I can feel you . . . yes,
And even *see* you with my mind's eye;
I can especially hear you sing
Your "SOUNDS OF SILENCE."

I can taste the cranberry
And the banana, and the lemon
Loaves of luscious bread
That you could not bake
Fast enough for me.

I ENVY THAT UNFATHOMABLE SOURCE
THAT HAS GATHERED YOU TO ITSELF.
I treasure your laughter, joy, and strength,
That legacy of "Doing now"
Which you prod me with.

I know that you now hover
Over your children
And those many of us
Whom you nourished and strengthened
And lifted up.

Well, for a short while
We won't be singing our duet together
But, friend Corgie,
Hang on fast to that challenging tune—
We'll all be joining you very soon.

Dr. Roberta Rosen

CHRISTMAS
(Twentieth Century)
(Nineteen hundred Seventy-Seventh Year)

The evenings come earlier, the dusk marks the end of the day,
The rising moon is much sooner, while the dawn seems further
away,
As the crisp morning air draws near, brisk steps of passers-by leave
tracks,
Activities seem played by ear, firewood being brought in on
racks.

Summer's reminiscence's sway the subconscious with its dear
dream,
With all of the mind's lost free play, vividly real, or so it seems,
Running wild with imagery, void of any inhibitions,
Plans for all future life to be, divinely ordained relations!

It seems only just yesterday, the new year had hardly begun,
Winter, spring, summer, then we say, fall, for the south now has
the sun,
And the seasons roll together, each with its peculiar nature,
Sequentially of each other, pleasing to God, and man's nurture!

Feathered friends are building their nests, beavers are repairing
their dams,
The mallards head south for their rest, leaving behind their
epigrams,
Without any formal reason, planet earth circles in orbit,
Ushering in the next season, in the centuries infinite!

Halloween, Thanksgiving ahead, snowflakes filling the darkened
skies,
Pathways formed by horse-drawn sled, kitchens filled with
homemade cakes, pies,
Greetings warm the air as friends call, from neighbors, and from
far away,
Holly, mistletoe deck the hall, garlands of arms signify gay!

May God be The Author, and The Finisher of this occasion,
Revered by all with Christmas tree, for The Only Begotten Son,
Our Redeemer, Lord, and master, Who died that all mankind
    may live,
For His grace to administer, our life to Him, we gladly give!

WHISPERS FROM AXUM

We are drawn to antiquity by the forces of age,
Encumbered by all the armies of Egypt
And Arabia searching for highlands.
Dancers whirl through the mist
Of Mohammed's prophecies oblivious;
Ivory down the Nile, gold across the desert,
Coptic chatter in the streets of Axum.
These are the foundations of magic,
With Byzantine masonry and noble hands
Secured against all time.
A lion stands at the gate of this city.

* * *

CASCADE MEMORY

It dwelt in darkness these long years,
Past centuries of rock and snow,
Wasteland upon wasteland turned inward.
It angered mournfully, yet never wept.
It dreamt of heights beyond imagination,
Yet never freed itself.
Seasons lost to seasons,
Happiness imbedded in the cliffs:
These days survive without end.

* * *

EROSION

Our monuments of sand had drifted into years
Of conceptual foundations that crumbled to the touch,
Introspectively demure.
This is the style that we chose:
Wind and water, gravity and heat—

We sifted through those years
Like legendary archeologists
Reaching for the fruits of Eden
In a statutory dream,
An unconscious form of art.

LET IT GO AND LET IT FLOW

I see sadness on a barren tree,
One leaf hangs on desperately.
Its summer splendor long has faded,
I feel its point of view is jaded.

Why, I wonder, does it linger on,
Family and neighbors are long since gone.
They lived their lives and did their best
At season's end they went to rest.

Through freezing wind and driving snow
The stubborn leaf still won't let go,
Somehow it doesn't seem to see
The overall futility.
Do I at times act like that leaf
By clinging to an old belief—
Do I prevent a normal flow
Resisting growth by saying ''No''?

Can I loose person, place and thing,
Must I possess and must I cling—
Or can I turn away instead
And leave a thing once it is dead?

There's no such thing as standing still
And it may take a lot of will,
But when I see a backward trend
I'll bring things to a gracious end!

LIVE WITH RIGHTEOUSNESS

Let it always be present in your heart.
The cradle rocks sweetly,
And already it is evening of life.

At daybreak, night haunts the mind.
Time is short, here comes spring—
And before we know it
Winter appears.

Pick your roses, the best,
Because life runs fast.
Go, my friend,
Meditate near the shore . . . think!

Nature, by its majestic dimension,
Inspiring in its beauty,
Dominates the soul.

See marvelous roses;
Pick at leisure;
Beware of thorns!

Live with righteousness.
Let it always be present in your heart.
So man approached the hive
And left with no honey,
Born unlucky, or perhaps lucky,
And called back to enigmatic nothingness,
To a grave, so early opened.
They left this world so young!
They tasted no sweetness,
Breathed no silencious brise,
And left the boat so early . . .

SOLITUDE IN THE GARDEN

Come in the garden.
The sun glows,
Unruly trees whisper
In crazy shivering sarabands.

Breathe this special aroma
In luxurious fields;
Take delight from exquisite sweetness.
This magnificient, impressive nature
Appeals to vibrating souls.
Come to the garden, meditate!

Hearts, heavy, drowsy,
Tired and sad, linger.

Life is right here, and now.
Lift up radiant smile,
Righteous, good, and strong.
Live, my friend, live!

BREATH OF SPRING

Oh, wondrous breath of spring,
You make the larks and robins sing.
You blow a kiss on barren trees,
And soon their branches sprout with leaves.

Blow gently, sweet breath of spring,
'Tis time to wake the slumbering.
You make the magic of God's creation
Come alive in wild anticipation.

Ah, refreshing breath of spring,
Your touch brings joy to everything.
You fill our hearts with a zest for life
And we forget our cares and strife.

Tell me, O breath of spring,
What the season changes bring.
Where do you hide from summer heat
And the cold of winter sleet?

Do you travel, breath of spring,
To the land where the angels sing?
If I die and journey there,
Will you be waiting for me there?

* * *

HAIKU

Spectacularly
They bloom so briefly and fall . . .
Wild cherry blossoms.

If you pray and ask,
God listens, and His mercy
Will overwhelm you.

DEATH

When shadows fall in twilight years
Our thoughts turn to death and tears.
How swiftly the years go by,
And soon we'll have to say good-bye.

Some people fear the call of death
And strive to keep their final breath.
They cling to memories of long ago,
Dreading the thought of letting go.

There are others who welcome death
For it is like a nice, cool bath.
It cleans their souls of mortal sins
And ends the pains that grieve their kin.

When eyelids close in final sleep
Our promise to the Lord we'll keep.
"We'll go home to you," we said,
In heaven where the angels tread."

Grieve not for us, for when we die
Our souls will journey to the sky.
Through a myriad of stars we'll soar
To eternal life forevermore.

* * *

NO CRY FOR ME, BRUDDAH

Hey, Bruddah:
No cry for me when I die
'Cuz maybe the good Lord going say to me:
"Wahine, be happy in my Kingdom of Heaven."
So, I going shimmy, shimmy here
And shimmy, shimmy there;
And I going make everybody happy
When I dance the hapa-haole hula.

663

SHULAMITH SALEM

A POEM

Gone are the days when the air was scented with laughter and
    bells;
Gone are the days when I heard swift and light-footed steps
Running in the hallway;
Gone are the rosy cheeks and smiling dimples that looks attracted;
Gone is my strength to walk in the pastures with a sure step and
    erect.

Gone is my sight to watch the stars and find sky's Milky Way;
All is gone, but my ability to think and meditate;
Meditate about life, its blessings and shortcomings;
Meditate and communicate with God,
For my days are numbered in His book.

The clouds are so shiftless, like a woman's thoughts,
And the stars peeking from behind them are like children at play;
Soon I will join them in their games, and in their wings
My thoughts will be forever sealed.

As the raindrops will tell you, and sun rays will whisper to you—
Particles of many thoughts and meditations follow us throughout
    our life,
From birth into eternity the cycle just never stops,
It revolves, revolves and revolves . . .

CONFINEMENT

The dry tears of a burnt-out life,
My short existence,
Visions of battles, swords, and then fatigue,
Feet running in dark hallways
While bombs explode and sirens wail,
Lives snapped in their midst—
All that, and myself also.

* * *

PLEASE, HOLD MY HAND FOREVER

I lie within a slowly dying darkness;
Dreams of love I carry in my bosom,
Secrets of life pulsate within my heart;
Then you alone are with me, love.

The skies debate with sad thoughts,
The stars flicker, so searchingly;
And under all that universe we stand,
Our hands clutching one to the other.

Please, hold my hand forever.

RUN, RUN

I am the goat of the mountains, running,
I hear my name called from a great distance
Yet I can't identify it;
My heart is thumping hard
To sounds coming up from the valleys,
A voice warning, begging, pleading—
But I have no name now.
Escape is only temporary
And my bewilderment is
Buried beneath the stones on the road,
And my eyes are misty as I wander
In a fog.
I struggle in and out of deep caves
But again it is all meaningless;
When I look out through my chained enclosure
There is one moment of complete awareness
And then only a shadow is left—
And a little worm in my hand.

MOTHER'S GRIEF

Gone are my children, and so I am left alone,
Forlorn in my penetrating sorrow;
Gone is my lover, and in his absence
My solitude is a burden
I cannot carry for long—

The valleys of my country are flooded
With oceans of tears and rivers of blood,
Mourning for my children
And for my lover they still cry—

And here I exist in my solitude,
Living a wasted hypocrite's life.
Pretending from day to day that all is well,
Eating, enjoying, while my heart is broken and hurt—

My nights are restless,
My dreams are tortures,
The days bring only sadness of heart
As the evenings carry their faded memories—

The dawn and the dusk are only
Faint reminders of days past,
When we all rejoiced together
And when love was amongst us—

These days are gone now,
And so is the past;
The present is sad and wasted
And the unknown future approaches slowly
For my hand to touch its wings soon—

Sad memories, sad memories . . .

PUG-NOSED DOG

I know a little dog,
He is kind of pug-nosed;
His face is wrinkled,
And so full of thought—

He had a lot of trouble with his stomach,
And even used to throw up a lot;
In circles only he walked,
Around and around the courtyard—

Although the world was wide and big,
In circles he walked, not even getting tired of it;
His owner kept him in a little enclosed yard,
And the only exercise he had was walking around

Until one day a new owner came along,
And the pug-nosed dog was freed
From his little confining courtyard,
And very sad he looked indeed—

Their house was big and spacious,
Their yard was bigger yet;
The pug-nosed dog was free to walk around,
Not confined at all, and not in circles only—

But as habit does it,
He still walked around in circles;
Many a day passed by before the vomiting stopped,
And also the circles became fewer and smaller—

He found out that all the doors were open wide,
He was free to choose other directions for his walks;
Yet once in a while he was still caught in a rut,
And in a little circle he walked around—

Just a little old habit . . .

STEREOTYPE? NO!

Yes, that's me—
Gone from gentle youth and spring
To fall storms and grief.
Still, I choose myself
As myself's chief,
From anger to tears
To some tranquility.
It's me, yes, me—
Imperfect, impractical,
Unhurried and unharried—
me, yes, me—
Using hours dreamily
Reading clouds
Spending words
Stroking cats
Collecting gourds
Confiding to my apple tree.
Yes, that's me;
Yes, I believe the vast unseen,
The Rosicrucians, the jumping bean.
Believing's good,
Feeling's keen;
Yes, I still play hopscotch
With Freddie Frog—
I also pet a mangy dog—
I search for secrets every day—
Sing the song of Mandalay.
Yes, that's me!
Studying a bumblebee
I'm here—
Here to think, to feel, to be—
And to be me!

SHARON SALISBURY

HANDS

Hands can say so many things;
    good-bye, hello, come near—
Beckon to a frightened man
    Or wipe away a tear.

Hands are strong and powerful.
    not long are they retired—
Molding clay into a form
    when their master is inspired.

Hands can soothe and comfort
    with a touch, they say I love;
Nakedly caressing, or
    when hidden in a glove.

Hands are capable of hurt,
    uncontrolled and used in hate—
Tearing apart, they can destroy,
    and viciously manipulate.

Hands can say so many things—
    in place of voice, they speak—
Offering a silent promise
    as a child drifts into sleep.

MY FRIEND

Thinks I'm beautiful
　　Though I know I am plain.
Patiently sharing my joy
　　And my pain.

I turn and she's there
　　The times that I sorrow.
She is my friend yesterday,
　　Today and tomorrow.

* * *

LITTLE ORPHAN

Little Orphan, don't you cry
　　because your mother's dead;
Your tears will go unnoticed,
　　as you painfully bow your head.

It seems, though you are very young,
　　you realize your fate;
Left to wander through the streets
　　to beg and steal—to hate.

Little Orphan, don't you know
　　you're just one victim of war
Who will slowly die of hunger—
　　your grave, an asphalt floor.

ARMOR

Invisible walls have been built
Through the years.
I've learned many lessons,
I've shed many tears.
Clawing and fighting my way to the top;
With stark realization, I must never stop.
For one simple slip, one minor mistake—
My whole world would tumble,
The vultures would take.

Not always a cold, heartless person was I;
Not always calculating, conniving and sly.

I once had the mistaken opinion
Most humans would care.
That peers and opponents would
Always fight fair.

I soon rudely awakened to
The intricate game
Of manipulating, bribery,
And drudging up shame.

So tune your ears carefully
To an experienced word.
Clothe yourself heavily with
Armor, Shield and Sword!

LOVERS AND FRIENDS

The world
is full
of lovers—
A song
is written;
a poem penned.
I love you
—not—
I like you;
Can a lover
be a friend?

Yes, my answer
as here
we lie,
Our passion
spent and gone.
It's good
to know
that you'll be there
With the cold
gray light
of dawn.

We play as
friendly children play
On a swing
or carousel.
Sharing ideas,
a photograph;
Across imaginary
seas we sail.

Love and like
synonymous—
We've learned
to stand
and bend.
Erasing that
elusive line
—between—
A lover and
a friend.

TELL ME WHY

Tell me why—   it seems to matter, the color
                    of one's skin—
                 in worldly competitions,
                    each side can't share and win;

                 we shouldn't show compassion
                    to less fortunate than we;
                 and bravely stand united
                    so the criminal must flee.

Tell me why—   the litle ones we borrow
                    so innocent and small
                 be abused and beaten—
                    and sometimes roughly mauled.

                 the Golden Rule is just some words
                    we practice with our lips;
                 between our words and actions
                    the meaning somehow slips.

Tell me why—   it's so hard to profit by others'
                    past mistakes;
                 we can't tolerate or understnd
                    what another heart dictates.

                 as friends from every nation,
                    holding hands around the world
                 can't we look upon each flag with pride
                    as it's majestically unfurled?

THE FLOW OF TIME

Today's events
like unjaded freshets
babble softly
drifting by
unnoticed and with
no fanfare,
accumulating and
crowding upon us
like water
by a dam impounded
to form a lake
of yesteryears;
there in retrospect
to be enjoyed
in portions
that may assuage
our thirst
for memories
yet within our ken.

* * *

AUTUMN TREES

The fury of an Autumn storm
roars down to clutch
their colored raiment
of gold and scarlet loose,
piling in sacred drifts
the full wardrobe
of God's annual rite
to leave them naked thus.

C. L. SAXE, JR.

YUMA BY THE SEA

City of Yuma, pause and ponder, but for chance you might be
    the Atlantic City of way out yonder.
What opportunity you lost in the name of security!
What wealth and fame did you squander
    by trying to stop the river that had to wander?

In 1906 the Rio Colorado began to flood;
You tried to stop it with tons of mud.
Then you called for railroad rolling stock
    and filled each car with more tons of rock.
The river found its way around
    that makeshift dam, and headed straight for lower ground.
It reached a depth of 280 feet, and the Rio Colorado came to be
    that desert miracle—the Salton Sea.

Ah yes, Yuma, but for your search for security
    you could be Yuma City on the sandy shores of the Salton
    Sea.
Today you would be a city of sun-baked boardwalk rambles;
    and years ahead of Atlantic City . . . as a city of gamblers.
And in the tradition of Western forces,
    you, naturally, would have handled divorces.

But, Yuma, you may get another chance,
You still may rise to fun-loving dominance.
When along the San Andreas line
    there comes that ominous rolling sign
    of earthquake motion,
You could become known as Yuma City . . . on the Pacific
    Ocean.

REVIVAL HOUR PRAYER

We send up thanks to Thee,
For the wonderful Father you have proven to be,
Blessings without number,
Whatever is best for men—
How oft we stand and wonder,
How great Thy planned handiwork has been.

Kindle in us anew
All that is good and tried and true
In this hour of revival,
While we in this age seek survival.

May Prayer—the mightiest force in the world—
Sustain us when darts against us are furled.
May the beauty of Thy encircling Love,
Be an inspiration from above.

To be a co-worker with Thee,
Truly, in the heart,
Does peace and joy impart.

* * *

A TOAST

To the Yucca, Candle of the Lord in the desert,
We give our toast to Thee.
Your tall spikes wave in the breeze so free;
You stand as a sentinel through the night,
To us a glorious sight!

LINA SCHREIER

GOOD-BYE, MOTHER

High up under blue sky
is where I awaken from this dream—
clouds looking like cauliflower,
humming of heavy machines,
hostesses with luncheon trays,
tiny beads of sweat on their noses,
red and blue uniforms with little hats,
motors humming monotonously.

good-bye, Mother,
maybe still standing at the gate,
lifting her finger,
warning, forbidding,
never-ending gesture.
A last hug; good-bye, Mother;
red carpet under my feet—
freedom at the end of the tunnel.

PERSON-TO-PERSON

I hear your voice
Across the miles,
Detached, impersonal,
And ask myself;
Where is the love
We have shared so long?
We speak,
Observing niceties,
Polite until the end.
Until mercifully
We say good-bye,
And humming wires
Disconnect
Two lives.

* * *

HUCKSTER

Will it sell?
Will it move?
You betcha it will.
Never mind
People,
What do they know?
It's the greatest,
The newest,
Best in the line.
So push it,
Hype it,
Promise the world.
They want a refund?
Give 'em another
Instead.

MARK A. SEAVER

SONGS OF THE ASTRAL PLANE

The clocks run fast,
Or maybe slow.
The stars fly by.
Or is it
Us by them?
The time is now.
Too late!
It is gone.
A moment, gone
And not replaceable.
Planets revolve,
Life evolves,
Time dissolves.
The ship stops
At a foreign home.
The sky is red.
We are blue.
Life is old.
We take off and
Time slips out of our hands.
We bow before kings
And kiss their feet.
We leave and
Decimate their planet.
We cry love and
Kill those who disagree.
Space is empty.
So seems life.
The clocks run fast—
Or is it slow?

JOHN THOMAS SERPA

VICTIM OF CHANGES

Victim of changes,
There are tears in your eyes.
Who will hear our cries?

Your love for fellow man is surpassed by none,
Yet who will love you in return?
You try to be good
But society is cruel,
You try to show tenderness
Yet life is full of violence.

Victim of changes,
I know your fears
And I can feel your tears.

Your mind is beautiful
But our world is full of lust and impurities.
You are a friend to everyone
Yet why aren't they that way to you?
You are struggling in this fast-paced world—
But haven't they heard of "peace of mind"?

Victim of changes,
Our understanding will be as everlasting as can be,
And I will wipe your eyes as you will to me.

You are a prince of God
Yet suffering in a world of false beliefs,
So now you sit down and pray
But please remember I am with you.
So go ahead and cry for now
Yet keep striving to be free.

Victim of changes,
I can tell that it's true—
That this earth doesn't deserve a person as beautiful as you!

JOHN THOMAS SERPA

NOW THAT YOU'RE GONE

Now that you're gone . . .
I know no peace inside my soul
With all this love for you I can't show.
Yet love is something you shouldn't repress;
Telling you will help the pain hurt a little less.
Now I know how it feels to have you gone—
So many beautiful memories still linger on
. . . And to think you said you'd never leave . . .

Now that you're gone . . .
It's really hard to continue.
It's the absence of so much pleasure, together, that makes me
    blue.
Thoughts of your tenderness will always comfort me.
I really do love you, can't you see?
So now you're hundreds of miles away,
I thought for sure you'd come back to stay
. . . And to think you said you'd never leave . . .

Now that you're gone . . .
I have so many friends who take care of me
But many sleepless nights by myself; are you thinking of me?
Coping with distress is something we all must do.
I realize I must live my own life, I have many things to do,
So time goes on. I'm over you. You live yours and I'll live
    mine—
May the world be good to you till the end of time!

TO BE LOVED

To walk a lonely day with a friend
And be surrounded with love,
To roll together in God's green grass
As if today is all that matters,
To lie under the sun
And feel the warm rays of our hearts,
To run down a mountainside
Being free, yet wanted . . .

To sit under a tree
Knowing our love is shadowed with trust and faith,
To feed a lovely animal
As to share our pleasures and fears,
To watch a running stream
As our dreams and memories flowing through our minds,
To be with each other as the sun sets
While the wind rushes through our hair . . .

To hope the day wouldn't come to an end
Yet knowing tomorrow you'll still be here,
To experience in a day
Feelings to last a lifetime,
To describe the most beautiful thing in the world
Is still difficult to do.
To be loved—I know it's happened to me,
And I pray it will happen to every one of you . . .

JUST A FREE SOUL

Just a free soul
Strolling through God's land,
Loving people along the way.

Such a soft touch,
Caressing us with
So much warmth and tenderness.

Just a happy face
Smiling all the time,
Brightening up our day.

Such a beautiful look,
Attracting affection with
The gleam in her eyes.

Just a child of God
Living life its fullest,
Sometimes fearing, yet always knowing.

Such a yearning mind,
Trying to please all
Although taking from no one.

So now time goes on:
Your river of love
Will never run dry.

All in all our lives
You have given us
Reasons for living,

So here you are in a beautiful world
Where you will always
Be in peace with God.

All we have is so many beautiful memories
Of happiness with you,
Always to be with us.

So it is said that all things must pass,
Yet in the hearts of your friends and relatives
Your unique quality of love will be eternal . . .

* * *

HOLD ME

Smiling
Touching
Kissing

Sensation
Anticipation
Expectation

Whispers
Dreams
Memories

Now and then
Tight and close
Soft and real

Moment of pleasure
Tears of joy
Peace of mind . . .

R. J. SHAFER

SEQUEL

The night was restless in fields once known.
The leaves were dressed in beads of dew,
And in the quiet of the lonely place
I thought I saw a wounded face.
And from the face there came these words
Spoken to another within the bounds
(Oh, such anxious, anxious sounds):
"What's that I heard? Is it true?
They built a cemetery at Hamm,
At Anzio, at Manila, at Guam?"
"Yes, it's true," the other replied,
"They built a cemetery at Hamm,
At Anzio, at Manila, at Guam;
And many more throughout the earth.
And they plan one in Korea,
And there is something about Vietnam."
"But did they not hear us when we prayed
In our fields so long ago?"
"Apparently not, apparently not."

A cold breeze brushed the lonely place.
A quivering remembering rose pleaded attention
To its color of red.

* * *

LISTEN!

Someone, alone, is quietly sobbing.
It sounds like a child,
Or a mother, perhaps a brother,
Or a young wife, a sister . . .
A father?

688

THE FIR AND THE PALM

Fir tree,
    Lonely and sad,
    Dreams of his slender Palm,
    Who, lonely and sad, dreams of her
Fir tree.

* * *

ODE TO A GREAT MAN

Was he born, or was he sculpt from fiery
Stones of Life on some Olympian height?
Heaven's gift he came, Prometheus-like, a
Lonely force in Freedom's smallish troop, and
Built his temples grand of noble tones with
Soaring strains of true, profound emotion,
Loos'ning ancient chains of lifeless form and
Leading man to dream aspiring dreams.

Was he born, or was he sculpt from fiery
Stones of Life on some Olympian height?
Heaven's gift he came, Prometheus-like, a
Lonely force in Freedom's smallish troop, and
Towered taller far than all his peers, the
Greatest Titan of his time—Beethoven!

STREET SOUNDS

There was a glitter from tinsel prancing and dancing in front of
him; as he reached out there was too much distance, lights
grew brighter and then the candle was blown by a heavy
breath; the sounds were deafening, like a drum roll—his
hand was still.

* * *

THE RING-TAILED CAT

There was a legend that I didn't wait to hear—
The hunt was more important at the time.
There were imagined trophies to be gained.
Life had hurried me through many closed doors;
I waited only for oncoming trains, conversation
was unimportant.
The drive to find the untamed and the need to be a winner—
All these are now done and the prize was only one
that had been reclaimed by life's tarnish.

* * *

DANGERS

The long bridge awaited us like the hungry tendrils from jungle
    life;
Faded lights made visions dim to those crossing;
There were screams of protest from the asphalt as it was heaped
    with unwelcome salvage;
Now it is time for the white scavengers to stake their claims.

DOROTHY A. SHEER

THE MIND

My mind sits in an encyclopedia,
Closed when the book is closed,
Opened when the book is opened,
Dusty when not in use.

Questions arise and so does my mind,
Answers are found when sought,
Taken out and debated;
Reason always wins the argument.

Challenge is its life support,
Boredom is its destruction;
Invention is its fancy,
Interest makes it grow.

DOROTHY A. SHEER

DEAR ORVILLE AND WILBUR

Many thanks for your flight,
Which is commemorated at your Kitty Hawk site.
We appreciate your wisdom, courage and invention,
A life history of your infinite perfection.

You gave birth to exploration in space,
Keeping us on top of the technology race.
To Mars and Venus we will zoom
In the time it takes a flower to bloom.

We speed across the sky toward the stars,
And soon shall have weekly trips to Mars.
Politics and the economy shall take on new dimensions,
The complexities of everyday life have no preventions.

Intergalactic communication evolved from your space ship,
From one dimension to another we will skip;
Your invention has made American life the best,
From the moment you took the first flight test.

INSIDE ME

Entrapped inside my body
are men of diffrent souls,
Where one man he does wander, the other has his goals.

He walks cocksure and confident
and knows just where he stands.
He likes to hold the future in the grasp of his strong hands.

The other prefers to sit back
and bask in the sun's warm rays,
Lie around untroubled, and waste away his days.

And sometimes I am fearful
for when there is a choice,
None stands above the other; both have an equal voice.

* * *

FOR ANGEL

Two people in love are
        Like the sun and the sky;
Separately they are nothing,
        Together they are of the greatest
Wonders of the world,
        Giving forth light, warmth, and beauty
To everything in reach.
And when love grows, as when
        The sun climbs in the sky,
The light grows brighter,
        The warmth grows warmer,
And life takes on a different,
        More beautiful appearance.

693

RUTH ROBINSON SHEPHERD

NEW BRIDE

June causes roses fair to bloom
and spread over earth a rich perfume.
Say, Sally, have you heard, there's a
rumor around town.

There's a new bride in town.
Have you seen her? She's little and neat
but mighty and sweet. Ain't you seen
her? No, not the bride or the bridegroom.

You are late, woman, her name is Myrtle, she's full
of fun, she lives at 2701.

Go on, gal, treasure your diamonds,
polish the gold, reach out to your
neighbor and keep the old.

DON'T WORRY

Walk tall and straight, here comes "78."
Don't worry, because worry grows loosely,
and the sorrow of decision makes no difference
who creates the division.

By the hour, often gives us a small or
large rain or shower; the entrance pay
on trouble before the due will set your
heart at ease, and make the compound
entrance equivalent, as today's mice
nibble on yesterday's cheese.

Never worry about a tide going out; stand
firm with your hands on the sack; the same
way you see it going is always the way it
turns back.

Never worry about the team going blind—
just keep on marching, marching, and
I'll stay in line.

GRANDSON NUMBER ONE

Your baby picture hadn't got quite out the envelope I tore—
I stopped. I told my startled self, "I've seen this *face* before!
Across the eyes, ah, yes! The head! But through the eyes, I
    know!
They speak of something from the gut and bone of long ago!"

New snow was down, I tracked it in that day you clicked in
    place,
That day the murmured magic said, "He's yours! The face! The
    face!"
Oh, sweet concern, and love to learn, for we have yet to meet,
To touch, and heft, and arms around; Oh, precious new
    heartbeat!

God keep you well and joyous, Ben; be credit to our clan
When time shall turn and I'll be gone, and *you* are come a man.

JESUS SAID?

The King's own shill slipped in such lines as "Turn the other
    cheek'';
Not Jesus—dead some thirty years—denied word God did speak.
He knew His Father's "eye for eye" and even "tooth for tooth,"
When Jesus dumped their tables moneychangers had that proof!

Come think of it, there's been small change—the symbiotic
    Church
Hath ever flourished close to Wealth, both leave the Poor in
    lurch;
And always priest, or parson, is dependent upon they
Whose greatest need is Holy Writ against their awful Day,
When they'll be stripped, turned inside out, and ordered up to
    tell,
In twenty words, *Why* they played God with loot from human
    Hell;
Why priestly laundered plunder paid for monk, or acolyte,
To sing their Praises, set their Crowns, in name of God and
    Right?

An *everlasting* fire, said God, an eye for *every* eye;
And Jesus *drove* the Changers out, as physical as I:
He felt my Hate; He knew my Fear;
Pain tore His heart; salt stung His tear.
In these are we as one.

* * *

31ST ON THE 28TH

Sweetheart, it seems but yesterday
I'd take your hand and softly say,
"I need you, dear; Come let us lay
Us down a while—
And talk.''
Past perfect? Ah, *sweet friend,* how true!
But still in love! All thanks to you.

IN THE GARDEN

The Widow Black doth lure for lust then eat her spider mate,
Directly he has seeded well her anxious eggs which wait
To hatch; and image parent face on silken filament.
Alas, poor Pop! Seduced, reduced, to mama-excrement!

From garden grim we'll split to make another scene, like, clear:
A sketchy, older, colder gal, a first-job engineer,
In rented church, and tux, and sound, and flashes, tie their knot;
Pretending ending, claws gave pause, he's looking back a lot.

He's piecing cold scenario: her self-invited move,
His never getting balance back before he hit the groove,
His dream of home and kids near kin, hamstrung by
      countermand,
His people's warmth, as garbage spurned; live burial, per plan!

Oh, missing daughter never gained, 'ere birth was empathy
The *lack* behind a fumbled mask of dire hypocrisy.
Another rushed a guy, moved in, and elbowed all aside;
Got tit for tat, and chucked a-lee, to wit: cast off! denied!

Said Solomon, "Let sword divide this child and half to each."
One cried, "*I* lied! Oh, hurt him not!" Tight lips betrayed the
    leech.
Whereas ye bid man "flourish," God, his dream lies starved and
    dies,
Nor woman warm who'll halo *him* with strength of tender ties!

  Where only *Peaches* grow?'' * Not kind!
A hoax from Hell! Ye made Love blind!
Thy garden path hath *web* to mind:
And slow the cruel feast!

(*"He picked a Lemon in the Garden of Love where only Peaches
    grow"—Pop song, 1912)

SPRING '79

Two days of sun and winter's done—forgot his final fling!
A push of leaf, a wing of song, and outflung arms to spring!
Then overnight a fresh of white locked all within a trice;
Took back each tender greening thing. Aw, Nature! Was *that*
    nice?

* * *

OSCODA FIRE—1911

In Michigan where forest fire and bitter cold began,
Where pulling on the long-johns is routine for miss and man,
Our place lies north of half the lines Iosco County cuts;
'Tis where at minus thirty-nine cold mercury spilled its guts
Straight out its busted bottom in the snowdrift 'cross our porch!
'Tis where the sun went out the day Oscoda got the torch.

'Tis where all night, in Huron wet, we agonized the burn
To ashes hot, of every all, and nothing left but turn
To mercy tent and blanket, and brave vow, "We'll build anew!"
And "Damn the preachers!" Why? Because their "hellfire" had
    come true.

Now all are "called" to sinful towns, where gross collections are,
All whiskey, whores, and lumberjacks, and members of the Bar.
Here every coin preempted is for shovel, axe or shack,
For soup to ease our bellies in survival's desperate lack;
So little left for sin that some half-wish a preacher back!
—In Michigan where forest fire and bitter cold began.

699

LOST AND ALONE

Lost and alone
I can't find my way,
searching for love
on each passing day,

High in the wind
I'm floating to see,
would somebody there
like to come along with me?

Come on, and nestle up to me,
can't you see I'm sitting here,
all by myself, so lonely;
I say, show me a little sunshine,
let me feel the warmth again
of your love one more time.

High on a hill
'side a clear mountain stream,
perched on a rock
I'm ready to dream.

Sun in my face
as the sky's looking down,
so lost and alone
when there's no one around.

* * *

WINGS

Sometimes I wish I could spend the day
Gliding through the breeze over waterways,
As free as a bird
I would do these things,
If I only had
a pair of wings . . .

HELENE CLAIRE SHUBERT

THE STAR

Midnight holds a wondrous STAR, in the
Eastern sky,
Radiant with holy light
      while angels sing on high,
Reechoing that precious phrase
      "Peace on Earth to Men"
Yearningly humanity dares to hope again.

Can there be Peace
Here on this Earth

      (while men still harbor Hate)?

Reach deep down in your heart and search
      for LOVE
It is not too late.
Still as of old
That STAR shines bright
Men's hearts can hold good will,
And once again the angels' song
Shall echo through each hill.

* * *

LET YOUR LIGHT SHINE THROUGH

Hold fast to your dreams
      Whatever you do,

For no one can dream
The same dream as you.

No one can fill the niche
      You have made,

701

Your role in life by you
Must be played.

Just as each snowflake
Has its own design,

You must live your life
And I must live mine,

So don't hide your talent
Whatever it be,

Let your light shine through
For the whole world to see.

FORTITUDE

What is fortitude when my heart breaks forth
At just the thought of my beloved?
A laugh so infectious,
Eyes that burn into my soul,
A touch that turns blood to fire,
To ice, to fire again,
A kiss that causes the stars in heaven
To bow down in humble servitude.

* * *

OFFERING

If it would move your heart,
I would gather all the tears
Of all the years,
And offer them at your feet
That you might bathe in them,
And each dazzling drop would cry
My love for you.

* * *

THE WALL

Not often does my heart respond,
Leaving its own cool, remote cell
To herald love with clarion bell,
But find, too late, again it's wrong.

With all this battering through the years
It has built a towering wall
That shields its wounds from curious all,
Yet still retains its sea of tears.

THE SEA OF LEAVES

I walked along the lonely road
After Autumn gave its birth;
I listened to the calls of birds
And joyous sounds of earth.
The leaves rustling with their kin
And falling off the trees;
Dancing and shimmering like lively folk
On Autumn days like these.
The maple in her rust-colored red
The oak in orange and brown;
The poplar trimmed in yellow dress
And falling to the ground.
And by and by when night has come
The leaves gather in a whirling mound;
The skies are pale and of amber brown
And different colored leaves are found.
The leaves go deep, as deep as the brine
And are soft as pillows.
They're swirling around like a storm at sea
As great as torrential billows.
When dusk has fallen the sea of leaves
Becomes peaceful, and hence
They stop their swirling, rustling, and swishing
And are followed by a stilled silence.
When days and nights grow colder
And frost visits the weather,
The leaves are stirred and blown away
And are suddenly gone forever.

BY THE FIREBOXES' RED GLARE

The coughin', poundin', shakin' the ground
Pantin', sweatin' boiler, what a sound!
The black smoke plumes in the air—
We all wish that steam locos were still there.
Progress pushes on, but remember steam well:
From the Atlantic to Pacific,
    Great Lakes to the Gulf,
The thunderous steam loco
    was like a living hell.
The whistle screams, vapor swells,
In the cab sweatin' by the fireboxes' red glare.
Stand up, salute all steam locos
    and the men who ran them,
Trains for all Americans as well as Uncle Sam.
Who can say what a hot fire—
Who dares call our steam engineers, our
    firemen liars?
The roar—stoke the coal while it's there—
Wipe the brow by the fireboxes' red glare!

J. E. SIMPKINS

STORY OF ARMY BOY

I'll sing this song softly, and play my guitar,
This is a sad story, I'll tell it beneath the stars.
It makes me blue every time I tell
Of an army boy died in Vietnam, war of hell.
Just a young man of twenty,
Married a Kentucky lass named Penny,
Got a baby the army boy never seen—
A bullet stopped all this young man's dreams.

This is a sad and sorrowful story,
The army boy's with Jesus, now in glory,
This young man loved the Nashville sound,
In Kentucky on a hillside, buried in the ground.
But shame on all us, shame—
At his funeral hardly no one knowed his name.

Penny's eyes full of tears and broken heart
Dear army boy, sad, just married, have to part.
Sadder yet, army boy didn't have no grave,
No plot of ground would the cemetery save;
"We have no room, bury him elsewhere."
Penny could only cry and stare—
Her army boy a fallen hero, flag half-mast waves . . .

America, would someone give him a grave?
An old couple offered their hillside;
Buried now, with Jesus he abides.
Tears come to my eyes when I tell this story,
Softly I sing of this army boy who went to glory . . .

ENDLESS SEARCH

What should we learn from history?
In the beginning it was filled with mystery.
Some of these mysteries are still believed true
And they are the cause of killing people like you.

Religions passed down for years on end
Are accepted as truth and worth killing a friend.
We should search for the truth about things that are old—
This will give us no reason to fight in the hot or the cold.

Christianity is built on Roman mythology,
Other religions on ancient theology.
What we need is a search for truth in beliefs,
And quit killing our neighbors as if they were thiefs.

THE JOY OF BEING

Because of Thee— I see the trees
   In all their greening majesty.
Because of Thee—I hear a concert
   Of full-throated melodies
Poured forth upon the breeze.
   From each and every tiny thing
I touch a poem of pure ecstasy—
   Not life—not death—just of Being.

For life and death are intermixed,
   The first is often latter.
So does it really matter
   Whether tears or whether laughter
Gather in the face of Being?
   Because of Thee, I welcome every sensation
Of joy—of fear—of sorrow—of cheer;
   'Tis just a form of Being,
Because of Thee.

TOGETHER

We travel many roads in life—to
where one never knows;
To seek and find peace of mind
and love that ever flows.
Your path has met and hearts
combine and two become as one,
As God guides you on your way
and His wish is done:
To care for one another, to cherish
each one's thoughts,
To right the wrongs and give the
strength that abides in God's great love.
Be always standing side by side
and constant in your faith,
Tho the hands of time turns the
years, your love will not erase.

* * *

SPRING TIME

Springtime nears and blooms
appear, in every nook and dell,
It beckons all the birds to sing
and makes us all feel swell.
It gives a lift to every one, to
think about the fun
That comes along with summer,
when winter's come and gone.
The trees begin to grow their
leaves, the grass and flowers, too.
As Springtime puts on her dress,
so lovely and so new.

709

TIME

Beat on! beat on! TIME:
Morn to morn not mine,
Neither foe nor friend,
Constant 'til the end,
Beating with rapture,
TIME defies capture!
Beat on! beat on! TIME.

Though body in chains,
The soul escapes reins;
Justice the treasure,
Soul knows no measure!
Time ever metered,
Soul still unfettered.
Beat on! Beat on! TIME.

Truth always in flight,
While eyes yield no light;
Endless fugitive,
TIME never captive.
Let the Light entwine
Fugitive and Time!
Beat on! Beat on! TIME!

* * *

EPITAPH

Do you think you'll write
An epic tonight!
Is your brain in gear?
Are your phrases clear?
Take your pen in hand!
Start your reprimand!
I'm ready to write,
Is the lighting right?

I have little strength;
Do you mind the length?
I've waited for long
To tell you what's wrong:

The world is all right—
The sun ever bright—
And fresh morning breeze
With bird-songs from trees
Should brighten the day
And cast cares away:
That tug on my heart
Warns me to depart;
Unable to rise
Or open my eyes.
Still birds are singing
A joyous ringing.

The death-blow you deal
Defies Time to heal;
One jolt to my leg—
To our God I beg,
Help me to the floor!
And then to my chore.

Sometimes I wonder
What weight I'm under;
As slowly I walk,
Unable to talk,
Held fast to my post,
Regardless of cost:
Wring blood to the most!
The Breath of Life lost!

PACE

My labor commands my life;
I cannot laugh for the money is gone;
I cannot cry for tears avoid concentration;
I penetrate the walls of empty duty; I must pace . . .

My lover demands my life,
expects my free time to be with him.
I cannot move forward without his advice;
I cannot stay behind for he will leave me;
I penetrate the walls of self-duty; I must pace . . .

My label misunderstands my life—
expected of me, is of woman;
I cannot exceed my companion but
I cannot restrain my ambition;
I penetrate the walls of self duty; I must pace . . .

My legacy withstands my life,
expecting to be received;
I cannot promise important funds;
I cannot leave without giving;
I penetrate the walls of family duty, I must pace . . .

EAGLE

You once roamed the countryside, the hills,
and mountain streams.

Your beautiful feathered head, your
vast wings in flight, reaching over the sky,
searching for a place to rest.

Your enemy is man, you know, for now you
are almost extinct. You once were free
to roam, but greed put a stop to your powerful flight.

Your beauty is far more than one
could phrase in one's expression of you.
your graceful appearance is now hardly
ever seen . . .

For your enemy has destroyed what was
once your fleet and left you almost
defenseless, with hardly a friend to guide
you to safety.

Since they will be sure to kill your flight,
save your strength for the future days,
for once again your flight will be stronger,
to withstand the guns that follow you.

Your powerful wings will set you free,
to carry on for those who are dead . . .

For now just survive on the land . . .
In time, you will seek those
who will provide for your existence
once again.

SHALL ALL . . .

Shall all the mighty mountains move
and dance as the stones they sing,
shall all the rivers flow with life
in honor to our King.
Shall all the trees bear golden fruit
that time shall never age,
shall all our names be writ in blood
on Glory's spotless page.
Shall all the seas give up their dead
and all the earth the same,
shall the morning sun shine ever bright
and never dim again.
Shall all the children fly away
and laugh from up on high,
shall all the old men become young
to live and never die.
Shall all the mighty mountains move
and dance as the stones they sing,
shall all the world in joyous praise
sing "hosanna" to the King.

* * *

HE WAS BORN TO BE

He was born to be crucified
for that was Divinity's plan.
He was born to be sacrificed
that Hope might be given to man.

SONGS OF MEMORY

So long as stars shall shine and wintry moon
Its glimmer of silver shed a wondrous light,
So long as words of love dispel earth's gloom.
And happy hearts beat high with glorious might,
A memory brings soft radiant eyes glowing.
Out of the past dear arms of love enfold
And sweetest tender smile is always showing
The love supreme, our hearts to speak and hold.
So memories of precious ones survive
A date or birthday thought of now and then,
A kiss, a smile, when special ones arrive;
The joy of days or hours have often been
Returned in joy or grief again and again,
Reminding us of happiness or loss and pain . . .

* * *

KANSAS MOON

The train rolled along through the night.
The Kansas sky looked the same as any other sky,
Except the moon seemed to keep in sight
From my window as land and rivers sped by.
Oh, Kansas moon, so near you seem,
Golden glow as if for some reason ablaze.
Are you real, or a fanciful dream?
A light penetrating earth's gathering haze,
Beautiful as the train speeds along,
Magnificent as a haunting song.
The moon seems larger in Kansas;
Has it enlarged itself since man ascended
To such dizzy heights, making plans as
He walked its surface contented?

715

EUNICE BAKER STEELE

YE SHALL HAVE A SONG

As in the evening when quiet hours come,
And holy solemnity pervades the scene,
When songs of gladness fill the heart at home;
Then light the fire and burn the backlog green,
And sit in atmosphere of peace and calm
So near the open fireplace winter fire;
And hear the many varied sounds, a balm,
In singing logs as they become much drier.
This tree in lonely forest lived so long,
Forever keeping silent in the wood,
To hear the birds on boughs continue singing song
That trilled the notes as only song birds could;
Imprisoned tones thus sank in to the tree
As breezes blew so happily and free.

These songs of many notes and tone
There slept until the oak was felled to ground.
Our fancy grows when backlog glows alone
On winter eve as flames rise all around.
A happy child sings snatch of melody sweet,
And hidden there in trunk of tree so grand
A penitent soul lifts heart a Savior to greet—
These many sounds come forth in music bland:
The carols of children; songs of birds in flight,
Or penitent prayer of souls in sorrow sad,
the hearts of gladness, hope, or faith at night.
So we shall have a song to make us glad
As thoughts return to life's fulfilled desire
When we hear sounds from backlog's open fire.

THE GOLDFINCH

Happy little yellow bird
    In undulating flight,
Flying through a cloudless sky
    That's deep and blue and bright.

At the crest of every wave
    He spills a bit of song,
Notes that kindle our delight
    For we, too, sing along.

Black spot on his wee forehead,
    A black barred wing each side,
Happy disposition, too,
    That makes him sing with pride.

Sunlight shining down on him
    Has made him golden bright.
He's a jewel among the birds.
    I've *never* seen him fight!

Love our little yellow bird
    For he distributes cheer.
When we know that he's about
    The whole world seems more dear.

* * *

A THOUGHT

I love my kith and love my kin,
    I love this old world we live in.
I love my dog and love my cat
    I love the birds and all of that.
I love the flowers of the spring
    And every other growing thing.
Without our understanding God,
    I'd sure be lost in blinding fog!

JESSIE M. STEVENSON

TRANQUILITY

There are two things we must learn to do
As in this world we travel through:
First and foremost for ourselves
We must never feel sorry;
If we do our lives will not be jolly.

The second thing I have in mind
Is that we must seek and find
A way by which we can make it so
We are able to live with Life's NO.

* * *

THE HEART OF CHRISTMAS

It's that time of year again
With all its tinsel and holly;
A time to laugh and a time to sing,
A time with good friends to be jolly,
A time for homecomings and such,
A time for giving and receiving much;
But let us not fail to see:
Without the Christ of Christmas
Christmas would never be.

BACK HOME

I was born in a place distant and past,
Where the air was clean, and memories last,

A place of colors, deep skies, and happiness,
Where people played and worked out their hopefulness.

I remember the Spring fields and the love,
The persons still dear, my mind wonders of

As I grew older, my job drew me away,
To fields of buildings and work most every day.

I went to a place where people grew as close as ament
flowers,
And the only thing that seemed to matter to some were
dollars.

Until one day, terribly sick, I knew that my time was
near and my life through,
Whereupon, I asked to be buried in a place both far from
land and time, too.

* * *

CREATIVITY

Space provides and different forms develop,
Expressions excel, and ideas converge,
Methods manipulate, and dreams envelop,
Performers assume, and their admirers urge.

A seed, an egg, and a person,
A bird, a thought, and an airplane,
A wheel, a road, and a motor car,
A fire and, hence, electricity.

719

Its arena is the mass of earth,
Ever onward the sweat of humanity extols its energy.
What of its origin—this great worth?
Human creativity, as constant, only dabbles after He.

SUNSET ON THE ALLEGHENY

When it's sunset on the Allegheny
I'm prone to think of God on high,
For his glories are there to see
Painted on yonder Western sky.

I'm grateful for the privilege.
To gaze across the Shenandoah
Where a sunset sky is my ceiling
And God's green earth my floor.

Yea! I treasure not my cottage
Nor the pictures on my wall;
For I'm painting in my memory
A sunset scene, masterpiece of all.

'Tis the transformations of the heavens
When the day has gone to rest.
Behold! It's a picture of glory
When the sun is settling in the West.

Each sunset models a new fashion
Crimson and gold mingled with blue.
The firmament declares the handiwork
That God has created for you.

When it's sunset on the Allegheny
Its glories human tongue cannot tell;
But drink its beauty through your eyes
In God's heaven all ends well.

THE MOON STORY: PROGRESS OF MAN

Thy celestial satellite, abode for the lover's heart,
Mysterious in the past when Diana did reign.
Home so distant and yet so near to the heart of her,
Home so near to this new breed of men, so remote now for the
    lover.
This breed has captured you.
My God!
Thy worship shall never more be reverent,
For men have touched upon your soul-like soil,
And given it sin and death, as this earth knew,
When He in his incestuous desire did debut.

* * *

I LOVE THEE

I loveth thee,
Thy loveth me,
Can't we unite
In perfect harmony?

I have a covenant with the Lord,
Please join me, there's room for more.
His love for me is divinely,
My love for thee is eternally.

THOUGHTS ON THE ROAD

Longing, on the road at night and in the early morn,
On an endless road it seems between two lives I'm torn.
Reaching for all I need the most and all I most desire,
Remembering the time has not yet come, the burden makes me
    tire.
Again the present holds me back, again I am confused;
In you will solace and refuge be, in you my strength renews.
No, I can't make my way alone—the worth would not be there—
Every step I take along the way I need for you to care.
So little I have to offer now, so much I want to be,
The future it seems holds much in store, when you are next to
    me.
Under the stars I'll find my path, and through the break of day,
Before the sleep has left your eyes I'll be far along my way.
But oh, how brief our time must be, how long the months
    between—
So I'll hold each moment preciously, to me, how much they
    mean.

* * *

IN LEAVING

Again the time has come for leaving
But myself I keep deceiving,
Hoping to make it last still longer
But I know it cannot be.

In every way my heart has grown fonder,
In leaving now it's time to ponder,
All we've lost and all we've won
And what's ahead for us to see.

Disheartened I will not be in leaving
So long as I can keep believing
Soon will come the time again
To know you better, as more than a friend.

SNOW SCENE

From a lounge chair by the window
I watch the snow swirl down,
make goosedown piles on fence rails
and the rooftops across town;
blossom evergreens with clusters
that crystal flowers seem,
sprinkle snow stars on the woolens
of an elfin sledding team.

One little one rolls a snowball
to a snowman's portly paunch;
apprehensive of the danger
the St. Bernard dog will pounce
and send the snowballs flying
with a giant, playful bounce.

Her brother comes to help her
and the snowman quickly grows.
He soon has chocolate cookie eyes
and a carrot for his nose.
A crimson apple peel provides
a smiling, jolly mouth.
But then a snowball fight ensues—
His snow monster to the South!

* * *

THE LIME JELLO FACADE

The patio lounge of the old hotel basked in the August sun,
The glare of its whiteness relieved by umbrellas in carousel
    shades,
making small cases for sweltering humanity.
Now and then a light, warm breeze drifted in from the sea.
A waiter wheeled out the piano on its little round stage.
A heavy man in his white linen suit mopped his brow and sat
    down.

724

He started to play a "striped-suit-Charlie" tune.
It livened things up a bit.
Guest began to drift in for lunch,
bored with their meandering occupations.
A portly dowager in pink linen, with lace trim,
and a full-blown flower hat came in, flashing diamond rings.
On her arm, was a sprightly distinguished chap,
rather thin, with a well-trimmed, graying moustache,
They ordered lobster thermidor and peach melba.
Suddenly, there was the lime jello scarf.
It appeared at the top of the stairs and sauntered down.
A few saw it first, and all eyes turned to it right away.
It was wrapped amazingly around a plain white Panama
and the model from New York, a la Dietrich.
Of course, there wasn't anything else in the buzz
for the rest of lunch. Her face had stared at them
from the newsstands for almost too many years now,
but it was still a magnet, they knew.
From the cover of *Vogue*, the cover of *Bazaar*,
the disinterested stare they all knew.
They were all quiet, except for two haggling businessmen
in the corner, when she ordered, "Half a lemonade."
She sat there with her legs crossed and sipped that.
One ruined lobster was, for once, picked at.

As the couple got up to go and passed the cashier,
There was a twitch in the clipped moustache.
He leaned over to her and whispered, loud enough,
"Never mind, my dear. The lime jello facade
had just half a lemonade!"
The cashier punched the key.
"That must be what love is," she thought.

* * *

LEGEND OF NASSAWANGO

Deep in the woods of Nassawango,
Where moss hung, cypress druids reach o'er a winding, murky
    creek;

There is a sudden, open clearing
And a crumbling, aged tower of stone and brick.
Vines of ivy and of creeper cling and clamber on its walls.
One can't help but pause and wonder;
The mysterious tower enthralls.
Was there ever anything else here?
If so, nothing else remains.
Just the plaintive cry of whippoorwill
And the rustling, sighing moan,
A breeze in the loblolly pines.

I startled, as a voice spoke from the bushes over there.
"This was a hustlin', bustlin', place once," it said.
My eyes searched yet awhile to find
From whence the voice had sprung.
Then I saw; an old man sat there, in the bushes, all alone.
Slouchy hat was pulled down, making shadows of his face,
But he seemed to mean no harm
And he might know about the place.

"That was the old iron furnace, and in eighteen thirty-eight,
There was a village of 400, clustered 'bout the gate.
There were 'round a hundred dwellings, a blacksmith shop and
        store,
A watermill, a sawmill and buildings just galore.
There was a place to go to school, a quiet little church,
A hotel for the visitors and the diggin's from the search.
Men bustled o'er a trestle with their barrowloads of ore.
The stack belched smoke from charcoal
And the furnace raged and roared.
The heavy bog ore melted.
The molten iron poured forth.
They made pots and toools and plowshares
And iron bars to ship the north.
'Twas a man's dream of the future,
Of a city great and grand,
On the banks of Nassawango,
On his 5,000 acres o' land.

FIVE YEARS OLD

I was a crying and Daddy
took me in his arms.
Looking down I saw a
tiny form, like my china doll;
she did not move.
They said she was in Heaven.
Sunless days and North winds'
breath left their ugly tracks.
They stayed forever.

* * *

FIREFLIGHT

A lone bold eagle
Fluttering, trembling,
rising from glass,
Beak shredding clouds,
soaring high
to keep the fire
from scorching her belly.

* * *

I TOUCHED

Your skin is coarse with age.
Our little girl helped us
plant you in a special place.
A Boy came, and they enjoyed your
calm shade, also the breeze that
made your leaves dance.
They are going, you will
stay—
Holding green memories.

(Reprinted by permission of *North American Mentor* Magazine,
    Fennimore, Wisconsin.)

LORD, WATCH MY COUNTRY

The night I was born
They said it was under a good star;
Being my mother's fifth son,
I was destined to be a great czar.

For a while I ran wild like a colt,
Through the vastness of my years,
Until I heard the bugle's call
For men to defend their ideals.

I had heard of Dutchland, Salerno, and Japan
During the years of my lonely youth,
But today, now grown, in Vietnam,
I have seen all my dreams come true.

It's good to hear the song of the guns,
And the cry of the eagles at war,
And see the great American sons,
Fight for their country, their homes, and the Lord.

I have heard, seen, and fought my foe,
With all the weapons known to man,
And, Oh Lord! They surely fight with love,
For a lonely country, they call Vietnam.

I wish my fellow citizens back home,
Would stand firm for our faithful rights,
For there surely a day will come,
When for our country we will have to fight.

And fight will be forever and a day,
Unless we stand together with our Lord,
Oh, Lord! Our country's safety is at stake;
If You don't bring us together, and stop the war.

Listen to our prayers, they come from our hearts;
Do it for me, and my countrymen's sake.

For this country I offer to Thee, before Your altar,
Because under Your shadow our country will be safe.

* * *

A CHILD'S HOPE

Mom, if one day I grow to be a man,
Like Armstrong, Collins, and Aldrin,
Whose names in the Hall of Fame today stand
As America's most greatest dream.

They flew the great Apollo Eleven together,
Thousands of miles into space,
Believed to be the longest ever
Attempted by man in this great race.

Americans were happy, they looked at the sky,
They forgot their foes, they forgot the war,
And millions and millions just sang and cried,
And they looked to the heavens, to thank our Lord.

Columbus had his doubts of the unknown;
He sailed his three caravels for the new seas
As did the Americans on their own,
Lookin' for new worlds and lookin' for peace.

Mom, now that man is on the Moon,
D'ye think it will be for the good of mankind,
Or d'ye think it will be man's doom,
Or the work of an evil mind?

Mom, would you answer my doubts,
Before that day, when I grow to be a man?
For now I am too young and too full of hopes,
For things that seem to hard for me to understand.

729

OUR SATELLITE, THE MOON

On sixteen July of nineteen sixty-nine,
A blast was heard a little after noon;
Was the beginning of history for mankind,
To put a man on our satellite, the Moon.

The Apollo Eleven was on its way soon,
Carrying three valiant American explorers,
They were happy, anxious, while others,
Feared for their lives on our satellite,
The Moon.

For centuries man wanted to explore
Other worlds that could be their doom;
At last, there were two men on the floor
Of our satellite, they call the Moon.

Save this country from our enemies, Oh, Lord!
For you wanted it for your church's base,
And in the near future, if not too soon,

Those three astronauts out there in space,
Will bring peace to this great world,
From our satellite, they call the Moon!

DIE VARMINT, DIE

his ring was hit by light as the sun
    moved 'cross the sky
and his hand moved to his gun as the badge
    caught my eye.
I hadn't seen the long red scar that
    ran across his hairy chin
nor the lame right side that
    made him look so thin.
the boots he wore began to jump and
    dust began to move
as the large black forty-four left
    his holster's groove.
his hat flew back as his head
    cocked up
and his brow began to glisten with
    enough sweat to fill a cup.

I saw the hammer pull back as his
    fingertip strained,
his arm came up with lightning speed
    as he steadied and aimed;
the bullet head came from its tube with
    smoke swirling around—
it moved so slow each inch made my heart
    take a pound.

it was half a foot from the gun on
    its way to the target
when once again I saw my life and
    I began to regret it;
my eyes were as tight as they could be
    and my nose began to close,
a tingling of nerves was felt from my
    head down to my toes.

another millisecond passed as the lead
    came closer and closer still;

even before the bullet hit I think it
      began to kill.
his eyes began to widen as he saw
      his aim would be true,
his lips began to part for a smile while
      the long heavy bullet still flew.

I felt the air pass my lips as I drew in
      a deep and heavy breath,
and thought for the first time—earnestly—
      of the possiblilty of death.
the lead hit pay dirt and the bone made
      a crispy crack—
just the sound of it sent a chill way
      down my back.

then I realized with quite a start as
      my eyes were opened wide,

that the aim and the bullet was not for me . . .
      but the rattler by my side.

MARY R. SWANSON

MY DAD

My father was a quiet man,
　I think I see him now.
A-workin' hard from dawn 'til dark,
　Behind a heavy plough.

There were three things he always said
　You had to keep in mind.
First, there was hope, then there was faith,
　And with it all be kind.

He taught me many, many things
　That money cannot buy,
Like truth and honesty and love—
　Oh! He was quite a guy.

I never heard him once complain,
　With anything he had.
He did just what he had to do,
　This man who was my Dad.

And when at last he went away
　It made me very sad,
But I thank the Lord for giving me
　This man to be my Dad.

YOU

You pray'd for darkness, you now in darkness abide.
God knows not you who 'gainst Christ did portray pride;
Pride 'gainst His Spirit, the Spirit of life.
Christ conquer'd death; you 'gainst Christ did make strife.

Satan is the darkness! Christ is the light!
You pray'd for darkness; you did Satan delight.
In death there's no victory. Christ's death was in vain
If in darkness you pray'd that you might 'ternal life gain.

MY LITTLE WIDE-EYED BOY LOOKED AT ME

"Mommy, can I be anything I want to be?
Is dreaming bad? Why should Jimmy say it is—to me?"
"Do not be afraid to dream," I said,
For dreams are worth while things within your head.
Dreaming helps us decide what we shall do,
Be it astronaut, fireman, or doctor, too."
"I'd like to explore, but what's left to discover?"
"Oh, so much, my dear, so listen to your mother.
There are stars, other planets, even satellites, to name a few,
But these are far, whereas there are things much nearer, too.
A world of microbes, tiny things which steal and cripple and
        maim.
To find a cure for these could bring you sure—but maybe
        grudging—fame.
So, determined you must be to cling to your dreams, as men
        scoff and
        laugh, for to discourage is their aim.
But when you succeed and prove them wrong,
By their weakness they will show that you are strong.
Remembering, somewhere in bygone years
They, too, had dreams, but theirs gave way to fears.
For, you see, they faltered while you carried right along.
So, dream, my son, dream LONG, dream STRONG!"

AGGIE M. TACTACAN

WITHIN YOUR MEMORIES

Only within your memories
Will you see me once again;
I'm hidden in your past—
Do you remember way back then?

If only for a moment
You are able to recall
A brief encounter with love—
Do you see me there at all?

Search and you will find me
For I'm hidden in the years,
Then when you remember
Gently wipe away the tears.

We shared love for a moment
Surely you must remember—
I've not forgotten you
Nor that long ago September.

* * *

HEAVEN BOUND

If heaven is missing an angel
I know where it can be found,
And if angels look like you
Then heaven is where I'm bound.

THOUGHTS, DREAMS AND NIGHTMARES
. . . A VIEWPOINT

There is a certain, sweet,
almost sickening
kind of laughter.
You hear it
only inside of yourself.
And it scares you.
And it hurts you.
And it always takes control.

It is a black and white pain
that engulfs your breath
and sucks every last drop
of air
from your brain.

Blindness,
Darkness,
and slow despair
are your only memories.
We become submerged
in an emotional drowning,
and then we are grasped
by a bony hand
to be slowly drawn and quartered,
And set on display.

There is a certain, sweet,
definitely sickening
kind of laughter.
And it will
slap you in the head
and turn your face quite pale.

We are struck
with a social withdrawal
and a solitude so loud
it will deafen you to the sounds of life.

And then there is nothing.

* * *

MIDNIGHT CONFESSIONS

I can only see as far
as my mind will let me.
And you can only understand as deep
as your heart will allow.

I can only say to you
what my words will deny,
But what my heart
can never forget.

And when we look at each other,
what will we see?
Is it the past,
or the future,
The joy,
or the pain,
The love
that once was,
or the touch of hate
that has taken its place?

We cannot deny
what we have done.
And we cannot deny
the feelings
that are now taking shape.

We will both try
and seek
other outlets,
for the frustration inside
is too great.

We have to let go,
or we will
choke
ourselves
with the memories.

SOMEWHERE IN A DREAM

Somewhere in a dream
I touched your smiling face;
It made me smile.
I looked into your eyes
And I saw.
I kissed your lips . . .
And I knew
That I loved you.

Somewhere in a dream
I felt your love all around me.
I heard you whisper "I Love You,"
And felt you touch me softly in the night.
And I knew
That you loved me too.

Then I awoke.
Afraid to open my eyes,
Afraid I'd see an empty bed,
And everything just as it had always been.
But instead I felt your body next to mine,
And your arms wrapped around me.
And I smiled and kissed your face . . .
Because I knew
That you were real.

DENISE

She used to hide
When she saw me,
Off to her mother she'd fly.
She'd peek out from
Behind her fortress,
Glare at me and cry.

Now she's older and wiser,
Thinks I'm the
Greatest godmother alive.
Ah, how wise, this child of five.

* * *

NONSENSE II

Platypus and fish
In the same dish?
A ridiculous sight to see!
But not as dumb
as a cookie crumb
Rolling after a honeycombed bee.

How droll, gasped the troll
As he quivered with glee
And giggled himself toward infinity.

Poor thing! Your wing
Has drifted away.
Such strife—'tis life!

Have a loverly day.

POR TI (FOR YOU)

I see you and I feel the warmth
Creep down into my soul.

I thought that I knew myself so well,
Knew all that there was to feel,
But then in one staggering moment,
I discovered what wes real.

Unplanned—Unrehearsed—Without thinking—
Apart from this world and my cares,
To a space in my life that was empty
Suddenly—You—were there.

Together we soared (on new thermals)
Mindless of all else around,
The force and the warmth of the moment
Suspended us clear above ground.

I've now been so deeply affected,
My emotions so greatly astir
With a love that's invaded my being
And made me acutely aware.

How I hope that you share just a fraction
Of what I attempt to describe,
And thank you, my friend, for awakening
A love that might surely have died.

* * *

SUSPICION

Oh, God—I feel so gooood today!
What's wrong?

WORDS FROM THE CROSS

Word One: *"Father, forgive them; for they know not what they do."*

If it was preordained, Jehovah, why,
    I ask, is prayer even needed?
Forgive for what? For driving nails home?
What choice had they anyway? The Psalmist
    has set the whole scene centuries before—
even down to the crap game for the clothes
    they'd ripped from His trembling body
        before the flogging . . .

And what's a hammer wielder anyway?
    A seedy little wage slave told to jump
at the sergeant's bark. You think the bastard's cruel?
He hammers nails as news hacks hammer typewriters—
    all in a day's work. It won't cost any sleep
        after a flagon of rotgut Jewish wine.

What need of prayer? The point, I suppose,
    is that our Lord was really pretty game,
blessing those hammer swingers as He did:
    a messianic precedent, I guess.
As Mediator-elect between the Father
and men, He took these weasels aside and asked
    that just this one the Father might agree
to play it cool—just once withhold the urge
    to hurl His heavenly high-powered thunderbolt
        at a stinking, angry, head-sick, sodden slob.

Word Four: *"My God, my God, why hast thou forsaken me?"*

They say that Jewish boys of Jesus' time
    were taught to commit the psalms to memory.
Lord Christ, it seems, this scorching cruel morning
    has done his homework, knows the psalm by rote:

JOHN F. TAYLOR

"My God, my God . . ." the words begin to reel
 across the laneways of His flickering brain
the way that tantalizing music runs relentlessly
and tortures the mind of the pain-wracked, sleepless invalid
 until the brain cells scream to be released,
  But the melody or words just move ahead,
 and other phrases start to flood His mind:

"I am a worm," the Savior seems to hear,
 "and no man . . . a worm . . . no man at all . . .
  O Eli Eli lama sabachthani!
The dog's hot breath is on my heart, O God,
and all my maddened ministry has failed!

"Thou hast indeed forsaken me, O Father,
as Thou wilt show the world far ages hence
 at Buchenwald, at Dachau, at My Lai.
Thou art, my Heavenly Father, dead indeed—and I?
 I cast my lot now with the drip-tongued dog
  and fetch him snarling to his seat
 within the Kingdom of my dying mind . . ."

KENT STATE, 1978

"The Goodyear Tire and Rubber Company has granted Kent
State $250,000 to establish a Professorship of Free
Enterprise." (News item)

Here where rosy, bullet-fathered streamlets
   oozed once, drop by little droplet,
    to the edge of those young eyelid-lowering days,
the spectres of the scarlet-spattered younglings
   still point their frowning fingers.

Now the flesh-charred stench of fiery jelly
lifts from the Asian paddies; gun stocks rust
    back to the earth;
   tin is safe, and tungsten
thrives where the slanteyed sweat is cheap;
    the rubber trees
drip radial-treaded treasure troves once more.

Listen, little phantom martyrs, listen:
what is that foot thump stirring the bloodcrust grass?
   Oh, it is the tread of treadrich robbers
   sprinkling venom raped from the dripping trees.

Quickly, phantom children, bleed afresh
and drench the new grass deep with weeping blood
   before the stainset of this poison flood.

GENTLE LOVER

So gently did he kiss me,
After loving me so,
I had no way of knowing
That he arose to go.
  So gently did he touch me
  When he arose to dress,
  I had no way of knowing
  It was the last caress.
So gently did he touch me
When he arose to go,
That why he chose to leave,
I simply do not know!

* * *

LINES TO MRS. BURNS

Whenever I feel sad, which is more often now
  Than it used to be,
I put on my red silk dress and go dancing.
The dress swirls round and round
And the music takes me to a world where
No soul hungers and no man bleeds,
And all the needs of the hungry children
Of the world are filled.
Suspended in time, the pain is less.
Excuse me! I must stop now and go put
  On my red silk dress.

ANNETTE MARIE TESAR

REFLECTIONS OF CHILDHOOD

'Twas then I ventured forth
Where willow branches hid me,
Inside a cozy nook
Beside a cool and shady brook,
To drift and dream
Until this placid little stream
Became the mighty Nile,
Afloat with barges of a queen;
Or, the winding Amazon,
Between dense jungle walls,
Where all the din and chatter
Soon gave way to roaring falls,
And the cares of this small world
No longer seemed to matter.
For I could slay my dragons,
Always winning in the end.
Oh, if only, after
So many years gone by,
Could I once more such moments spend,
Then I would surely try.
But they come but once, and then,
Not to one as old as I.

LOVE'S LABOR, NOT LOST

When in reflecting, in quiet moments,
A mood of creativity sometimes comes.
Arranging words is comparable to the carpenter's art:
Both, if done properly,
Produce a work of beauty,
An entireness greater than the sum of the parts,
Each is the product of careful labor
And without love would have no
Reason for being.
A less than masterful poet
Might be forgiven his shortcomings,
For sincerity is there,
Even if craft is not.
The urge to create is universal.

* * *

MY HUSBAND, WHILE SLEEPING

Wrapped in dreams he lies,
His face that of a babe in its innocence.
All cares are drained away
And kept at bay by the mantle of sleep,
His body eloquent with the hard-won
Reward of peace.

A camera can record the physical form,
But only the mind's eye
Can detect the soul.

HONORED ESTATE

There lies beyond the wall of hedge
Enshrouded to the very edge
By leafy branches lush and green,
What vast estate but dimly seen?

Here overhead and all around
Comes rushing cacophonic sound
Of early morning folk, work-bound,
Disturbing not this silent way
Nor yet again at close of day
Where stillness broods the hours away.

In Arlington the fair green Earth
Awaits serene her honored sons,
Their arms laid down, their anguish stilled,
Her arms enfold these treasured ones.

LOST

Quite often I find Myself out on a stormy sea.
The night is so blackened, but short and next to me,
Like a ship tossing and turning, I the victim do,
Praying the guidance of a calm wave, to be subdued.
Just about to settle the pounding surf, the untamed,
A mighty wave whips itself across the vessel's frame.
Will there ever be a moment of quietude or peace?
Well, cautiously I'll sail, for the lost must be reached.

* * *

SECLUSIONS UNKNOWN

Oft' time I recline and permit my thoughts to wonder,
Questions both evitable, inevitable I ponder.
I attempt to obliviate doubts, but on the other hand,
Being curious to the suggestive subject's trance
Suddenly I find myself in a spatial stare,
Strangely fighting, wondering, what is this fear?
Slowly reality focuses upon life's screen.
Leaving seclusions unknown, I know not what was seen.

SMALL THOUGHTS

Many drops of water,
  Few grains of sand,
Makes the great mighty ocean
  And our big gracious land.

Even the little moments,
  Big or little they be,
Make the longing ages
  of LOVE eternity.

Although our small errors
  May lead the soul away
From the path of righteous
  Far in sin to stray,

Small deeds of kindness,
  Small words of LOVE,
Help to make this world happy
  As the stars shine above.

So, do all the good you can,
  In all the ways, places, and times
You can, to all the people you
  know and meet for as long as you can.

To love others and be kind,
  In every way we find,
Is our purpose and God's plan:
  To live here on earth with our fellow man.

ROBERT THORNTON, JR.

THE POT OF GOLD

I look into the sky and see
A marvelous thing called beauty.
Colors across the sky flow,
They call this a rainbow.

They say that at the rainbow's end,
Far across the gleaming heavens,
There's a pot of gold to be found
For those who let their dreams abound.

It's but a myth, the realists say,
Nothing more than a child's imagination at play.
There's nothing up there to be seen,
Save the sun's everlasting beam.

I have at times, been guilty of chasing rainbows
And of searching for the mystical pot of gold.
It's been more than a game or fantasy with me;
It's been my lonely search to be happy.

Will I ever find my rainbow?
Will I every find that dazzling pot of gold?
Where will I find this wonderful work of art?
Maybe, just maybe, it's there in your heart.

(For Sandy)

A TRIBUTE TO POPE JOHN XXIII
(1881–1963)

In the majestic Papal Gardens amidst shady trees,
　Pope John XXIII wrote his peaceful memories.
Amid fragrant flowers and aromatic bay leaves,
　He left his mark of greatness in complete simplicity.
He proved to be a famous Sovereign Pontiff of Christianity,
　While revealing himself as Master of mankind's dream.
"Peace On Earth" was His Holiness' greatest concern;
　His writings were a lesson for every nation to learn.
In these secluded and exotic gardens ever so rare,
　He penned heaven's wise peace plan right there.·
This Pope's Peace Plan was the calm before the storm;
　Now, the world feels its need with more care and concern.
His legacy of brotherly love was truly angelic and warm.
　But the foes of peace had taken it with great alarm.
Peace on earth men weep and pray for night and morn;
　Yet, no "Peace On Earth" for the wicked and stubborn.

A great tribute everyone on this saintly Pope can bestow,
　If Pope John's "Seeds of Love" we sow, water and grow.
"Good Pope John" everyone learned to love and to know;
　No, not for his wisdom and smile but his glowing halo.
He lived each day with joy and peace to his very last breath;
　So, he welcomed the arrival of "Sister Death" at length.
He prayed for peace ever from the earth's length and breadth;
　This was his "Labor of Love" until his day of death.
Man's innermost craving, we hope someday to receive;
　It will come all the sooner, if we are good and none deceive.
It comes but rarely as the treasure at a rainbow's end;
　It is very slippery and elusive, unless all men do amend.
True peace is ever within man's goal, if others he does not
　　offend.
　Peace comes to those of good will; glory to God without end.
Darkness of soul is akin to sin; this choice belongs to everyone.
　Work for God's glory, and peace will come when life is done.

In Pope John's life story—*Journal Of A Soul*—
   Lies written his undying love and unique earthly role.
Angelo Guiseppe Roncalli was his given family name;
   Though he stated never was he an "Angel" by any claim.
Full of wisdom, wit and learning; Faith, Hope and Charity.
   As Christ's Vicar on Earth, he practiced true humility.
He decided once the Vatican windows to open without any din;
   So, he ordered Vatican Council II: "To let fresh air in."
This ecumenical meeting was called for all tensions to release;
   This meant a united effort to implement world-wide peace.
He laid down a firm principle: "To reach peace, teach peace."
   This was a lesson of meekness, not weakness to increase.
Thus, he taught God's greater honor and glory first in our
      Universe.
   This was the Golden Key to the door of "Peace on Earth" so
   terse.
Pope John XXIII still holds out this key as he enjoys eternal rest;
   His Legacy of Love, as the interim Pope, is a Statesman's test.

* * *

IN MEMORIAM: POPE PAUL VI
(1897–1978)

In the diocese and province of Brescia, Italy,
   A noble son of destiny was born to Judith Alghisi.
His father was a lawyer, editor and Senator George Montini;
   Born of an upper middle-class, deeply religious family.
In his birthplace of Concesio, he left his immortal memory;
   A famous and rare niche in Mankind's Halls of History.
John Baptist Montini saw a new era with the light of day;
   These were turbulent times of change and moral decay.
Anticlerical days of agitation to his utmost dismay.
   Such were the hallmarks of his country, more so today.
His indomitable spirit and courage remains forever to stay;
   This was his share of his parental heritage in God's way.

Beset with frail health problems for the most part of his life;
　　He prevailed over great odds with sheer courage in strife.
His illness merited for his blessings in "the discipline of the
　　cross."
　　His heroic self-discipline proved him a genius without gloss.
He defended the helpless and hopeless, unborn in life's way;
　　He was a true Champion of Peace and Justice in our day.
His genius and learning prepared him well as a diplomat-priest;
　　He served tirelessly and humbly for thirty years, saying the
　　least.
He gave his fullest under three Popes, amidst the worst
　　calamities;
　　This prepared him best to assume one day similar difficulties.
As the Shepherd of Historic Milan, the world's largest diocese,
　　The future of Bishop of Rome ruled His Flock with great ease.

Despite many contradictions, Providence guided him as the Pope;
　　To steer the "Bark of Peter" on life's stormy seas with hope.
As a golden link in the endless chain of Apostolic Succession,
　　He found moral bankruptcy in the world's greatest recession.
He chose the name Paul VI to imitate the Apostle of the Gentiles;
　　With such determination, he did battle with the world's wiles.
As "The Pilgrim Pope," His Holiness traveled the world by air;
　　He inspired the cause of humanity with unity in faith
　　everywhere.
He became Christ's "Ambassador of Peace" to avert all-out war;
　　He pleaded before the United Nations for world order to
　　restore.
"No more war, no more war!" this timid Pope begged in vain;
　　Deaf and blind statesmen ignored his pleading in all his pain.

Pope Paul VI traveled the world over by air on his mission plan;
　　To unite all nations and men in the brotherhood of man.
Without a vacation, laboring all hours of the night, day and
　　morn;
　　His Crown became heavier, deeper dug each sharp thorn.
His foes were countless, subtle, as many as crosswinds air;
　　They assailed him mostly for "Human Life" dignity so few
　　share.

In spite of adverse winds and rough seas everywhere, a stormy
    career
    Made him a ''Beacon of Hope'' in despair—a skillful Mariner.
In facing death itself, he proved himself a Good Shepherd and
    genius;
    Wearing his Pontificate's Crown of Thorns despite the
    impious.
His dignity was unique with his Vatican Council II final decrees;
    This made him The Twentieth Century Herald with human
    liberties.

At the start of his reign, he flew to the Holy Land to lift schism's
    veil;
    He met the Patriarch of the East, Athenagoras, in their travail.
He kissed the other, this historic gesture pardoned all past scores;
    They prayed for Christian Unity and to heal all mankind's
    sores.
Constantinople, Rome and Jerusalem were united as long-lost
    brothers;
    Opening the doors of friendship, they closed to prejudice all
    others.
At the end of his earthly career, his health became steadily
    worse;
    He predicted ''Sister Death's'' coming, emptying his life's
    purse.
His fabulous riches were spiritual triumphs in life as in his death;
    He served Jesus Christ's Flock to his life's very last breath.
No epitaph was needed for his simple burial place in Mother
    Earth;
    Now, His Holiness awaits the Resurrection and Eternal
    Re-Birth.

* * *

IN MEMORIAM: POPE JOHN PAUL I
(1912–1978)

An angel flew down from Heaven's Paradise:
    So swiftly and suddenly, he streaked to the Earth.

He landed down quietly on the Apostolic Palace,
  To snatch away the Holy father from his Birth.
All mankind was left stunned, shocked and fatherless;
  Lacking the wisdom of the world, vibrant and nonetheless,
The vicar of Christ, simply and warmly, was anecdote-full;
Promising, wise and witty, left the world doleful.

A Johannine-Pauline Pope for the first time was elected;
  He left millions of people, world-wide, wonderfully elated.
Trembling with awesome fear, this Pope soon became ill-fated;
  Though Solemnly Reigning, he felt at home in Rome.
This challenge he coped with under the huge Basilica Dome;
  Then, he retired one night in Meditation with Christ alone.
"The Light of the World" a serene smile had shown,
  When the Pope fell asleep eternally to everyone unknown.

Pope John Paul's name none ever on earth shall efface;
  His Holiness' memory lives on forever in Eternity with grace.
His journalistic and intellectual prowess, we will always miss;
  His unwritten volumes of Love's Legends, we would caress.
His solemn simplicity in the war of love against hatred,
  Forever remains a Mystery no man can fully relate.
Brotherhood and Fatherhood are now in Eternity reunited;
  His Holiness continues to pray for all mankind still blighted.

A month's reign in time made him a world-favorite Pope,
  As Pope John Paul I's infectious smile gave endless hope.
Death, as a thief in the night, silently took him at an eerie hour;
  September 28th, 1978, is hardly forgotten for stealing God's
    Flower.
A saddened, shocked and bewildered mankind seemed still worse;
  "The Angel of Death's Shadow" left us under its spell's
    curse.
Doubtless, this Pope left us orphaned in prayer but not without
    Hope,
  While he carved an image of himself as "The Smiling Pope!"

(Notation: This poem can be read from top to bottom by alternating the lines; similarly, the opening and closing lines can be read at the discretion of the reader in prose as a resumé of the context with a minimum of words and phrases for this purpose.)

IN MEMORIAM: POPE JOHN PAUL I

The preceding poem is dedicated in loving memory of the author's brother,
Pvt. 1st Class Charles J. Tomalonis (1914-1978), a World War II Veteran,
who served his country in the Barrage Balloon Outfit at Bremerton and
Seattle, Washington, while stationed at Fort Lewis. Later he was asked to
volunteer for the copper pit mines at Ruth (one of the largest Glory Holes in
the mining world), while stationed at Camp Douglas near Ely, Nevada.
After suffering serious, permanent, crippling mining accident injuries, he
was honorably discharged. He was a member of the American Legion Post
667 and Catholic War Veteran Post 1079, New Philadelphia, Pennsylvania.
He died suddenly from natural causes on October 1, 1978 similar to those of
the subject of this poem. R.I.P.

* * *

LO! THE PEOPLE'S POPE

L - et all men on earth his sudden passing mourn!
O - ft His Holiness' memory recall each night and morn.

T - hirty-three years his Master among us here trod.
H - is Vicar on Earth that many days reigned so with God.
E - ach nation and all their people sadly heads bowed.

P - erplexed is our human race with God's mysterious way.
E - veryone wonders with bewilderment and dismay.
O - ften their faith wavers as lost sheep going astray.
P - atience and perseverance must be the rule of the day.
L - et all men await salvation and heaven's real thrill.
E - ven Pope John Paul I in life could not remain still.
S - uch was his Providential destiny by God's holy will.

P - ope John Paul left mankind suddenly distressed.
O - nly once men die to rejoice forever with God's Blessed.
P - ray that in dying, Death will increase his greater glory.
E - ach then will compare and share "The Book of Life's" story.

HAIL! POPE JOHN PAUL II
(1920—   )

In mournful words we whispered "Eternal Rest,"
  As news flashed *round about* the new Holy Father.
The College of Cardinals chose Poland's very best;
  To succeed "The Smiling Pope" as mankind's fondest.
The vast, anxious crowds filled Saint Peter's Square.
  Hailed they the brilliant, surprised successor to Peter's Chair.

His Eminence, Karol Cardinal Wojtyla, the finest Prince
  And Good Shepherd; found it not hard the world to convince;
"Who enters a papal conclave a Pope, comes out a Cardinal!"
  Most Romans related this truth once and for all.
The Pope-Elect, John Paul II, took the name as predicted;
  That his predecessor's memory be honored by the Elected.

A holy, humble, astute and wise, strong and younger successor
  Of Saint Peter smiled buoyantly as a great Pope but lesser.
This Pope's name among Cardinals was so seldom heard;
  He accepted the world's highest honor with the chosen word.
His grave duties weighed down an historic Pope from Poland,
  Who comes to lead His Flock with his staff in his firm hand.

This most gracious Chief Shepherd hails from a University City,
  Krakow—Europe's oldest learning center in its antiquity.
A pastoral pope, hale and hearty with the courage of a lion;
  He came from afar with the Falcon's outspread wings so fine.
A rare symbol and linguist; uniquely Roman-tutored and sublime;
  Now, his burden surpasses human understanding in our time.

His Motto—"All Thine"—bespeaks his goal both far and near.
  "Long live the Pope!" resounds joyously for all to hear.
May His Holiness follow Christ's call faithfully year after year!
  His wisdom and patience will inspire all to persevere.
His native courage, heritage and culture will ever motivate him;
  To follow his immortal predecessors and final victory to win.

JERUSALEM THE GOLDEN

Jerusalem the Golden is the City of the Lord our God;
   God chose it ages ago before Christ His Son there trod.
It bespeaks the "Peace of God" from its mountains to Rome;
   It re-echoes that "Peace" with its greeting always "Shalom!"
Bethlehem nearby is where the "Prince of Peace" was born;
   It reechoes that "Peace" with its greeting always "Shalom!"
Christ chose neither city as His earthly home but for His sojourn.
   In Nazareth, His humble home, He chose to work, pray and
      roam.
In this obscure town, He led "A Solitary Life" all His own;
   He practiced Obedience to His Father with Whom He in One!
He labored thirty years as a carpenter and God's Only Begotten
      Son;
   His three years of public ministry was then only begun.
His mission on earth was but a very short, powerful and fruitful
      one;
   In being rejected by men, His peace plan was never won.

The glitter of Jerusalem, the Golden City, touched men's hearts;
   By the command of Moses, pilgrims came from all earthly
      parts.
Yearly, they traveled great distances to pay homage to God;
   But, in the Holy of Holies, none but a few dared to trod.
Glorious Jerusalem and Solomon's Temple none would profane;
   God's Presence there gave them reason forever firm to remain.
The Holy City thus became a vast treasure and world-sought
      prize.
   It lured the world's greatest powers; its riches ravished all
      eyes.
At the "Crossroads of Civilization," many caravans daily passed;
   They sold the world's best riches; sought not God's peace
      which lasts.
The "*Pax Romana*" was tribute paid to Caesar to avert all war;
   Purchased peace became a battlefield for their freedom to
      restore.

Down through the centuries, this scene has not changed in
    history;
  Worship of the Golden Calf gave rise to stark death and
    misery.

The Son of Man came down from heaven to restore all things;
  He laid down His Life as a Lamb of Sacrifice with His
    Sufferings.
As a Victim of Divine Love, He died to triumph over the sins of
    all men;
  This was His only way to redeem mankind from the power of
    Satan.
Thus, the "Peace of God" was purchased at no small price;
  This gives deeper meaning to the Eternal High Priest's
    sacrifice.
At the Last Supper, Christ gave us Himself as testimony of His
    Love;
  It found its fulfillment in His Crucifixion as willed from above.
Christ forever gained a final victory over sin, Satan and hell;
  This took place on Calvary's Hill outside of Jerusalem known
    so well. This "Peace of God" vanquished the forces of evil
    and the devil;
  But, the powers of darkness still struggle in endless works of
    evil.
The wars on earth against "Peace On Earth" among men will
    never cease,
  Despite the heroic efforts of world leaders for permanent
    peace.

JOSEPH OF ARIMATHEA
(When East Meets West)

Joseph of Arimathea, our Tourist Guide,
   Hired a taxi cab for a Mount Olivet ride.
"The French and Germans trudge up this hill,
   But we'll ride up and downhill go in stride.
Wisely, we'll save our energy at our will."
   Thus, spoke an Arab Christian gently for a bill.

This clever advice was nice for an agreed price;
   It worked out like a jewel, not a crafty device.
The experience was priceless twice and thrice
   He went out of his way; it truly measured up.
Into the Valley of Gehenna, three marched up;
   What a hike to the Old Wall City for to sup!

Jerusalem was sizzling at the end of October.
   Without a drop of water, all seemed sober.
He offered a modest meal as his free treat;
   At the ancient Monastery, he could not cheat.
The Way of the Cross was just outside the door.
   Wasn't it nice to treat us both, he being poor?

The fates were kind with God's blessings supreme;
   We entered the hostelry; we fulfilled a life's dream.
Two Chinese priests and a Mexican sat at the table;
   I was the real stranger; I did not need a label.
The handshakes and greetings met with warm smile;
   I felt as in a dreamland and not in the aisles.

Across the long table sat the dignified Chinese;
   The Mexican Padre beside me, near touching knees.
My mind quickened suddenly as being quite alert;
   It seemed one Chinese Guest was down to earth.
Didn't we cross paths in the distant past by a resort?
   I strived to recall him for a still better rapport.

The letters of the alphabet flashed from A to Z;
   Yet, for the moment his strange name failed me.
Baffled at length, I hesitated for such an inquiry;
   A big discovery might be made, if I could hurry.
I made an unusual, desperate and final plea:
   "Did you every work in Coney Island with me?"

His face was radiant and eyes bright with delight;
   After fifteen long years, I was never more right.
We recognized each other as a target on the moon;
   "One giant step forward" did not come too soon.
The joy of past freindship was the biggest thrill;
   It started a new chapter like the nectar of life will.

This surprise meeting had nothing like it to compare;
   When East met West around the globe there.
After his World Tour of thirty days or even more;
   Taiwan met New York with a record score.
With no more time to spare, he returned home by air;
   On the morrow in parting, the joy we still ever share.

His pictures of exotic places filled a big scrapbook;
   But, our snapshot on the front page is the first look.
Two exuberantly smiling faces can never be mistook;
   They give fuller meaning to life with God's Presence.
This happy reunion was the work of Divine Providence;
   To be always present at the right place is not mere chance.
Christ said: "He who has ears let him hear . . ."
   I say: "This is the reward of a stormy career!"

DEDICATION

The author wishes to dedicate this poem to all believers in Divine Providence, especially his very distinguished friend and world-traveler—the Rev. Msgr. Anthony Kuo-Fan, Ph.D., the President of Providence College, and Vicar General of Taichung Diocese, Taiwan, the Republic of China. As the pastor of the Catholic Church at Chunghsing New Village, the center of the Taiwan provincial government, he collaborates with most of the government dignitaries in matters of church and state. After building a high school, he became president of the college where he is engaged in a large expansion program. The date of this

most memorable meeting was October 25, 1975, on the occasion of a
pilgrimage to Rome and Jerusalem during the Holy Year Jubilee celebration which takes place every twenty-five years in the Roman Catholic
church. Statistically, Jerusalem, the State of Israel, is 7,885 air miles from
New York City.

* * *

THE TEMPLE OF THE SUN GOD

High above the lonely Peruvian altiplano,
   The rugged Andes leave scars in its ridged rills.
Rippling and bubbling streams flow softly down its hills,
   Plunging rapidly through ravines in hazy mists.
Winding along deep valleys for in the ocean it spills,
   While the Temple of the Sun God stands sentinel to all ills.
     LO! THE TEMPLE OF THE SUN.

The vast expanse of the boundless Pacific Ocean
   Looms beyond its horizons in its bounty deep.
Here the Humboldt Gulf Stream's icy waters sweep,
   To affect its climate with its chill, foggy, salty air.
This panoramic view of mist and fog prevails everywhere
   To dampen human spirits; to spread gloom and despair.
     LO! THE TEMPLE OF THE SUN.

Nature is strange and too unfeeling without a smiling sun;
   It lifts the soul from depths of darkness and man's despair.
This Incan temple mound stands all alone as a witness there;
   While nature's elements act not in harmony with cold-hot air.
Thus, the Incan priest and pagans tried the Sun God to appease;
   So, the price of a human sacrifice was laid down for peace.
     LO! THE TEMPLE OF THE SUN.

Around the human sacrificial victim stood the entourage
   Of solemn pagan priests, chieftains, princes and virgins.
They stared there in grim silence to pardon their sins,
   While the plunged dagger gushed with innocent blood spills.
Heaven seems to mourn this blood scene and dead landscape:
   Dark and dreary, slatelike sand and soil, rocks opaque.
     LO! THE TEMPLE OF THE SUN.

These shocking scenes of ancient times change not in our age;
   They appear in different headlines and the sporting page!
Victims of violence and the glory of men's shame tell the tale.
   Could this not be a fish story: sun, sucker, carp, or whale?
The realities of life are strange but true, not ordinary allegory;
   The law of self-preservation fills the pages of all history.
      LO! THE TEMPLE OF THE SUN.

One last look at the ancient Temple of the Sun God;
   It left a grim reminder of tribal customs beastly and bold.
This gave rise to nostalgic feelings of friends dearer than gold;
   The memory of no less a folly as running up stone steps so
   old.
In seeing nothing there, I saw everything that could be told:
   I gazed across "The Shadow of the Valley of the Moon!"
      LO! THE TEMPLE OF THE SUN.

* * *

AN ODE TO DOM

You may not be a Cardinal;
Surely, you're not a king.
But, a friend so ever gentle,
When doing the right thing.
It's not the Gifts you offer;
It's the love you kindly share.
This Ode to you I proffer,
To prove you always care.

You may not be a genius rare;
Yet, a noble peer and priest.
Silence is gold, all do declare;
Speech is silver, saying the least.
Selfless to all your needy who see:
'Tis the essence of real Charity.
To human suffering, you hold a key;
It opens Heaven's Gates to Eternity!

DEDICATION

The author wishes to dedicate his poetic contributions to *New Voices in American Poetry* anthology for the past five years in loving and grateful memory of his beloved parents: Simon A. (1874-1949) and Rose Helen (1881-1972) Tomalonis, born in Lithuania under Czarist Russia. Their lack of formal education, indomitable spirit of courage, and self-sacrifice, have enriched the author in sharing with others what both parents considered as their greatest loss and deprivation. In retrospect, after long lives, they may well have had the equivalency of a college degree in wisom *or philosophy*. Likewise, a special token of gratitude to his late brother Stanley A. Tomalonis (1919-1969) whose generosity, financial and moral support mainly, made possible the author's reaching his lifelong goal—The Eternal Priesthood.

BECAUSE OF YOU

Dear Jim:
 Just for you a rose is blooming,
 unto you this day is born:
 Just because of you some children
 wave a flag or blow a horn.
 Just because of you a farmer
 plows his fields, a painter paints,
 Teacher teaches, Christians worship
 free of tyrants or restraints.

 Just becuase of you we're walking
 unashamed and unafraid;
 Just because of you our children
 face their problems undismayed.
 Yes, because of you a smile is
 etched in glory on each face—
 Smile that shapes because we're grateful,
 smile that fear will not erase.

 Sure, you'll hear those childish voices
 shouting praise we'd not restrain,
 Just because of you, their hero,
 whom this day they'd entertain.
 Parents, too—the folks we live with—
 proudly kneel and say a prayer;
 Prayer that means they do remember
 ev'ry soldier ev'rywhere.

 No, it's not a day of sadness
 as we place a garland here,
 But a day to show our gladness
 for a mem'ry we revere.
 Yes, because of you we're happy—
 happy in the lives we lead—
 Older folks and, too, the young folks,
 matters not the race or creed.

As we march the way in freedom,
heads erect and void of fear,
It's because of you we're able,
yes, because of you we're here.
So, today we honor all the
lads who wore a uniform—
Lads in life from ev'ry station
lads for whom our hearts are warm.

* * *

ROSES FOR MY MOTHER

A little lad— no more than six—
    with tousled curly hair
Came in my flower shop today
    as I was standing there.
His blouse was open at the neck,
    his cheeks were rosy red,
And in a timid sort of way
    looked up at me and said,
"Please, Mister, here's a quarter and
    it's all I have to pay:
So could you fix some roses up
    into a nice bouquet?

"I want them for my mother and
    I wish you'd fix them nice,
With pretty colored ribbon wrapped
    around them once or twice.
And would you, Mister, please just write
    a note and make it say,
'A Happy Birthday, Mother Dear,
    although you've gone away.'
And if you'll let me take them out
    to where she's resting there,
I'll kneel down on her grave again
    and say a little prayer.

"I've tried so hard to do the things
   she wanted me to do,
And promised her I'd do my best
   to make her dreams come true:
But then I get so lonesome 'cause
   she isn't here to love
Since when she went away to live
   with God up there above.
She said that she'd be happy there
   where angels always sing,
And where each day is Sunday and
   the church bells always ring.

"She promised, oh so many times,
   while teaching me to pray,
That God would want to have me there
   to live with her someday.
So, Mister, please don't laugh if there
   are teardrops in my eyes,
Because I think so much about
   the grave where Mother lies,
And how she often talked to me
   about when she'd be gone,
Explaining why her son should be
   so brave and carry on."

SO MANY COMMON FOLKS

It takes a lot of common folks,
   the kind who say "Hello,"
To make a world worth living in,
   where friendships overflow;
And they must do some laughing,
   as contented people do,
For sun to shine and roses bloom
   where weeds and thistles grew.

It takes a lot of common folks
   with faith in one another,
To mold a world where every man's
   defender of his brother;
And they must be the kind of folks
   whose greeting is a smile,
The ordinary "howdy" folks
   to shape a world worthwhile.

That's why there are so many of
   the common folks around
To make this world a place in which
   so many smiles abound;
And just as long as we can have
   our share of gentle folks,
We'll have a world invested with
   the strength of mighty oaks.

LOVER

Love dwells in me forever,
since our solitudes met in the evening.
Love dwells in me forever,
since that kiss you gave me by the window.
Love dwells in me forever,
since your eyes and my eyes were both captured
in the intricate web of our feelings
which, no matter how hard we suppressed them
were bound—destined—to conquer and vanquish.

* * *

THOU ART

Thou art my love,
my only love in life.
Thou art my love
'til death and after death,
unto eternity.

771

THE LORD'S DAY

I am the Lord's own day:
I am six days younger than Earth's light,
My days are five less than His firmament,
Plants and dry land are four sunsets older than I,
Sun, moon, and stars have three sunrises on me.
Creatures of the clean waters and fowls of the pure air,
Swam and flew two sin-free days before my time.
Land animals and man were made at my door;
For everything was so good, God had kept me in store.
Man, created crowning-creature, was before I came,
And had given all other of Earth's creatures their name.
My first sunset rest, kept by God and man,
When everything was perfect, was most holy and grand.

Creation groans under man-caused violence and aches and
    longs for rest;
Man needs "the Son of Man . . . Lord also of the Sabbath" to
    come and bless.
My first sunset to sunset, holy God kept with sin-free man,
Then everything "was very good," most holy, happy, and grand.
I long for the Son of Man to bring such sunset to sunset again,
For that can only be true when, as was, there is no sin.

God's finger wrote me on stone in His Ten Words and Will.
I am still and ever shall be the Lord's Day still.

Scriptural Basic Basis
(Gen. 1, 2; Mark 2:27, 28; Isa. 58:13-14; Heb. 4; Rom. 8:22, 23; Exod.
20:8-11; 31:18)

THE STRANGER

Where I come from no one knows,
Where I go everyone goes.
What I say no one believes,
But I have done something only I can achieve.
If people would only listen before they scorn,
They would hear of a great power that has just been born.
No one cares to listen and hear their fate
But if they wait any longer it will be too late.
Danger is near but why can't they see?
Open their eyes and they will panic and flee.
Yet, why worry the fools? Let them by happy!
Why tell them they are so close to death?
Where I come from no one knows,
Where I go everyone will go.

* * *

MY FATHER

It seems my words can't express
My love, my admiration
To such a wonderful man,
Strong, with emotions, well-hidden,
He is the one I can lean on.
Having gone so far to achieve his goal,
How can one measure pride?
I love this man and I hope he can see
The admiration in my eyes.

MARY ANN TRACY

MOUNTAIN EVE

When golden dreams lie o'er the hills
With shadow-mists of memories,
When twilight on the mountains fills
The whisper wind with melodies,
When western skies are wide aflame
And tumbled clouds are golden-bound,
Then splendor reigns once more that came
'Fore mankind ever walked the ground.

Such majesty! A silhouette
Of mountain's edge against the sky,
Of brooding monarch pines that yet
Remember sunsets long gone by,
And whisper of them. Time stands still.
All ages past and those unborn
Are living now on purple hills,
Are almost tangible of form.
Remaining just enough beyond
A mortal's grasp through dusky light.
Then shadows close their timeless bond
And silken comes the touch of night.

But now cold murk and dreaded fear
Oppress the soul? Look up! Afar!
There mankind's glimpse of God appears:
The blessed hope, the evening star.

CYNTHIA M. TRICKEL

REMEMBER ME

To Her:

I loved your voice;
I loved your hair;
I loved the way you made me care.

It was long, long ago
When I decided to say,
We will run off and get married someday.

I knew not then I was going to die
But now I know, so please do not cry.
Always remember I will be around
And I hope you will never be sad and down.

I will be with you each night and day
And I wish you so much to be happy and gay.
It does not matter where I will be
As long as you remember me.

Please tell our baby when she grows up,
That I loved her so very, very much.
Tell her so many things about me
And what we used to do, we three.

So remember darling, before I die,
We will meet again somewhere in the sky.

From Him . . .

TWO ACORNS

An acorn cast upon the ground
   In time became a tree
And spread its beauty all around
   For all who passed to see;
But one who lived upon a shelf
   Complained that times were hard
And spent much pity on itself
   Because success was barred.

The acorn falling on the ground
   Was not afraid to die
And quiet be without a sound
   While months were passing by,
if only in the years that passed
   The life it gave could rise
And point a tribute that would last
   Toward God's eternal skies.

So often someone fails to find
   The joy there is in life
And comes to think the fates unkind
   Because their heart has strife,
When other men of lesser breed
   Have pockets lined with gold
And have supplies for every need
   And shelter from the cold.

If we would have the prize that waits
   For those who do their part
And live secure behind the gates
   That guard a thankful heart,
We must with valor run the race
   In progress past our door
And do our task with smiling face
   Until our journey's o'er.

ERNEST EUGENE TROWBRIDGE

TASKS WELL DONE

There is a joy that comes to me as life's mad race I run,
And that's the joy that comes because of tasks I leave well done;
I find no peace can calm my mind if I have quit the race
With tasks unfinshed all about and staring in my face;
There is no place that I can go and just enjoy the game
If tasks I leave unfinished bring dishonor to my name;
No night can bring me sweet repose and courage for the day
If I have painted pictures that will quickly fade away.

I like to do the tasks that come to me with thought and care
So I'll be glad to meet the job that I've done anywhere,
For word of pen can ever tell by weight or mammoth size
What can be told by tasks well done—they rightly advertise.
There's always joy in seeing things I have begun complete
With all that goes to make the job look finished up and neat;
For what's a dream if I cannot transpose the thing I feel
From just a picture in the mind to something that is real?

No recompense can e'er be mine if I my vision lose
Or fail to quite complete the tasks I dream of as I muse;
So let me do them one by one forever and a day
Until the light of setting sun forever fades away;
Let me find in accomplishment the joy I rightly crave
And let that joy extend to life that's lived beyond the grave,
For in this life we just begin the tasks we love to do,
And finish them in realms beyond where all is right and true.

BEVERLY M. TRUDELL

MY LORD AND MY GOD
(Here Is Thy Stay)

To whom relates when the world is well read?
Where seen among the hills, dales and valleys—
Who heard talk and clamor though Christ was born—
Listen and knew early that it was He.
The prophets spoke word and thought ages in time:
Left her heart for hearth and from home to preach,
Took retreat, forty days cavern saved grace!
How many figs he grasped in hand that thirst,
In whose presence where thronged the multitude?
Least of riches could not deny the maimed,
Crippled, blind, sick, man, son of God, retold;
Whom chose to follow the way of the cross.
And there was Simon, one friend, stationed near
One foe, death, but faith grows, and lives with Him.

* * *

SATELLITE

Hadn't I sate with windswept car
These mobile wings of moon and star,
An airy urge of port and sea
A driving thought of reverie—
Cruse the convert mind thus far.
Thoughts of bland verse relating are
The answer to his rite Vicar,
That its needs sound words errantly—
   Hadn't I sate?

We clothe our dreams like a stellar—
Its laden beauty knows its share!
Pious in hope, faith, charity!
Age conceived its own disparity:
Winds obscure its child avatar.
   Hadn't I sate?

778

SEASCAPE

Sky, sand, shells and sea . . .

In the distance gently moving shimmering waves
With their surface-scintillating countless diamond bits,
And way off, as far as the eye can see, the horizon . . .
At the shoreline the pounding surf rushes in with its on and off
    bubbly foam.

I'm stretched out on the sand;
The sounds and feel of the sea envelop me
       gushing surf
       caressing breezes
       all-embracing sunshine warmth
How it touches me . . .

The crescendo of the rolling, roaring sea
Orchestrates to a symphony of the ages.
I close my eyes; contemplation and then contentment take over;
I'm lost in nature's wonderment,
A hypnotic reverie.
Everything blends together and I too become a part of it all.
As in a trance there is just the sea and me:
We merge, the sea and I.

Alas, but for an instant . . .

There's water lapping at my feet—
Wouldn't you know—the tide's coming in—
Oh, rude awakening—gone the mystic spell . . .

WILLIAM G. TUBBS

CHRISTMAS PRAYER

Christmas is the time of year
We think of fun and games.
We hope the Lord will give us snow
Instead of chilly rains.

We all are busy these last few weeks
Making cookies and good sweets
To stuff the Christmas stockings
With those Christmas treats.

We are hanging shimmering tinsel
And bits of ribbon, too,
While the boughs are heavy, laden
With ornaments of many hues.

The lights are all a-twinkling
Like the stars up in the sky,
And the baby at the window
Is waving at all the passers-by.

Father is up the ladder
Hanging the star upon the tree,
While Mother is in the kitchen
Stuffing that great big golden turkey.

At night when we come home from school
The air is full of Christmas tunes;
They sure sound a lot better
Than the call of that great big bird they call the loon.

What is Christmas all about?
It isn't tinsel, games, or toys;
And even if the Lord does bring,
Instead of snow, those chilly rains,
It is the birth of Jesus Christ
That we celebrate this Christmas night.

If we follow the Lord's command
To love our brothers throughout the land,
There will be a bigger noise than any band.
For out of the heavens we will hear
Angelic choirs with a great big cheer:

* * *

GLORY TO GOD IN THE HIGHEST
AND PEACE TO MEN OF GOOD WILL!

Upon this land the Lord will walk
And there will be no need for talk;
For love will have conquered all that day,
War and strife will be no more.

For out in the streets people will shout with joy,
And there will be no need for a great big band;
For on this day the light will come
As Jesus Christ does walk the land.

When Christ has come,
To all He will call,
As the Father beckons to us all.
So, brothers and sisters, heed the call;
The gifts of the Spirit are for all.
These gifts which the Lord does bring:
Joy and peace, good will towards men,
Is my Christmas prayer for all.

A MOTHER'S LEGACY

Another mother did without today
    not to mention yesterday,
Her children are her bank accounts,
    they are always there on a rainy day;
Pillows of memories are her savings,
    they draw more interest, she'd say.
Blood, sweat and tears her contributions,
    as hope seems to look astray.
Like her mother, and her mother before,
    providing, dividing, and watching
    the children play;
Doing without earthly goods and leaving
    a will of "don't-forgets,"
    that's just a mother's way.

* * *

A REVELATION

I shall not want that which is not mine to have,
I shall not want recognition if it means isolation.
I shall not want to live if living is without loving.
I shall not want to know the secrets of the universe
or the wonders within, for it is through dying that
the secrets unveil.
Yet knowing as I do of the alternatives, I cannot
live except by wanting!

AFTERTHOUGHT

I have a fondness for remembering,
Especially days of happier mien,
When just the proper wine
Enhanced the palate's joy,
And conversation flowed.
Now only one is left,
And long-remembered joy
Creates a quiet pause,
As each recalled emotion
Demands a civilized response
Of silence, with no tears.
And there appears a false
Veneer to hide the scars
Of loneliness and time.

* * *

MEMORY

The chair I gave you
For your birthday
These long years ago
Stands idle where you
Left it and last sat in it.
I like to think
The ghost of you
Still makes it move
And rock.
But only kittens
Play at hide and seek,
And take priority
Where once you sat.

783

TRIBUTE TO OUR GENTLEMAN BING

Who's going to sing us "White Christmas" this year?
Who's going to bring us those sweet sentiments in song
    since our dear Bing has gone along?
To his loving family we send our regrets, knowing full well how
    much they miss their Dad's bright wit and affectionate,
    "Oh, Pet!"
To lessen all our pain best, we can remember this great man was
    first a gentleman and never a ham;
Though he could make us laugh, sigh, and cry through practically
    one song or one scene,
He was always a perennial and his popularity never waned.
He could dance with a straw sailor and cane-nimble and quick,
His sense of rhythm was so clean.
Or as a priest in *Going My Way*, he continued to top his
    performance year after year.
We know in history in years to come, this man's talents for
    living
    and giving, as well as his beautiful singing, will never ring
    out!

SOLITUDE

White sandy beaches everywhere,
for me to walk on.
Hours and days of burning sun,
for me to lie in.
Sea waves eternal roar,
for me to listen to.
Air that smells of salt,
for me to breath.
And sometimes rain,
for me to feel upon my face.

I found my island and
I'm free again.
All except my heart, perhaps,
And that will come in time.
Or so they tell me.

And though I know
I'll never really dream again,
I wonder.
Do you remember when we shared
an island dream?
And do you know,
if it hadn't been for you
I wouldn't be here?
Alone . . .

WEDNESDAYS

I'll just skip over Wednesday,
this week.
And all the inbetween days
too,
for a long, long time.

Someday—when Wednesdays are in
my week again,
and all the inbetween days
fall into place—
I'll know that you really
said good-bye.

Then, perhaps, the emptiness
of missing you won't be
so all-consuming.
But, I'll miss you every Wednesday.
And all the inbetween days,
too.

And I'll remember all things.
Everything we shared on
all those inbetween days.
Before there ever was a
Wednesday.

BEYOND THAT MOUNTAIN

In the quiet darkness of night
I watch for the sunrise.
In dimness about me, the signs foretell.
In shaded grays and pinks,
Over the mountaintop,
I watch the night change
Into colorful underlined clouds.
The dark retreats and brightness grows.

Beyond that mountain a force awaits,
Lighting the clouds with pink,
Then blue at last. Divergent rays
Spread over the sky
As I await the burst of new day,
Already exposed in its brightness
To those who are now
Beyond that mountaintop.

EMILY HOMES VOWELL

LET ME GROW

Let me grow scales o'er my eyes
That I may no longer see
The misery, dirt, squalor
Endured most everywhere.

Let me grow forgetful mind
That I may no longer know
The results of crime and drugs
So prevalent here and there.

Let me grow a deafened ear
That I may no longer tell
The cries of loneliness,
Of hunger, fear, and pain.

Let me grow a calloused heart
That I may no longer care
If little ones are unhappy
Sorrowful, troubled, and weak.

Or else, Lord, grant me greater strength
To discharge the load of my awareness.

REVERIE

When I sit at the console of my organ
And my fingers wander over the keys,
Oftentimes I fall to thinking
And let my dreams do as they please.

I hear the tinkle of a fountain,
The beat of angel's wings,
The laughter of a little child,
And within me my heart sings.

There'll be organs up in Heaven,
There'll be harps and singing, too,
And the music will go on forever—
God planned it for me and for you.

* * *

BURDENS

Did you ever get up in the morning
And with the sunrise came a burden or two?
And you wondered as the day progressed
How you ever were going to get through?

Then as you took out your Bible
And God spoke to you through His word,
The load once so heavy now was lighter
And you said, "Thank you, Lord, thank you, Lord."

A SONG FOR PETER

I'll hear your voice in wind and rain,
    From this day forth and evermore;
Soft music of the wind and rain,
    Beside a river and lake shore.

You'll hear my voice in wind and rain,
    On wings of dreams,
My love refrain;
    I'll hear your voice as winter dreams
Inspire again
    Symphonic theme.

Look for me in the wind and snow,
    From this day forth and evermore;
Hear music of my heart and soul,
    Beside a mountain and lake shore.
                (Petr Ilich Tchaikovsky, 1840-1893)

* * *

RHYME ROYAL

Now set between us here the players' board,
    Each side according to the rule lined up,
They of the white look few, the black a horde,
    Would seem a simple matter with some luck
To draw aside the queen, the king be struck;
    Yet life is more than any game of chess,
And those that love instead of hate, are blessed.
        (Based on the Rhyme Royal rhyming pattern introduced
            into English by Geoffrey Chaucer, ca. 1340-1400)

CANDLELIGHT

As seasons go by I remember
　　Most of all your face in candlelight
Encircled by marigold amber;
　　As seasons flow by I remember
Fall apples, cozy fire embers,
　　Fresh spring flowers, and warm summer nights,
But as seasons go I remember
　　Mostly your dear face in candlelight.
　　　　　　　　(Based on a Triolet rhyme scheme.)

EVERLASTING

The morning brings a golden cloud
　　Like a child with a flying kite;
Every day as a promise vowed
　　Dawn returns at the end of night.

By my window a budding tree
　　Seems a-hum with a bumblebee,
As happily a gentle breeze
　　Sighs of spring, and eternity.

* * *

WINDOWS

With his fingers on a frosted window
　　He idly pictured racing horses wild,
And one he had seen, a bucking pinto,
　　Until tumbled in bed a sleepy child.

He dreamed of rivers with roaring water,
　　Green wide grasslands beneath an azure sky,
Manhood, marriage, and a lovely daughter,
　　Morning waking him with a happy sigh.

791

SONG OF THE BUMBLEBEE

Years ago, one early morning
    The hungriest of cannibals
Instruction gave the bumblebee
    To bite world 'round all flesh therein:
"Tell me the sweetest of them all,
    And I'll eat nothing else," said he.

The bumblebee flew round the earth
    And bit a dog, a cat, a horse
Eventually it bit a man
    So hummed in joy for all its worth:
"Man has the sweetest flesh, of course,
    Man is sweetest of all," it sang.

"Ah, bumblebee," the people cried,
    "Don't tell the ogre anything,
He's bound to eat up all of us."
    "Man is sweetest," the bee replied,
And continued to hum and sing:
    "Man is sweetest of all," it buzzed.

"Is that so?" the people's prince sighed,
    And removed the tongue of the bee
In flight to the cannibal's den:
    So bumblebees only reply,
"Mm-m mm-m, mm-m mm-m,"
    To anyone's questions since then.
                (Based on a Khakassian legend.)

ACROSS THE RHINE

Across the Rhine on foot they came,
　　Men, women, children, animals,
And so the story still remains
　　In written Germanic annals:

We walked on water all the way—
　　If you would like to try the same,
It's not so difficult today
　　To sing, and dance, and have a game.

As long as it is firm, and cold,
　　Upon the water with children
Just like folk did in days of old,
　　We can walk on water frozen.
(Germanic migrations fourth to sixth centuries A.D.;
　　　　　　　　　　　　A Rhine crossing 406)

* * *

SONG OF MY HEART

Whenever all else seems to thrive and grow,
　　The summer roses fade, begin to wilt
From heat, their velvet petals scatter, spilt
　　Upon the ground like forlorn flakes of snow;
And melting with the sun's rays final glow,
　　The light withdrawing in thin shafts that tilt
Night shadows, the songbirds' trailing hushed lilt
　　Almost sounds to echo of some sorrow;
At times my dreams like summer flowers fade,
　　Dispersed by bleak winds into ocean foam,
But over near the tree of life in shade
　　My soul knows no desire to ever roam;
The love within the circle firmly made
　　Of your arms will forever be my home.
　　　　　　(Inspired by Marcus Tullius Cicero, 106-43 B.C.;
　　　　　　"There is no place more delightful than home.")

SONETTO*

My Dear Beloved, if I could write you
    All my heart holds in original rhyme,
Every thought placed in each lyrical line
    To express love, and composed just for you,
As fledglings flying would tell something new
    With each endearment to last for all time,
Pleasing you always as the lovely shine
    In heavenly color of rainbows may do;
All words I would gift wrap, but iambic,
    However poetic for your darling eyes,
Elusive ever, evading metric,
    Drift quickly by me like blue dreaming skies
Seem to forever go beyond music
    And, softly smiling, remain lullabies.
(*A rhyme pattern from the verse form called ''Sonetto,''
      meaning a little song, that originated in Italy.)

* * *

SONG OF LOVE

Once upon a dream, Stone Ages away,
    I seem to recall in a wilderness,
Together we shared times of quietness
    When we were younger in a yesterday;
Sleeping in my soul as a summer day
    Filled with golden sunshine and happiness,
The dream only waits for your soft caress
    To awaken it like a song today;
All of our tomorrows your embrace holds
    With a melody singing silently,
Truly, tenderly, as I loved you then,
    I will always love you, and now enfold
Fully, faithfully, as you once loved me
    My heart giving you all my love again.
        (A variation of Sonetto rhyme.)

DAVID'S LAMENT*

Look, and you will read on Scripture's pages
　　A terrible lament from King David
For the death of Saul in former ages,
　　A record of treacherous, and sordid
Plots of other men with hearts most horrid:
　　"Nay," you answer as if shy, then reply,
"The weeping was done well by King David.
　　Why should I cry, and shed tears from my eyes
For anything that now is long gone by?"
　　But somewhere in the music of the wind
A voice can still be heard within its sigh,
　　Distance not making it faraway thin:
The vileness of lies cleanse from King Saul's shield
　　For died he as his son died in the field.
　　　　　(A rhyme pattern derived from the Sonetto by the
　　　　　　　English poet Edmund Spenser, c. 1552-1599)
　　　　　　　　　　　　　　　　(*2 Sam. 1:17-23)

* * *

SINCE BABYLON

The answer tossed upon the sea of time
　　In symbols bold, yet baffling to the mind
Remains a strange enchanted pantomime,
　　A riddle with no key that I shall find.
Others, the Scriptures explanations give
　　To dreams like Daniel had upon his bed,
Of days in Babylon when he did live,
　　But of his visions leave some part unsaid.
There locked forever hidden in mystery
　　Bewildering things beheld within the night,
Reason directed me turn to history,
　　Reality to grasp for better sight:
Since Babylon on earth four empires reigned,
　　The Persian, Greek, Roman, and the Christian.

　　　　(An English rhyme pattern derived from the Sonetto,
　　　and at times used by William Shakespeare, 1564–1616)

DARLING PAPA

I'm only a child afraid of the dark,
   O please, my darling Papa, bring me home,
Though reason rules the woman, in my heart
   I'm only a child afraid of the dark;
Without love no sunlight, nor moon, nor star,
   Without you it's lonely living alone,
I'm only a child afraid of the dark,
   O please, my darling papa, bring me home.
           (An arrangement of rhyme pattern from a
             verse style called a Triolet.)

* * *

PAS DE DEUX

And overhead the stars at night
   More wonderful than fairyland
Shone all about, made crystal bright
   The earth with snowy feathered plume;
And through the clear still night there came
   The joyful song from wedding band;
With jingling bells and horse-drawn sleigh
   They brought the shy young bride and groom.

And laughing they did pull in rein
   Before a house with open door,
Wherein the guests in bright array
   Had gathered for the marriage feast;
And though the party mood was gay
   The couple vowed forevermore
In love they would remain, and stay,
   The passing years their love increase.

ARMS OF THE SEA

On a downhill causeway leading to the sea
     There's a lovely little popular café
Where, when I first met you, long before we knew,
     Our two coffee cups had carried us away.
As I took your hand and led you to the beach
     We then wandered to the jetty on the strand
Where a rowboat bore us over rising swell
     To the sailing vessel anchored near the land.
So from that time forward all our days have been
     But a voyage in the lives of you and me,
And we owe it all to coffee in the shop
     On a downhill causeway leading to the sea.

* * *

MORE OF YOU

When I vowed you had taken my heart
     There appeared no more love to impart,
But through day to day life,
     With its rapture and strife,
You have torn all that theory apart.

For the longer we draw breath, and live,
     All the more you determine to give;
Till the day that it's done
     You're a million in one,
And our love we will never outlive.

AURORA

Dew fell gently in the nighttime;
    Dawn gave way to powerful sun;
Brilliant color came with daytime;
    Vibrant morning had begun.
Prismic light from hanging droplets
    Each aflame, reflective pools,
Turned the world to living gem-sets,
    All transformed to treasured jewels.

RESOLUTIONS

The New Year is a clean white page
Spread out before us. Let's engage
Not in small meannesses but dissolve
All enmities, and let's resolve:

No matter what new vows we make
Or what old vices we forsake,
To climb forever far above
Our present selves, let us resolve.

We reach for ink and pen to write,
The scroll's begun in black and white,
But there's a blot! Wrong lines evolve
Without a plan, so, let's resolve

To fill each day from first to last
With better deeds than haunt our past;
To make this page close-lined with love
And kindliness, let us resolve.

MABLE WARNKE

THE MISSING BODY

When Mary to the garden went
    On that first Easter day
The tomb was almost empty,
    Almost, not all the way;

For in it lay the linen cloths
    Which had Christ's body bound,
The napkin, too, but Christ Himself
    Was nowhere to be found.

She quickly hurried back to tell
    That Christ, her Lord, was gone,
She knew not who had taken Him,
    Nor what great deed was done.

If in our day it happens that
    A body disappears,
It means bad news and usually
    Results in grief and fears.

But with Christ's missing Body, which
    Itself rose from the tomb,
We have the joy of great Good News
    Which drives away all gloom.

For us His missing Body has
    Great meaning, since it proves
The truth of all God's promises,
    The greatness of His love,

The empty Cross! The empty Tomb!
    Have but one thing to say:
"We have a LIVING SAVIOR, WHO
    IS WITH US NOW! TODAY!

MABLE WARNKE

DARE TO SHARE

Folks are crying all around
    The world, and they are asking
Questions about life itself,
    While busy with its tasking;

"Why am I here? What purpose
    Has been planned for me to fill?"
These questions need an answer,
    If we'd know and do God's will.

We have some of the answers
    And if we would really care
We'd heed the Gospel message
    And with others *dare to share*

The news that Christ is living!
    And so, also we shall live
And gladly share the blessing
    Which He, by His grace does give.

Our source of Joy is Jesus,
    He's our Light for every day,
Our Hope for each tomorrow
    As we go along life's way.

To fight the power of evil,
    We need the greater Power
Found in the Word of Jesus,
    To gird us every hour.

We also need each other,
    As we hold Christ's banner high,
And follow in His footsteps
    Serving others, far or nigh.

We have Christ's precious promise,
    To be with us everywhere,
Pray! Praise! Give thanks! and gladly
    GO! His Gospel DARE to SHARE!

THE INNKEEPER

Too busy with his busy-ness, the keeper of the inn,
He had no time, he had no room, to take the Christ-Child in.
    But wait, before we censure him for what he failed to do,
    Let's take a look at our own lives; we may neglect Him,
    too.
The inn of life to each of us by our God has been given;
Do we have room to take Him in, this Child, the King of
    Heaven?
    For He still seeks to enter in the hearts of men today,
    Do we have room to welcome Him, or push Him far away?
We get wrapped up in worldly things, we rush with growing
    speed,
Too busy to extend a hand to someone else in need.
    For each time we help someone who's in need, whose days
    are grim,
    Our kindly act of helpfulness is done as unto Him.
This Advent time belongs to Christ, take care, prepare your inn,
Your heart a waiting cradle make and take the Christ-Child in.

* * *

CANCELLED!

Our schedule was planned carefully, and all was timed so well,
The meetings o'er, 'twas homeward bound, but then the curtain
    fell!
    Arriving at air terminal, our separate ways to go,
    One single word upset all plans: CANCELLED! because of
    snow.

The crowds grew large and larger, folks stood or milled around,
And sought to get new schedules for wherever they were bound.
    'Twas all in vain; in spite of new and scientific tools,
    There's one thing man cannot control, no matter what the
    rules;
And that's the weather, which is in God's wise and mighty Hand,
Reminding us not to forget—HE STILL IS IN COMMAND!

KEEPING PACE

At times life seems like a speeding train
Clambering up mountains and over rough terrain,
A laborious journey that one would never choose
But since there are no stops one has to see it through.

Should anyone attempt to apply the brake
Havoc and confusion would certainly take place,
For others on the track are speeding just as fast
And one must keep the pace or allow them all to pass.

* * *

SEARCHING

One is alone and wanting even on familiar base
For one is always searching for someone or some place.
From childhood on through life, just like a lost sheep,
Needing assurance, fulfillment, something that flows deep.

What each is searching for has all gone on before,
Through eons and eons of time and locked within man's core.
This inner core, this "Light," this "Spark of Divinity,"
To comprehend its full meaning is the aim of humanity.

* * *

THE CYCLES OF TIME

To understand the nature of things;
To feel what the silence is saying;
To sense the decree of destiny
The cycles of time are conveying.

OLD WOMAN

Your spirit is strong, flesh is weak
Your face is wrinkled, youth you seek.
    Age has bathed her hair in gray,
    She sits and thinks of far away.
Old woman is she, her brows are bent,
Her life of past has now been spent.
    As I ponder a thought, I wonder why
    Of all living things, you should die.
In my dream appears the old woman clear;
I know this woman, she's my mother dear.

* * *

OLDTIMER

An oldtimer, sitting on a chair
Not doing much, not even on a dare.
    His face is wrinkled, hair is white,
    He sits and thinks till the night.
Amid the trees on a shaded hill,
Carving a branch, hears a whippoorwill.
    Through heat of day, his thoughts are flowing,
    Amidst deep-dyed leaves winds are blowing.
Leaning back, taking big sigh,
Thinks of days that passed him by.

THEY'RE DOWN, THEY'RE UP, THEY'RE DOWN

There was a time, my friend,
When ankle-length dresses were in
And a pretty face was all we could admire.

They're still as pretty as can be;
What a pleasure it would be to me
To see them in much shorter attire.

The dresss were getting shorter
But most didn't think they oughta
And a big ado about nothing came about.

When the issue was finally settled
The innovators got a medal
For those awful ankle-lengths were finally out.

They would hang above the knees—
Some fine-looking knees, if you please,
And I wonder what idiot invented the long dress?

If they ever return again
I'll have to take it on the chin;
Very distressing, very depressing, a blow to progress.

Now they barely cover the hip—
Those fine legs stop at the slip,
Those fine thighs get all the eyes with no recant.

But those awful long dresses are back,
And they've added those pants to the rack.
I guess it's "Down with short dresses; long live stupid pants."

ANGELS WEEPING WATER

. . . and the sun machine rays were blocked by overlapping
    clouds
the drops of moisture hit with a large boom
the Gods let off their love sounds as the angels weeping water
    turned down their cheeks
not the time of the season—but our feelings are not counted by
    way of time
so some sat by windows watching the angels weeping water
others enjoyed it . . . singing in the rain . . . the rain . . . the
    rain proves the heavens are not so heavenly
just normal . . .
don't blame it on Adam or Eve
there never was a perfect—never will be
Theories never proved anything—just time
maybe there is a perfect . . . combustions of the Gods'
    thundering never cease to amaze me
they believe in the eyes of the beholder—most of the world sure
    to hell
well let's quit the theories and wait till the clocks tick their way
    to the point. . . .

* * *

TWO DIFFERENT WORLDS

Throw me in the closet
Throw me in the back
Turn your head
I wish you dead
Leave me
I'll become an object
Leave me
I'll become a wall
Onto you
Which I fall
Close your ears
Close your eyes
Pretend as if
I wasn't here.

806

To heck with ya
Who wants ya
Instead of good
We got bad
Another world
Has his own
A frown
A smile
Make it
All worthwhile
Two sides
Two faces
Different kind
Of persons
A world that
Can hold one
Yet can't hold
Another one.

Daddy likes
A sport
Me likes
A music
Football?
Ahh, to heck with it
Rock-n-Roll?
Don't leave my side
Him like jock
Me like sound
So just come
Turn me off
It doesn't matter
It don't matter
I got a life
Don't get on my nerves
You live on your planet
I'll live on mine.

YOU SPOKE TO ME

You spoke to me with music
But it's doubtful if I heard,
While the tones played out the story
I was listening for a word.

You spoke to me through motion:
Dragging step and lowered eye,
But the message failed to register,
I was listening for a cry.

You spoke to me a thousand ways
Before you went away,
And now I hear it clearly
Calling out from yesterday.

Let me widen up my focus
To include all sentient things;
Let me feel the hidden meanings
That bare awareness brings!

I need to know that you forgive
My blindness to your fears,
I need to know you'll comfort me
Through many, lonely years.

BURNS

O flower of elfin song or knell,
O bloom of night or asphodel,
Which flower the best portrays his art?
For each could be a counterpart.

The Scotch broom in his friendliness,
The heather bell for home address,
The lint white thorn with plighted love
Among the braes the tall foxglove.

In prominence the hills of stars
For fragrance meadow flowers,
The applewhite for choice perfume
The lilies with their varied bloom.

Finality of bleeding hearts,
Hay flowers training loaded carts;
One night I saw a rare moonblow
One day two bows nature did show.

Both flags dip low on ways of Clyde
Where Highland Mary does abide
But most of all the rest was he
The red, red rose of poetry.

* * *

TANGO

"I'm sick, send help to Lemiti"
A message scrawled in bullet's lead.
"Tango, your talk must really fly,"
Was all the shepherd said.

A warning bark the ranger roused,
The message sought and found
A pan of oats where Roanie browsed,
His hoofbeats scorned the ground.

A first-aid kit, a record run,
Tango barked hard at quackery—
Ptomaine emptied its gun—
Again hisself was free.

The shepherd rose to herd again
But stood amazed, aghast
For lying in his bed of pain
Poor Tango breathed his last.

The woods will never be the same
Tho Tango left his brood—
But graven on one heart, a name
Still echoes through the wood.

* * *

COWBOY SUNSET

We passed the hat for Colowash
The day he made that ride,
He roped his innards in, by gosh,
To keep himself inside.

The sunfish and the coy sashay,
The pitch and buck and whirl,
Would hold a Brahma steer at bay
Before a shy maid's curl.

He rode him out plumb to the brim,
He sulks in the corral.
We raised ten-gallon hats to him
And gave a cowboy yell.

At night our saddles form a ring
About the dying fire,
The stars about our blankets cling
Old Colowash aspire!

MY FRIEND

The desert sun shone down upon us,
    high spirits enjoying life.
We were different, but we were the same.

We swam together, and slept together,
    and shared a warm embrace.
And when I held you, your blue eyes
    looking in mine,
I felt your tenderness and compassion.

It has been many days since that wonderful
    September morn,
Oh, how I miss you so.
Not a day goes past that I don't wonder how you are
    and wonder where you have been.

Each evening before I go to bed, I take one
    last glance at the picture of the
    one I'll always love and admire.
And I'll often wonder if we'll ever see each other again.

I needed you. You needed me.
We were different, but we were the same.

A BOY NEEDS SOMEONE

He never knew his father, never had someone who cared.
He never had someone to show him the way,
    or play ball with him on a sunny day.

Never knew what it was like to ride a horse,
    hike up a mountain, or walk in the forest.

Never had someone to hold him, someone to love him,
    someone to scold him.

Never had someone to talk to about the pains of growing up,
    never someone to rush home to and show the victory cup.

But now there is someone to be with, and talk about being a
    man,
Someone to encourage him to do all that he can.
He is no longer alone. He is no longer just one.
Because now there is someone, someone who treats him like a
    "son."

* * *

GALACTIC PROPHECY

The future of tomorrow is what we live today.
A vision of prosperity and kindness in what we do and say.
Where no man is a stranger, where we all work as one,
Positive beings united together, living under one sun.
To boldly go to the far reaches of our mind, to push and to
    excel,
Spreading laughter, spreading freedom, spreading justice so all
    the universe is well.

WENDY

At times it seems so strange to me
Why God won't let my special friend see.
Why for some life seems so carefree and gay,
And for others it's taken so painfully away.

I look in your eyes and I see your love,
How you trust in God, the Lord above.
And while people complain each and every day
You never have qualms to express or say.

I know your mind is fuzzy and unclear
But you've heard heartbeats that I'll never hear.
I'll search for answers and rack my mind;
For the knowledge you have that I'll never find.

What I'm trying to say, my retarded friend,
Is that the feeling you gave me won't ever end,
For you have taught me so many wonderful things
And you'll never know what happiness that brings.

And when you're gone and so is your pain
I'll think of you when I hear the rain.
And when it's my turn, I hope I'll be
Right up there with you and you with me.

(by Jan Fisher)

(This poem was written for Wendy Welch before she died in
        1978 at the age of 22.)

HIGH FLIGHT

Today, I decided.
Decided to fly, fly in my own way.
I will glide with the wind
Alone, with no help.
Climb, I must.
Danger is evident in such a decision,
But I hope I do not know fear.
I must prove to myself I can do it.
Many will never know the taste of victory unless they try.
It is the fear of defeat that makes us stop.
I do not know such a word.
All I know is the sky is mine.

* * *

MY RACE IS NOT YET RUN

As a kid I had fun, when you let me.
In high school I developed as myself without your help.
I am gone from you. I am far. I am now me.

I do not need you any longer.
You are no longer my friend.
You never were.

My life is just beginning.
Others need me. Others need me and want me.
They accept me for what I am.
I represent a new spirit.

As we live together, we become one.
The spirit has united into one.
And all because my race is not yet run.

CHRISTIE

Snow-plum blossoms
    softly caress the greening ground,
        Oh my Love . . . Oh my Love . . .
The sky is blue,
    gray shadows flee, for I have found
        Oh my Love . . . Oh my Love . . .
Dark and shining opals
    so glisten in your eyes.
Moist tender lips
    more soft than I could realize.
        Oh my Love . . . Oh my Love . . .
You drove the aching pain
    from deep within my heart;
You taught me faith
    could once again restart,
        Oh my Love . . . Oh my Love . . .
Quickening of my breath,
    a touch of tenderness.
The welcome of a smile,
    the thrill of happiness.
        Oh my Love . . . Oh my Love . . .
I wonder at the touch that brings me life anew . . .
I wonder at the gift from God Who gave me you. . . .
        Oh my Love . . .

STRIVING ONWARD

Sometimes we hope, but somehow hope too much;
The hopes we hope, the dreams we dream,
Are much too high or too far gone to touch.
No matter if circumstances could be changed,
And no matter how much our lives could be rearranged,
Nothing would ever be perfect and nothing could wholly satisfy.
It is so foolish then to fret and brood,
And so you see that is the reason why.
Why not instead, if we must meditate and dream,
Why not think on the good in life and on those better things?
Only making certain that those goals so earnestly sought
Might someday bring reward for every obstacle so long fought.
That every struggle might prove in time worthwhile,
And we might live life to the fullest and in faith,
Fighting every fear with triumph and each tear with a smile.

* * *

LIFE, AS A GIFT

Each fleeting moment in Time is precious,
For not one mortal soul can boast of time to spare.
The hours pass so swiftly; the days go quickly by;
And soon so many transient years have gone
As mere memories, before our unbelieving human eyes.

Yes, Life is a gift to be cherished and treasured;
Not to be spent in idleness, to be wasted in folly.
The hours are sanctioned; one hope for a mission is granted
By the Author of Life itself, as a seed of hope that is planted.

PATTERNS

i will return
    thru the eyes of tigers
        to the river city and finished dreams;
i see no mistakes and still,
    there are mainstreams of words unmasking
a star system beyond our mother's eyes,
    and gathering the storm
      her atoms reveal
        the meaning of love,
          her thoughts i will decode
          with my poetry.

the roar of the locust
    and its deep sleeping
      thru this country multiplies;
we must redream the perfect deserts
    to transfix the patterns,
      and seal the permanence
        of touching,
          bond inside bond.

* * *

BETWEEN US

your body so hot with the summer
    seeping through the screens into our lives;
at night the prickle of heat,
    the sweat between your legs,
      such pools we slide into—
      such innocence—
you are in the breath of me, pamela,
    heart of hearts.

AKATHRIEL

I found a canopic urn . . .
                but it is empty,
And the Chöd apparition will not whisper his secret
Of Redemption,
Nor will the windflowers speak their prelude.

I stumbled on temporal dust
                and became its image . . .
The heavens look down,
But laugh at the folly
And unearth my seed in poetic contingency.

I reached into memory to touch a girl once loved . . .
But the pages are unharvested,
And the nakedness tragic fantasy
Of emotions so real yet shadowy,
                as promises
Pollinic that end on winds in a desert dawn.

I found a canopic urn . . .
                but it is asymmetric
And barren as the tears that moistened the clay,
And its sacredness uncertain,
Its age long past . . .
                or yesterday ephemeral;
It slips from my hands and breaks upon my soul.

TUAT

"I have longed to move away but am afraid."
    —Dylan Thomas

I desire to be an Audian poet
On the metaphysical stage,
Fabric about the estrogenic flow
That anoints incarnate ethicalities,
To suffer and love, to be enwombed
In the distal dream before I was;
        But my sleep is shallow
        And the night is long.

I desire to be an Audian poet
On the metaphysical stage,
A haruspex defiant of ingenerate gods
Who quaff the Macedonian cup,
To stand upon an aeonian mound
touched by the eternities . . . and *man;*
        But my sleep is shallow
        And the night is long.

Come lie beside me in this subtle grave,
For the sleep is shallow and our night quite long.

* * *

IMMISCIBLE

To come so silently amidst the multitude
In nakedness and exception upon a tear . . .

To rise so thetically from dream to claim
Through emotions no man defy or understand . . .

To be within that tear the cause and receptor
Of a fantasy so silently fading into the unconceived.

819

CREED

Man has echoed it
Yet he has said nothing—

Man has envisioned it
Yet he has understood vestiges—

Childhood lurks as a demon in his heart
Seeking to betray the illusions he worships—

Reality preys upon the substance of his soul
Releasing moments of light that enact his madness—

Man has known the daughters of Allah
Yet he has never loved them.

* * *

PERSONAL

I fall into despair,
Corridors narrow,
The river Jobel knows not my hand,
Sleep comes to deceive unremembered reams.
I sit in these shadows
And weep too silently for solace;
I am not perceived,
My soul translucent,
A Vaisakh moon in my fantasies
In a coldness of poetic effect.

CLOSE ENCOUNTERS

Economics

And the rigid, uncompromising, golden
Sword of truth shall plunge . . . deep
Into the flexible, pliable, paper
Quicksand of illusion . . . but
What manner of thing might rise
From the passion of this union?

Education

They banished truth—enshrined the lie
And wouldn't even tell us why.
Harsh, unspoken, lesson learned—
Seek you all and every other thing
But fly from truth—
'Twill find you soon enough!

Of Another Kind

Oh, ever so softly I silently scream
For the face of the Devil I've seen in a dream.
Terrible monster, incredibly mean,
Loved by the people that I would demean,
Evil incarnate, which cannot be seen,
Suckling its children on poisoned ice cream.
Oh, ever so softly I silently scream:
The name of our Demon is Super Machine!

A LOOK AT *MYSELF*

When upon the windowsill, I see
    A sign of life—a sparrow looking up to Thee;
The sound of a mockingbird in a distant tree—
I'm alive! Someone is speaking just to me.

I stepped out of my old self
    And when I looked back at me,
I had to be the awfulest mess in His eternity—
'Twas nothing but a bag of flesh;
'Twas anything, but fresh.

It told the story of my plight—
    The wrinkled mass—the losing fight;
The horror of a selfish life—
    Result of greed, and lust, and strife.

I looked at it; it looked at me;
    One of us must flee—
before it crumbled back to dust,
    It smiled good-bye—gave nod of trust.

Fear had no place in the new me
    Nor in my longing to be free;
My soul was filled with much delight—
    The old self bowed gracefully from sight.

This was me—my second chance—
    To play my part or flee,
Forever into eternal darkness,
    Or go on stage with glee.

I am grateful to all
    Who helped prepare my curtain call;
I never knew just when 'twould be—
    But I did know that call was He.

Again, to friends and foe alike,
    Wherever you may be—
You'll be remembered prayerfully,
    As I claim my Victory.

Victory is the faith—
    The plug-in to the Divine;
The security of feeling safe,
    When tuned into His mind—
A vast—endless network—
The only one of its kind.

THOUGHTS OF A DRIFTER

I have nothing, and no one to give that nothing to;
I don't even have a place from which to bid adieu.
As I drift along from place to place,
    I feel apart from the human race.

Too long, I dreamed my life away;
'Twas long filled with rot and decay—
There's no turning back, I've lost too much ground;
Unless, of course, I turn myself completely around.

My yesterdays were dreadful; my todays are the same;
Tomorrows hold no promise, other than being lame.
Everything I ever knew has long left my mind,
With no roots to sustain me, there was nothing to leave behind.
Since I have nothing to return to, 'cept what I had before;
Could it be that somewhere out there on a distant shore,
A welcoming awaits me, if I'll just drift some more?

I never knew my mother, and my father, he stayed gone;
I was my own captain from the day that I was born—
The ol' captain's had his day—and wayward winds did havoc
    play
With him and his old raft as it drifted 'long the way.
Everything looked so big and bright when I was ridin' high;
The mighty waves tempted me to reach up for the sky—
But, just as life itself is just one breath away,
So it was with the waves, and down with them went I.

Should I have had a destination all mapped out for me;
Maybe Fate would still have come—to shape my destiny.
Who am I? Same as you. I fit into a plan—
The same One who put me here is still in command.

HOLD ON

Hold on, hold on, my friend;
Dare not yet to envision the end—
Too much is left undone;
Too much is left unsaid;
God will tell you when,
        And, only then—
Close your eyes and reminisce,
        Of happiness again.
'Tis not of this world,
        Nor the pilgrimage therein,
That you will find a resting place—
'Tis at the journey's end.

Hold on, hold on, my friend,
Although you hang by a thread;
Look! There's a light up ahead;
And, Home is just around the bend.
Home, sweet home—
        Where the heart is light and gay;
        Where the children come from play;
        Where the toilers come to rest,
        Where love is at its very best,
        And kin come to join in prayer
        Of Thanksgiving that God lives there.

Hang in there, my friend,
As each day blends into night;
The peace and quiet are worth the fight—
And, with all your might,
Welcome Victory! It's in sight!

HEAVENLY CONNECTION

Oh, God in heaven,
I praise Thy holy name;
Thou who looks down upon us
And blesses us each the same.

We thank Thee, blessed Jesus,
For the daily bread we eat,
For the water with which to quench our thirst
And the space to plant our feet.

We thank Thee every day and night
For the stars cast in the skies;
We bow our heads to Thee, dear Lord,
Who forgiveness of our sins supplies.

We have eyes with which to see all things
But yet we're cruel and blind;
In this sea of thoughtlessness
Thou alone art kind.

Tread upon our many sins,
Help! Forgive us, Lord, I pray
That our new tomorrow
May be a better day!

MOTHER'S BIRTHDAY

You did not notice, as you sat in the chair   .   .   .
Your precious hands folded with greatest of care.

You knew not my thoughts, as I saw you that day . . .
So I'll write on this paper what I wanted to say.

The white of your hair looked the purest of snow . . .
I wondered, that moment, where did the years go.

The reflection of sunbeams danced in your eyes . . .
Did you know, Mother, they are as blue as the sky?

Have I told you, Mother, you have delicate hands . . .
A pure soul, and a heart as big as this land?

You didn't know, Mother, your presence that day . . .
Was a refreshing song on a harp to be played.

I am mindful of all the sweet things you have done . . .
Special words you've said, a smile like the sun.

You have wisdom, beauty, charm and such grace . . .
Reminding me of things like fine satin and lace.

On your special birthday, I want you to know . . .
How much I will always love you so.

Many years will come, as they must fade . . .
But your wisdom and love shall not abade.

Such a lady you are, there is no other . . .
That could compare with you, dearest Mother.

(Notation: Written especially for Annie Laura Long Meers, by
      her Honey Bee, Maryellen)

OUR THING

Spread your wings,my friend,
As you soar through the sky.

For I now lie calm and watch
As you come from shore,
To play with me and my waves.

Playful you are today,
As you swoop and touch
The friendly swells.

I'm so happy I can provide for you,
For that's my job, you now,
And it is yours to wing the skies and fly.

For I am the sea,
And you the sea gull.

* * *

NOEL

She's now so very, very, far away
But my thoughts of her are deeply embedded
Yes, embedded in my heart to forever stay

You know as I think back,
She really never asked for much,
Just a bit of my time, a kind word,
A touch

I've never found her equal.
No, and I guess I never will

For there was but one Noel,
Now beneath the ground she lies still.

MY OLD HOUSE

I drove by it the other day
And noticed the lawns were velvet green—
The trees grown strong, straight and tall;
I drove by it the other day and my eyes were filled with tears.
I wanted to stop and look around
But I kept on driving;
I wondered if the roses still bloomed at the back.
Was the giant evergreen still stately and proud?
The sheltered patio with fireplace of brick
And red wooden table and chairs;
But I kept on driving.
Does the pathway still lead to the white garden gate?
And the leaves crunch under your feet
When Autumn frost freshens the air.
I drove by it the other day and my eyes were filled with tears.
In the golden days of Summer's delight
Are the raspberries ripened and red?
I remembered the kitchen window I loved—
Those high-beamed ceilings and chandeliers,
Yes, the pictures of loved ones at rest
But I kept on driving and my eyes were filled with tears.
Dear old friends and "Fluffy," the cat we so loved;
Then holiday gatherings when all were back home,
With neighbors so wonderful still—
Our children all grown in distant lands now,
God called them to lead their own lives;
But Time passes on, great changes take place,
So I kept on driving,
For my old house is no longer my old house—
And my eyes were filled with tears . . .

APPALACHIAN YEARNING

Over in the mountains, east of the O-Hi-O,
There is a special feeling that I've come to know.
It's really oh, so awesome, it takes my breath away
When the mountain sun rises on another day.

It's calling out to me, APPALACHIAN YEARNING,
Washing my senses clean
It's coming from inside, APPALACHIAN YEARNING,
Reflections in my eyes.

In the midst of the hardwoods, there so tall
Above ferns of feathery splendor,
The paintbox leaves of mountain fall
Aren't all that nature renders.
Lo, the cottony fog upon the pink, sweet laurel
Brings my nose to dazzle and my lungs to twirl.

When creatures repose to ponder
A winter-frozen brook,
My heart soon grows fonder betwixt a second look.
And before sap starts creeping up the maple's waist
I'll stack up the boiling fires indeed with haste.

It's calling out to me, APPALACHIAN YEARNING,
Washing my senses clean
It's coming from inside, APPALACHIAN YEARNING,
Reflections in my eyes.

SIMPLICITY

Have you ever really listened to a child?
Planted a flower or a tree?
Felt free and wild on a sunny day?
And looked up to Heaven to pray?

Teach us to become a babe again,
Full of innocence, not wanting to hurt;
To love without pain;
Is that possible, Lord, TO LOVE AGAIN???

* * *

CORRALING THE THUNDERING CLOUDS

I wonder if I could lasso those clouds
And bring them home with me?
To gaze at, dream by, and rain upon us both;
There's just you, me, remembering our oath.

Staring at the fire
And the thundering rain against the pane;
The two of us alone without the crowds.

Just sitting there, not a word is spoken,
Nor does it have to be;
That warm electrical feeling's OURS—
While a wee bit o' Heaven flo'ers.

Photographs

Rose Elizabeth Andrews (15)

Lily Arbab (17)

Louise B. Armstrong (18-19)

Estelle Barlow (38)

Iris Bartolot (40-47)

Eva Beaver (52-55)

Camilia Joanne Belcher (60-62)

Dorothy Bush Belden (63-66)

Paul N. Bickford (72-81)

Edward Hussey Binns (82-85)

Ricky Kay Bennett Blas (90)

La Nora Bloom (91)

Bessie Taylor Brown (124-125)

Calvin Reed Brown, M.D. (126-127)

Sena Ethel Bucy (138-139)

Rose Burgess (142-143)

Colette Josephine Burre (144)

838

Bette Davis Burris (147-149)

Salandra A. Butler (154-156)

Beulah Thomas Carey (162)

Fermin L. Cariño (163-164)

Steve Carlson (165)

Jeri Cary (169-170)

Frances Ann Chierico (182)

Larry Wayne Clay (183)

Bernada Cooley (184-185)

Judy A. Crowell (191-192)

Richard F. Dallam, Sr. (196-197)

Helen Del Valle (211-215)

Lucille Stroud Due (221)

Anne Pardue Ellenberger (239-244)

Judith Elliott (245)

Tom Evans (257)

George Leonard Farmakis (261-262)

Kay Flemming (286-287)

Frances M. Florio (288-289)

David Frank (294)

Richard Paul Goodyear (312-313)

Frances Ewing Grayson (315)

Betty B. Greenberg (316-320)

Louis U. Guthrie, Sr. (328-329)

Eleanor C. Hamel (334-335)

Pat Hampton (336-339)

Alberta Anna Hannaman (340)

Keith R. Harris (349)

Gina Hawrych (354-355)

Elizabeth S. Hayes (356-358)

Gary J. Heasell (359)

Harry C. Helm (363-364)

846

Herman A. Henderson (365)

Isabella Aldrich Hoffman (375)

Maryida Horn (385)

Enrique Irizarry (398-399)

Violet A. Janz (406)

Dorothy Johnson (415)

Israel Katz (418-427)

Donna S. Keursteiner (442)

Tobi J. Kumar (443)

Evelyn Lahaie (444-445)

Sir Walter Robert Lettieri (454-455)

Vida Linden (464-465)

Adeline Huggins Loftis (466-467)

M. May Lovelace (471-477)

Adaline Lincoln Lush (482-483)

Elna McBee (484)

Artie Nettles McCoy (488-489)

William T. McEwan, Jr. (491-492)

Lavinia Fern McKinney (496-497)

Jean Mathews (506-508)

Irene Maxwell (509-515)

George Mac Mendenhall (517-518)

Louis George Merry (519-520)

Edward Paul Miles (521)

Wilber J. Milliner (524-528)

Anne Marie and Rasheed Mohammed (530)

semarie and Tina Marie Mohammed (531)

Michael A. Molander (532-533)

Frank T. Mort, Jr. (543)

Cassandra M. Mullen (544-546)

Wilfred G. Munroe (547)

Anne Ruth McDade Murphy (548-549)

John Patrick Murphy (550-552)

Lois Nicholson (557)

Robert J. Norton (563)

Cathy Smith Patton (583-588)

Elizabeth Pavich (589)

Gregory David Paxton (590)

Byrle Payne (591-597)

Rodney Deane Payne (599-600)

Lynda C. Pellegrino (604)

Beatrice Petty (607)

Le Van Phuc (608)

Master Lawrence W. "Beanie" Pina (609-614)

Wynema Jacqueline Poarch (618)

Corina L. Popp (620)

Bonnidean Petty Purchase (622)

Rita Pyles (623)

Linda Edwards (623)

Carl Desidor Rachel (624-626)

Florence Dora Rapp (631)

J. Cutler Roberts, M.D. (642-643)

Shulamith Salem (664-669)

Anna V. Salerno (670)

Sharon Salisbury (671-676)

William F. Sands (677)

Dorothy A. Sheer (691-692)

J. C. Shellhammer III (693)

Ruth Robinson Shepherd (694-695)

C. David Stiff (722)

Sol Sudeten (728-730)

John F. Taylor (743-745)

Annette Marie Tesar (747)

Nancy C. Thomas (748)

Mary L. Thompson (750)

Stella C. Thompson (751)

Rev. John J. Tomalonis (753-766)

Pastor Richard E. Tottress (772)

Margaret Tucker (782)

Mable Warnke (800-802)

Troy Weber (806-807)

Al West (815)

Mable Turner Witzgall (822-825)

William P. Yurak (828)

Index of Authors

867

869

Mc

M

N

O

P

Index of Titles

882

883

887

888

Y